PHILANTHROPY AND THE FUNDING
OF THE CHURCH OF ENGLAND, 1856–1914

Perspectives in Economic and Social History

Series Editors: Andrew August
Jari Eloranta

Titles in this Series

Forthcoming Titles

PHILANTHROPY AND THE FUNDING
OF THE CHURCH OF ENGLAND, 1856–1914

BY

Sarah Flew

Routledge
Taylor & Francis Group

LONDON AND NEW YORK

First published 2015 by Pickering & Chatto (Publishers) Limited

2 Park Square, Milton Park, Abingdon, Oxfordshire OX14 4RN
52 Vanderbilt Avenue, New York, NY 10017

Routledge is an imprint of the Taylor & Francis Group, an informa business

First issued in paperback 2020

BRITISH LIBRARY CATALOGUING IN PUBLICATION DATA

Flew, Sarah, author.
Philanthropy and the funding of the Church of England, 1856–1914. –
(Perspectives in economic and social history)
1. Church of England – Finance – History – 19th century. 2. Church of England
– Finance – History – 20th century. 3. Christian giving – Church of England.
4. Religion and sociology – Great Britain – History – 19th century. 5. Religion
and sociology – Great Britain – History – 20th century.
I. Title II. Series
254.8'0941-dc23

ISBN-13: 978-1-84893-500-6 (hbk)
ISBN-13: 978-0-367-66906-5 (pbk)

Typeset by Pickering & Chatto (Publishers) Limited

CONTENTS

The following prayer, written by Bishop Tait, appeared in every annual report of the Bishop of London's Fund and in the front of collection books in an abbreviated form:

A Prayer
which may be used, either privately or in their families, by those who are interested in the Bishop of London's Fund

O Lord, our Heavenly Father, Who hast made all men, and lovest all whom Thou hast made; Who hast sent Thy Son Jesus Christ into this world of sin and woe, that He might seek and save those who were lost; look mercifully, we pray Thee, on this great City, wherein are a hundred and fifty score thousand human souls. Have pity especially upon the vast crowd of men, women, and little children who are wandering amongst us uncared for, as sheep without a shepherd. O Lord, Thou hast designed the Gospel of Thy Son to be preached to the Poor; stir up the wills of all to whom Thou hast given any portion of this world's wealth, that, spending Thine own gifts in Thy service, they may seek to multiply the means of grace to those that are destitute. Give us in all our plans zeal, and wisdom to direct our zeal; a ready mind and a liberal hand; that we may not only undertake but perfect somewhat in our day and generation to instruct the ignorant, and guide those who are out of the way, to check vice, and spread in many dark and wretched homes the comforts which Thou hast prepared for suffering souls in Jesus Christ.

O Lord, give us truly grateful hearts for all the spiritual privileges Thou hast placed within our reach. Make us to use them to the Christian regulation of our own lives, so that by word and good example, as well as by schemes of public charity, we may labour to advance Thy kingdom. Guide and bless all Christian people in London who desire the good of souls. Look especially upon this effort of ours, undertaken in Thy Name. May every step in its progress be made in the spirit of prayer. Bless all the Clergy, with those who labour under them, and help them in their pastoral work. Impress on the hearts of all who take part even in the common business of our scheme a due sense of its sacred ends. Grant that we may remember always in whose Name we are acting, how deep is our responsibility, and how we must do all in a truly Christian spirit, if we would win souls to Christ.

O Lord, may the efforts which we make for others deepen in our souls the sense of what the Lord Jesus Christ has done for us; and do Thou unite us daily closer to Him whose blood cleanseth from sin, and who will send His Spirit to lead us to holiness and to Himself.

Hear us, we beseech Thee, through the same Jesus Christ our Saviour. Amen.

ACKNOWLEDGEMENTS

Many people have helped me to produce this labour of love. First of all I would like to thank the many academics that have encouraged me in my work. I am greatly indebted to my three PhD supervisors (Professor John Wolffe, Professor Arthur Burns, and Dr John Maiden) for their patience, guidance and encouragement through every stage of the research and writing up of the thesis upon which this work is based. Thanks are also due to Professor Anne Laurence and Dr Frances Knight, my PhD examiners, for their helpful comments. Secondly, I would like to take the opportunity to express my gratitude to the friendly and helpful staff at the many archives visited. Especial thanks go to Sister Teresa Joan White of the Community of St Andrew; Jeff Gerhardt of the London Metropolitan Archives; the staff of Lambeth Palace Library; and the staff of the London City Mission. Thirdly, I would particularly like to thank the British Association of Victorian Studies for kindly awarding me a research grant that enabled me to visit the special collections of the universities of Birmingham and Glasgow. And lastly, and by no means least, I wish to give my everlasting gratitude to my friends and family for politely pretending to be interested in my research.

LIST OF ABBREVIATIONS

AD	*Ancilla Domini*
ACS	Additional Curates' Society
BGCSF	Bethnal Green Churches and Schools Fund
BLF	Bishop of London's Fund
CMS	Church Missionary Society
CRL	Cadburys Research Library
CP-AS	Church Pastoral-Aid Society
CSA	Community of St Andrew
ELCC	*East London Church Chronicle*
ELCF	East London Church Fund
ICBS	Incorporated Church Building Society
ICES	Islington Church Extension Society
ICHM	Islington Home Mission Society
LCM	London City Mission
LCMM	*London City Mission Magazine*
LDA	Ladies' Diocesan Association
LDCBS	London Diocesan Church Building Society
LDDI	London Diocesan Deaconess Institution
LDHM	London Diocesan Home Mission
LDM	*London Diocesan Magazine*
LHA	Lay Helpers' Association
LHAC	Lewisham History and Archives Centre
LMA	London Metropolitan Archives
LPL	Lambeth Palace Library
LSE	London School of Economics and Political Science
MCF	Metropolis Churches Fund
PMWA	Parochial Mission Women Association
PGU	Proportionate Giving Union
SBS	Systematic Beneficence Society
SHSC	Senate House Special Collection
SPG	Society for the Propagation of the Gospel in Foreign Parts

SRA	Scripture Readers' Association
SRJ	*Scripture Readers' Journal*
STG	Society of the Treasury of God
TNA	The National Archives
WDA	Women's Diocesan Association

LIST OF FIGURES AND TABLES

INTRODUCTION

It is curious that an institution as large as the Church of England should have received so little attention from scholars of the modern period in respect of its funding mechanisms. Unfortunately, historians of modern religion seem to regard such a subject as outside of their skill set and conversely economic historians of this period (who do have the necessary skill set) have shown very little interest in the subject of religion. This book is therefore a contribution to bridging the gulf between these two distant fields and its ambition is to highlight the contribution that can be made by examining religious bodies through the functional and analytical lens of accountancy and financial management. The very few published books on the subject of church finance have tended to concentrate on the institutional aspect of finance and have thereby managed to avoid actually discussing the 'grubby' subject of money itself. In fact, such is the reluctance of church historians to discuss the issue of money that some authors are openly apologetic in bringing up such a sensitive subject. Michael Wilks, for example, admits that: 'The theme ... in many ways ... could hardly seem less appropriate to that institution whose founder commanded his followers to take neither silver nor gold'.[1] I even suspect that some historians of religion feel that such a detached and functional analysis of religion is almost inappropriate, as it is not the mechanistic side of religion that draws their interest but rather the experiential, intellectual, ideological and ritualistic aspects of religion. In respect of the subject of this book, I make no such apologies for my interest in money: as the song reminds us 'money makes the world go round' and religious bodies are no different in their need for money than other charitable institutions.[2] The reasonable assumption thereby taken by this work is that modern religious bodies have to function as economic agents, and that they need steady sources of income supported by funding mechanisms that will raise sufficient funds on an annual basis.

The starting point for this discussion is an assertion from the eminent sociologist Bryan Wilson. He reflects that: 'Religious economics is a neglected field, but it can readily be stated that the proportion of the Gross National Product diverted to the supernatural has diminished in the course of the centuries'.[3] It was this germ of an idea – to quantify the funding of religion – that forms the basis of this research. Needless to say, given the time-consuming nature of such a task, it has been necessary to limit the scope of this work to an illustrative case study. The subject chosen for such a study has been an examination and analysis of the funding of a range of Anglican home-missionary organizations in opera-tion in the Diocese of London during the period of 1856 to 1914. The old adage 'put your money where your mouth is' makes the point that serious dedication is demonstrated with actions and not just words, and that if you really are commit-ted to a cause you will back up your words with financial support. Specifically, this book takes the view that a decline in financial commitment can be a meas-ure of changing public attitudes towards religion. This analysis will therefore evaluate the financial commitment of the laity to Anglican diocesan home-mis-sionary organizations in London in the period 1856 to 1914 and judge whether this commitment remained stable. Consequently, the two main themes that run through this book are philanthropy and secularization.

The nineteenth century saw an explosion in the population of England and Wales which was particularly concentrated in urban centres, such as London.[4] In response to this growth, both Charles James Blomfield (Bishop of London between 1828 and 1856) and Archibald Campbell Tait (Bishop of London between 1856 and 1868) supported and developed a range of diocesan organi-zations with the purpose of evangelizing the unchurched masses of London. The Church did not itself have the funds to finance these organizations and was, therefore, forced to find alternative sources of money. Its response was to turn to the laity. Edward Lewes Cutts (1824–1901), perpetual curate of Billericay, made this point in a plea on behalf of the Additional Curates' Society in 1860: 'What is lacking? Chiefly money to carry out the work; and that God has given in unprecedented abundance to the laity of England; and now he calls upon them to provide that which is lacking to carry out this new Reformation'.[5] The finan-cial resources were there; all the Church needed to do was to persuade people to give, and to give generously. Accordingly, it is the laity's financial relationship with the Church of England through the funding of its diocesan home-mission-ary organizations that is the central topic of this work.

Sources and Scope

London, in the period of this study, makes a suitable case for the study of both philanthropy and Anglican home-missionary provision. Firstly, the problem of spiritual destitution was amplified in the Diocese of London due to its dramatic population growth at a rate of about 40,000 people a year. Consequently, several statistical surveys were carried out in the nineteenth century which give accounts of the level of religious provision in London. Secondly, London tended to take the lead in charitable concerns, with provincial branches being set up at a later date. Thirdly, philanthropy in London involved the wealthy elite on a national scale; this was due to the fact that the upper-classes typically had a second home in London where they lived during the London season. Fourthly, philanthropy in London was not dominated by wealthy industrialists or Nonconformists as in provincial cities, such as Bristol. In contrast, London contained an unrivalled concentration of wealthy Anglicans employed in professions such as finance and brewing.[6] Fifthly, and practically, a wealth of primary source material has survived relating to this subject. These are in the form of the minute books, printed annual reports, working papers, sermons and the publications of the home-missionary organizations. Additionally, this material is supported by the personal papers of bishops and wealthy individuals, and a range of metropolitan charitable directories dating from the latter half of the nineteenth-century. Finally, and most importantly, case studies on London have previously led the debate on the secularization narrative.[7] Consequently, London, in this period, provides the ideal vehicle to study changing patterns in philanthropy from the middle- and upper-classes towards religious voluntary organizations.

Specifically, this book will examine the funding of a range of Anglican religious voluntary organizations, established to serve the Diocese of London across the period of 1856 to 1914. Archibald Campbell Tait was installed as Bishop of London in 1856 and correspondingly this date has been chosen for the commencement of the study. The majority of the organizations chosen for this study were established during Tait's episcopate (1856–68) and all were still in existence in 1914, the closing date for the period of study. The commencement of World War I has been chosen as the closure date of the study because of the significant economic changes as a result of the war and the consequential impact on philanthropy. Furthermore, 1914 was also the year that the Church of England introduced a dramatic restructuring of its financial system with the creation of the Central Board of Finance and individual Diocesan Boards of Finance. After 1914 the London Diocesan Board of Finance took on responsibilities for managing aspects of the funding of some of its diocesan societies.

This research has drawn on a range of primary source materials which have so far received little attention. The principal tool of communication for any charitable organization was the printed annual report and, crucially for the purposes of this research, these printed reports typically contained lengthy subscription lists which reported every subscription, donation and bequest received by the society in that accounting year; in some cases longer accumulative lists included every sum given by a particular individual. Virtually complete sets of annual reports are available for three of the six organizations subject to this study. However, it has been possible, in the case of the other three societies, to supplement the annual report information with additional material from a variety of other sources. The subsequent analysis of these combined sources has made it possible to illuminate the following two areas of interest. Firstly, the analysis has set out to identify the individual funder-base of each society. Writing in 1965, David Owen claimed that 'the generality of contributors to late Victorian charity must remain an anonymous mass, for there is little evidence as to their identity, their numbers, and their motives'.[8] However, Owen is wrong in his assertion as a detailed analysis of the subscription lists does make it possible to identify the financial supporters as individuals. Indeed, it is noteworthy that the literature on philanthropy contains hardly any discussion of the actual philanthropists themselves.[9] Generally, those philanthropists that are mentioned are those of great fame, such as the first Duke of Westminster (1825–99) or Baroness Angela Burdett-Coutts (1814–1906). This deficiency in approach will be addressed in this work which will consider and analyse the demographic base and identities of the funders of the selected Anglican home-missionary organizations. Secondly, the analysis has been able to illuminate and examine the financial health of the organizations chosen for this study, with the specific aim of evaluating the trends in the individual funding streams in the context of the overall financial state. It is fair to say that this is an area that has been completely neglected and avoided by historians. Robert Wuthnow and Virginia Hodgkinson state that 'we remain in the dark about most of the connections between religion and giving in our society'.[10] This comment is also true in the case of the historiography of modern British religion, particularly in respect of the Church of England and giving. Accordingly, the main thrust of the book is an analysis of the finances of these selected organizations. The initial four questions examined are: how did the Church societies raise money; who did they solicit support from; to what extent were the societies successful in soliciting financial support to carry out their aims; and did the funding revenue streams remain stable? These questions are posed with the main purpose of evaluating the Anglican laity's support of these organizations in relation to who gave financial support and how this had changed by the end of the period.

This book is organized in three parts. Part 1, comprised of Chapters 1 and 2, reviews the form of home-missionary work in the nineteenth century and the funding models which supported the different organizations. Although this study is concerned mainly with an analysis of the funding of the diocesan home-missionary schemes in operation in London in the latter half of the nineteenth century, it is necessary to contextualize the development of these organizations within the overall development of home mission as a new initiative in the nineteenth century. Chapter 1, therefore, explores the gradual development of home-missionary schemes in the first half of the nineteenth century and charts the funding changes in the period as a consequence of the cessation of state funding of church building. This approach is continued in Chapter 2 which describes the main features of the new home-missionary organizations established during

Bishop Tait's episcopate in London. The focus of Part 2, comprised of Chapters 3, 4 and 5, is an analysis of the funding of these organizations. Chapter 3 analyses the mechanisms by which money was raised for the different organizations. Chapter 4 presents the overall results of the analysis of the data gathered from the subscription lists. It then analyses the financial health of the voluntary organizations chosen for this study, by looking at income figures and analysing their funding streams and how they changed through the period. This chapter also in turn analyses how the funder-base changed through the period by examining who the funders were and how the funder demographic changed. Chapter 5, in turn, profiles the prominent individuals that funded the home missionary organizations in this study. The final part, Part 3, comprised of Chapter 6 and the conclusion, sets the preceding discussion within the context of a theology of giving and the changing nature of the Victorian culture of philanthropy. Chapter 6 considers the mid-century renaissance of the doctrine of Christian stewardship and its subsequent decline. Furthermore, it highlights the increasing concern by clergy, at the end of the nineteenth century, that new generations of Christians were not being educated in stewardship and that, consequently, they were more likely to view money as being their own property rather than God's property. Finally, the Conclusion analyses how the philanthropic impulse to give to Anglican home-missionary organizations had changed within the period and argues that there was an across the board trend of decline in financial support. It argues that the Church of England was an unwitting player in the secularization of Christian culture through its reluctant acceptance – in the absence of the ethic of Christian stewardship – of a new culture of secular modes of fundraising. This conclusion is supported by the finding that crucially, at the turn of the century, the Anglican home-missionary societies could no longer rely upon the support of the wealthy businessman. And that in particular, with the passing of a certain generation of wealthy philanthropic businessmen, these societies lost their financial security as a new generation of male philanthropists failed to come forward to fill this funding void. This finding therefore builds upon the work of other historians concerned with the themes of gender and class in relation to the secularization thesis.

1 THE EARLIER STAGES OF HOME MISSION IN LONDON, 1800–56

In 1887, Reverend William Walsh (1836–1918), published a survey of church extension in London entitled *Progress of the Church in London During the Last 50 Years*. Looking back on the previous fifty years of church extension in London, he acknowledged the debt to the earlier generation of church extensionists:

> A great revival of missionary ardour is everywhere to be observed; agencies and methods for applying spiritual necessities, more numerous and more varied than any which our forefathers employed or thought of, are producing results of which they never dreamed; but the life and activity of the present generation must not blind us to the life and activity of many who have gone before, or lead us to think comparatively little of their zeal and earnestness in diffusing religious truth.[1]

In this survey, Walsh acknowledges the portfolio of national and diocesan schemes that had revolutionized church extension in London.

National Church Building Schemes

The first half of the nineteenth century witnessed the birth of a great many initiatives in Anglican church extension directed towards evangelizing the burgeoning populations of the cities. Initially, the greatest concern of the Church was the problem of inadequate levels of religious provision.[2] The Church's approach to solving this problem in the cities was to take the traditional rural model as its ideal: this model was of a community of different classes being overseen by the incumbent and squire. The approach taken in London and other cities was to break the large overpopulated and unmanageable parishes into smaller, more suitably sized units, with each unit being provided with a church and clergyman.[3] The cry for more churches began at the turn of the century and accelerated through the first decade, culminating in a High Church campaign in 1815.[4] This was led by the wealthy layman John Bowdler (1746–1823) and was supported by 120 prominent laymen, including Sir Robert Harry Inglis (1786–1855) and the merchant William Cotton (1786–1866). The campaigners argued that it was Parliament's duty to fund this increase in church accommodation: 'Parliament alone can do it; and we conceive it to be one of its chief duties to provide places of worship for the members of the established religion.[5] This coincided with the publication of Richard Yates' (1769–1834) pamphlet *The Church in Danger* (1815) which, with an impressive use of statistics, argued for increased church accommodation in London.[6] The campaign was rewarded, in 1818, with a Parliamentary grant of £1,000,000 for church building in London and large provincial towns to commemorate the recent victory at Waterloo.[7]

A new body, the Church Building Commissioners, was appointed to super-intend these funds, in addition to being given powers to propose schemes for the subdivision of parishes. An additional sum of £500,000 was granted by Parlia-ment in 1824.[8] The first grant of £1,000,000 produced only 98 churches at an average cost of £10,000 each; consequently, the second grant of £500,000 marked the beginning of an era of economy and cheaper churches.[9] In conjunction with the establishment of the Church Building Commissioners, the year 1818 also saw the establishment of a national Church Building Society, which later, was incorporated to become the Incorporated Church Building Society in 1828. This society collected voluntary donations from the Anglican laity nationally, and also gave aid to parishes that could not raise the partial funds needed to meet the cri-teria to receive grants from the Church Building Commissioners. Its committee was High Church and shared many members with the Church Building Com-missioners, for example, the wine merchant Joshua Watson (1771–1855) and William Cotton. The society was very successful in its first year, raising £54,000 from voluntary subscriptions and donations, but this success was short-lived and the society was in financial difficulty within ten years. This financial situation was mirrored in the accounts of the Church Building Commissioners which by the early 1830s had granted away virtually all of its capital.[10]

Further efforts to obtain additional grants from Parliament were stalled by the advancement in the voice of Nonconformist lobbyists. The emancipation of Nonconformists and Roman Catholics in 1828 and 1829 gave birth to the voluntaryist movement in the early 1830s. Voluntaryism is the principle that all forms of association should be voluntary, and specifically that religion should not be supported by the state. From this point onwards, the Church of England expe-rienced a reduction in the privileges granted to it, in conjunction with an increase in the rights granted to people of other religious faiths. In 1868, for example, after a long campaign, the anti-establishment pressure from Nonconformist lobbyists secured the abolition of the compulsory aspect of the church rate.[11] Despite these increased privileges to other denominations, the Church of England continued until the mid 1840s to hold the view that further state grants for Anglican church building were still a possibility. In connection with this, in the 1830s and 1840s, the Church of England overhauled its administration through a long series of church reforms implemented by the Ecclesiastical Commission which was formed by Parliament in 1835.[12] Many in the Church held the view that if it was actively seen to be overhauling its administration and finances, Parliament would look on it more kindly when asked, in the future, for public money for church extension.[13] This series of reforms, implemented by the Ecclesiastical Commission, rationalized the administration of the Church through a reorganization of the dioceses (through the redrawing of boundaries, amalgamation and creation of new dioceses) and through a review of existing Church of England resources. This financial rationalization freed up capital from the cathedral establishments which the Church could then divert to needy parishes. However, despite these efforts the Church was not successful in obtaining further Parliamentary grants to aid church building. The final major attempts to secure further Parliamentary funding for church extension came in the 1840s with Sir Robert Inglis's unsuccessful campaign for new Parliamentary funds between 1840 and 1842.[14] This attempt marked the definitive end of the campaign for Parliamentary funding of Anglican church extension. Occasionally individuals continued to raise the subject but generally the view that it was Parliament's responsibility to finance new church building for the Established Church was abandoned.[15]

The fortunes of the Incorporated Church Building Society improved, however, due to the introduction of the mechanism of the royal letter in 1828.[16] Only three charities (all High Church in character) were officially granted the right to collect monies under the terms of a royal letter; these were the Incorporated Church Building Society, the Society for the Propagation of the Gospel and the National Society.[17] The practice was to collect for each of these charities in succession every three years.[18] In the period between 1828 and 1851, £258,009 was collected through the royal letter mechanism for the Incorporated Church Building Society.[19] Unfortunately, this period of prosperity only lasted for 25 years; in 1853 the mechanism of the royal letter was abolished by the government on the grounds that it made too close a link between Church and Crown. In 1853, on the advice of Henry John Temple (1784–1865), third Viscount Palmerston, then Home Secretary, the three societies which had licence to collect monies from this mechanism were given notice that the scheme would no longer be recommended.[20] The High Church newspaper the *Guardian* in 1855 condemned the abolition as 'an unmixed evil', squarely laying the blame on Lord Palmerston, with Lord Shaftesbury 'at his elbow'.[21] The practice of royal letters had been condemned by the Protestant Alliance, an evangelical interdenominational Anti-Catholic political pressure group of which Shaftesbury was President. Their condemnation of the practice was due to the fact that royal letters solely favoured High Church societies.[22] This dispute highlights that, as well as Nonconformist lobbying, growing party tensions in the 1850s also impacted on the state sanctioned funding of the Incorporated Church Building Society. As a consequence, by the 1850s there were very limited funds available for national church-building schemes.

Localized Church Building Schemes

With the cessation of parliamentary grants in 1824 and the dropping off of income to the Incorporated Church Building Society in the late 1820s, there was very little money available in this period from the national church-building organizations. Consequently, in the mid 1820s, diocesan church-extension organizations began to be established in order to supplement and eventually replace the work of these national funding bodies. Such diocesan schemes became more common-place in the 1830s.[23] The most influential precedent for urban church extension was the initiative established by Thomas Chalmers (1780–1847), Church of Scotland minister, in St John's parish in Glasgow in 1819. Chalmers wanted to create in the city parishes of Glasgow the sense of community that he had experienced in rural Fife. The key to this scheme was the subdivision of the parish into smaller more manageable units, each unit being supplied with district visitors and parish schools.[24] In 1835, the publication of Baptist Wriothesley Noel's (1799–1873) pamphlet, entitled *The State of the Metropolis Considered,* started the process that led to the establishment of a diocesan church-extension scheme in London in the following year. Noel, a Church of England clergyman and later Baptist minister, argued that the government needed to give a far larger sum than previously given in order to fund this church extension.[25] Furthermore, he argued that new methods, such as open-air preaching, were necessary to overcome the extent of the spiritual destitution being experienced in London.[26] In the same year, the Reverend Edward Bouverie Pusey (1800–82) wrote an article for the *British Magazine* entitled 'Churches in London: Past and Present Exertions of the Church and her Present Needs'.[27] Pusey's paper sought to remind individuals of their Christian duty to financially support the Church. Shortly afterwards, in early 1836, Bishop Blomfield set out his proposal for the creation of a church-extension scheme for London to be known as the Metropolis Churches Fund, in the pamphlet *Proposals for Creation of a Fund.* Its aim was 'to divide the moral wilderness of this vast city into manageable districts, each with its place of worship, its schools, and its local institutions'.[28] Blomfield's proposal highlighted the 'liberal assistance of the Christian public' which had supported comparable schemes for church extension in Glasgow and Manchester.[29] Following the standard of church accommodation set out in the second report of the Ecclesiastical Commissioners, which aimed to provide church accommodation for one-third of the population, Blomfield calculated that there was a deficiency of 279 churches, his standard being one church and minister for every 3,000 persons.[30] In some of London's worst parishes, with populations in excess of 10,000, he estimated that there was only enough church provision for ten per cent of the population.[31] The object of his new society, the Metropolis Churches Fund, was to erect a modest fifty new churches at an estimated cost of

£250,000.[32] An extended version of Pusey's pamphlet, published in 1837, criticized Blomfield for only cautiously aiming to build only one sixth of the needed provision: 50 churches out of the 279 required. Pusey suggested that £500,000 would be a more desirable sum to raise and argued that if people responded generously to the scheme, Blomfield might feel encouraged 'to undertake the whole of this great task'.[33] Thomas Chalmers, in contrast, was astonished by the scope of Blomfield's plans, and dismissed them saying that, 'but if he insists upon expatiating over the whole metropolis by building fifty churches at once, his whole scheme will be nothing more than a devout imagination, impossible to be realized'.[34] The committee of the Metropolis Churches Fund, being formed of interested individuals who had attended the society's launch meeting, was of mixed Church party and included prominent individuals from either side: High Church laymen such as Joshua Watson and William Cotton (both of whom had been actively involved in the Incorporated Church Building Society); and Evangelicals such as, Anthony Ashley Cooper, 7th Earl of Shaftesbury (then styled Lord Ashley Cooper) and the Reverend Baptist Noel.[35]

By this point in time, Blomfield was doubtful that any more money would be forthcoming in the way of further Parliamentary grants. Instead, he initially suggested that the work proposed in this pamphlet could be funded by a 2d a ton duty on coal, but this suggestion was rejected.[36] Consequently, the Metropolis Churches Fund was to be entirely funded by contributions from the Anglican laity. The Fund particularly targeted 'owners of large property in the metropolis', 'great companies and commercial establishments' and 'merchants, bankers and opulent tradesmen' in its appeals.[37] People responded generously to the fund in its first year. The King (William IV) was the society's patron; as was Queen Victoria who personally donated £1,000.[38] Pusey, himself, gave £6,000 to the Fund: £1,000 publicly in his name and £5,000 anonymously under the description of 'from a clergyman seeking treasure in heaven', a phrase he uses in his 1835 pamphlet *Churches in London*.[39] This generous sum was matched by Bishop Blomfield who gave £6,200 in total during the life of the fund.[40] Income stated in its first annual report recorded that by June 1837 £117,423 had been subscribed.[41] By the fourth annual report for the accounting year of 1839-40, accumulated contributions (including promised subscriptions) totalled £149,439.[42] Individuals giving large amounts (categorized as over £100) were given the option of paying in four annual instalments; and when these payments ceased in the society's fourth year, the Metropolis Churches Fund stopped producing annual reports.[43] It was not surprising, however, that income had declined so quickly; individuals had responded to the Bishop's scheme as if it was an appeal, which in effect it was, and there was no intention to make the Fund a permanent scheme at this point. The committee reported, in 1849, that "their resources were entirely exhausted;" and again in 1853, that they had received in the four intervening years but £18,000, of which £14,500 was made up of the contributions of only four individuals; the number of annual subscribers had fallen to just three individuals.[44] In March 1839, a new off-shoot appeal, entitled the Bethnal Green Churches and Schools Fund, was launched with the aim of creating ten additional districts within the parish of Bethnal Green.[45] The plan was to supply each of these new districts with a newly built and endowed church, complete with a parsonage and school, at a total estimated cost of £75,000. This object was achieved when the tenth church, Saint Thomas, was consecrated in July 1850.[46] The *Final Report of the Metropolis Churches Fund* (1854) summed up the achievements of the Metropolis Churches Fund and Bethnal Green Churches and Schools Fund and showed that the two organizations had surpassed the objective of erecting 50 churches at a cost of £250,000. During the eighteen years of the Fund, £266,000 had been raised: this figure included all monies raised by the offshoot Bethnal Green Churches and Schools Fund. The report also estimated that, with the additional sums elicited from local sources, a grand total of more than £536,000 had been raised. Collectively, 78 churches had been built with the aid of the two funds (with an additional seven churches through the generosity of individual benefactors), thereby increasing church sittings by 106,000. Additionally, 146 additional clergymen had been employed in the new districts, and new schools had been established for over 20,000 children.[47] Blomfield's scheme had therefore surpassed its target and established a model for future church extension in London.

The 1840s also saw the flowering of various other local efforts of church extension in London. In 1842, the St Pancras Church Building Fund was established by the wealthy High Church printer William Rivington (1807–88). The Rivington family owned the well-established printing company of the same name, and became closely associated with publishing for the Tractarians.[48] This building fund was invigorated in 1846, when the Evangelical Reverend Thomas Dale (1797–1870) was appointed incumbent of St Pancras. In addition, the Westminster Spiritual Aid Fund was established in 1846 by the High Church Archdeacon Christopher Wordsworth (1807–85). It provided additional clergy and schools in the Westminster parishes of St Margaret and St John.[49] These local societies were aided with the simplification of district formation through the passage of Peel's New Parishes Act of 1843 (6 and 7 Vict. c. 37) which made possible the constitution of new districts, out of any part of a parish or parts of parishes, before the building of a church.[50] Once a new church had been provided for the new district, it would become a separate parish for ecclesiastical purposes.[51] Previously, the procedure to create a new parish had been the 'expensive and troublesome machinery of special acts of parliament'.[52] This new act, therefore, not only simplified the process but it eradicated the need of a costly act.[53] The endowment for these new districts was provided by the Ecclesiastical Commissioners.

Alternative Approaches to Home Mission

Other new Anglican initiatives that took place in the 1820s to 1840s were the introduction of temporary churches, the increased use of additional clergy and lay agency, and the tentative use of women with the revival of sisterhoods. Additionally, Blomfield began to relax his High Church notions of acceptable forms of home mission through his acceptance of the occasional use of lay agency and unconsecrated rooms in the 1830s.[54]

The 1830s saw the formation of voluntary organizations established with the aim of supporting the clergy in their work. First, in 1828, the District Visiting Society was established and controlled by Evangelical laymen. It was similar in character to the Nonconformist London Christian Instruction Society established in 1825.[55] Secondly and more importantly, in 1835 the evangelical interdenominational London City Mission was formed by David Nasmith (1799–1839), who had previously established the Glasgow City Mission in 1826. B. I. Coleman argues that Baptist Noel's 1835 pamphlet was partly responsible for the formation of the London City Mission.[56] Consequently, in response to the establishment of the London City Mission, in 1835, a group of London Evangelicals offered to raise £150,000 for church extension if Blomfield formed a diocesan society modelled on the organization formed in Chester in the previous year.[57] Blomfield, however, declined the offer and encouraged the group of Evangelicals to found the first Anglican home-missionary organization in February 1836: the Church Pastoral-Aid Society's object was to provide funds to support additional clergy in populous districts, and to encourage the use of laymen as non-ministerial helpers to the clergy.[58] In 1837 High Church members broke away from the Church Pastoral-Aid Society to form the Additional Curates' Society because of their opposition to the use of laymen. The Additional Curates' Society consequently only endorsed the employment of ordained curates.[59] In 1842 the City of London's Young Men's Society for Aiding Missions at Home and Abroad was formed by a group of Evangelical clergy who wanted a group for young men involved in their Sunday School. It became the Church of England Young Men's Society in the 1850s and by this time had become national in its scope.[60] In 1844, the Scripture Readers' Association was formed in response to the activities of the London City Mission. Towards the end of 1843, the London City Mission proposed to concentrate its efforts by appointing twenty missionaries to the Bethnal Green district; this initiative was backed financially by the wealthy Evangelical Anglican brewer Robert Hanbury (1796–1884).[61] With Blomfield's encouragement, Hanbury and a raft of other prominent Evangelicals (principally those involved in the founding of the Church Pastoral-Aid Society) consequently formed the Scripture Readers' Association in March 1844 under the patronage of Bishop Blomfield and Charles

Sumner, the Evangelical Bishop of Winchester. The purpose was to provide 'for the Metropolitan parishes in the diocese of London and Winchester, Lay Scripture Readers, whose duty it shall be to read the scriptures from house to house'.[62] Within a few months, the society had scripture readers working in association with several of the Bethnal Green churches. [63]

Finally, the 1840s also saw the innovation of the use of temporary churches. The first use of these was in 1841, when a large wooden structure was built to accommodate the needs of an expanding congregation of the Episcopal Chapel at Kentish Town.[64] This temporary building acted as a model for many wooden and iron buildings that followed.[65] This innovation was low in cost and could be quickly erected in a new area, both great advantages to the slow and costly procedure of church-building.[66] The 1830s and 1840s were, therefore, decades of great innovation in terms of the shaping of home-mission as a new missionary concept. This period saw various forms of home-missionary work being employed to address the problem of the 'spiritual destitution' of the masses; in addition to the development of both localized and diocesan church-extension societies, new societies were established (in both High Church and Evangelical form) which provided additional curates to over populated parishes and which advocated the use of lay agency.

These new methods were also advocated in Horace Mann's report on the 1851 Religious Census (published in 1854) in which he declared that the Church needed to launch an 'aggressive' missionary campaign in order to tackle 'the terrible emergency'.[67] The census had been commissioned in order to obtain figures regarding the provision of church accommodation for public worship. The report suggested that about 58 per cent of the population were able to attend worship (having allowed for the non-attendance of the young, the sick and elderly). Therefore, as a result of the information tabulated in over 250 pages of data, the report concluded that the Christian churches needed to provide another 1,644,735 sittings in the form of approximately 2,000 churches or chapels.[68] Mann argued that the Church of England should look to Nonconformist successes with the working-classes for ideas and recommended the use of licensed rooms initially, with churches being built once the congregations had been formed.[69] Above all, he implored the Church to employ aggressive measures, advocating the employment of additional lay agents and street preaching.

This last suggestion was facilitated in 1855, with the passing of Shaftesbury's Religious Worship Bill which made it legal to hold a religious meeting in an unlicensed place. In the early 1850s the practice of open-air preaching began to be more widely discussed and became generally more acceptable amongst interdenominational groups. In 1854 the London City Mission introduced open-air preaching as a direct result of Horace Mann's endorsement of street preaching in the census report which it felt had made the practice more publicly acceptable.[70] In addition in 1853, the Evangelical John MacGregor (1825–92), a lawyer and traveller, founded the interdenominational Open Air Mission; another prominent committee member was the Recordite lawyer Alexander Haldane (1800–82).[71] MacGregor was also the honorary secretary of the Protestant Alliance. Its principal objects were to 'encourage, regulate, and improve open-air preaching' and it was funded entirely by donations and subscriptions.[72] The *Second Open-Air Mission Annual Report* (1855) described the flowering of open-air preaching in London. It reported that the London City Mission had removed its restriction on open-air preaching; that the Archbishop of Canterbury had approved its use; that the Bishop of Winchester had advocated its use in his last visitation charge; that the Christian Instruction Society were holding Tent Meetings in the suburbs; and that the Bishop of London had sanctioned the work of the Islington Church Home Mission.[73]

The Islington Church Home Mission was founded in November 1854, by the Reverend Daniel Wilson junior (1805–86) in the Evangelical parish of Islington.[74] Wilson was Vicar of Islington, as his father had been before him, and President of the Islington Association of the Church Missionary Society. The true innovation of this society was that it was not a church building society in the form of the localized societies formed for St Pancras and Westminster. Instead, its objects were to promote the sub-division of large overgrown districts; to supply additional clergy and lay agents; to establish schools; to supply more school room services and cottage lectures; and to employ methods such as open-air preaching.[75] In such tasks as open-air preaching, its missionaries were assisted by the students from the Church Missionary Society College which was based in Islington.[76] An article in the *Christian Observer* in December 1856 remarked that the Islington Church Home Mission was the only Church of England society that was employing open-air preaching as a missionary approach.[77] Blomfield in his final charge of 1854, written before the practice of open-air preaching had been legalized, said that he would not forbid its practice, but that he doubted 'whether it will succeed to any considerable extent, and whether it has any important advantage over the plan of preaching in school-rooms or other convenient buildings'.[78] In the following year, however, Blomfield expressed his approval of the work of the Islington Church Home Mission in a letter to the Reverend C. F. Childe (Principal of the Church Missionary Society College in Islington), and sent a donation.[79] Such developments highlight the development and growing acceptance of new missionary techniques in the 1850s.

London Diocesan Church Building Society

In 1854, Blomfield reconstituted and relaunched the Metropolis Churches Fund under the new name of the London Diocesan Church Building Society.[80] By this time, the traditional sources of funding church-extension activities in London had dried up. The funds of the Church Building Commissioners were exhausted and the income of the Metropolis Churches Fund was inconsequential. Furthermore, the Incorporated Church Building Society's financial situation was now seriously limited by the recent abolition of royal letters. The impetus for Blomfield's act had come firstly from the reawakening of the Metropolis Churches Fund in consequence of the establishment of the Church Extension Fund in 1851. This Fund was a short-lived national funding body established in response to the Papal Bull of late 1850. This action, emotively entitled the 'Papal Aggression' by *The Times* newspaper, reinstituted the Catholic hierarchy with the creation of twelve Catholic dioceses with corresponding bishops.[81] In reaction, in January 1851, the Church Extension Fund was established with a mixed High Church and Evangelical committee who were united in combating the 'Papal Aggression' in their campaign of church extension. The launch appeal of the Church Extension Fund, in *The Times* in April 1851, opened with the words:

> Much has been heard of late respecting Papal Aggression. The Protestant spirit of Englishmen has been roused from one end of the country to the other; and so far as public feeling can be collected from meetings and manifestoes, the nation has declared itself unequivocally against the arrogant pretensions of the Church of Rome, and its unscriptural and pernicious doctrines.[82]

The committee included several Bishops, such as: the Evangelical Charles Sumner (1790–1874), Bishop of Winchester; the High Churchman John Lonsdale (1788–1867), Bishop of Lichfield; and the High Churchman Charles Longley (1794–1868), Bishop of Ripon. It chiefly, however, consisted of the main players in London church extension from the 1840s and 1850s.[83] The meetings of the society were chaired by Bishop Blomfield and the society operated from the same address as the office of the Metropolis Churches Fund.[84] Although based in London, and expecting to raise most of its money through London, the aim of the society was to fund church extension nationally. Its purpose was to galvanize the funding of church extension and to act as a central channel for funding. It therefore accepted either general contributions or those for existing diocesan church-building societies.[85] Funds would then be given out generally in grants or would be redirected to a particular diocesan organization as specified by the donor. The appeal stated that the intention of the Fund was that it would run for a limited time and this is confirmed by the society's minute book, which record regular meetings until March 1852 and then just occasional meetings until March 1856. The society's letter book also records that by January 1852 the society's funds were exhausted.[86] The Fund raised just over £65,000 in its first year; most of this amount (£61,000) was earmarked to be applied to localities specified by the donors.[87] And it is exactly in this respect that it acted to reawaken the Metropolis Churches Fund.

The second impetus to the Metropolis Churches Fund was the publication of a pamphlet in 1853 by William Rivington, the wealthy printer who had established the St Pancras Church Building Fund.[88] Rivington hoped that by publicizing the neglect of the Metropolis Churches Fund he could rally new support and bring about its revival.[89] Instead, in May 1854 a new society, the London Diocesan Church Building Society, was instituted as a permanent institution to replace the temporary Metropolis Churches Fund.[90] There was a degree of continuity from the earlier committee of the Metropolis Churches Fund with members such as William Cotton, John Duke Coleridge, William Ewart Gladstone (1809–98), and Anthony Ashley Cooper, seventh Earl of Shaftesbury (1801–85) all continuing on as London Diocesan Church Building Society committee members. The objects of this society were initially to build and endow new churches and to supply these churches with parsonages. Under Bishop Tait, it expanded its objects to include the use of missionaries and multipurpose buildings, such as school-churches.

The launch of this new endeavour in 1854 was well-timed, coinciding with both the publication of Horace Mann's report and Blomfield's 1854 charge.[91] Despite this, the launch was unsuccessful and failed to gain a high level of financial support from the Anglican community. Receipts in the first year were disappointing with income for the year 1854–5 amounting to only £4,302. Three combined factors are the possible cause for this lacklustre relaunch. Firstly, part of its failure may have been in its name which implied that it was just a church-building society.[92] Secondly, Blomfield was increasingly frail at the end of his episcopacy. In December 1855, when the London Diocesan Church Building Society published a *Special Appeal to the Landowners*, Blomfield was unable to personally launch the appeal because of illness.[93] Thirdly, the society itself suggested that the public had been disappointed in the speed of results from the earlier church-extension work and that had resulted in widespread 'general apathy on the subject of church extension'.[94] The quarterly magazine of the London Diocesan Church Building Society, *Church Work among the Masses*, observed in 1862 that: 'People expected some immediate and visible effects to follow from so great a movement. They had yet to learn that the benefits of Church Extension, carried out in localities previously neglected, can be only gradually realised.'[95] So correspondingly, in the wake of the publication of the census report and with the issue of the spiritual destitution of the masses prominently in the public mind, the London Diocesan Church Building Society was the only diocesan organization that existed in London to co-ordinate church-extension efforts and it was struggling financially from lack of support. These limited financial resources, in turn, had a significant impact on the scale of the home-missionary work that the London Diocesan Church Building Society was able to provide in the last couple of years of Blomfield's episcopacy.

Conclusion

Within this period there was a shift both in the form of church extension and the method of funding church-extension work. As increasingly sophisticated forms of home mission developed, the model gradually progressed from being simply church-centred in the 1810s, to being an ensemble of church building, missionary clergymen and the use of lay agency by the 1850s. Experience had shown these early church-extensionists that the erection of a church needed to be part of a co-ordinated approach. Blomfield, himself, recognized that it was 'not enough to build a church' for 'the profane, the careless' and 'the miserably poor'; the poor needed a more hands on and direct approach.[96] Blomfield's son, Arthur William Blomfield (1829–99), speaking of his father late in his episcopacy, said that 'he had become increasingly alive to the fact that in the work of church extension, the men are even more necessary than the buildings'.[97] During Blomfield's episcopacy, church extension in London had developed to encompass the use of new forms of home mission: church building (in the form of temporary churches); the use of missionary clergymen and scripture readers; and the advent of open-air preaching.[98]

Blomfield's episcopacy witnessed the building and consecration of around 110 new churches and the establishment of a wide range of Anglican national, diocesan and local home-missionary organizations.[99] However, despite the extensive efforts of Blomfield to extend religious provision in London, his efforts had not kept pace with the rapidly expanding population. The *Final Report of the Metropolis Churches Fund* in 1854 concluded that, 'it is manifest that the increase of Church accommodation during these eighteen years has scarcely kept pace with the increase of population. The original evil remains in almost all its intensity'.[100] In November 1856 the mantle was passed to Archibald Campbell Tait as the new Bishop of London. The scale of his church-extension efforts would be dependent upon the financial generosity of the Anglican laity. Tait's challenge was to garner the necessary sustained financial support to invigorate diocesan church-extension activities.

2 THE CONSOLIDATION AND FURTHER DEVELOPMENT OF HOME MISSION UNDER BISHOP TAIT, 1856–68

Archibald Campbell Tait was consecrated Bishop of London in November 1856, at a time when the issue of the mission of the Church of England to the working-classes had been firmly on the public agenda in the previous two years: Horace Mann's report on the 1851 Religious Census had been published in 1854; open-air preaching had only recently been legitimized in 1855 and was still in its early stages; in Islington the innovative Islington Church Home Mission had been formed only two years earlier; and the Metropolis Churches Fund had recently been reconstituted as the London Diocesan Church Building Society. Tait, however, brought his own additional impetus to this situation with his active support of evangelical interdenominational organizations and his willingness to embrace evangelical methods of preaching. Tait took a 'hands on' approach and led by example. Writing in his journal in 1867, he reflected back upon the beginning of his episcopate:

> I bore my own part in such work, preaching, for example, to the half gypsy popu-
> lation of the Potteries, Kensington, in the open air almost by moonlight, to the
> Omnibus men in their yard Islington by night, to the people assembled by Covent
> Garden Market on a Sunday afternoon in summer, and once to a great assemblage in
> the quadrangle here at Fulham, while our church was closed'.[1]

Such was Tait's zeal for these activities that, in the first month of his episcopate, commentators remarked upon 'the Bishop's undignified and almost Methodist proceedings'.[2] Tait recounts that he acted in this way because he felt that it 'gave the impetus to the clergy and encouraged them to break through the old routine rules which cramped their energy'.[3] Three factors, then, came together to reinvigorate home-missionary techniques in the mid 1850s in London: the installation of a younger and healthier man in his forties as Bishop of London; the employment of new home-missionary techniques in London; and Tait's willingness to embrace these new techniques. Under Blomfield a new complex model of urban church extension had been pioneered in London; Bishop Tait's task was to further extend this model through the creation of an even greater range of male and female diocesan organizations.

London Diocesan Church Building Society

In 1856, on becoming Bishop of London, Tait inherited from Blomfield the rather lacklustre and recently reconstituted London Diocesan Church Building Society. The *Third London Diocesan Church Building Society Annual Report* of 1856–7 already showed the organizing committee's disillusionment, with the society's income for that year being only £7,002.[4] By 1859, however, the *Fifth London Diocesan Church Building Society Annual Report* had taken on a more optimistic tone, reflecting the society's pleasure in the fact that the issue of spiritual destitution in the metropolis was prominently in the public arena.[5] This was due firstly, to the presentation of Bishop Tait's first charge as Bishop of London, and secondly, to the publication of the report of the Select Committee of the House of Lords on the spiritual condition of the large towns.[6]

The deficiency in church accommodation in the large towns had been particularly highlighted in the census report which calculated that London only had enough church accommodation on average to provide for just under 30 per cent of its population.[7] In some areas the standard of provision was even lower: St George-in-the-East, which had a population of 30,507, only had enough church accommodation for 2,830 people, less than 10 per cent of its population.[8] The report's disclosure of the extent of the spiritual destitution of London and other large towns, prompted the formation of a House of Lords Select Committee to enquire into the 'deficiency of means of spiritual instruction and places of divine worship in the metropolis, and in other populous districts in England and Wales'. This Select Committee reported that church sittings provided by all denominations only accommodated 29.7 per cent of the population of London, instead of the 58 per cent standard established in Horace Mann's census report. From this, it concluded that an additional 669,514 extra sittings were needed to raise the percentage to Mann's standard.[9] Bishop Tait and the wider committee of the London Diocesan Church Building Society were involved in the collection of information for the Select Committee: Tait, himself, was a member of the Select Committee, and the Reverend Thomas Fraser Stooks (1816–74), in his capacity as secretary to the London Diocesan Church Building Society, provided the committee with statistics on church accommodation in London.[10] The report made eight recommendations to remedy the problem of spiritual destitution: the use by the Ecclesiastical Commissioners of income formerly belonging to the Chapter of St Paul's Cathedral; the union of certain benefices in the City of London; the sale of the sites of the old churches; the use of more short services in the church; voluntary donations from employers of labour towards the spiritual provision of their employees; a more sufficient endowment of livings in large towns, in order to encourage clergy to want to minister in these town churches; the establishment of 'parochial missions'; and finally, and 'above all, liberal voluntary aid from the public'.[11]

Unfortunately, this increased public awareness did not impact favourably on the income of the London Diocesan Church Building Society: receipts for the year 1859–60 were still only £6,661, including £579 in repaid loans. To put this figure into context, £5,000 was the estimated cost of supplying a church at this time: £1,000 for the site and an additional £4,000 for the church building.[12] In an address to Tait, the society's committee reported on how the 'scarcity of funds' was limiting its work:

> The development of Church Extension in London can only be in proportion to the lib-
> erality with which it is supported by the community at large. For, my Lord, it is necessary
> that we keep steadily in view the certain truth, that the efforts we make for the spiritual
> benefit of London must depend upon voluntary contributions. It is clear from the Report
> of the Committee of the House of Lords that no aid will be given by Government.[13]

The problem was, the society felt, one of perception; the very name 'London Dioc-esan Church Building Society' implied that it was just a church-building society. Consequently, in March 1860, Tait issued an appeal with the aim of dispelling this idea, arguing that the society should be thought of as a 'parochial extension society' rather than a church-building society.[14] Tait's appeal stressed the society's recent innovation of using missionaries; this progressive development had been introduced as a new object in 1857 at the instigation of the Evangelical Robert Grosvenor, Baron Ebury. With this introduction, the society increased its objects to include the allocation of grants for the stipends of missionary clergymen 'to labour in Districts where, as yet, there is no Church, but where it is intended at some future time to build one'.[15] This innovation to fund men as well as buildings was new. The additional curates at work in Bethnal Green had not been funded by the Metropolis Churches Fund or the Bethnal Green Churches and Schools Fund, but instead by the Additional Curates' Society and the Church Pastoral-Aid Society.[16] In 1857, the London Diocesan Church Building Society also further extended its objects to include the purchase of sites, the purchase or build-ing of temporary churches, and the building of school-churches.[17] This expansion of the society's objects coincided with the launch of the London Diocesan Home Mission, the first of the new diocesan home-missionary organizations to be established during Tait's episcopate. Although the London Diocesan Church Building Society had expanded it objects to include missionaries and the use of a variety of buildings, its fundamental limitation was still that it was not attracting sufficient funds from the Anglican laity. Tait addressed this problem by launch-ing two new societies as substitutes: firstly, the London Diocesan Home Mission in 1857, and then the Bishop of London's Fund in 1863.

New Male Home Missionary Societies

It was the employment of clergymen to act as home missionaries that formed the basis of the London Diocesan Home Mission. This society was funded by contributions from the laity and from the churches to which the missionaries were attached; after 1863 it received additional funds from the Bishop of London's Fund. The inspiration for the London Diocesan Home Mission had come from the pioneering work being carried out in the Evangelical parish of Islington. Tait's first public engagement as Bishop of London had been to chair the inaugural meeting of Islington Church Extension Society in December 1856. The bishop declared at this event that he was both surprised and pleased to hear that Islington had two different types of society attached to it: one for church building and one for home mission.[18]

> I rejoiced to find that every principle which I thought ought to be carried out in preparing the ground for the building of the church of stone and lime had been carried out here in the attempt first to build the living Church of Christ. When I read a sermon which was delivered by the vicar, in the parish church here, a short time ago, I rejoiced to find that there was a cattle-shed which was used as a church; I rejoiced to hear of a garden which had its walls raised, and a roof put over it that it might be used as a church; I rejoiced to hear also of three or four school rooms, in districts lately formed, being so used as to serve the purpose of temporary churches. I rejoiced to hear of a wooden church, and of an iron church, in an adjoining district; and I rejoiced perhaps even more to hear that in an omnibus yard there are meetings on Sunday mornings, of those whose occupations, carried on for our benefit, too much deprive them of the ordinary means of grace; and that in this omnibus yard, prayers are offered, and praises to God are sung, as heartily as within any cathedral in the land.[19]

His praise was particularly reserved for the work of the Islington Church Home Mission (established in 1854), which had laid down the ground work for the complementary Islington Church Extension Society (established in 1856) whose ambition was to erect ten churches in six years.[20] Tait agreed with the Islington model, that the best method was to first build up the congregation and then build the physical church; this model thus shaped the form of Tait's own diocesan model of church extension.[21]

The London Diocesan Home Mission was established on the premise that the existing parochial clergy in London were so overstretched that it was unrealistic to expect them to also evangelize the masses.[22] Tait explained that the Church 'cannot wait till churches are built and parishes formed. Let missionary efforts be directed to this work at once, and churches and parishes, and all their due appliances for regular worship and instruction, will follow in God's good time.'[23] Overall its strategy was to build up a community before attempting to build a church; in Tait's opinion this was the way to get the poor to attend church. The missionary was to go into densely populated areas where the existing parochial machinery was inadequate and to promote the Gospel:

> When you have sent the right man, and he ministers amongst them, and has gathered them one by one to attend on his ministrations, whether in the open air or in a saw-mill, or wherever it may be, then when you have a permanent church he walks into that church at the head of his already formed congregation.[24]

The Evangelical Dudley Ryder (1798–1882), second Earl of Harrowby, report-ing at the society's annual meeting in 1865, articulated the benefits of this new missionary-led approach. He argued that the old model of focusing on 'perma-nent work' (i.e. church building) often resulted in the first incumbent 'preaching in a kind of desert'. Instead the more successful approach, following the methods employed by the apostles, was 'transient work' (i.e. addressing the multitudes where ever they may be) followed by later 'permanent work'. This new form of approach would ensure that the new incumbent would already have an estab-lished community both to attend church and to support him in his work.[25] The added advantage of this missionary-centred, rather than church-centred, model of church extension was that it was thought to be more cost effective in the long term. The missionary would build a community of people who would in turn help raise some of the money needed ultimately for the church building.

The Mission at St Paul's Church in Deptford was one of the earliest success stories for the London Diocesan Home Mission, taking just five years to estab-lish a new congregation and church. In 1859, the Reverend John Polkinghorne Courtenay (d. 1882), held his first service under a railway arch to a congregation consisting of only five people. Over a period he held more open-air services in most of the streets around Deptford, with crowds gradually swelling to large numbers. Soon the congregation was large enough to merit the hiring of a saw mill for regular services, with average morning attendances of 400 and evening attendances of 600 to 700 people. The *Eighth LDHM Annual Report* reported that 'the great majority of these people had not been in the habit of attending any place of worship previous to the period that the Missionary commenced his labours amongst them.' In April 1863, a committee was formed to raise the funds to enable the community to build a permanent church. Shortly after in December 1864, the new Christ Church, with accommodation for 1,200 peo-ple, was consecrated by the Bishop of London. Attached to the church were a range of activities: bible classes for working men and young women; mothers' meetings; clothing clubs and coal clubs.[26]

The London Diocesan Home Mission was inaugurated with a series of experimental Sunday evening services held for working people in the parish churches of north and east London at the end of 1857.[27] The society also car-ried out special missions aimed at particular workers, such as navvies, cabmen, omnibus men and railway labourers. Tait felt that the immediacy of the society's work was particularly well suited to tackle the urban problem of temporary work forces.[28] The London Diocesan Home Mission also played an important part in the general missions which were the main innovation under Tait's successor, John

Jackson (Bishop of London between 1869 and 1885). These campaigns were conducted over several days, the objective being 'the evangelization of the masses'. Such large-scale missions, which generally lasted between eight to ten days, first occurred in 1874 and became regular occurrences from the mid 1880s.[29] Following the mixed-party model of organization established under Blomfield, the committee of the London Diocesan Home Mission was also of mixed Church party. It included: Evangelicals such as Daniel Wilson junior; prominent High Churchmen such as William Cotton; and Tractarians such as the Reverend Bryan King (1811–95), Rector of St George-in-the-East.[30] Highlighting the continuity between diocesan organizations, about one-third of the London Diocesan Church Building Society committee were also committee members of the London Diocesan Home Mission. In terms of reception, the High Church *Guardian* welcomed the work of the London Diocesan Home Mission at its inauguration.[31] The Evangelical *Record*, however, expressed its concern over the mixed Church party constitution of the society: 'Here we have together some of the most faithful heralds of the pure Gospel of JESUS CHRIST linked together with others who preach "another gospel"'. This concern, however, was short-lived, and otherwise the paper reported approvingly on the work of the society.[32] The mixed Church party of this society (and subsequently the Bishop of London's Fund) is noteworthy as it is evidence of different parties working together in a time of party tensions caused by the rise of ritualism.[33] Tait was aware of the immensity of his new role as Bishop of London and made concessions to both Evangelicals and the High Church. For example, he allowed Evangelicals to hire theatres to hold services and also endorsed High Church practices in churches providing that they were not too provocative.[34] P. T. Marsh argues that he took this stance because 'he knew that the church needed all the zeal that it could command to make headway against the spiritual destitution, blank secularism, and social misery prevalent in London'.[35] Tait explained the underlying principle that bound the different parties together in the work of the London Diocesan Home Mission in his 1858 charge: 'But I will not believe that we ministers of this one great national Church of Christ, bound to aid and sympathize with each other in the difficulties of contending with an ungodly world, can have so magnified our points of differences as to be unwilling to co-operate one with an another in the work of saving souls'.[36] Later in the 1860s, Tait again justified the mixed-party committee constitution of the Bishop of London's Fund to a committee member by citing both the 'comprehensive' nature of the national Church and its consequential 'imperfect state'. He argued that 'the Church of England is on the side of this comprehensive charitable view of the comparative unimportance of lesser differences ... we are great believers in the unity of the Faith held even amongst great diversities of opinion'.[37] This mixed-party model, therefore, continued to demonstrate the ability of men of different positions of overlook their contentious differences and to work in unison on certain diocesan schemes.

In 1862, having just declined the Archbishopric of York on the grounds that his work in London was still too much in its infancy, Tait issued his second charge. This set in motion the events that led to the establishment of the Bishop of London's Fund which his biographer regarded as being 'the greatest and most memorable act of Tait's London Episcopate'.[38] Tait's prime concern was that the spiritual destitution of London was being constantly exacerbated by its expanding population. The census of 1861 had recently been issued, showing that in the previous decade the population of London had grown by over 400,000 people. The Church, in the past ten years, had only managed to keep pace with the growing population and had not made any inroads.[39] Writing in 1862, a committee member of the London Diocesan Church Building Society described the Church's attempts to keep pace with the rapidly expanding metropolitan population as being comparable with 'that of a ship's crew pumping for their lives, and water rushing in nearly as fast again as they can keep it under.'[40] The article highlighted the Church's inability to keep pace with the burgeoning population of London and calculated that 'when Bishop Blomfield closed his great church-building career, London was left in want of 110 churches more than when he commenced it!' By 1862, this deficiency had increased further to 148.[41] Bishop Tait's charge of 1862 echoed this sentiment in his review of the Church's efforts in the period 1851 to 1861: 'the appalling fact accordingly transpires, that, whatever were our spiritual wants in this respect in 1851, all our great exertions have not lessened them, but have at best but prevented the evil from growing worse.'[42] This lack of progress highlights the scale of the challenge that Tait faced during his episcopate.

Tait's charge prompted Charles Girdlestone (1797–1881), Rector of Kingswinford in Lincolnshire, to suggest that Tait should specifically approach London's landowners for funds. Girdlestone, who was himself a property owner in London, commented that he had never been approached to make a donation to any charitable scheme in the metropolis.[43] After having referred the letter to the committee of the London Diocesan Church Building Society, it was decided that an appeal should be launched. Tait gathered together a large meeting of the most influential men in London (men who owned property or employed labour in the metropolis) in April 1863, with a view to discuss the best way of addressing the 'spiritual needs' of the metropolis.[44] His plan was to raise £500,000 from the laity over a ten-year period but such was the enthusiasm for his scheme that a target of £1,000,000 was set. *The Times* was quick to condemn the proposal as simply being yet another church-building scheme; Alexander James Beresford Beresford Hope (1820–87) and the Reverend Thomas Fraser Stooks, both committee members of the London Diocesan Church Building Society and Bishop of London's Fund, wrote letters to *The Times* to correct this misapprehension, stressing the use of missionaries and laymen in the scheme.[45] Shortly afterwards, on 20 June 1863, Tait issued a pastoral letter to the laity of the Diocese of London to launch the Bishop of London's Fund.[46] The appeal set out the objects of the Fund: missionary clergy or additional curates; scripture readers; mission women; clergymen's residences; schools; mission rooms or school churches; endowment of old or new districts; endowment of curacies; and building of churches. Tellingly, the provision of missionary clergy was put at the head of the list and the building of churches at the end; no doubt this was with the aim of dispelling the notion that this was just another repackaged church building society. The new society did not itself carry out this work. It funded the work carried about by other organizations and communities, giving grants to organizations such as the London Diocesan Home Mission for the salaries of its missionaries.

The initial intention was that the Bishop of London's Fund would be a temporary institution lasting for ten years, and that it would be carried out in connection with the existing machinery of the London Diocesan Church Building Society. The success of the society's launch and its public prominence is observable in the size and status of its committee which dwarfed previous diocesan committees. The *First Bishop of London's Fund Annual Report* listed its 149 committee members, many of which were high status men: the committee included two dukes, one marquis, eight earls and five viscounts.[47] Its committee followed in the mixed Church-party model that had been established by Blomfield. *The Record*, by 1863, was able to report the benefits of this mixed-party model whilst still retaining its scepticism:

> It is delightful to see men holding different opinions on circumstances uniting together, because they have one common standing on the foundations of eternal truth ... We are the friends of Union in a large and liberal sense, but we cannot shut our eyes to the perils of indiscriminate comprehension, or hope that men, who would destroy the foundations of the Church of England by sweeping away subscription to the Articles, would work together harmoniously in dealing with the spiritual destitution.[48]

The evolving progression of the church-extension initiatives from Bishop Blomfield to Bishop Tait can also be seen in the continuity and cross-over of the committee members between the different societies; many of the Bishop of London's Fund committee members had been involved in the earlier incarnations of the Metropolis Churches Fund and the London Diocesan Church Building Society. This was the case, for example, with William Cotton, Anthony Ashley Cooper (seventh Earl of Shaftesbury), William Ewart Gladstone and Robert Grosvenor (first Baron Ebury).[49] Likewise there was a great deal of partnership between the London Diocesan Home Mission and other committees, with over half of its committee being members of either the London Diocesan Church Building Society or Bishop of London's Fund committees.

The Fund's first action was to appoint a Special Committee to report on the religious condition of London. The detailed report, published in 1864, related the current metropolitan population to the existing provision of church accommodation, the amount of lay agency, and the amount of school provision.[50]

From this data, the Report extrapolated the deficiency of provision according to a desired standard of provision that the Committee had adopted as necessary to provide an adequate standard of parochial service: one clergyman for every 2,000 people; and church accommodation for 25 per cent of the population of the diocese.[51] The figure of 25 per cent was derived from a reworking of Horace Mann's figures from the census report. Mann calculated, after making allowances for the aged and infirm, that 58 per cent of the population were able to attend church. The Bishop of London's Fund report determined that in the Diocese of London the existing provision was for only 29 per cent of the population; 18 per cent was supplied by the Church of England and 11 per cent by Nonconformists. The society calculated that if the Church of England were to provide its proportional amount of the 58 per cent; it would need to provide 36 per cent, with Nonconformists providing the other 22 per cent.[52] Instead the society's committee proposed a more moderate and achievable 25 per cent as its standard of provision. This is a clear indication that the Church of England accepted that the Nonconformists had a role in providing church accommodation in the diocese. From this basis, the Report concluded that another 500 clergymen and an additional 250,000 sittings were required. As stated, this calculation was formulated on two standards of provision: one clergyman for every 2,000 people and church accommodation for 25 per cent of the population of the diocese.[53] For context, Bishop Blomfield's objective for a standard of church provision, when he launched the Metropolis Churches Fund in 1836, had been one church and clergyman for every 3,000 people.[54] The reduction in the number of people that one clergyman could minister to was taken from the Select Committee report which stated that '2,000 are as many as can be tolerably be visited by one clergyman'; this highlights the fact that clergymen in this later period were expected to have a more active role.[55] Working on a suggested standard of one lay agent to every 2,000 people, the report concluded that another 600 lay agents were required. Again this calculation acknowledged existing levels of Nonconformist lay agent provision from societies such as the London City Mission and the Ranyard Bible Mission. It also reported that 92 parishes were without a parsonage, and it calculated that the Church of England should provide school provision for 100,000 children. The Church Pastoral-Aid Society estimated that £3,000,000 would need to be raised to address the deficiencies quantified in this review.[56] Having calculated the scale of deficiency, the next step undertaken by the Bishop of London's Fund was to implement a strategy and to raise the requisite funds.

The strategic arm of the Bishop of London's Fund was the Origination Committee, so called because its purpose was to 'originate measures for accomplishing the objects of the Fund' and to devise different schemes of work for different situations.[57] The committee set out three different approaches (called schemes A to C) that could be taken in a parish in need of the Fund's assistance. Scheme A was to provide mission rooms or schools, and if necessary, sites for churches in districts where missionary clergy were already at work under the supervision of different agencies. Scheme B was to divide the most populous parishes into conventional districts. Under this scheme 10,000 people were to be left under the jurisdiction of the mother church. The rest of the parish would then be arranged so each new district would have a population of around 4,000; each new temporary district would be provided with two missionary clergy. Working with the London Diocesan Home Mission, the Bishop of London's Fund would provide the monies for a mission station and if possible a site for a church.[58] After two years, the success of the temporary district would be reviewed to see if it was suitable for constitution as a permanent district. Steps would then be taken to obtain an endowment from the Ecclesiastical Commissioners.[59] Parishes judged suitable for this scheme in 1864 were St Peter's, Walworth (with a population of 34,000); All Saint's Poplar (with a population of 33,000); St George-in-the-East (with a population of 30,000); and Christ Church, Marylebone (with a population of 22,000). The *Ninth Bishop of London's Fund Annual Report*, reporting on the year 1872, gave progress reports for financed initiatives in all of these proposed areas; all had progressed successfully to having new permanent districts constituted. For example: the parish of Christ Church (Marylebone) had been divided into three districts, with the two newly built and endowed churches of St Barnabas and St Cyprian; and the parish of St George-in-the-East had also been divided into three districts, with the two newly built and endowed churches of St John's and St Peter's.[60] Finally, Scheme C was to provide missionary clergy, scripture readers and missionary women in parishes where the population was too large for the existing staff to manage. This scheme was used in cases where the population size did not warrant division.[61] This strategy was implemented by working with a number of different agencies, such as the London Diocesan Home Mission and Scripture Readers' Association.

The Bishop of London's Fund differed from the London Diocesan Church Building Society and Metropolis Churches Fund in an innovative new way by making payments of annual block grants to a number of Anglican voluntary organizations. Annual grants of between £1,000 and £2,000 were allocated to the London Diocesan Church Building Society, London Diocesan Home Mission, Scripture Readers' Association, Additional Curates' Society, Church Pastoral-Aid Society, and the Diocesan Board of Education.[62] Smaller grants of just a few hundred pounds, which varied year to year in size, were given to the Parochial Mission Women Association and London Diocesan Deaconess Institution.[63] In respect of the Lay Helpers' Association, variable small annual grants were made in order to cover its running costs. These societies all carried out home-missionary work that addressed the objectives of the Fund, either in terms of funding the missionary work of men and women, or the provision (hire or build) of buildings. In addition, grants were given directly to specific projects, such as the building of a church, the purchase of a site for a church building or the purchase of an iron church. The Bishop of London's Fund was, therefore, the central funder of all aspects of diocesan home-missionary work. In 1907, the Bishop of London encapsulated the importance of the Fund by describing it as being 'the central war-chest of the Diocese'.[64]

In the first annual report, which presented income until 31 December 1864 (eighteen months from the launch of the appeal), the Fund had received £100,457 with a further £72,000 pledged; and many of the subscribers had pledged amounts for the envisaged full ten-year period.[65] At the end of the Fund's first five-year run, in 1868, Bishop Tait was promoted to the Archbishopric of Canterbury and was succeeded by John Jackson (1811–85), who had been Bishop of Lincoln. At the end of this period, the amount received by the Fund stood at £284,189 with an additional £66,558 promised, making a grand total of £350,747.[66] An analysis of grants given in this first five year period shows that grants totalling £214,017 had been made, of which the majority still related to buildings in different forms. The category breakdown of these grants was as follows: £4,000 for 20 parsonages (2 per cent of grants); £17,184 for schools (8 per cent); £15,204 for mission buildings and rooms (7 per cent); £1,218 for the endowment of two districts (1 per cent); £61,244 for permanent churches (29 per cent); £52,587 for sites relating to churches, schools, mission buildings and parsonages (24 per cent); and £62,580 on clergy and lay agents (29 per cent).[67] To contextualize this expenditure, a statement by the Executive Committee of the Bishop of London's Fund in 1865 estimated unit costs for the society's grants. In respect of living agents, it estimated that the cost of a missionary clergyman or additional curate was £100 to £200 per annum, that a scripture reader was £70 per annum, and that a mission woman was £40 per annum. It respect of building works, it estimated that the building cost of a parsonage was about £1,500 to £2,000, that a church was £5,000 (£1,000 for the site plus £4,000 for the fabric and fittings), that a mission church was £2,000, and finally that a school building should be costed at £2 to £3 for every scholar, plus an additional £1,000 for the site.[68] The Bishop of Ripon suggests a similar sum when in 1895 he complains that the income of the BLF (£24,000) is barely sufficient to build four churches.[69]

In 1873, Jackson confirmed the Fund as a permanent institution and calculated that the nearly £500,000 given out in grants, had raised an equivalent £1,500,000 in supportive funding for projects, with an additional £1,000,000 capital from the Ecclesiastical Commissioners for the endowment of new parishes.[70] Reviewing the work of the first ten years, Jackson commended the society and estimated that through the building of 110 new churches, the enlargements of other churches, the service of an additional 200 clergymen, and the work of various lay organizations, new provision had been made for half a million people in the diocese.[71] The population increase, in that ten-year period, had added an additional 350,000 people to the diocese. Fortunately, however, this increase had been matched by an equivalent loss of 340,000 to the Diocese of Rochester when a number of parishes were transferred in 1867 on the death of Bishop Wigram of Rochester; this was under the terms of the London Diocese Act of 1863.[72] Taking these adjustments into account, Jackson judged that the Diocese of London had consequently made a 'marked impression upon the destitution' within the previous ten years.[73] Setting out the society's objectives for the future, Jackson judged that there was not much need at present for further parish subdivision. Correspondingly, the Fund's committee decided that their priority should be strengthening missionary work in poor parishes that were not yet large enough for subdivision. In such areas it was estimated that an additional one hundred mission buildings would be required, with the usual supporting cast of bible classes and mothers' meetings. In addition, it was calculated that there were still 140 parishes without parsonages.[74]

In 1913, the Bishop of London (Bishop Winnington-Ingram, Bishop of London between 1901 and 1939) preaching at the Fiftieth Jubilee thanksgiving service, estimated that in its first fifty years, the Fund had raised nearly £1,500,000 and had drawn forth about another £3,000,000 in supportive funding.[75] From this £1,500,000 raised, an estimated 46 per cent of the funds had been spent on mission clergy, curates and lay agency; 28 per cent on church building; 18 per cent on mission buildings; 5 per cent on schools; 2 per cent on parsonages and 1 per cent on endowment.[76] In summary, 54 per cent of funds had been granted for capital projects or 'permanent work' and 46 per cent for salaries or 'transient work'.[77] This was a clear increase on the 29 per cent allocated to salaries in the first five years of the Fund and is evidence of the shift in emphasis introduced by Jackson. The anniversary booklet of 1913 reviewed the work of the Fund during its first fifty years and reported that the Fund had helped finance the erection of 240 churches and several hundred mission rooms, in addition to supplying curates and lay workers to many parishes.[78] In contrast to the low income levels experienced by the London Diocesan Church Building Society, the Bishop of London's Fund was successful in establishing a steady income stream of at least £20,000 per annum through the period. Despite this, Bishop Winnington-Ingram wrote a letter to all incumbents in 1911 stating that his 'one great disappointment' was his failure to increase the Fund's income to its required level; at the beginning of his episcopacy he had suggested that the fund needed around £50,000 a year to meet its duties to accommodate the continuously expanding population.[79] Annual income figures in this region were routinely achieved by the interdenominational London City Mission from the late 1870s onwards.

In 1865, in accordance with a recommendation of a sub-committee of the Bishop of London's Fund, the Lay Helpers' Association was established under the presidency of the Bishop of London, with a mixed committee of laymen and clergy.[80] The aim of the association was to support existing lay workers and to attract new ones. It did this by organizing local meetings, lectures and services for its members, thereby creating a support network for the lay workers. The Lay Helpers' Association arranged training sessions in preaching and doctrine for their members. Every year a four-week residential course of training was available to lay helpers at Keble College. This course gave the lay readers the opportunity to attend theological lectures and sermons, and to meet other lay agents. Some of the lay readers were sanctioned by the Bishop to be missioners, but the majority acted as parochial readers, under the supervision of their incumbent, in mission services. To be admitted into the association, the laymen had to be a communicant who engaged voluntarily in Church work, and they had to be recommended by a clergyman or two existing associates.

Looking back on its origins, the Lay Helpers' Association later stated that the period from the 1860s to the 1880s had seen a complete transformation in the use and appreciation of the skills of the layman: that the ground for laymen had been 'ploughed' by Bishop Blomfield, 'planted' by Bishop Tait and 'watered' by Bishop Jackson.[81] It was, however, for Bishop Tait that they dedicated their greatest praise. In the first issue of *London Diocesan Magazine* in 1886, the Lay Helpers' Association entry commented that: 'It was reserved for Bishop Tait – the "Bishop of the Laity" as he was sometimes called ... to enlist the laity at large under the standard of the Bishop of the Diocese'.[82] The society argued that under previous bishops, laymen had been appreciated simply for their 'money qualification' and their contribution to committee work. In contrast, they credited Bishop Tait for being the first Bishop to wholeheartedly appreciate that the laity had valuable spiritual attributes that could be utilized practically.[83] The unstated economic aspect of this development was, of course, that lay help was a low-cost way of supporting the clergy. The society's limited financial needs, of a few hundred pounds a year, were initially funded by the Bishop of London's Fund but over time it became self-supporting through membership contributions.[84] By the 1880s, the society had nearly 4,000 members; by the 1890s this number had risen further to 6,000.[85] In 1909 the Lay Helpers' Association was reconstituted under the new name of the Readers' Board and Association of Readers for the Diocese of London.[86] In 1880 a similar organization, entitled the Lay Workers' Association was established for the Diocese of Rochester.[87]

In 1880 the work of the Bishop of London's Fund was expanded further with the creation of the East London Church Fund. In 1879, the post of Bishop Suffragan of Bedford was created, the first Bishop being William Walsham How (1823–97). His responsibility was the East of London, specifically the three rural deaneries of Hackney, Spitalfields and Stepney (with a population of 700,000); and the parish of Tottenham (with a population of 46,000).[88] In 1888 responsibility for Islington, Saint Sepulchre (not including the two city parishes), Shoreditch and Enfield was added to the Bishopric, which equated to a responsibility for an additional 700,000 people.[89] Again following the committee model established by earlier diocesan church-extension organizations in London, the society was of mixed Church party in its constitution. This facet was described in *The Times* in 1882 which stated that the 'council had refused to be influenced by any of the party distinctions which so unhappily prevailed in the present day'.[90]

The object of the Fund was 'not to build Churches, but to build up the faith of Christ in the parishes of the East London Church Fund District.'[91] In parallel with the Bishop of London's Fund, it functioned as a funding body. It differed, however, in that it only funded living agents (missionary and additional clergy, curates, and lay agency) in the geographical area under the supervision of the Suffragan Bishop. The Bishop of London (Bishop Winnington-Ingram) speaking at the 1902 annual meeting nicely summed up the work funded by the society:

> The East End Church is a visiting Church. It wins by visiting'. He implored the church workers in the East London to: 'Knock at your people's doors. Persevere. Climb up their narrow stairs. Know the lodgers hidden in the back rooms. Comfort the sick. Pray for the dying.[92]

Its missionaries and lay agents evangelized through a variety of means: they held mission services in common lodging houses; carried out thrift, temperance and purity work; promoted emigration; ran guilds, classes, unions; organized mission services illustrated by magic lanterns and pictures; held Church history lectures; ran public nurseries and various other agencies 'to redeem children'; and carried out missionary work amongst the Jews and foreign immigrants.[93] It did not give funds for the building of churches, mission buildings or parsonages; these were still covered by grants from the Bishop of London's Fund.[94] The East London Church Fund did not completely relieve the Bishop of London's Fund of its financial responsibilities relating to living agents working in the north and east of London until 1891 when it began to take on its relevant portion of the Bishop of London's Fund's annual block grants: for example, grants to the London Diocesan Home Mission, London Diocesan Deaconess Institution, Parochial Mission Women Association and Scripture Readers' Association.[95] And again, in parallel with the Bishop of London's Fund, its objects were funded entirely by contributions from the laity.

Thus, under Tait church extension activities within the diocese continued to build upon the groundwork established by Blomfield. Tait's new male home-missionary organizations continued the mixed portfolio approach of using both buildings (churches, parsonages and mission rooms) and missionaries which had been established by Blomfield. However, under Tait and his successors, more emphasis and money was directed towards the use of people in the form of scripture readers, missionaries, mission women and deaconesses. This is highlighted by the fact that three of the four male societies were solely concerned with the use of people to evangelize the masses. Furthermore, nearly half of the expenditure of the Bishop of London's Fund was directed towards the use of missionary agency. The greatest advancement, however, was the Bishop of London's Fund's role as the central source of financial support; this brought the different agencies at work in the diocese together and made them all part of a more co-ordinated diocesan scheme. Supplemental to the efforts of these large male societies, were a small number of female home-missionary societies. It is this galvanization of female lay help and their organization into missionary societies that was one of the greatest innovations in this period.

New Female Home Missionary Societies

The first of the new Anglican female missionary societies was the Parochial Mission Women Association which was established in 1860. A few years earlier in 1857, Ellen Ranyard (1810–79), a Congregationalist, had established the inter-denominational and evangelical Bible and Domestic Female Mission. The Ranyard Bible Mission, as it was later known, was innovative in its use of both working-class lay men and women as missionaries.[96] Inspired by Ranyard's book *The Missing Link*, published in 1859, four upper-class ladies decided to establish an Anglican version of this society. Their objections to the Ranyard Bible Women were that the women were often Nonconformist and that they were independent of the parochial system, hence the prominence of the word 'parochial' in the new society's name.[97]

The society was founded by four close friends, two of which were related: Lady Charlotte Hatherley (1804–78); Lady Laura Selborne (1821–85); Lady Cecily Susan Montagu of Beaulieu (1835–1915); and Caroline Jane Talbot (1809–76), the aunt of her co-founder Lady Montagu of Beaulieu. All four women were married to politically prominent men.[98] The society's presidents were: Caroline Jane Talbot, from 1860 to her death in 1876; Lady Montagu of Beaulieu, from 1876 to her death in 1915; and Lady Maud Caroline Hamilton (1846–1938), from 1915 until the society's demise in 1923.[99] The Parochial Mission Women Association was managed by a committee of Lady Managers; this governance was supplemented by a 'Committee of Reference' which consisted of eight gentlemen, generally family relations of the Lady Managers. Their role was to audit the annual accounts and to advise the all female management committee on financial matters.[100] Unlike the mixed Church-party model established by the diocesan male societies, both the female committee and all male finance committee of the Parochial Mission Women Association were predominantly High Church and Conservative. And also in contrast to these male organizations, the committee had no clerical presence; the only clerical association was that their annual reports stated that they worked under the official sanction of the Bishop of London and the Archbishop of Canterbury. Consequently, the committee membership was limited to a close group of friends, relations and colleagues. Poole, in her analysis of the unusual constitution of the Parochial Mission Women Association, stresses that throughout the society's existence 'no churchman ever corrected, reproved, chided, or over-ruled them or asserted any authority whatsoever over them.'[101]

The Parochial Mission Women Association was constituted on three principles: that its mission work would be part of the parochial system of the Church; that the mission women would be supervised by their Incumbent and by an assigned Lady-Superintendent; and that no alms would be given. The society carried out its work by employing working-class women to act as mission women. These women carried out house-to-house visiting and, through personal influence and example, taught thrift, economy and cleanliness.[102] The value of the mission woman's work is described in a small pamphlet which details the work of one mission woman named Elizabeth:

> She began at first by calling on all the poor people, and leaving the parochial cards, and making friends with them. She invited them all to come and meet the Lady Superintendent at the Mission room every Monday afternoon. She found numbers of children unbaptized, and soon persuaded the mothers to bring them to be baptized. The town was in many parts very dirty indeed. Elizabeth cleaned and helped to clean a great number of the rooms; and the courts and yards were soon quite different places, after she had been a little while in the parish. She used to encourage them to keep up clean habits, by telling the poor women that she would bring the Lady Superintendent to see their clean cottages, and many of the houses you would hardly know again after she had been there.[103]

Another special feature of the mission woman's work was to help the poor to save, by means of a Penny Bank, for new clothing or items for the home. In the region of £14,000 was collected annually through this means; between 1860 and 1914 £588,000 in small sums had been collected.[104] This feature did more than just assist the poor with their financial management:

> They must deny themselves something, and when they experience the pleasure of new clothes for themselves, their husbands or their children, or some article of comfort for their homes, the apparent fleeting pleasures of the gin-shop are lessened, and they are encouraged to seek the comfort of good and respectable surroundings rather than again indulge in sensual gratifications. They feel more inclined to go to church, and more ashamed of being seen in the public-house. As a collector the mission woman's visits give her an entrance where she would not otherwise be admitted. She can often help in cases of sickness, clean up the house, make the children tidy. She reads and talks of God when opportunity offers: she seeks out children who ought to be baptised; she tries to induce the drunken and profligate to see the error of their ways; she loses no chance in rescuing young girls and taking them into refuge; she brings under the notice of the clergyman cases requiring his ministrations.[105]

The mission women were only placed in districts where the incumbent had applied for them. They worked under the supervision of a Lady Superintendent who held weekly mothers' meetings either in the afternoon or evening. In addition, there was a strong domestic element to the mission woman's work:

providing a few hours of respite care for a mother with very ill children; washing the bedding of a bedridden invalid; nursing the sick; and making tea.

In 1864, the Bishop of London's Fund minute book records the approval of an annual grant to the Parochial Mission Women Association because it was 'chiefly of a Diocesan character'.[106] The society started off as a home-missionary organization within the Diocese of London, and although it expanded its geographical area in 1862, it was still mainly confined to the dioceses of London and Rochester. In November 1862, it opened a western branch (covering Cornwall and Devon) and in 1871 a northern branch (covering Northumberland).[107] In 1884 the society reported that they were employing 187 mission women: 140 of these were situated in the Dioceses of London and Rochester.[108] Additionally, in 1868 Countess Charlotte Spencer (1835–1903), wife of John Poyntz Spencer, fifth Earl Spencer (1835–1910), formed a 'Supplemental Ladies Association' to the work of the Parochial Mission Women Association with the object of carrying out work in the East End. Its aim was give material assistance in East End parishes in a way that did not infringe the society's principle of not giving indiscriminate alms. Examples of the sort of aid given by this supplemental association were: admittance orders for hospitals; material; outfits for girls going to service; and the hire of a bed, mattress, or pail and brush for whitewashing walls.[109] The objects of the Parochial Mission Women Association were funded by a combination of contributions from the laity, mission payments (from the parishes in which the mission women worked), and grants from the Bishop of London's Fund and East London Church Fund.

In the subsequent year of 1861, the London Diocesan Deaconess Institution was founded with the original name of the North London Deaconess Institution. In the previous decade a small number of Anglican sisterhoods had been founded in England, the first being the Park Village Sisterhood (near Regents Park) which was established in 1845. The public response to sisterhoods was to treat them with suspicion because of their association with the Oxford Movement and their independence of Episcopal authority.[110] In acknowledgement of this general mistrust, the name of the deaconess institution was altered in 1868 to include the word 'diocesan'; this was in order to make clear that it was not a sisterhood and that it was part of the diocesan machinery and therefore under Episcopal supervision. Tait, speaking in 1875 as Archbishop of Canterbury, sought to clarify that the orders of deaconesses were not sisterhoods: 'A Sisterhood, was a private society, whereas deaconesses were grafted into the framework of the Church.'[111]

The London Diocesan Deaconess Institution was co-founded by Elizabeth Catherine Ferard (1825–83) and the Reverend Thomas Pelham Dale (1821–92), with the official approval of Bishop Tait. The community was initially supervised by Dale, a relation of Ferard by marriage, as the community's first Chaplain.[112] Elizabeth Ferard was set apart, in July 1862, as the first deaconess in the Church of England under this revived order. Despite the fact that the organization was modelled on the German Protestant Deaconess Institution of Kaiserswerth (founded in 1838), the London Diocesan Deaconess Institution was undoubtedly of High Church character. In 1868, the Reverend Pelham Dale, himself High Church, resigned his position with the Institution, following various disagreements with the Elizabeth Ferard. Her personal desire was for the community to become more like a sisterhood and she wanted her role (as the Head Sister) to have more independent control of the management of the Institution. In contrast, Dale's founding intention had been that the organization would 'provide a home and organization for women who, having no vocation for the life of a "Religious," yet wished to devote their energies to charitable works'.[113] By the late 1880s, the society had become more explicitly High Church: the deaconesses had taken the title of 'Sister'; the Head Sister had taken the title of 'Superior'; and the term novice was introduced in the late 1890s.[114] These developments highlight the very aspect of sisterhoods that aroused public suspicion, their independence and Anglo-Catholic character.

The work of the deaconesses had three aspects: medical, educational and religious. The principal work of the institution at its opening was within its nursing ward where the deaconesses cared for both the patients' physical and spiritual provision.[115] The deaconesses also assisted in other external nursing activities: helping in the Great Northern Hospital; assisting in Bethnal Green missions during cholera pandemics; and through the establishment of their own nursing home (which later moved to Westgate-on-Sea near Margate).[116] The balance of their work changed as the century progressed, with the deaconesses doing less nursing as the field of nursing developed into its own profession. The nursing ward based at the deaconesses' home changed its purpose in 1881, to become St Gabriel's Industrial Home for Girls which taught the girls skills such as embroidery, lace-making, weaving and rug-making. From the 1890s, the educational work of the deaconesses shifted from being in charge of the running of church schools to concentrating on scripture lessons instead and on Sunday school teaching.[117] Finally, in 1897 the industrial school closed when the space was needed to house the expanded number of deaconesses.

The first annual report of the society outlined the results of the mission work carried out in its first year: 'a population of 3,000 has been visited; nearly 70 children brought to baptism; children have been induced to attend school; parents have been induced to attend public worship'.[118] Typically, the work of the deaconess was concentrated upon supporting a clergyman in his missionary work, for example at the Christ Church Mission, College Park (which was funded by the Bishop of London's Fund in 1888). In missions such as this, the deaconesses supported the incumbent in his work by carrying out district visiting, and organizing mothers' meetings, and women's and girls' Bible classes.[119] They also participated in the larger-scale missionary events, such as a concentrated ten-day mission held in February 1895, conducted in the parish of St Clement's, Notting Hill; these campaigns, with had different agencies working in co-operation in focused locations, were initiated by Bishop Jackson.[120] From 1888, the deaconesses also took on the responsibility for the management of the Lily Mission, a lodging house for women and girls based in the St Clement's parish of Notting Hill.[121]

The deaconess orders were not a movement of significant size. In 1863 the society was composed of three deaconesses, six probationers and eight associates.[122] By 1899 there were 34 deaconesses, three probationers and 36 associates in the Diocese of London.[123] The London Diocesan Deaconess Institution's register of deaconesses records that in total, by 1913, 80 deaconesses had been ordained for West London and 80 for East London home.[124] The total numbers of official Church of England deaconesses in the English provinces of Canterbury and York were 60 in 1882, 300 in 1920, and 216 in 1930.[125] Following the financial model of the Parochial Mission Women Association, the objects of the deaconess society were funded from the same sources: a combination of contributions from the laity, contributions from missions in which they worked, contributions from the deaconesses, and grants from the Bishop of London's Fund and the East London Church Fund.

The final female innovation of the period was the establishment of the Ladies' Diocesan Association in 1864. This pioneering Anglican society for laywomen predated the establishment of the equivalent male society (the Lay Helpers' Association) in the Diocese of London by one year. Curiously, its very existence and importance has eluded most researchers who have stressed the importance of the Girls' Friendly Society (established 1874) and the Mothers' Union (1887), both established in later decades.[126] Its importance has finally received some recognition in Andrea Geddes Poole's book *Philanthropy and the Construction of Victorian Women's Citizenship* (2014) which looks specifically at networks of philanthropy through the activities of Lady Lucy Cavendish and Miss Emma Cons. Poole argues that through the works of the Parochial Mission Women Association and Ladies' Diocesan Association, 'women were able to create pockets of power for themselves within the Church of England.'[127] The Ladies' Diocesan Association was established at the instigation of Catharine Tait (1819–78), wife of Bishop Tait and daughter of William Spooner (1778–1857), the Evangelical Archdeacon of Coventry.[128] Hannah Baud, in her research on bishops' wives, characterizes Catharine's example as 'trailblazing' because her efforts spearheaded the organization of women's work in the Church of England and were widely influential to the later wives of bishops.[129] Her model of what a bishop's wife could achieve, in particular, inspired the work of the more widely celebrated Louise Creighton (1850–1936), the wife of Mandell Creighton (Bishop of London between 1897 and 1901).

At the society's inception it had been unusual for institutions to admit such organized workers because 'Committees and Boards of Guardians feared the introduction of zeal which might not be tempered with discretion'.[130] The Ladies' Diocesan Association, however, with its official backing from the Bishop was granted exceptional access to these institutions. Previously, voluntary work by women had been considered unsuitable in the early nineteenth century as it took them away from their true domestic vocation.[131] Lady Lucy Cavendish (1841–1925) a member of the society's Executive Committee, reiterated this point in an address to the Ladies' Diocesan Association in May 1897.[132] She said that in the late 1850s it was very unusual for a young lady (the exception being a clergyman's daughter) to work amongst the poor, and commented that daughters were no longer shielded from social issues in the way that they had been in the past. Reflecting on her own grandmother's youth, she claimed that her grandmother was not even aware that there were poor people in London.[133] Consequentially, the value of the society was that it opened hospitals and work-houses up to 'spiritual influences' and made this type of female philanthropic work standard practice by the end of the nineteenth century in such institutions.[134] The Ladies' Diocesan Association was the only organization, of this type, in London for upper- and middle-class Anglican laywomen.

Catharine's inspiration for the association had come from a sermon preached in St Paul's Cathedral by the Reverend Thomas James Rowsell, the society's first chaplain, who criticized those who came to London for the season but did nothing spiritually to benefit themselves or London.[135] Catharine's response was to systematically organize such ladies in London who wished to do 'distinct work for Christ beyond the limits of their own families – in workhouse visitation, and in hospitals, and in ministering to the wants of the poor in their own houses'.[136] Furthermore, the ladies also collected funds on behalf of the Bishop; this role was given prominence in the society's rules.[137] The women involved in the organization were very high profile and included eminent figures in London society: Louisa Twining (1820–1912), philanthropist; Catherine Gladstone (1812–1900), wife of the Liberal Prime Minister, William Ewart Gladstone; Angela Burdett-Coutts, philanthropist; and Georgiana Russell (1836–1922), daughter of the Whig Prime Minister, John Russell, first Earl Russell (1792–1878).[138] The Vice-Presidency of the society was a duty inherited by the subsequent wives (or daughters) of each Bishop of London, the role of President being held by the Bishop.[139]

The society was relaunched by Louise Creighton, in May 1897, under the new name of the Women's Diocesan Association. In her memoir Creighton said that the organization had stagnated to become 'a rather dwindling lifeless body' in the years after Mrs Tait.[140] The objects of the reconstituted society were principally to 'bring together women Church workers throughout the Diocese, and give them opportunities for united prayer and conference', and 'help provide workers for the various parishes and institutions where women's work is needed.'[141] After its reconstitution, it was organized along the lines of the rural deaneries and organized meetings to revitalize and organize women's work in the diocese. The society had a General Committee and Executive Committee. The General Committee had a representative from every parish and from all of the women's Church societies working in the diocese, such as the Girls' Friendly Society, Church of England Temperance Society Women's Branch, Women's Help Society, London Council for Rescue Work, and the Mothers' Union.[142] From this General Committee a smaller Executive Committee of 12 to 16 ladies was appointed.[143] The Women's Diocesan Association also spawned the very successful daughter organization, the Girls' Diocesan Association which was established by in 1901 by Beatrice Creighton (1872–1953), daughter of Louise Creighton.[144]

The Ladies' Diocesan Association used the *London Diocesan Magazine* (published between 1886 and 1927) as its principal organ of communication, sending a copy of each monthly issue to each of its members as part of their return on their annual subscription of five shillings.[145] Its notices also included information such as the establishment of the North London Ladies' Settlement and the courses available to ladies at King's College London.[146] The society used the magazine to advertise positions for lady volunteers: in July 1889, the Reverend Henry Fawcett of St Thomas, Bethnal Green advertised for Sunday School teachers and for help with Girls' Evening Sewing Classes and Temperance Meetings; and in 1892, the Reverend John H. Scott of Spitalfields Parish Church advertised for 'Lady Workers' who could speak German, to work amongst the Jews.[147] The society also organized regular meetings for its members where they were addressed on such subjects as: 'Africa's Claims on English Women' by Eugene Stock (1836–1928), secretary and historian of the Church Missionary Society; 'The Needs of North and North-West London' by Alfred Earle (1827–1918), Bishop of Marlborough; and 'Tactics in Teaching' by the Reverend Frederick Ponsonby, Vicar of St Mary Magdalene, Munster Square.[148] The crucial value of the society was its role as the central hub of information in respect of women's work in the diocese. Together with the Girls' Diocesan Association, these two lay societies were instrumental in both organizing and galvanizing women's work in the diocese.

The establishment of female home-missionary organizations was a new development within Tait's episcopate. In the late 1840s and early 1850s, a small number of sisterhoods had been established, directly in response to the Oxford Movement. These sisterhoods, however, were tarnished by their association with Catholicism. As a result, the Anglican Church strove to form its own form of female missionary work in the 1860s. The office of deaconess was introduced as a vow-less form of sisterhood and the parochial mission woman was developed to be an Anglican form of the interdenominational bible women. Both organizations stressed through words in their organizational name ('parochial' and 'diocesan') that the female workers would be under the superintendence of the Bishop. In addition to the organization of female missionary workers, the establishment of the Ladies' Diocesan Association was a pioneering organization that coordinated, for the first time, the voluntary activities of the female laity (of a certain class) in the diocese.

Conclusion

The latter half of the nineteenth century saw the full development of a model of urban mission which appreciated the specific challenges of urban parish life. Unlike the rural clergyman, the metropolitan incumbent had to cope with the complex situations caused by temporary working populations and shifting populations as people were either relocated due to city development or moved out to the suburbs. Under Bishop Tait's leadership, new diocesan Anglican home-missionary organizations were created which tackled the problem of urban mission in a myriad of ways. These organizations had both traditional and innovative dimensions. The Bishop of London's Fund continued to fund church building and pay the salaries of ordained clergy in a revamped continuance of the work of the London Diocesan Church Building Society but it was also innovative in the giving of grants to other diocesan organizations. The London Diocesan Home Mission was modelled on the earlier work of the Islington Church Home Mission in Islington, but stimulated a major diocesan campaign to plant missionaries throughout the densely populated parishes of London with an aim to build up new congregations. The establishment of both the Ladies' Diocesan Association and Lay Helpers' Association was innovative in its organization of laymen and laywomen in the diocese. Additionally, the Parochial Mission Women Association, London Diocesan Deaconess Institution and Ladies' Diocesan Association were all forerunners in their organization of Anglican female workers, both paid and unpaid.

These bodies exemplify three different approaches to voluntary Anglican organization. First, the Bishop of London's Fund and East London Church Fund were grant-making bodies and raised their funds from voluntary contributions. Second, the London Diocesan Home Mission, London Diocesan Deaconess Institution and Parochial Mission Women Association were societies which carried out missionary work; they raised their funds from voluntary contributions and grants from the Bishop of London's Fund and East London Church Fund. And finally, the Lay Helpers' Association and Ladies' Diocesan Association were organizations to coordinate and support the work of lay helpers; they were either funded by grants from the Bishop of London's Fund or were self-financing through membership. Crucial to the success of these societies was the generosity of the Anglican laity.

3 THE MECHANICS OF FUNDRAISING

The nineteenth century experienced a dramatic change in the way that charity was organized. In particular, it saw the decline of the traditional endowed charity set up by an individual in their will.[1] The creation of an endowed charity allowed the individual philanthropist to have complete say over how their money was spent through the strict terms of the trust; this form of charity, however, required the philanthropist to have direct knowledge of both the geographical area and the problem that they wanted to alleviate. In contrast, in the nineteenth century it was difficult for the individual to have such direct knowledge of the diverse social problems being experienced in the rapidly expanding urban centres. This led to the development of a new form of collectivist charity: the voluntary organization. This new charitable form acted as the intermediary between the philanthropist and the beneficiary. This change from endowed charity to collectivist charity meant that the individual had less direct influence on the charity; relegated to the position of just being one subscriber amongst many. Inevitably though, the wealthiest men and women were still able to influence the work of the charity through stipulations attached to their large donations. Importantly, though, this new form of charity made it possible for more ordinary people to get involved in charitable giving and to collectively have an impact. Charitable magazines of the period were quick to publicize gifts, from the rich and poor alike, in order to solicit more subscriptions and donations. In 1891, the East London Church Fund reported that:

> Some interesting gifts have been received. A young sailor brought nearly a pound to the office which he had collected round about Whitechapel during his few weeks' leave from the man-of-war on which he serves. Three Lancashire mill hands, who spent Whitsuntide in East London, sent us ten shillings on their return home. One of our cards – issued in our own district – found its way back across the Atlantic with a five-dollar note, and, best of all perhaps, the boys in the Mission School of Norfolk Island, Melanesia, recently forwarded £10, an annual gift, to they themselves said, clothe and Christianise a white boy.[2]

This period, with its spectacular growth in the number of voluntary organizations, was undoubtedly a great philanthropic age. A letter to the editor of the *Times*, in 1884, reflected upon the 'immense ocean of charity' at work in the metropolis.[3]

Indeed, the periodical *The Philanthropist* suggested that the metropolis could be better named 'Philanthropis'.[4] Various charitable directories, such as *The Classified Directory to the Metropolitan Charities* and *Herbert Fry's Royal Guide to the London Charities*, detailed the millions of pounds being raised annually by the charities at work in metropolis; the 1885 edition of *The Classified Directory to the Metropolitan Charities* reported that the 1,103 charities operating in the metropolis had an annual income of £4,447,436.[5] Charitable fundraising was, therefore, a competitive endeavour and the diocesan home-missionary organizations at work in London were entirely reliant upon a regular flow of private donations for their survival. They needed therefore to implement strategies that would maintain a public profile in order to generate a regular flow of support from the public.[6]

Form and Financial Administration

The Quaker banker and philanthropist Samuel Gurney (1816–82), speaking at the International Philanthropic Conference in 1862, outlined the typical form of the philanthropic voluntary organization:

> London is the headquarters of agencies which are at work throughout the country. Here the central bodies deal with the funds remitted from charitable residents in all parts of the United Kingdom. These are raised by bringing the objects of each society under the notice of the benevolent by personal canvass, by circular, or by public advertisement; occasionally by public dinners and fancy fairs; or in the case of missionary societies by a comprehensive system of local associations. The central executive consists usually of paid and unpaid officers, the unpaid being a president, treasurer, committee, and perhaps an honorary secretary, the paid being secretary, collectors and other subordinate officers. Generally the president is a nobleman or gentleman of influence in the philanthropic world, the committee meets from time to time to pass accounts, draw cheques and direct the management of affairs; and issues to subscribers annually a report of the year's proceedings, with a statement of expenditure.[7]

Both the male and female diocesan organizations conformed to this business model described by Gurney, operating to a high standard of professionalism with bank accounts and audited annual reports. The male societies were the most business-like in their administration; all had a paid administrative secretary and an office to conduct the administrative aspects of the organization. Payments to the societies were made either directly to the society's office or through the society's bank.[8] They also all demonstrated good business practice, having reserve funds, funds placed on deposit or invested in stock, clear budgets and very little evidence of malpractice. The organization of the female societies was less rigorously formal. Whereas the Parochial Mission Women Association had a rented office and paid administrative secretary, the deaconesses managed all of their financial and administrative aspects in-house. The administration and finances of the deaconess institution were, nevertheless, still effectively managed. Susan

Mumm's endeavours to analyse the finances of the sisterhoods stalled because of the sisterhoods' neglect of record-keeping, lack of good business practice and general 'fiscal ineptitude'.[9] The London Diocesan Deaconess Institution, in contrast, presents an exceptional example in its adherence to good business practice from the outset. It had a finance committee, bank account, printed annual reports (including accounts produced by the society's treasurer), and the position of treasurer was held by a succession of wealthy businessmen or clergymen. In contrast, the Parochial Mission Women Association occasionally gave the impression that its financial operations were lax, mainly through its abuse of its overdraft facility at the bank; at one point the Lady Managers seemed to be slightly confused regarding the way that interest was charged on its overdraft.[10] Additionally, the society experienced two cases of financial misconduct: the secretary (Mr O'Brien) embezzled money from the society by arranging to have the business post delivered to his home address; this enabled him to take cash sums amounting to nearly £50; and again in 1892, one of the society's mission women (Mrs Jones) was discovered to have been systematically, for many years, pocketing small sums from the penny bank collecting system.[11] The BLF experienced one small theft of just under £14 by its accountant, Mr Cooper.[12] Both parties repaid the stolen sums to the society. Such difficult matters, however, were always passed to the Gentlemen's Committee of Reference which assisted them in all financial matters. This committee mainly consisted of the husbands, fathers and brothers of the Lady Managers. Examples of matters dealt with by the Gentlemen's Committee include the investment of assets, dealing with the fraud committed by the society's secretary, setting a limit on the society's expenditure, advising on the ideal size of the society's reserve fund, and advising on suitable courses of action to deal with the society's longstanding overdraft. These administrative arrangements suggest that the female societies operated on a rather more semi-domestic and less professional level.

The principal way of publicizing the charitable organization was through the printed annual report. It acted, in a business sense, as a marketing tool for the voluntary organization by publicizing all the good works that the organization had achieved in the past year and by emphasising how these were dependent upon a regular flow of income. A typical annual report contained the following: a list of trustees; the objects of the fund; the rules of the fund; a full list of subscribers and donors; a list of bequests; a report of the good work of the fund for the previous year; a summary of grants made; and a summary of the annual accounts. The reports were produced for the societies' annual meetings which were part of the Season's calendar of 'May Meetings' which were, in the case of the larger male organizations, reported in newspapers such as *The Times*. The publication of the annual report, in conjunction with the public annual meeting, was therefore both a way of reporting on progress and expenditure in the previous year and a way of soliciting funds for the future.

Both the male and female societies made every effort to solicit charitable bequests; the formal form of wording to make a bequest was included in their annual reports. The charitable bequest provided the voluntary organizations with an important additional income stream that could either be spent or invested. A survey in *The Times* in 1899 suggested that an average of £1,250,000 was being left annually as charitable bequests.[13] The historian David Owen, however, suggests that a higher figure of £2,000,000 a year is a more likely figure for this period.[14] Not unexpectedly, research into charitable bequests and wills made in this period has concluded that women were more likely than men to leave a substantial percentage of their estate to charity. Owen's analysis of the 466 wills (316 men and 150 women) published in the *Telegraph* between 1891 and 1898 found that women generally bequeathed a higher proportion of their estate to charity: in his analysis women bequeathed on average 25 per cent of their estate to charity, whereas men bequeathed a smaller 11 per cent.[15] Likewise, Prochaska's sample analysis of one hundred wills from the 1860s also showed that women gave a larger proportion of their estate to charity. He found that women bequeathed on average 13 per cent of their estate to charity compared to men bequeathing 3 per cent. He also found that spinsters bequeathed an even higher proportion of 15 per cent.[16] An analysis of a sample of 87 individuals who left money to the societies in this study also confirms these findings. This examination found that women bequeathed, on average, 15 per cent of their estates; whereas men gave away a much lower proportion (four per cent) of their estates in charitable bequests. *The Times* reported that there were two main sources of charitable bequests; these were individuals that had been charitable during their lifetime and individuals without dependents.[17] Analysis of the bequests to the diocesan organizations in this study shows that at least 40 per cent of bequests came from individuals who had been either donors or subscribers to the society concerned. In addition, the analysis also shows that the bequests from women were mainly from spinsters. This confirms the suggestion in *The Times* that people without dependents were more charitable. It therefore also suggests that the societies with the more predominantly female funder base would garner a larger number of bequests. However, analysis of the bequests made to the female organizations shows that these societies received very few bequests during the period 1860 to 1914.[18] Instead, the key factor in determining the volume of bequests received by any society was the size of collecting infrastructure, as demonstrated by the large number of bequests harvested by the London City Mission (see Table A.5.1). Therefore, the societies that had a geographically wide collecting infrastructure gained in two ways through their wide subscriber and legator funder-base.

Voluntary organizations were, by their very nature, entirely reliant upon a regular flow of private donations for their survival. They needed therefore to implement strategies that would maintain a public profile in order to generate a regular flow of support from the Anglican laity that would sustain their financial needs on an annual basis. In order to achieve this, they represented themselves and operated in a precise and businesslike manner: they published annual reports to coincide with their public annual meetings; they produced audited accounts; the societies' treasurers were professional men, usually high-status bankers; and generally they employed administrative staff. The male and female societies were, therefore, very similar in the way that they conducted their financial administration. They differed, however, in the ways that they raised and solicited money; this was to a great extent determined by the collecting infrastructure at their disposal.

Fundraising Strategy: Promotional Activities

One of the most powerful promotional tools at the disposal of the male voluntary organizations was the Bishop of London, or in the case of the East London Church Fund the appropriate Suffragan Bishop. Principally, the Bishop, through his patronage, gave the organization official sanction; the public could, therefore, feel confident that they were giving their money to a trusted organization which was acting within diocesan guidelines.[19] The Bishop was able to publicize the good works of these organizations by speaking at public meetings and through his bishop's charge. Bishop Jackson, for example, in his 1884 charge, gave updated statistical information on the work of the London Diocesan Home Mission and Bishop of London's Fund, and wrote about the value of lay helpers, deaconesses and parochial mission women.[20] Furthermore, the Bishop could also issue pastoral letters on the organization's behalf.[21] He was, therefore, a powerful advocate for the diocesan organizations. The female societies also made some limited use of the Bishop as a promotional tool and figurehead. He could publicize the organization's good works at meetings; both the Bishop of London and the Bishop of Stepney spoke on behalf of the Parochial Mission Women Association at annual meetings.[22] And in terms of official sanction, the Bishop acted in an official capacity as Visitor to the London Diocesan Deaconess Institution; with the Parochial Mission Women Association stating on their annual reports that they worked under the official sanction of the Bishop of London and the Archbishop of Canterbury.[23] In the case of the female societies, it was the Bishop's wife who was their most prominent ally, particularly in her role as the Vice-President of the Ladies' Diocesan Association. By way of example, Beatrice Temple became Lady President of the London Diocesan Deaconess Institution on her husband's promotion to the Bishopric of London in 1885. As Vice-President, she supported the work of the society by publicizing its work: in 1887 she presided over a large meeting of about 200 persons at Fulham Palace; and in 1888, the High Church Canon John Festing (1837–1902) spoke of the work of the Parochial Mission Women Association at a Ladies' Diocesan Association meeting presided over by Mrs Temple.[24] These examples suggest that the female societies had easier access to the Bishop's wife and also that her role was suited to the more domestic events, such as opening sales of work, carried out by the female societies.

In addition to the self-promotion by figure heads, the diocese itself also made efforts to support its own voluntary organizations. This was an important part of the overall 'diocesan revival' of the nineteenth century which saw the diocese develop its own 'diocesan consciousness' through a process of church reform that culminated in the establishment of a diocesan financial body in 1914.[25] This long process of reinvigoration involved the formation of new dioceses and the reorganization of existing dioceses, the revival of rural deaneries, the development of the office of archdeacon, the establishment of the new role of suffragan bishops, the creation of diocesan organizations (such as the London Diocesan Church Building Society), more effective use of visitation returns, and the development of diocesan conferences. The Funds Committee of the 1884 London Diocesan Conference considered the subject of the organization and finances of the Church's diocesan voluntary organizations and recommended the publication of a diocesan periodical which would act as publicity for the work of the diocesan organizations.[26] In consequence, a monthly periodical called the *London Diocesan Magazine* was published from May 1886. The magazine acted, principally, as a marketing vehicle for the diocesan organizations, reporting on their good works and income; more generally, it also included diocesan news, obituaries, reports on bequests, and reports of diocesan conferences and the bishop's charge. It was the male diocesan organizations that made the fullest use of this opportunity, with notices appearing in every issue for the Bishop of London's Fund and East London Church Fund, and in frequent issues for the London Diocesan Home Mission. As the *London Diocesan Magazine* was an Anglican publication, it did not include notices for the interdenominational London City Mission. These articles focused mainly on finance: the state of the funds; lists of large donations; and grants paid out. Notices from the London Diocesan Deaconess Institution and Parochial Mission Women Association in the *London Diocesan Magazine* were rare, though notices from the Parochial Mission Women Association increased at the start of the twentieth century when the society's income was declining. Furthermore, some of the lay organizations, such as the Ladies' Diocesan Association and Lay Helpers' Association, used it as their principal means of communication. The Ladies' Diocesan Association used the magazine to report on: its annual meeting; the state of its finances; details of the annual excursion; appointments and resignations; workers wanted for certain positions; and a programme of events.

In terms of other avenues of promotion, the male organizations advertised regularly, across Church-party divides, in the classified advertising pages of the newspapers. For example, the London Diocesan Home Mission advertised its special services for the working-class, in December 1857, in *The Times,* the High Church *Guardian* and the Evangelical *Record*.[27] The breadth of advertising can also be seen in the Bishop of London's Fund advertisements, in 1869, which spanned: *The Times, Morning Post, Daily Telegraph, Echo, Pall Mall Gazette, Standard, Rock and City Press, Daily News,* and *Star*.[28] It was the Parochial Mission Women Association that made the greatest use of advertising and direct mail to solicit new subscriptions.[29] Again, the society advertised widely across periodicals and newspapers that represented all Church parties: *The Times;* the High Church *Guardian;* Evangelical *Record; Morning Post; Philanthropist; Charity Record; Charity Organisation Society Annual Report; Guide to Church Congress;* Mackeson's *Guide to the Churches in London; Quarterly Review; Englishwoman's Yearbook; Pall Mall Gazette; Crockford's Clerical Directory;* and the *London Diocese Book*. However, with diminishing funds the society cut back on its advertising in the early twentieth century because of poor results.[30] This in turn further perpetuated the society's decline as it was no longer financially able to promote itself widely. The minute books of the Parochial Mission Women Association repeatedly record the thoroughness of the society's attempts to publicize the society's work. In 1890, upon discovering that it had not been mentioned in Charles Booth's (1840–1916) *Life and Labour,* the society arranged an interview with Booth to ensure their inclusion in future editions; the interview with Booth occurred in March 1890 and the minute book records that Major Fitzroy (from the Gentlemen's Committee of Reference) had 'had a satisfactory interview with Mr Booth, who had been very glad to hear about PMW and had read the report with great interest'.[31] A similar case occurred again in 1893, when the committee clearly express their dissatisfaction at the size of their entry in Angela Burdett-Coutts' book *Woman's Mission* (1893).[32] Another way of publicizing the work of the society was through the 'Letter to the Editor' newspaper columns. By way of example, William Macdonald Sinclair (1850–1917), Archdeacon of London, wrote a letter to the editor of *The Times* in 1906 promoting an appeal that the Bishop of London had just launched on behalf of the Bishop of London's Fund. Sinclair's letter emphasized the close relationship between the City and the Bishop of London's Fund, in terms of City organizations and City bankers.[33] The Parochial Mission Women Association was also successful in having several letters to the editor published in *The Times*.[34] The common factor in these letters to editors and entries in books was that the societies used high-status supporters to leverage publicity for the society's good works.

Half of the voluntary organizations bore the expense of producing their own magazine. The East London Church Fund published a quarterly magazine, the *East End Church Chronicle,* which it published from 1888. The London Diocesan Deaconess Institution, from 1887, produced a quarterly magazine *Ancilla Domini* (which translates as 'handmaid of the Lord'), using it as a substitute for advertising. And the London City Mission produced its own monthly magazine, aptly named the *London City Mission Magazine,* from 1837. These magazines gave the organizations the opportunity to talk about their work on a much more detailed level and with a more engaging anecdotal tone thereby keeping their supporters actively involved in its work on a regular basis. For example, the April 1908 issue of *Ancilla Domini* included: news of the annual retreat for associates; a thank you for the hospital letters and for money given in support of Jimmy Minch (a choir boy at St Matthew's, Oakley Square); promotion of the London Diocesan Deaconess Institution's book of Eucharistic Offices; the balance sheet and subscription list for 1907; a list of material gifts given to the London Diocesan Deaconess Institution; news from the convalescent home in Westgate-on-Sea; a plea for white linen cloth, clothes for the poor and contributions for a forthcoming sale of works; an account of the society's distribution of toys amongst some poor children; and finally, a report from the Lily Mission in Notting Hill.

These magazines also gave the organization the opportunity to speak directly to their supporters about lack of funds. The *East London Church Chronicle*, in particular, often had quite desperately worded front covers: in December 1909, the front cover simply stated (in large letters filling the page):

> URGENT. If the present grants to be made by the Fund are to be continued and not reduced, £2,500 must be received before the books for 1909 close on JANUARY 12th. The matter is really urgent. Please send a contribution to The Secretary'.[35]

The organizations that did not have their own magazine published 'Occasional Papers' to publicize their work. This was the method preferred by the Bishop of London's Fund: in June 1868, it used such an occasional paper as a marketing device, sending a paper to 1,449 subscribers (of other religious societies) who did not give to the society.[36] After 1890, the Bishop of London's Fund's promotional material became more sophisticated with the publication of a regular illustrated booklet showcasing the work it had completed in the previous year, with case studies on individual churches.[37] Booklets were also produced to publicize the jubilees of both the Bishop of London's Fund and London Diocesan Home Mission; these reported in functional terms the achievements of the societies over the decades.[38]

The male and female societies approached their readership in different ways. The male societies made more use of functional reporting; they listed the number of churches built, missionaries employed and districts formed. Although the female societies also reported in this way on the good works in the previous year, they were likely to supplement this information with the use of stirring success stories and emotional pleas that would hopefully tug at both the heart strings and the purse strings. This may have been because the committees of the societies were female (or partly female) or because they were aware that such an approach would engage their female funder-base. These stirring stories recounted the reclamation of the fallen. For example, the Parochial Mission Women Association wrote a series of articles for the periodical *Mission Life* which publicized the work of the society through such 'success stories'. This success story was followed directly with an emotive plea for funds:

> Mrs K (Mission-woman) is particularly successful with the fallen girls, and they let her go amongst them, in their own haunts, where no respectable person ever went. There is a vast deal of drunkenness too to contend with, and Mrs K has been a most valuable helper to the Clergy in watching over cases where a beginning had been made in better ways, and there were temptations to relax. Her strongest point of all is her earnestness in bringing people to Baptism, never leaving them till she had brought the children and all the members of the family who had not yet been baptized. The numbers she has brought could hardly be counted.[39]

Likewise, *Ancilla Domini* often included emotive success stories; in July 1888 an article entitled 'Being a Few Experiences in the Life of a Parish Deaconess' focused on examples of returning people to God. This example, one of many described, references a man who was tenderly nursed by the deaconesses; the man had, in health, been a skilled mechanic but had fallen ill with consumption:

> I then sent him to the Isle of Wight, and while there, he told me afterwards, the Sisters washed the patients' feet, and wanted to wash his too. Their conduct to him was simply inexplicable. He said, "I knew they were *ladies*, and why should ladies trouble to wash my feet?" I remarked that they were only acting out the principles of Christian faith ... Not until the last hour of his life did I see the slightest change in him, and then I thought I detected, though he was too weak to speak, a softened expression in his face not there before. How I hoped that, even in the very last hour, the God without whom he said he had lived, and without whom he said he would die, in His infinite mercy had reclaimed him as His own![40]

Distinguished patronage was also an important boost to any organization either as a donor or committee member. Patronage from a member of the royal family gave a huge advantage to the society's chances of survival, acting as a badge of success and legitimacy.[41] Likewise, public meetings held at the homes of prominent personages and with prominent speakers would also guarantee a higher attendance. The Duke of Westminster lent Grosvenor House for many charitable drawing-room meetings; including the Bishop of London's Fund, Parochial Mission Women Association, London City Mission, Bishop of St Albans' Fund, Rochester Diocesan Association and the Church Army.[42] Attendance at these prominent London meetings was strictly by invitation or by ticket only, in contrast with the annual service which was open to all.[43] Notices regarding the society's meeting would be placed in the Court Circular column of *The Times* or would be placed in the classified adverts. These notices would often mention who would be chairing the meeting and the names of the high profile speakers.[44] The London Diocesan Home Mission held most of its public meetings at London House (the City residence of the Bishop of London) or at the homes of its leading supporters: Granville Augustus William Waldegrave, third Baron Radstock (1833–1913); Arthur Fitzgerald Kinnaird, eleventh Lord Kinnaird; and the businessman George Moore (1806–76).[45] Other popular venues for public meetings were Fulham Palace (the country residence of the Bishop of London) and Mansion House (the official residence of the Lord Mayor of the City of London). Meetings were also held at the Mansion House for both the London Diocesan Deaconess Institution and Parochial Mission Women Association.[46] These meetings held at City venues, such as Mansion House, were generally for the purpose of appealing to wealthy men and City firms.[47] In contrast, the small local association drawing-room meetings held by the male societies in the provinces would have been more informal in character. Likewise the drawing-room meetings for the London Diocesan Deaconess Institution and Parochial Mission Women Association were generally more of a domestic affair and were held in the home of a supporter or committee member: the Parochial Mission Women Association held drawing-room meetings in the homes of Mrs Jay (the wife of Willie Parkinson Jay, an Eastbourne incumbent who had previously been Vicar of Christ Church, Watney Street).[48] The purpose of these meetings was to draw individuals together with the express aim of publicizing the society's work and thereby gaining new subscribers.

The novelist Charles Dickens (1812–70) satirized the use of distinguished patronage in *Our Mutual Friend* (1865). Here the nouveau riche Mr Boffin is targeted by a charity which invites him to become a steward in return for the minimum fee of three guineas. The invitation to subscribe is by means of a 'large fat double letter, sealed with ducal coronet' from the Duke of Linseed. Likewise, another charity informs Mr Boffin of the offer from a lady to donate £20 if ten other individuals offer the large sum of £100; this letter comes from 'two noble Earls and a Viscount.'[49] Such methods can be readily viewed in the minute books and magazines of the voluntary organizations in this study: retired committee members and generous donors are listed as vice-presidents in the annual report and the technique of matched funding was frequently employed. For example, the midsummer issue of the *East London Church Chronicle* in 1904 reported that eleven supporters had come forward to match the offer of £100 from a Walter Johnson. The magazine exclaimed: 'How they have all come so quickly we hardly know, except that God has indeed answered our prayers and stirred up the hearts of His faithful people.'[50]

For the female societies, the distinguished patron could be used for greatest effect in the opening of special events. The fundraising guide *Bazaars and Fancy Fairs* (1896) recommended that 'some lady or gentleman of considerable influence open the bazaar EACH day', and that free entrance tickets be 'given to those who are likely to spend money.'[51] The Parochial Mission Women Association always ensured a good turnout at its annual fundraising art exhibition by securing a prominent society lady for the opening. In 1913, its art exhibition was opened by Queen Amelia of Portugal on the first day and by Princess Lichnowsky, wife of the German Ambassador, on the second day.[52] Correspondingly, a Grand Concert in aid of the London Diocesan Deaconess Institution's Lily Mission, held at Paddington Baths in Bayswater in February 1893 was patronized by a number of distinguished lady patronesses. These were Janet Sinclair, Countess of Caithness (1829–1906); Georgina Gascoyne-Cecil, Marchioness of Salisbury (1827–99) and wife of the High Church Prime Minister; and Beatrice Temple, wife of the Bishop of London.[53] The financial value of such prestigious patronage can be demonstrated by the fact that the Parochial Mission Women Association's art exhibitions with prominent patronage were the society's most financially successful events. The use of a distinguished person or their home in connection to a society's event was important to draw in a guaranteed audience of old and new supporters. The male and female societies, however, made different use of these distinguished assets: the male societies used the homes of high-status individuals for meetings whereas the female societies used society ladies to draw crowds at events which raised money.

Fundraising Strategy: Collecting Money

Voluntary organizations needed to do more though than just promote their good works, the single most important factor in their financial success was the size of their collecting network. The most useful tool for the larger male societies was the local association which as well as soliciting donations and subscriptions, also held public meetings and generally drummed up support. The interdenominational London City Mission was supreme in this area, having (in addition to its metropolitan associations) a comprehensive network of nearly 350 provincial associations arranged into county auxiliaries. The Anglican collecting networks were much more modest in scope, of which the most successful was the East London Church Fund. Its collecting infrastructure grew rapidly between 1890 and 1910, beginning with just a few small associations in provincial towns organized by individual churches. By 1910, a network of local associations had been established in the provinces, mainly in the south east and south west, but still only numbered a modest 30 associations. So, whereas in 1913 the London City Mission raised £20,714 from its metropolitan associations and a further £6,130 from provincial associations, the East London Church Fund, in the same year, raised only £8,613 from local associations and church collections combined.

Unlike the London City Mission, the local associations of the East London Church Fund were contained to the south and south-west of England, with a few isolated associations in towns such as Malvern, Newmarket and Ross-on-Wye. Those based in sea-side towns (such as Bournemouth, Eastbourne and Torquay) were particularly vigorous in publicizing the plight of the East End poor to the local residents. In this respect, the Fund was able to employ the status and talents of its Bishop to great effect; Bishop Walsham How regularly undertook annual preaching tours of these towns, as did his successors. In 1899, for example, the East London Church Fund held campaigns in Eastbourne and Torquay: sermons were preached in six Eastbourne churches and four in Torquay.[54] These funds raised by the seaside towns were so important that in 1908, the East London Church Fund reported that if it were not for Brighton and Hove 'the Fund would indeed be in a sorry plight'.[55] Likewise, the Bournemouth campaign of 1906 raised an impressive £900 for the Fund.[56]

The East London Church Fund's most successful provincial associations were in the towns of Bournemouth, Tunbridge Wells, Brighton, Eastbourne and Torquay.[57] The relationship with these provincial towns can be explained by three factors. Firstly, the spa towns and seaside towns were middle-class enclaves: many of these towns had been developed by the landed gentry on their own lands. This was the case, for example, in Tunbridge Wells, Eastbourne, Torquay and Bournemouth.[58] These towns were developed to appeal to middle and upper-classes with assembly rooms, theatres, public parks with bandstands, promenades and wide tree-lined roads.[59] The south coast of Devon was marketed in the nineteenth century as the perfect winter resort due to its mild climate which made it ideal for those suffering from lung diseases.[60] Consequently, these towns were popular destinations for retirement.[61] Writing in 1917, Robert Chancellor Nesbitt (1868–1944), a solicitor and High Church layman, commented that the East London Church Fund had made 'valuable connections' in towns such as Brighton, Eastbourne, Bournemouth and Torquay 'where so many Londoners reside'.[62] The second factor that led to a relationship with these provincial towns was a connection with London incumbencies. For example, Charles Edward Ricketts Robinson (d.1881), Vicar of St John's Church in Torquay from 1870, had formerly been the Chaplain of Price's Patent Candle Factory in London; and the honorary secretary of the Brighton and Hove Association was Ridley Daniel Tyssen (1840–1917), Vicar of St Patrick Hove from 1885. Tyssen had formerly been Rector of South Hackney and was described as having had 'a large place in his heart for East London ever since.'[63] The London City Mission also raised money from these middle-class seaside and spa towns. And mirroring the East London Church Fund, its most successful local associations were based in Bournemouth, Leamington Spa, Eastbourne, Torquay and Cheltenham.[64] The third factor was that the plight of the East End of London was prominently in the national public eye in this period. This was especially so in the 1880s with the publication of *The Bitter Cry of Outcast London* in 1883;[65] the sensation of William Thomas Stead's (1849–1912) exposé of child prostitution in the *Pall Mall Gazette* in 1885; and the notoriety of the Jack the Ripper murders in the period 1888 to 1891. The attention being directed to the East End in response to the 'terrible murders in Whitechapel' was referred to in the journal of the Scripture Readers' Association.[66]

Both the London City Mission and the East London Church Fund, for example, used the public debate regarding *The Bitter Cry of Outcast London* to publicize their work. This influential pamphlet, published in 1883, by the Congregationalist Minister Andrew Mearns (1837–1925) expounded the criminality, immorality and desperate conditions of the London rookeries.[67] The East London Church Fund was quick to capitalize on the great reaction awakened by the publication of this pamphlet by writing letters to the newspapers publicizing the work that it was already doing to alleviate the 'temporal as well as spiritual' afflictions of the destitute in these very parts of London.[68] And the *London City Mission Magazine,* in 1884, expressed its thanks to the Bournemouth branch which had, in response to the publication of *The Bitter Cry of Outcast London,* promised to finance two missionaries in 'outcast districts'. In response to this proposal, the London City Mission offered to send a deputation to any other town interested in the society's work.[69] It is this particular connection that the London City Mission and East London Church Fund both had with the East End of London is the most plausible explanation for their success in raising funds from the provinces. An incidental outcome of these successful collecting networks was that the societies also harvested bequests from members of the local association; of the traceable bequests to the East London Church Fund, about a fifth had addresses that related to the largest provincial local associations.[70] And correspondingly, approximately half of the London City Mission's bequests came from individuals who lived outside of London. These regional associations were, therefore, of vital importance to sustaining the short and long-term finances of both the East London Church Fund and the London City Mission.

The other societies, in this study, did not have extensive supportive collecting infrastructures. In comparison, the Bishop of London's Fund (described previously as the 'war-chest' of the diocese) had an identity that naturally represented the diocese in its entirety. Consequently, it did not employ the East End as a marketing tool. Despite its high public profile as the Bishop's Fund, it had a very limited network of local associations. These were initially quite a piecemeal affair; in 1876 the Fund had 36 small church-based local associations mainly in the north and west of London. It was not until 1893, when the society had been in existence for thirty years, that the Fund expanded its small network of local associations systematically throughout the diocese by appointing a clergyman as honorary organizing secretaries for each of the rural deaneries.[71] In great contrast to the London City Mission and East London Church Fund, the Bishop of London's Fund did not have any local associations outside the diocese and did not actively solicit funds from the seaside and spa towns. The London Diocesan Home Mission, in even greater contrast, had no collecting system and relied upon subscriptions and donations being sent directly to its office. Likewise, the female societies had very limited support in terms of a collecting infrastructure. The Parochial Mission Women Association had two local associations in the form of its Northern Fund (covering Northumberland) and Western Fund (covering Cornwall and Devon) which acted to fund mission women in these regions; these regional funds were organized by friends and family relations of committee members and were quite small in scale.[72] In the mid 1890s, Arundall Whatton (Curate of All Saints, Notting Hill) acted as the organizing secretary of the London Diocesan Deaconess Institution and arranged occasional meetings. Reports in *Ancilla Domini* show that in 1894 he arranged meetings in Folkestone, Clifton and Fulham Palace.[73] These initiatives, however, were principally the efforts of individuals rather than on the systematic scale of the larger male organizations. Consequently, these efforts were not as vital in funding terms to the female organizations.

In addition to the local association, many of the male societies had female associations that raised awareness on behalf of the society and collected funds on its behalf. This use of female auxiliary groups, from the beginning of the nineteenth century, to fundraise for male societies has a long tradition and was a precursor of the establishment of independent female societies.[74] The Ladies' Diocesan Association had since its inception (in 1864) been supportive of the Bishop of London's Fund but this connection was particularly reinforced with its reinvigoration as the Women's Diocesan Association under Louise Creighton. In 1900, the association took on, at the request of the Bishop, an increased responsibility for raising money for the Fund and for publicizing its works and the association appointed a second honorary secretary with this specific responsibility.[75] Contributions to the Bishop of London's Fund through the Women's Diocesan Association rose year-on-year between 1900 and 1911, with the association collecting £708 in 1911.[76] The association was supported by the additional collecting of the efforts of the Girls' Diocesan Association from 1905.[77] The East London Church Fund also established, in 1893, a women's association called 'The Women's Union in Aid of East London Church Fund'.[78] The female associations were important, therefore, in both promoting and financially supporting the male societies. The female organizations also made full use of female associates as promoters and fundraisers. The London Diocesan Deaconess Institution had a band of ladies called associates or assistants who carried out work on behalf of the society and raised money for it.[79] In the late 1880s and 1890s these associates numbered around 30 ladies, rising to 40 at the turn of the century. Virtually all of these associates were annual subscribers to the institutions.[80] The Parochial Mission Women Association also had a band of associates that assisted it in their work and in fundraising on its behalf.[81] The associate would enlist new subscribers to collect small sums, assist with sales of works, and generally to raise the profile of the society.

An additional value of these associations, both local and female, was their ability to raise funds through the use of collecting cards and collecting boxes. The only organization that made wide-scale use of collecting cards and boxes was the East London Church Fund which regularly received around 1,000 sums (typically for very small sums of less than £1 in total per card) each year from this source.[82] In contrast, the London City Mission's use of collecting cards and boxes was surprisingly small considering the society's large-scale use of local associations at around 600 per year.[83] The voluntary collectors were predominantly women; on average 81 per cent of collecting cards for the East London Church Fund came from women, and likewise 77 per cent for the London City Mission. Other than through the Women's Diocesan Association, the Bishop of London's Fund did not receive large amounts through the medium of collecting cards and boxes; only 50 sums contributed in 1867 came from that source. Surprisingly, the supporters of the female societies made little personal use of collecting cards or boxes. The Parochial Mission Women Association annual reports only list a handful of collecting cards each year in their annual reports. And likewise, the use of collecting cards by the London Diocesan Deaconess Institution was also fairly limited, peaking in the period 1871 to 1876 (at a rate of 20–40 each year); this was when the society was busy fundraising for its new home in Tavistock Crescent. Collecting cards did not, therefore, raise large sums for any of the organizations. Due to the small sums collected by this method (typically around ten shillings per card), this method of raising funds only ever accounted for a few hundred pounds of annual income at the most.

Instead of making use of local associations and female associations, the Parochial Mission Women Association and London Diocesan Deaconess Institution were more likely to make use of a paid collector. The deaconesses relied mainly on a paid collector until 1897 when the collector died; after this date all donations were sent directly to the Mother Superior at the deaconess home. The society had tried briefly in 1870, for a two-year period, to go without a paid collector but found that that their finances suffered as a result. This was partly due to the fact that the task of collecting subscriptions was 'found to be most disagreeable to the ladies.'[84] In parallel, the Parochial Mission Women Association employed two lady collectors in the 1870s, and in the 1880s shared a collector with the Charity Organisation Society.[85] One possible explanation for the small number of collecting cards used by the female societies is that women were less inclined to act as unpaid collectors when they could play an actual managerial role or practical role in the society's work. In contrast, the male societies made little use of paid collectors; presumably this is because they already had a complex network of local associations and female associations to collect money freely on their behalf. Neither of the two larger societies, the Bishop of London's Fund and East London Church Fund, employed paid collectors. In contrast, the London Diocesan Home Mission, which had no local associations, employed a collector from 1866.[86] This suggests that the use of a paid collector was used as a substitute to a network of associations.

Another valuable source of funding for the male societies was the church collection, which had the double benefit of raising money and raising awareness of the society. This took two different forms. Firstly, each male society held an annual service (either at Westminster Abbey or at St Paul's Cathedral) and at these an anniversary collection would be held. Secondly, the larger societies such as the

Bishop of London's Fund and East London Church Fund had a fixed Sunday when all churches within the diocese would be asked to collect for that specific charity.[87] The money raised annually by diocesan-wide church collections was significant in terms of income: in 1893 the Bishop of London's Fund raised £6,503 from church collections in 417 churches; and in 1901 £7,096 from 480 churches.[88] In 1889, the East London Church Fund raised over £1,200 from collections just held on 'ELCF Sunday' and £6,043 in total over the year.[89] The London Diocesan Home Mission did not raise particularly large sums from this source, despite requesting that collections be held in churches that had grown from its mission districts.[90] In 1891, the Bishop of London's Fund and London Diocesan Home Mission came to an arrangement whereby in return for a larger annual block grant, the London Diocesan Home Mission would no longer have church collections carried out in its favour. Bishop Temple had instigated this measure because he recognized that these two diocesan societies were competing to solicit funds from the same sources.[91] In contrast, the female societies raised only occasional sums of money from church collections, principally from the societies' annual services though there were also occasional special sermons by high profile speakers. Additional funds were also raised through the publication and sale of sermons preached in the societies favour. In one more successful example, the popular preacher Henry Parry Liddon (1829–90), Canon of St Paul's Cathedral, preached a sermon 'Phoebe in London' in aid of the Parochial Mission Women Association at the Parish Church of Kensington in June 1877. The collection after the sermon raised £96; the society then arranged for 500 copies of the sermon to be printed which were then sold at one shilling each.[92] Sermons were also printed in the societies own magazines, occasional papers and magazines such as the *London Diocesan Magazine*.[93] Whereas the female societies only raised small amounts from church collections, the male societies raised significant sums from this source. This reflected both the size of the collecting infrastructure behind the male societies and the weight of influence of the diocese and the Bishop.

Fundraising Strategy: Other Forms of Fundraising

There is very little evidence of the male societies raising funds through forms of entertainment. Significantly, the East London Church Fund makes only a few mentions of fundraising through alternative means; these were mainly small initiatives carried out by schools.[94] Other than these few solitary initiatives mentioned in the society's magazine, there was only one mention of entertainment fundraising in the society's minute book. In 1913, Lady Katherine Fitzroy (1865–1933), wife of Sir Almeric William Fitzroy (1851–1935), asked the Fund if it would like to share in the profits of a dramatic performance. The minute book simply notes, with no explanation, that the 'Council decided that it would not be possible to accept the offer made by Lady Fitzroy of a share in the management and proceeds of a dramatic performance'.[95] Correspondingly, there are only three references to the Bishop of London's Fund having received money from entertainment-derived sources; these were two concerts and a sale of works, two of which had a direct connection with the Women's Diocesan Association.[96] In the latter half of the nineteenth century, there was a wide debate on the suitability of various form of entertainment being used to raise money for religious objects, with charitable bazaars coming in for particular condemnation. It is therefore noteworthy that these three fundraising entertainment events for the Bishop of London's Fund all occurred in the early twentieth century when commercialized forms of fundraising became more acceptable. This suggests that either the male societies did not approve of such methods or did need to resort to this form of fundraising.

Instead, the practice of using forms of entertainment to raise money was more prevalent in the female managed organizations. The London Diocesan Deaconess Institution raised money through such means principally in order to acquire additional funds for the Lily Mission and for the nursing home in Westgate-on-Sea. Examples of such fundraising activities were: a dramatic performance; a 'masque of flowers' (a theatrical performance that involved dancing and singing); a concert; a bicycle parade; and a jumble sale.[97] There are also regular mentions of sales of works in aid of the deaconesses from 1880 onwards. A sale of work involved individuals donating items that they had made which could then be sold: generally items such as needlework, china, pictures, jams and potted meats.[98] The London Diocesan Deaconess Institution principally used such methods to fund outreach projects and plug funding deficits. Pre-eminent in this area of fundraising was the Parochial Mission Women Association which organized regular entertainment based forms of fundraising from the mid 1870s. Between 1877 and 1921, the society annually received income from an amateur art exhibition. This was usually held at Lowther Lodge, the home of William Lowther (1821–1912), Conservative MP, and his wife Charlotte Anne Lowther (d. 1908). A small entrance fee was charged over the three-day period of the exhibition and in total the event generally raised in the region of £200 to £300 each year for the association.[99] The society also received income from entertainment based fundraising forms. Examples include: a reading, in 1877, by the folklorist William Ralston Shedden-Ralston (1828–89) which raised £96; a photographic lecture, in 1882, which raised £54; and a performance by the Romany Dramatic Club, in 1907, at the Albert Hall which raised which £213.[100] The use of a distinguished personage was, if possible, employed at such events. In 1888, the minute book records the society's attempts to secure the Duchess of Albany's (daughter-in-law to Queen Victoria) attendance and the Princess of Wales' (who later became Queen Alexandra) agreement to become patroness at its fundraising concert.[101] Lady Hamilton (the society's President from 1915) also regularly held sales of work on behalf of the society; in 1893 her two sales raised nearly £200.[102] In the case of the Parochial Mission Women Association, fundraising through entertainment means was a significant stream of funding.

The two crucial factors that shaped the fundraising initiatives of the Parochial Mission Women Association were firstly, that the main management committee was entirely composed of society ladies; and secondly, and that there was no clergyman on the committee to caution against the use of such fundraising practices. In contrast, the mother house of the London Diocesan Deaconess Institution received a negligible amount from such entertainment-based fundraising sources. This form of fundraising was used more by their outreach programmes, such as the nursing home at Westgate-on-Sea and the lodging house at the Lily Mission in Notting Hill, which had a ready band of lady volunteer helpers who would step in and organize an event to help fill a deficit in funds or in response to a special building appeal.[103] As the period progressed, both societies made more use of such commercially-based fundraising methods. This may have been because it was a financially productive way to supplement diminishing subscriptions and donations. Equally, it may have been because such methods were becoming more acceptable and widely used in the late nineteenth century.

Conclusion

The mainstay of all of these organizations was the money raised through subscriptions, donations and bequests from the Anglican laity. The male organizations had a number of useful weapons in their promotional arsenal, having both the influential support of high-status patrons and the weight of the diocesan infrastructure behind them. The value of this infrastructure was that it facilitated the collection of funds across a wide geographical area, through local associations, female associations and church collections. Additionally, the East London Church Fund significantly established a wide network of local associations outside London by publicizing the destitution of the East End through the vehicle of its magazine and through promotional tours. Together these methods ensured that the male societies had a much larger funder-base, both numerically and geographically. Correspondingly, the female societies shared many of the standard charitable fundraising strategies employed by the male groups. They produced annual reports, held annual meetings, sold printed sermons by high profile speakers, placed adverts in newspapers and periodicals and used associates to collect money on their behalf. Their weakness, however, was that they did not have a large-scale infrastructure that could be employed for collecting purposes and holding church collections. This made the female societies more likely to use a paid collector, to advertise and to use emotive accounts to raise funds. The female societies were more dependent upon self promotion through drawing-room meetings, the use of publicity literature and advertising. In contrast to the male societies which had the weight of the diocesan infrastructure behind them, the principal weapon that the female societies had at their disposal was their social contacts. This is possibly the reason why female societies were more likely to use fundraising events to raise money.

4 WANING FINANCIAL SUPPORT

Church Finance and Secularization

The value of interrogating the connections between the disparate fields of religion and finance was highlighted by a pioneering American research project in the 1990s. The 'Financing of American Religion' project, carried out by the Institute for the Study of American Evangelicals, researched individual giving in a variety of different ways: the relationship between giving and income; the relationship between giving and involvement; the connection between giving and pledging; denominational differences in individual giving; and historical trends in giving.[1] Although the project was principally concerned with examining the contemporary financial issues being faced by religious groups, it also sought to contextualize trends within the tradition of voluntary giving that emerged in the nineteenth century. The historical subsidiary project concentrated on a historical examination of American evangelical religion.[2] The project found clear links between high levels of per capita income and the institutionalization of giving through practices such as tithing and pledging cards. In connection with this, it also found that the use of such practices reflected theological differences.[3] A correlation was also found between levels of involvement and finance and, in particular, that the financial decline of a religious body generally reflected a decline in church membership or involvement.[4] These themes, in conjunction with the connection between gender and giving, are of direct bearing to the questions being addressed by this work and will be examined in this and subsequent chapters. Areas that will be examined are: the Church of England's teaching of the theology of Christian stewardship in the nineteenth century; the degree to which Anglican home-missionary organizations secured their funds from committee members; and, in particular, trends in male and female giving.

The financing of religious voluntary organizations is one area of history that would seem to fall naturally within the remit of historians of modern religion. However, this particular aspect of research has received little attention from British historians. The literature, so far, has mainly concentrated on the development of the Church's large financial institutions, such as the Ecclesiastical

Commissioners and the Queen Anne's Bounty.[5] Other works have explored different aspects of interplay between religion and economics: the influence of evangelicalism on social and economic thought; the problem of the acquisition of wealth by both the Church and the individual, as expressed in the biblical teaching 'Ye cannot serve God and mammon' (Matthew 6:24); and the relationship between business and religion.[6] Not one of these major works has focused specifically on the financial relationship between the Church and its laity.[7] This is surely an aspect of church finance which is as equally important as the revenues superintended by the Ecclesiastical Commissioners or the mechanics of parish finance.[8] The aim of the remainder of this book is to put an evaluation of the financial support of the Anglican laity at its core, rather than making it a peripheral and incidental concern. The merit of this approach is its ability to consider the dominant issue of secularization from an innovative new angle, the laity's financial relationship with the Church of England.

Secularization has been a constant theme in the historiography of modern religion since its articulation in the 1950s and its dominance has been criticized by some historians. Jeffrey Cox terms it the 'master narrative of religion in modern history' and argues that there is 'something about the theory of secularization that leads repeatedly to the stripping away of the legitimacy of the religious point of view of individuals in the modern world.'[9] Nevertheless, despite the contentious nature of the theory of secularization, it continues to be a central narrative within nineteenth- and twentieth-century Anglican and Nonconformist church history.[10] Scholarship on secularization is divided between those who continue to strive to illuminate the critical phase of secularization, in either the nineteenth or twentieth century, and those who stress the enduring and adaptive nature of religion. The dominant themes in these discussions have been the religiosity of both the working-class and women.

Historians have engaged with secularization theory by interrogating different sources and by employing different methodologies: some have examined 'religiosity' whilst others have examined 'religious behaviour'.[11] Many of the case studies in the initial decades of the 1950s to the 1970s, focused on institutional church life and measured levels of church membership and church attendance as indicators of secularization. These early studies concentrated on urbanization and industrialization as causes of secularization.[12] Next in the historiography came the revisionists. These historians were concerned with challenging notions of broader decline and portrayed instead the vibrancy of the church in local case studies.[13] Jeffrey Cox's and Simon Green's local studies, of Lambeth and Yorkshire respectively, were concerned with the status of the church in society, and placed particular emphasis on the high levels of community services provided by the Church through a multiplicity of voluntary organizations in the period at the end of the nineteenth century and beginning of the twentieth century. Cox, for example, in his study of religious life in Lambeth, demonstrated the vibrancy of the Church at the local level and therefore the deficiency of previous accounts of church history. In contrast, Sarah Williams' account of popular religion in Southwark in the same period moves beyond the wall of the church and concentrates instead on popular religion in the home and family. Her research, derived from a study of folklore and oral history, examines the more 'elusive and amorphous aspects of religious culture' and therefore accords a more central role to the religious practices and beliefs of working-class women.[14] Callum Brown took a new approach both in terms of methodology and chronology. His two books *The Death of Christian Britain* (2000) and *Religion and the Demographic Revolution* (2012) are part of his planned trilogy on secularization which will cover discourse, demography and testimony respectively.[15] Both of Brown's books have focused on female religiosity. The first book approaches secularization through his notion of 'discursive Christianity', which is 'the way in which Christianity infused public culture and was adopted by individuals, whether churchgoers or not, in forming their own identities'.[16] Brown argues that people subscribed to this Christian discourse until the 1960s and that Britain was until this point 'a highly religious nation'.[17] In particular Brown identifies the 1960s as being the period 'when women cancelled their mass subscription to the discursive domain of Christianity'.[18] His second book sets out to continue the secularization narrative with a heavily statistical analysis of religious decline in the context of the demographic changes in the period after 1960. He argues that the demographic changes in this period revolutionized family structures and thereby perpetuated religious decline. Taking a different approach, Dominic Erdozain's book *The Problem of Pleasure* (2010) is interesting because it returns to the idea that religious decline started in the late nineteenth century. Erdozain's research has, through an investigation of sin, studied the ideological dimension of religion. He argues that, at the end of the nineteenth century, the 'internal concept of sin' was conceptually supplanted with the 'external concept of vice'.[19] Leisure time, it was thought, posed a danger to the individual because it was an opportunity for sin. Consequently, the churches increasingly marketed and provided sport as a safe activity to fill that leisure time. He argues that the churches were themselves an unwitting player in the 'secularisation of the Christian culture'.[20]

These approaches have therefore analysed divergent aspects of religious life. Jeremy Morris comments that, as the historiography has advanced, historians have extended 'their discussion of religion beyond the institutional parameters' as a result of the shift 'in what historians are prepared to accept as religion'.[21] One of the key difficulties in discussing secularization is in the actual definition of religion. The sociologists Charles Glock and Rodney Stark in *Religion and Society in Tension* (1966) address this difficulty of quantifying religiosity and changes in religiosity. They explain the elusive nature of the term 'religion' and its derivations:

> Yet, if we carefully examine the imagery which the words stimulate, it is not that people disagree on definitions so much as that they use these words, which are multi dimensional in meaning, in an unidimensional way. They tend to equate religion with

belief *or* with practice *or* with experience without recognizing consciously that the other dimensions exist.[22]

Glock and Stark argue that we should replace our unidimensional model of religion with a multidimensional model. They propose five dimensions of religiosity. Firstly, the 'experiential dimension' is an emotionally characterized dimension encompassing experiences such as conversion and felt communication with God. Secondly, the 'intellectual dimension' relates to an individual's knowledge of their religion in the form of the sacred scriptures of their faith. Thirdly, the 'ideological dimension' relates to the specific beliefs that an individual will hold in relation to their faith. This is, for example, through belief in the virgin birth or original sin. Fourthly, the 'ritualistic dimension' relates to the rituals of faith: attending church worship, prayer, rites of passage. Fifthly, the 'consequential dimension' relates to the behaviour of people as a consequence of their faith; so how people live out their Christians standards or ethical stance in their day-to-day lives. This is, for example, through good works and giving money to charity.[23] It is this final dimension which is the focus of this work. These different dimensions are echoed in Ninian Smart's 'Seven Dimensions of Religions', in which the 'Ethical and Legal Dimension' encompasses charity.[24]

The great body of literature on the subject of secularization has examined this dominant issue mainly through the themes of gender and class. This work continues to develop these themes through an examination of the inherited sense of duty of the upper- and middle-classes to support the Church. Although the religiosity of the working-classes has been studied in great detail at parish levels in recent years, there is a need to illuminate secularization theory with substantive accounts of the changing religiosity of the middle- and upper-classes.[25] This is because they were arguably the group funding religion in this period and any decline in their financial support would impact on the Church's ability to function. The subsequent chapters will, therefore, investigate the individual's financial relationship with religion. This is a key aspect of Glock and Stark's 'consequential dimension' which has previously been largely unstudied: the behaviour of people as a consequence of their faith, in this case in the form of financial support.

In *Religion and the Demographic Revolution*, Brown suggests that secularization before the 1960s was almost entirely a male phenomenon:

> Until the sixties, the secularisation of which historians and sociologists speak was almost wholly male. If you look at the quotations cited as evidence of religious decline, the vast majority are to do with men 'backsliding' in their religious duties – 'lapsing' from churchgoing, 'descending' into immoral behaviour, and abstaining from proper conduct in the family. Though unremarked, social historians of religion are invariably speaking of secularisation before the 1960s as a male thing.[26]

This work reinforces Brown's suggestion. It argues that the home-missionary organizations in this study lost the support of the wealthy Anglican businessman in the late nineteenth century and early twentieth century. This decline in male support had a significant impact on the society's finances because, as will be discussed in later chapters, men typically gave larger individual sums than women. Both McLeod and Erdozain have argued that religious decline arose from trends that originated in the late nineteenth century. McLeod argues that: 'around 1880 is a significant turning-point in the history of middle- and upper-class attitudes, because it is about then that the "Victorian" façade of religious consensus began to crumble.'[27] Simon Green also argues, in his recent book *The Passing of Protestant England: Secularisation and Social Change, c. 1920–1960* (2010), that evidence of decline in the Church of England was apparent well before the 1960s, arguing that clear indications of decline can be discerned from the 1920s. Green argues that even though church membership levels remained stable in the period 1900 to 1950, it was 'the underlying foundations of that membership, more still of those concerning the relationship of the membership to adherence and authority, that diminished so swiftly during these same years'.[28] This chapter, and subsequent chapters, will consider the financial dimension of the 'foundations of membership' and will highlight a changing financial relationship between the Anglican laity and its Church. In doing so, it will revisit this crucial earlier period of 1880 to 1910 identified by McLeod and Erdozain.

The heart of this book (and this chapter) is an analysis of the finances of these home-missionary organizations. This is with the view of evaluating the Anglican community's support of these organizations during the period of study, in terms of who gave financial support and how this changed. Having addressed the topic of fundraising in the previous chapter, this chapter concerns itself with the stability of the funding revenue streams within the period. This is with the aim of arguing that a decline in giving to Anglican home-missionary organizations is evidence of a significant change in the relationship between the laity and the Church at the end of the nineteenth century.

As explained at the very start of this book, the ambition of this work is to highlight the contribution that can be made to scholarship by examining religious bodies through the functional and analytical lens of accountancy and financial management. The purpose of this particular chapter is, therefore, to evaluate the financial health of the diocesan organizations. The information contained in the subscription lists of the societies' annual reports will be analysed in a variety of ways in order to identify whether there were any demographic changes in the source of contribution and level of contribution. This is with the purpose of identifying any significant funding trends across the organizations, in terms of Church party, class or gender. To expand upon this, the analysis will contrast the funding of the High Church female organizations with the mixed Church party male organizations. Additionally, it will analyse whether any decline in financial support can be attributed to a particular class or gender. The methodology and terminology employed is explained in full with the Appendix of Tables.

The Financial Experience of the Diocesan Home-Missionary Organizations

Voluntary societies were dependent for their survival upon a regular stream of contributions from the public and not unexpectedly, their income rose and fell according to the number of its supporters. The laity's support of the Bishop of London's Fund was strongest in its first decade when the total number of contributions remained consistently in the range of 2,200 to 2,700 each year. Correspondingly, income in this period was relatively stable in the £30,000 to £40,000 range. Despite a falling-off in support in the 1870s and 1880s and a slump in income, overall support gradually revived and by 1912 the volume of contributions had again risen to 2,700 with a total income of over £35,000. The East London Church Fund, with its wide network of collecting local associations, received a much larger number of donations and subscriptions than its sister organization; the volume of contributions peaked at some 3,900 in 1905, the society's silver anniversary. Despite this, the society's typical income levels never reached much more than £20,000. The income and supporter network of these two large Anglican societies was eclipsed, however, by the efforts of the interdenominational London City Mission. The breadth of its collecting network (which was well in excess of 10,000 supporters) was reflected in its income which was typically over £50,000. The three smaller societies lacked the extensive collecting infrastructures of the large male societies and consequently had much more limited funds at their disposal on an annual basis: the London Diocesan Home Mission had a typical income of £4,000 to £5,000; the Parochial Mission Women Association £4,000 to £5,000, and the London Diocesan Deaconess Institution £1,500 to £2,000.

The Bishop of London's Fund and East London Church Fund both received its income from three sources: voluntary income (donations, subscriptions and legacies); church collections; and investment interest. As the interdenominational London City Mission was not an Anglican organization it could not utilize the diocesan infrastructure for church collections. Consequently, it received all of its income from voluntary sources and investment interest. As the period progressed, the societies typically received a larger proportion of their income from sources other than subscriptions and donations; this was due to legacies and interest on accumulated capital, often in the form of legacies that came with the stipulation that the capital could not be spent. By 1912 the Bishop of London's Fund, for example, had a large amount of cash temporarily invested and a large amount of stock which it had accumulated through bequests. Consequently, in 1912 investment income was responsible for 10 per cent of income (£3,546). Stock holdings for that year amounted to nearly £90,000 in different securities, principally in the form of different Railway Stocks, Metropolitan Consolidated Stock and Metropolitan Water Stock.[29] Investment income for the East London Church Fund (£821 for 1913) and the London City Mission (£1,250 for 1913–14) was of a more modest amount.

The Bishop of London's Fund also experienced increased income from church collections in the early twentieth century. Various factors can be suggested for this increased support. Firstly, there were more churches in the diocese to hold church collections by the end of the century.[30] Additionally, by this point in time a large number of the churches in the diocese would have received some sort of financial support from the Bishop of London's Fund and would have been obligated to hold an annual collection in aid of the Fund. More crucially, in 1893, the Bishop of London's Fund expanded its small network of local associations systematically throughout the diocese by appointing organizing secretaries for each of the rural deaneries.[31] In 1912, income from church collections was in the region of £6,539 (18 per cent of total income). Unfortunately, it is not possible to review the East London Church Fund's church collection revenue because this income is combined with local association income in the society's accounts. However, the *East London Church Chronicle* reported that the society had received around £6,000 from church collections, in 1889, over the course of the year.[32]

Legacy income was also an important funding source for these societies. Obviously the amount received varied from year-to-year but it was still a reliable source of funding. The Bishop of London's Fund typically received in the region of £2,000 to £4,000 per annum, with 1906 being an exception year due to the receipt of over £4,000 in cash and £18,000 in investments from the estate of John Lockwood who had died in 1872, his wife having had a life interest in his estate. The East London Church Fund was the only organization that apportioned its legacy income on an annual basis; this was in order to prevent large fluctuations in annual income and, therefore, to assist with annual budgeting.[33] The London City Mission, as a consequence of its large collecting network, secured a much larger number of legacies than its Anglican contemporaries and routinely secured annual legacy income in the region of £15,000 (about a quarter of its annual income).

The smaller societies had more complex financial models. As with the large male organizations, they received money from voluntary income (donations, subscriptions and legacies) and church collections. They also, however, received funds from: fundraising events; grants from either the Bishop of London's Fund or the East London Church Fund; mission payments (a contributory payment from the mission the society was working in conjunction with); investment income; and in the case of the deaconess institution, contributions from the sisters themselves. Income from these alternative sources became proportionately more significant as the period progressed. For example, the deaconesses experienced a large increase in its income from mission payments (which rose from £57 in 1865 to £516 in 1914) and deaconess contributions (which rose from £211 in 1865 to £923 in 1914). Likewise, the income of the London Diocesan Home Mission was transformed with the receipt of a significant legacy in the early 1880s which alone earned in the region of £3,000 in interest each year.[34] Unfortunately, the annual reports for the Parochial Mission Women Association in this period have not survived; it is, therefore, not possible to provide comparable analysis in terms of the society's funding streams. Evidence from the minute books and a later annual report suggests that this society also received more a higher proportion of its funding, in the early twentieth century, from interest and fundraising events.

The life blood of these organizations, however, was voluntary income from subscriptions and donations from the public and it is this source that is the real focus of this chapter. Despite the overall financial buoyancy of the majority of these organizations, the stability in their total annual income figures masks the fact that all of the societies were suffering some form of decline in financial support from the public. In some cases, there was a complete decline or even collapse in financial support. In other cases, the decline in support can be identified as being mainly a male phenomenon. The analysis that follows will categorize the financial experiences of the diocesan home-missionary societies through two models: 'Model 1' representing a decline in the number of male supporters and 'Model 2' representing a decline in the number of both male and female supporters. The Bishop of London's Fund, East London Church Fund and London City Mission all experienced a decline or change in financial support that can be categorized as 'Model 1'. The fortunes of the London Diocesan Home Mission, London Diocesan Deaconess Institution and the Parochial Mission Women Association, however, suffered a more complete collapse with both the number of male and female supporters declining: their experience was that of 'Model 2'.[35]

Model One: A Decline in Male Support

It is important to firstly acknowledge that the male supporters of these organizations typically gave larger sums than the female supporters. It is this simple fact that explains why economically the male supporters were of such importance to the financial health of charities. To take an extreme example, it would take the collective contributions of over a thousand women to equal the amount given by a wealthy landowner such as the Duke of Devonshire. So for example, whereas in the first year of the Bishop of London's Fund, 83 per cent (382 out of a total of 460) of the subscriptions and donations came from men, this equated to 94 per cent of the financial value of these contributions. Likewise, in 1897, when the male proportion had dropped to 52 per cent (492 men and 447 women), their contribution still equated to 71 per cent of the financial value. It was therefore disastrous for a society to experience a decline in its number of male supporters. This, unfortunately, was the experience of the Bishop of London's Fund, East London Church Fund and London City Mission; Figures 4.1 to 4.3 clearly show a downward trajectory in the annual number of male supporters giving subscriptions or donations each year to each of these organizations.

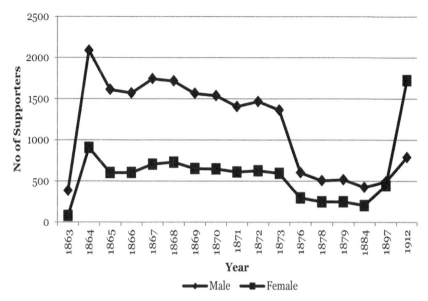

Figure 4.1: BLF Financial Supporter Analysis

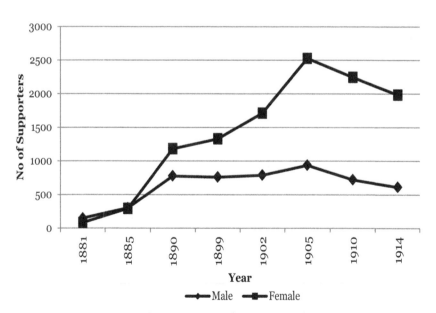

Figure 4.2: ELCF Financial Supporter Analysis

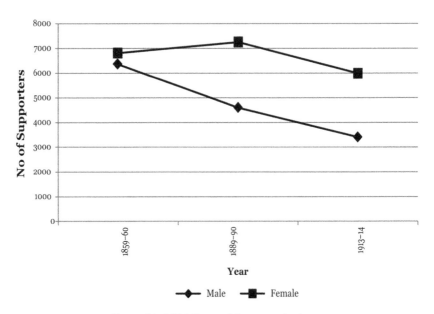

Figure 4.3: LCM Financial Supporter Analysis

In the first fifteen years of the Bishop of London's Fund, men made up on average 71 per cent (full range 67–73 per cent) of the gender identified supporters.[36] By 1897, the male proportion had dropped to 52 per cent, and by 1912 the percentage had fallen further to make up only 31 per cent of contributors.[37] The gender shift was also experienced by the East London Church Fund. Men made up the majority of funders of this organization only for the first few years: in 1885, 51 per cent of the funders were men.[38] After this date, the majority of funders were female with the proportion gradually increasing from 60 per cent in 1890, to 76 per cent in 1914. So by 1914 only 24 per cent of its funders were male; a figure comparable with the Bishop of London's Fund male funder proportion of 31 per cent for 1912. This shift was to some degree matched by proportional changes in financial value terms. In 1881, 81 per cent of the financial value of individual contributions for the East London Church Fund came from men; by 1914 it had fallen to 33 per cent. In contrast, the male proportion (31 per cent) of the Bishop of London's Fund supporters in 1912 still contributed 67 per cent of the financial value of gender identified sums. This highlights the fact that the male supporters of this Fund were high profile men giving large sums. This phenomenon was also experienced by the interdenominational London City Mission. Between 1859 and 1913 the society lost nearly 4,000 supporters (14,504 in 1859–60, 10,773 in 1913–14). Gender analysis shows that the bulk (about three-quarters) of these 'lost' supporters were men. The proportion of male supporters therefore declined from 48 per cent in 1859 (6,366 men and 6,814 women), to 36 per cent (3,409 men and 5,988 women) in 1913.[39] The proportion of the London City Mission's female supporters therefore increased in the period from 52 to 64 per cent. Again very much in line with the proportions stated for the Bishop of London's Fund (31 per cent male, 69 per cent female) and East London Church Fund (36 per cent male, 64 per cent female) for the period just before World War I.

One possible explanation for the increase in female contributions, in this period, is the passing of the Married Women's Property Acts of 1870 and 1882. These acts separated women from their husbands as distinct legal entities thereby giving married women the same property rights as unmarried women. However, analysis of the marital status of the female funders shows that there was also a shift within the female sector with more of the funders being spinsters at the end of the period. In 1865, 39 per cent of the Bishop of London's Fund's female supporters were spinsters; the comparable figure for 1912 was 53 per cent. The more plausible explanation for the increase in the level of contributions from women, specifically to the Bishop of London's Fund, was the reinvigoration and reconstitution of the Ladies' Diocesan Association under the superintendence of Louise Creighton. Brian Heeney describes Louise Creighton as being 'the leading woman in the Church of England during the first two decades of the twentieth century'.[40] In 1900, the Women's Diocesan Association took on an increased responsibility for raising money for the Bishop of London's Fund and for publicizing its works. The association appointed a second honorary secretary with this specific responsibility. Contributions to the Bishop of London's Fund through the Women's Diocesan Association rose year-on-year between 1900 and 1911.[41] This money came from personal subscriptions, road collections, collecting boxes, drawing-room meetings, and concerts in aid of the Bishop of London's Fund. In August 1905 the Girls' Diocesan Association also joined with the Women's Diocesan Association in supporting the Bishop of London's Fund. It is this reinvigoration that is the most likely explanation for the increase in female contributions. However, this upsurge in female support does not in any way account for a parallel decline in the actual number of male supporters.

Frank Prochaska also noted, in his classic work *Women and Philanthropy in Nineteenth Century England* (1980), an increase in female contributions during the course of the nineteenth century. In forty-five of the fifty societies that he investigated, the proportion of female subscribers increased as the century progressed. However, it is worth emphasising that Prochaska's comment related to the proportion of contributors not the volume. In some of his examples, the proportional increase in female supporters does not indicate a great revival in female philanthropy but rather a decline in male contributions. For example, Prochaska calculates that the percentage of female supporters rose from 12 to 40 per cent between 1805 and 1895 for the British and Foreign Bible Society.[42] However, close analysis of Prochaska's figures for this charity shows that the number of supporters had fallen significantly between 1854 and 1895. Within this period the number of female supporters remained quite constant but the number of male supporters fell by a third. Likewise, Prochaska calculates that the percentage of female supporters rose from 12 to 49 per cent between 1801 and 1900 for the Church Missionary Society. However, the number of female supporters of the Church Missionary Society was very similar in the two selected years of 1825 (535 female subscribers out of a total of 1,868) and 1900 (522 female subscribers out of a total of 1,064), whereas the number of male supporters fell from 1,333 to 542. In conclusion, the fact that a bigger percentage of the supporters were female in some cases reflects the decline in male supporters rather than an actual increase in the number of female ones.

So in the case of all three of these organizations, the identity of the typical funder changed within the period. And in parallel with this change, the standard amount given also changed. In the 1860s and 1870s, the typical supporter of the Bishop of London's Fund was a man giving an amount in the '£2 to <£10' band. The situation in 1912 was completely different, the typical funder then was a woman (more likely a spinster) giving a small amount of less than one pound. In parallel, the typical funder of the East London Church Fund also changed within the period. The profile of the typical funder in 1885 was that of a man giving '£2 to <£10' (closely followed by a woman giving the same amount). By 1910 this had changed, the typical profile being a woman (more likely a spinster) giving less than £1. In contrast, although the London City Mission also experience an increase in its proportion of female supporters, the identity of the typical supporter did not change within the period: it remained a woman (more likely married) giving under £1.

In the case of the Bishop of London's Fund, the upsurge in female support offset the decline in male support and consequential decline in the size of the typical contribution.[43] This additional female support, combined with the increased income from legacies and investment interest meant that the society's income remained buoyant. The East London Church Fund was not so fortunate; the upsurge in female supporters did not financially compensate for the loss of the male supporters. Instead in the later years, its relative financial buoyancy was being maintained by anonymous donors who gave large sums in order to balance the end of year books. In 1914, the *East London Church Chronicle* reported upon the financial difficulties it had suffered from the turn of the century, stating that there 'had been a steady falling off of ordinary receipts since 1900'. It reported that the 'year 1913 has proved to be the worst in the history of the Fund' and that its deficit had only been avoided in the past because of 'special gifts.' In the accounting year of 1913, 'no special gift' had come to 'their assistance, with the consequence that there was a difference of over £5,000 between receipts and expenditure.'[44] This trend of emergency special gifts is observable in the East London Church Fund subscription lists. Often given at the end of the year, more likely as a response to the desperately worded articles in the society's magazines than as a genuine Christmas gift, these large sums were given presumably to prevent an end of year deficit. For example in December 1911, the *East London Church Chronicle* declared that it was 'Simply miraculous! that the Fund had received a cheque for £3,000 from an anonymous donor'.[45] Again in December 1912, the *East London Church Chronicle* reported that a donation of £5,000 from 'A Friend' had got rid of their deficit worries.[46] These large donations were not necessarily from committee members. The £5,000 donation had come from 'a friend who had long subscribed £50 yearly, and who, in view of that large donation, would no longer be able to continue the annual subscription'.[47] The friend in question was Miss Emily Ann Maynard (d. 1920), the daughter of a solicitor.[48] These large one-off donations highlight the fact that overall the income from 'subscriptions and donations' was declining. Overall, the East London Church Fund experienced stable income from 1880 until 1910 when a marked decline commenced in its subscription and donation income. After 1910, the income from this source was often being supplemented by one large donation from an anonymous benefactor with the purpose of preventing an end of year deficit.

The desperate appeals employed by the East London Church Fund could not be more at odds with the satisfaction and contentment expressed by the London City Mission within the same period. In contrast, the size of the London City Mission's supporter network cushioned it from feeling the full financial impact of the loss of some male funders. The consequential loss of income can be particularly noted in the fact that the funds being received from its metropolitan societies were over £3,000 lower in 1913 than in 1875. However, unlike the East London Church Fund, its income from this source was stable between 1910 and 1914.[49] Income from provincial associations, however, remained relatively constant hovering around the £6,000 figure. The most striking disparity between the Anglican societies and the London City Mission was in the tone of language used in their annual reports and magazines. The buoyant tone of the London City Mission, in respect of its financial morale, was generally one of overwhelming optimism, with comments that it was 'cheered' by the state of the funds being typical.[50] In 1884, for example, their annual report notes the committee's 'thankfulness that the assistance they have received has thus increased at a time when the trade of the country at large has been in a state of unusual depression'.[51] A key feature in the financial stability of the London City Mission was the fact that it had a much larger network of supporters both geographically and numerically. This vast network typically gave very small sums: of the 38,224 payments analysed, 20,726 (54 per cent) were for under £1. Unlike the Anglican organizations, the London City Mission did not rely upon large contributions: only 114 of the 38,224 payments analysed were for £100 or more (0.3 per cent). This reliance on a mass of supporters giving small sums meant that the London City Mission was not dependent upon the support of a few wealthy supporters for its general livelihood. This falling away of male supporters was important to the charitable organization for two reasons. Men typically gave larger contributions than women. This is the main reason that the trend experienced by these organizations was for the size of the contribution to diminish over time. Also the decline in male supporters impacted on the number of corporate bodies that subscribed or donated, with the Bishop of London's Fund and the East London Church Fund both experiencing a decline in income from corporate sources.

The term 'corporate body' is used loosely, in the statistical analysis, to refer to all contributions which were not made in the names of individuals or groups of individuals (e.g., 'Mrs F. G. Davidson's servants'). The category encompasses businesses, charities, educational establishments, livery companies and public bodies.[52] Contributions from livery companies were a regular and stable source of income through the period, with many of them giving by annual subscription. The Bishop of London's Fund received five contributions from livery companies in 1866, eight in 1897, and six in 1912. Many of the livery companies gave money to the Bishop of London's Fund in the form of an annual subscription.[53] The East London Church Fund received three contributions from livery companies in 1885, five in 1902 and six in 1910. Overall, grants from livery companies were one of the few types of corporate funding that continued through the period. The obvious reason for this sustained support is that one of their main functions was to dispense charity. It is, however, the decline of giving by commercial organizations that is of note.

Thirty-seven financial institutions gave money to the Bishop of London's Fund either in the form of a one-off donation (e.g. Baring Brothers gave £1,000 in 1863) or in the form of annual subscriptions (e.g. Barnett and Company gave £500 between 1865 and 1869). In addition to this, contributions came from insurance companies (such as the Pelican Life Insurance Company and the Phoenix Fire Office) as one-off donations in the period 1864 to 1871.[54] These contributions to the Bishop of London's Fund from financial organizations were short-lived and had mainly ceased by the 1870s.[55] The Bishop of London's Fund's support from financial institutions was confined to the first decade of the Fund. The East London Church Fund received contributions from only seven financial institutions, of which Hoares and Company and Fruhling and Goschen were the most generous; contributions from these two organizations were also over a longer period.[56] In 1912, the Bishop of London's Fund only received eight sums from corporate sources that were for sums of over £2: six of these were from livery companies.[57] In contrast, the East London Church Fund received seventeen contributions in 1910 from corporate sources, of which only six were livery companies. This more sustained support came from commercial companies that were located in the East End and therefore felt a greater sense of obligation for the people of the East End. The volume of its support was, however, still very modest when compared with that of the London City Mission. In 1913–14 it received 193 sums from corporate sources, reflecting the much larger size of its collecting infrastructure. This included large sums from several metropolitan railway companies and gas companies. Corporate funding of the Bishop of London's Fund was only significant in the first ten-year period, falling to a volume of only 9 to 13 contributions a year after this date, the majority of which were from livery companies. The East London Church Fund was slightly more successful in retaining local business support, but corporate contributions had also fallen to the level of only 13 in 1914. This contrasted with the more buoyant corporate funding of the London City Mission.[58] Overall, therefore, corporate giving declined within the period. The firms that continued their philanthropic relationship over a long period were those superintended by successive generations of religiously committed partners. For example, the support of the Buxton family as channelled through the family brewing firm of Messrs Truman, Hanbury and Buxton. This, therefore, suggests that the religious commitment of businessmen was key to the consequential level of corporate contributions and that any decline in male giving would have a consequential impact on corporate giving. And this is indeed what the analysis suggests, that male and corporate giving declined in parallel.

Various social and economic factors had the potential to impact on male levels of giving, both positively and negatively. Firstly, there is no indication that the increase in wealth-holding had a positive impact on the societies' income levels; the historian W. D. Rubinstein found that there was an increase in the number of very wealthy men in the second half of the nineteenth century.[59] Secondly, the population increase slowed at the end of the century as people deliberately acted to limit their family size; this reduction in the number of children, from the 1870s, meant that the family had more disposable income and was better fed.[60] Again, this development did not have a positive impact on the level of contributions to the societies. In respect of an event which could have had a negative impact, it is also worth reiterating that the agricultural depression did not impact on the level of contributions made by titled people to these organizations.[61] Finally, again relating to economic measures which could have had a negative impact, the introduction of national insurance contributions and the super tax (in the period 1909–11) would have impacted on household incomes and therefore affected levels of giving but not to the degree that it would have impacted greatly on the disposable incomes of the very wealthy. The impact of the new taxes was commented upon by the Lord Mayor at the East London Church Fund's annual meeting in early 1914. He lamented that 'everyone felt how in these days unnecessary taxation seemed to drive deeper into people's pockets than ever before'.[62] The society did indeed report that 1913 had 'proved to be the worst in the history of the Fund' with expenditure being £5,000 in excess of receipts. However, it blamed 'a steady falling off of ordinary receipts since 1900' and added that previous deficits had only been avoided through the receipt of large donations in the last few years. The period 1896 to 1914 also experienced moderate inflation caused by a large increase in the world's gold stocks due to the development of the South African goldfields.[63] This had an impact on the prices of goods, meaning that real wages (the purchasing power of the wage) declined in the period 1900 to 1914.[64] However, the decline in male giving in all instances had commenced long before these events happened.

Model Two: A Decline in Both Male and Female Support

The fortunes of the London Diocesan Home Mission, London Diocesan Deaconess Institution and the Parochial Mission Women Association experienced a more complete collapse with both the number of male and female supporters declining: their experience was of 'Model 2'. Figures 4.4 and 4.5 clearly illustrate a dramatic decline in the number of people supporting these societies on an annual basis. From the perspective of an examination of total income, the London Diocesan Home Mission's income levels remained fairly stable within the period 1857 to 1914, with income reliably in the region of £4,000 to £5,000. Despite this, the financial support of the Anglican laity had pretty much disappeared by 1914, with only £55 of income coming from subscriptions and donations in 1914.[65] This short fall was offset by the annual block grant from the Bishop of London's Fund (of around £1,500) and increased income in the form of dividends. The society's minute book first started recording concern for its diminishing income in the 1870s. Throughout the 1870s, the minute books expressed the Council's concern that they would end the year in deficit. Fortunately, this deficit was often met by a timely anonymous donation, presumably from a committee member.[66] In the 1880s, the organization's ongoing concern with money disappeared with the receipt of one large bequest in 1881.[67] Consequently, after this date the society's principal source of income came from dividend income. This one bequest from Maria Mary Fussell (1834–81) single-handedly rescued the society's fortune. In the later period, the number of annual contributors was negligible: 90 in 1893 and then falling year-on-year to only 30 in 1914. The influx of money from the Fussell bequest did not mean that the committee was content with its level of income. Newspaper reports of the London Diocesan Home Mission annual meeting repeated the society's pleas for new supporters to come forward.[68] The society, in 1899, expressed its concern that financial support was low for two reasons: public perception that the society had a steady income (through the Fussell bequest and annual Bishop of London's Fund grant), and because of the 'pressing claims' of the Bishop of London's Fund and East London Church Fund.[69] In the early twentieth century, Bishop Winnington-Ingram was a particular champion for the society and made frequent appeals on its behalf, arguing that the lack of financial support was limiting its work.[70] In 1901, *The Times* reported that the Bishop believed that 'there was no other society in the Diocese of London doing more to advance the Kingdom of God than the London Diocesan Home Mission'.[71] Despite this and other appeals there was no increase in contributions from the laity. By 1914 the laity's support of the society had virtually dried up, with essentially all income coming from dividends and the Bishop of London's Fund block grant.

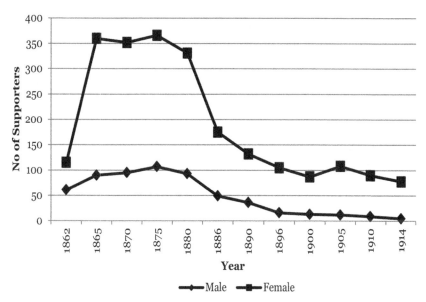

Figure 4.4: LDDI Financial Supporter Analysis

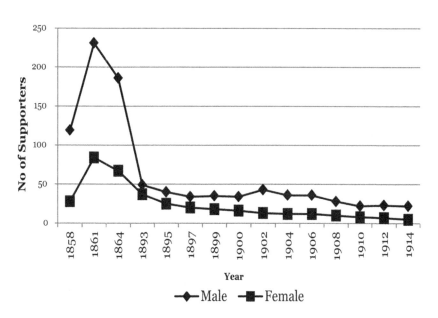

Figure 4.5: LDHM Financial Supporter Analysis

Likewise, the income of the London Diocesan Deaconess Institution was also stable within the period, remaining constantly within the region of £1,500 to £2,000. However, this stability also masked a collapse in financial support from the laity. Virtually all London Diocesan Deaconess Institution income came from four sources: payments from deaconesses; mission payments; dividend income; and voluntary contributions. However, the financial importance of these different funding streams varied considerably through the period. In 1865 subscriptions and donations accounted for £705 of total income, but by 1914 they had fallen to only amount to £87.

Again, this loss in subscription and donation income was compensated for by rising income in other categories. The reason for this shift was not because the deaconesses were comfortably off and had stopped soliciting new subscriptions and donations. In fact, the very reverse was true, with the society's financial books often ending the year with a very small amount in hand. The state of their finances was a constant underlying concern with the persistent possibility of an end of year deficit. In 1904, *Ancilla Domini* stated that the society was living 'hand to mouth'.[72] In 1910 the society ended the budget year with a carry-forward balance of only £14. An article in *Ancilla Domini* commented on the fragile state of the society's finances: 'We have had no donations, and other smaller sources of income have diminished. What would have made a serious deficit has been avoided by an increase of nearly £200 in the Sisters' contributions, which amounted to more than half of the whole available income.'[73] In 1912 the society again expressed its concern regarding the diminishing sum being subscribed to them saying that even a small subscription to receive the society's magazine *Ancilla Domini* would be of assistance.[74] The state of the society's funds affected the work that the deaconesses could carry out. For example, in 1881, the institution was forced to close its nursing ward because 'funds were insufficient to maintain so costly a work'; in its place it opened a cheaper industrial home for girls.[75] The biggest demand on their annual budget was the cost of building repairs, in particular the ongoing problem with the state of their drains. Throughout the years 'Special Appeals' were launched to meet these additional burdens. In 1889, the cost of the drain repairs was £389, nearly half of this sum being donated by an anonymous donor.[76] Just a few years later, in 1894, new building repairs were again placing a burden on the society.[77] It should also be borne in mind that the society was increasing in size in this period; the number of deaconesses had risen to 34 in 1899. So mirroring the financial position of the London Diocesan Home Mission, by 1914 despite numerous appeals the laity's support of the society had virtually dried up; with essentially all income, in the later period, came from deaconess payments, mission payments and interest. Contributions to the organization peaked in the period 1865 to 1880. This peak coincided with the fundraising campaign to build the new deaconess home in Tavistock Crescent. The number of contributions then declined on an annual basis from the mid 1870s, with only 88 contributions being received in 1914.

It is not possible to provide the same degree of analysis for the Parochial Mission Women Association as very few of their annual reports survive. However, the annual income figures, reported in the charitable directories of the period, indicate a clear decline in income from a peak in 1885: £4,077 (1870); £6,196 (1875); £5,756 (1880); £7,247 (1885); £5,322 (1895); £3,887 (1905); and £2,899 (1914).[78] This decline is mirrored in comments in the society's minute books which illustrate the society's constant concern regarding money from the 1880s onwards. So much so, that by 1892 the society was considering closing some of its missions.[79] William Frederick Danvers Smith, second Viscount Hambleden (1868–1928), Chair of the 1899 annual meeting, expressed his concern at the decrease in subscriptions and donations; this decline meant that the association had to refuse requests for mission women.[80] This shrinkage in funds was reiterated in 1906 again by the Chair of the annual meeting.[81] In response, an extensive appeal to elicit new supporters, endorsed by the Bishop of London, was carried out in 1907 but the response was not 'encouraging'.[82] In 1908 again the society appealed for new supporters saying that its 'income has been seriously diminished by the death and removal of old subscribers'.[83] Even an attempt to hold an appeal in aid of the society's fiftieth jubilee in 1910 failed to solicit new funds.[84] By 1914 the committee was forced to withdraw some of its mission women from a number of parishes.[85] And in 1917, the society committee began to consider winding up the fund, finally closing the Parochial Mission Women Association down in November 1923.[86] In 1900, the *Daily Express* stated in an article titled 'War Injures a Charity' that the society was suffering a loss in income because 'the claims of war funds have diverted money away from it'.[87] The Parochial Mission Women Association may have been affected by the war but, as already stated, the society's income figures were already in decline before the Boer War (1899–1902) started and declined continually from 1885 onwards. By 1888 the society had practically exhausted its £1,500 'Working Fund': a separate account created to ensure that the society always had reserves to meet payments.[88] This 'Working Fund' had not been replenished when used and instead had been gradually emptied by payments to meet annual deficits. The society made regular use of the society's overdraft facility from 1897, with this becoming a virtually permanent monthly feature from the end of 1912. At the end of 1914, the Parochial Mission Women Association managed to pay off most of its overdraft by selling nearly £1,000 worth of stock.[89] Despite this, the overdraft continued to feature nearly every month and was not cleared until the society sold all of its stock in the months prior to the winding up of the society at the end of 1923. Mirroring the profile of the London Diocesan Deaconess Institution, the bulk of the Parochial Mission Women Association's financial supporters were women, with an average of 73 per cent (544 out of a total of 748) of the gender identified contributions coming from women.

'Model 2' therefore represents those societies that experienced an overall decline in public support, experiencing a decline in the number of both male and female supporters. Both of the female societies received the bulk of their contributions from women. The volume of contributions to the deaconesses was at its highest in the mid 1870s (557 in 1874); this support then declined year-on-year, with a particularly sharp fall-off occurring after 1882. Over the whole period, the society received 79 per cent (8,379 out of a total of 10,619) of its gender-identified contributions from women. The proportion of female supporters remained fairly level, at a range of 70 to 80 per cent until 1892; this gradually increased until it reached 94 per cent (78 women and only 5 men) in 1914. The profile of the typical funder only changed subtly throughout the period; it remained constant as a woman giving a small amount annually. The only change was that the woman in the latter part of the period was more likely to be a spinster, reflecting the fact that the deaconesses were personally contributing additional sums of the society's subscription list. No long-term data is available within the period to give comparable information for the Parochial Mission Women Association but their typical funder in the 1860s was a woman giving between £2 and £10. In 1918, in line with the other organizations, the typical funder was a woman giving less than £1. It is therefore likely that the experience of this society is of 'Model 2' which represents a decline in both male and female supporters. In contrast, the majority of the supporters of the London Diocesan Home Mission were men; in total 71 per cent (1,323 men compared to 529 women) of the gender identified contributions came from men. Its typical funder did not change within the period; the profile remained that of a man giving between '£1 to <£2'. The London Diocesan Home Mission was the only organization which proportionately retained the support of male supporters but it must be stressed that with only 30 contributions in 1914, its support was practically nonexistent. Its experience was however, that of 'Model 2': one of absolute decline in the number of financial supporters, a decline that was mapped across all demographics and also saw a diminution in the typical size of contribution. Analysis of the 30 supporters remaining in 1914 shows the lack of support from the laity. Many of these 30 were committee members, relatives to committee members and prominent Evangelicals, with names such as Sir Thomas Fowell Buxton, third baronet, and Sydney Buxton, Earl Buxton.[90] Unsurprisingly, this overall decline in financial support from individuals was also matched by a decline in giving from corporate sources. Corporate funding of the London Diocesan Deaconess Institution, Parochial Mission Women Association and London Diocesan Home Mission was never significant and had pretty much dried up by the early twentieth century. By 1900 all of the support from commercial companies had ceased, leaving only occasional support from livery companies and the Corporation of London.

Conclusion: The Loss of Financial Support

This analysis has proposed two different models of change in funder support in this period. 'Model One' was experienced by the Bishop of London's Fund, East London Church Fund and the London City Mission. These societies all experienced a decline in the number of male subscribers. This change was most pronounced in the subscription lists of the Bishop of London's Fund which managed to retain its level of supporters but also experienced a shift in its supporter base, with a move from the supporters being predominantly men to being predominantly women. The East London Church Fund experienced both a decline in the health of its finances and a decline in the number of supporters, and like the Bishop of London's Fund it also experienced a shift in its funder-base. Finally, the experience of the London City Mission was one of no significant funding shift in terms of its supporters or in terms of the level of financial support, although it did experience a decrease in its proportion of male supporters but not to the same degree as the Anglican organizations. In contrast, 'Model Two' experienced by the London Diocesan Home Mission, Parochial Mission Women Association and London Diocesan Deaconess Institution was one of straightforward decline, both financially and in terms of its support numerically; the numerical decline was seen across both male and female supporters. In conjunction with this decline and shift in supporter base, the societies also experienced a change in the size of contribution. In conclusion, bringing these different elements together, the typical funder of the Bishop of London's Fund, East London Church Fund, London City Mission, Parochial Mission Women Association and London Diocesan Deaconess Institution in the latter years was a woman giving a very small amount. Only the London Diocesan Home Mission, with its negligible number of supporters, retained a predominantly male supporter base.

Overall, by the end of the period the Anglican laity's financial support for the organizations had declined or in some cases virtually ceased altogether. The phenomenon of overall decline of supporters numerically is noteworthy because the population was expanding rapidly in this period. The principal cause of this population explosion was a decline in mortality; the life expectancy in London increased from 30 years in 1811 to 52 in 1911.[91] In conjunction with this the population size of the Diocese of London grew accordingly, from 2,143,340 in 1851 to 3,811,827 in 1911 (see Table A.7). This growth was also within the context of major diocesan restructuring within the period which diminished the geographical size and population of the Diocese.[92] This increase in population did not result in increased support for these societies. By 1914, both the London Diocesan Home Mission and the London Diocesan Deaconess Institution had ceased to receive any noteworthy income from the laity. Also the East London Church Fund, which still received the bulk of its funding from the laity, was by 1914 worried about its declining support. The only society that bucked this trend is the Bishop of London's Fund which had increased its number of subscriptions and donations by 1912. In summary, these home-missionary organizations had all experienced significant funding changes within the period. Analysis of these changes has highlighted the disappearance of the middle-class man from the society's subscription lists in the later period. In contrast, the fortunes of the interdenominational London City Mission had not experienced the volatility of the Anglican organizations and had remained quite stable within the same period.

This is because the London City Mission was not dependent upon the support of the wealthy businessman and therefore did not experience this funding shift.

The analysis has highlighted an increase in the overall proportion of female supporters increased during the period. This was the case with the Bishop of London's Fund, East London Church Fund, London City Mission and London Diocesan Deaconess Institution. This proportional increase in female supporters did not always mean that there had been a corresponding numerical increase. A numerical increase in female supporters only occurred in the Bishop of London's Fund subscription lists. Analysis of the East London Church Fund subscription lists shows an increase in the number of female supporters coinciding with the society's twenty-fifth anniversary in 1905, but with the number of female supporters declining from this point. Several factors could have impacted on female contributions within the period. Mrs Creighton's presidency of the Women's Diocesan Association exactly covered the period which witnessed an increase in female supporters to the Bishop of London's Fund. Sean Gill argues that, during the Victorian and Edwardian period, all parties of the Church of England experienced increased participation by women. He terms this the 'the feminization of the Church'.[93] At the start of the twentieth century, the *Daily News* census surveyed church attendance in Greater London in the period November 1902 to November 1903. In terms of gender, the *Daily News* census calculated that women made up 65.5 per cent of adult Anglican worshippers. The figures showed that more women than men, numerically, attended both the morning and evening services, with attendances for both sexes being higher in the evening.[94] The female proportion was more pronounced in West London where women made up 69 per cent of morning adult worshippers and 70 per cent of evening adult worshippers. The explanation given for this was that wealthy Anglicans that resided in West London had more female domestic servants.[95] Charles Booth in *Life and Labour of the People in London* (1903) noted that: 'Throughout London the female sex forms the mainstay of every religious assembly of whatever class.'[96] Jeffrey Cox also commented, in *The English Churches in a Secular Society,* on the higher proportion of female church attendance in Lambeth.[97] However, this increased religiosity of women would reasonably be expected to impact on all of the finances of these organizations. Instead, the increase in female supporters (in terms of volume) was only experienced by the Bishop of London's Fund and briefly by the East London Church Fund. As previously stated, it is reasonable to argue that this increase in female numbers was as a result of the galvanization of the female associations in this period. The crucial point, however, is that the analysis of the subscriptions lists has shown that it was the decline in male supporters that is the noteworthy phenomenon in this period.

Having established that all six societies either experienced an overall decline in giving or a more specific male decline in giving, the next chapter will examine the demographics and identities of the principal philanthropists who funded home-missionary organizations in this period.

5 THE VICTORIAN PHILANTHROPISTS

Writing in 1965, David Owen in his classic work *English Philanthropy* claimed that 'the generality of contributors to late Victorian charity must remain an anonymous mass, for there is little evidence as to their identity, their numbers, and their motives'. This is, however, a simplistic view as the names (and often addresses) of this 'anonymous mass' are listed in thousands of printed charitable subscription lists. Detailed analysis of these lists does make it possible to identify the financial supporters as individuals and to observe patterns and stereotypes of philanthropy. It is remarkable that books on philanthropy have very little discussion of the actual philanthropists. Olive Checkland, for example, in *Philanthropy in Victorian Scotland* refers to the Dick bequest as 'one of the most interesting of the educational endowments in Victorian Scotland' and yet supplies only brief information about James Dick.[1] Generally, the philanthropists mentioned are those of great fame, such as Baroness Angela Burdett-Coutts (1814–1906). This chapter portrays a gallery of philanthropists, including: the 'usual suspects', such as the first Duke of Westminster (1825–99); the lesser known philanthropists, such as the merchant George Moore (1806–76); and completely unknown philanthropists, such as Maria Mary Fussell (1834–81) and Richard Foster (1822–1910). Many of the prominent philanthropists identified in this study can be found in the *The Charitable Ten Thousand*: Duke of Bedford, Richard Benyon, Baroness Burdett-Coutts, The Misses Doxat, Lord Ebury, Richard Foster, John Saunders Gilliat, Charles Morrison, Elizabeth Von Mumm, Duke of Portland, Viscount Portman, Henry Warner Prescott, Lady Wantage, Duke of Westminster, Earl Wharncliffe. This publication, produced in 1896 and 1904, was an A to Z list with addresses of philanthropists drawn up from subscription lists. The historian David Owen gave this publication the apt description of a 'sucker-list'.[2]

The funder-base for the different societies reflected their different mechanisms for collecting funds. The profiles of the prominent supporters of the Bishop of London's Fund and East London Church Fund were unsurprisingly, given that they were sister organizations, very similar in makeup. Both organizations received their largest contributions from a mixture of titled people, bishops of London and commoners (mainly bankers). However, within these similarities there were slightly different balances. More of the Bishop of London's Fund's prominent supporters were titled or clergy, and more of the East London Church Fund's prominent supporters were commoners. In contrast, the London Diocesan Home Mission received no large sums from London clergymen themselves; its prominent supporters were principally titled landowners, bankers and commoners related to clergymen. The members of the Anglican laity that appear prominently in the subscription lists of these three male organizations, therefore, shared a common background. The factor that linked many of these financially prominent philanthropists was their position in London, either professionally or in society. The large contributions came from hereditary titled landowners with London property, individuals who were high-ranking London clergymen or were related to London clergymen, and individuals who were City bankers. The principal funders of the interdenominational London City Mission did not share this profile (see Table A.4.1f). Firstly, the prominent London City Mission funders were mainly a mixture of Nonconformists and Evangelical Anglicans who had close Nonconformist connections through earlier generations. Secondly, the philanthropists that funded this organization were mainly wealthy businessmen connected to businesses in either banking or brewing.[3] The top funders of the London City Mission included several members of the Buxton brewing family and members of the Barclay and Bevan banking families, all of whom shared Quaker roots. In contrast, the two female societies solicited their largest contributions from the society's own committee members, volunteers and their extended family and friends. Consequently, the funders of these organizations matched the High Church profile of the committees of these organizations. This suggests that the Parochial Mission Women Association's efforts to advertise widely in both Evangelical and High Church publications failed to bear fruit. The network of support for the two female societies was, therefore, actually more semi-public in nature because on the whole they drew funds from a more limited field of acquaintances. The female societies lacked the supportive diocesan infrastructure of local associations and this made them more dependent upon the contacts either in the immediate locality or through social contacts. The funder-base of the London Diocesan Home Mission shared characteristics of both the female societies and the large male societies. Like the large male societies, its funding came from commoners, clergy and landed nobility. And like the female societies it lacked an extensive diocesan infrastructure, making it more dependent upon its committee for support.

The philanthropists profiled in the remainder of this chapter share one common attribute. They are all individuals with ample fortunes who choose to give away large sums either during life or at their death. They come, however, from a true cross-section of the middle-class and upper-class, with some inheriting their wealth, some deriving their wealth from property rental, and some from commercial pursuits.

Titled Philanthropists

It seems only right that a discussion on giving by titled individuals should commence with the Royal Family. Such philanthropists were not unsurprisingly listed at the head of the charity's subscription list. Queen Victoria, for example, donated to the Metropolis Churches Fund (£1,000), London Diocesan Church Building Society (£500) and Bishop of London's Fund (£3,050). Other members of the Royal Family who gave to the Bishop of London's Fund in the period 1863 to 1912 were: King Edward VII (1841–1910), £1,063; King George V (1865–1936), £42; Prince George, second Duke of Cambridge (1819–1904), £120; and Ernest II, Duke of Saxe-Coburg and Gotha (1818–93) and brother of Prince Albert, £100. Such names do not appear in any of the other subscriptions lists for the organizations examined in this study, thereby highlighting the prominence and prestige of the Bishop of London's Fund. The names of the prominent London landowners such as the William Henry Berkley Portman, second Viscount Portman (1829–1919) and Hugh Lupus Grosvenor, first Duke of Westminster (1825–99) appear more widely across a the range of organizations. Viscount Portman contributed £13,595 to the Bishop of London's Fund and £2,400 to the East London Church Fund. His wealth was derived from a large rental income from the Portman Estate in central London. The Grosvenor family were financially very supportive of home mission in London and sat on many committees. Richard Grosvenor, second Marquess of Westminster (1795–1869) and father to the first Duke of Westminster, was a committee member of the London Diocesan Church Building Society and supported its work through a donation of £10,000. Richard Grosvenor's brother, the Evangelical Robert Grosvenor, first Baron Ebury (1801–93) was a committee member of the Scripture Readers' Association, London Diocesan Home Mission, London Diocesan Church Building Society and Bishop of London's Fund. In 1869, upon the death of the second Marquess, Hugh Lupus Grosvenor inherited the vast estate of London property and the title. In 1874 he was elevated from the position of Marquess to the position of Duke of Westminster, the only dukedom conferred by Queen Victoria to a non-royal. His wealth was principally derived from income on his property in London, particularly Mayfair and Belgravia; between 1870 and 1899, his rental income on this property rose from £115,000 to £250,000 per year.[4] The first Duke of Westminster, reputed to have been the wealthiest man in Britain at his death, was a generous supporter of home-mission and his name appears in most of the subscription lists for organizations in this study: he contributed £35,050 to the Bishop of London's Fund, £6,000 to the East London Church Fund, £4,500 to the London City Mission, and £170 to the London Diocesan Home Mission.[5] In respect of the female associations, he gave at least £100 to the Parochial Mission Women Association but did not subscribe to the London Diocesan Deaconess Institution. His biography calls him a 'devout churchman' and a 'model landlord' and notes the numerous London sites that he gave freely or at a peppercorn rent for the building of churches (All Saints Church in Pimlico and St Philip's Church in Buckingham Palace Road), rectories, schools and a public library.[6] Other favoured causes of the Duke were hospitals, temperance, and the protection of animals. The first Duke was succeeded in 1899 by his grandson, Hugh Grosvenor, second Duke of Westminster (1879–1953) whose name also appears in the subscription lists for both the Bishop of London's Fund (giving £6,700 up to 1912) and the East London Church Fund (£200 up to 1914). Upon the first duke's death in 1899, *The Times* reported:

> At his express wish the management of the estate was conducted with great generosity to all kinds of charitable and religious institutions. Freehold sites and money for the erection of buildings, for the pay of curates, and for other helpful work were freely granted, and at no time was the slightest distinction ever drawn between Churchmen and Dissenters ... He was, indeed, the best of landlords – alike to all classes of his tenants and to the public at large.[7]

The Bishop of London's Fund had a higher proportion of titled supporters than the other societies; this reflects the fact that wealthy London property owners were specifically targeted by the society (as did its predecessors of the Metropolis Churches Fund and London Diocesan Church Building Society).[8] In 1854, at the launch of the London Diocesan Church Building Society, the society appealed to property owners. In response, the three principal London property owners all pledged £10,000: Richard Grosvenor, the Marquess of Westminster; Francis Russell, seventh Duke of Bedford (1788–1861) and the Commissioners of Woods, Forests and Land Revenues (which superintended the Crown Estate) all pledged £10,000 each.[9] The Duke of Bedford's successors also supported the Bishop of London's Fund. William Russell, eighth Duke of Bedford (1809–72), inherited from his father (the seventh Duke) in 1861 and gave the Fund £10,000. Herbrand Arthur Russell, eleventh Duke of Bedford (1858–1940) also gave the Fund £1,000. Likewise every generation of the dukes of Devonshire maintained their financial support of the Fund in the period up until World War I: William Cavendish, seventh Duke of Devonshire (1808–91) gave £2,800; Spencer Compton Cavendish, eighth Duke of Devonshire (1833–1908) gave £1,500; and Victor Christian William Cavendish, ninth Duke of Devonshire had given £500 by 1912 in the form of an annual subscription of £100. Rubinstein lists these three English titled families (Westminster, Bedford and Devonshire) as having the largest income from property.[10] Other London property owners such the Earl of Cadogan also appear in the subscription lists: Henry Charles Cadogan, fourth Earl of Cadogan (1812–73) gave £625; and George Henry Cadogan, fifth Earl of Cadogan gave (1840–1915) £1,330. The fifth Earl was a Bishop of London's Fund committee member and rebuilt the beautifully decorated Arts and Crafts church of Holy Trinity in Sloane Square, in the 1880s at a cost of £20,000. The other great London property owners, in the form of the City's livery companies, were also generous supporters of all of the organizations. It is noteworthy that the names of these great London property owners do not appear prominently, if at all, in the subscription lists of either of the two major foreign missionary societies (the High Church Society for the Propagation of the Gospel or the Evangelical Church Missionary Society). Contributions from livery companies to these two organisations were also very modest in contrast to the amounts that these companies gave to home-missionary organizations.[11] The repeated giving to home-missionary organizations by several generations of the great titled propertied families of London, emphasizes their sense of obligation as landlords to provide for the spiritual needs of their tenants. It is fair to surmise that they did not feel the same obligation to the foreigner abroad.

Support of the Parochial Mission Women Association was also a family affair but for a different reason. Not unsurprisingly, given the high number of titled ladies on its committee, the society had a much higher proportion of titled supporters (see Table A.2.2e). The average proportion of titled contributors for the Parochial Mission Women Association was very high at 44 per cent of total supporters. The reason for this is that the society itself had a predominantly titled committee. The typical profile of the principal funders therefore closely matched the committee profile. Many of the society's prominent funders (see Table A.4.1e) were committee members or were relatives of committee members. For example, the society's co-founder and President, Lady Montagu of Beaulieu was one of the top funders of the Parochial Mission Women Association; as was her mother, Georgiana Elizabeth Stuart-Wortley-Mackenzie, Lady Wharn-cliffe (d. 1884); her cousin Lady Victoria Welby-Gregory (1837–1912) and her cousin's husband the Conservative MP, Sir William Earle Welby-Gregory (1829–98). Likewise, several of Lady Lucy Caroline Cavendish's (1841–1925) family subscribed to the Fund. Lucy was a Lady Manager of the Parochial Mission Women Association for over forty years between 1877 and 1921. She tried, unsuccessfully, to resign from the committee in 1914 because she did not have the time to visit her missions; her resignation was not accepted.[12] In 1864 she married Lord Frederick Charles Cavendish (1836–82), son of the seventh Duke of Devonshire. Lord Frederick Cavendish was Lord Secretary of Ireland and was assassinated in Dublin in what are called the "Phoenix Park" murders. They had no children.[13] The fund was supported by her father (George William Lyttelton, fourth Baron Lyttelton, 1817–76), grandmother (Sarah Lyttelton, Dowager Lady Lyttelton, 1787–1870), aunt (Miss Caroline Lyttelton, 1816–1902) and uncle (the Honorable and Reverend William Henry Lyttelton, 1820–84). The funders of the Parochial Mission Women Association, therefore, generally came from a small network of family, friends and society contacts. The funder-base of this society was principally drawn from the family and friends of the committee. Likewise, this was the only society that had a proportionally large number of titled legators: four of the 18 (22 per cent). Again this reflects the society's funder-base. For example, Lady Charlotte Hatherley (1804–78), one of the society's founders, left instructions for her husband to sell her jewels and to give the money raised (£500) to the Parochial Mission Women Association. In contrast, the London Diocesan Deaconess Institution hardly received any subscriptions and donations from titled individuals and received no bequests from this source. Again in the case of the London Diocesan Deaconess Institution, the few titled supporters were connected to the society through its committee members. Lord Josceline William Percy (1811–81), Conservative MP and the second son of the George Percy, fifth Duke of Northumberland (1778–1867) was the society's chairman from 1867 to 1872 and gave £345. His spinster sister Lady Louisa Percy (1802–83) also gave £155 between 1871 and 1883.

A survey of wills in *The Times* newspaper in 1899, noted that it was rare for the landed gentry to leave charitable bequests.[14] This is because, in such cases, strict settlements were commonly drawn up to ensure that the main estate was preserved intact for each generation. Only 13 of the 263 bequests made to the Bishop of London's Fund, London Diocesan Home Mission and the East London Church Fund came from titled legators (eight women and five men); 12 of these bequests were for the Bishop of London's Fund.[15] The amounts from titled men were quite modest, falling in the range of £50 to £450; the (mean) average of titled male bequest was £310. For example, George Rushout, third Baron Northwick (1811–87), Conservative MP and son of the Honourable Reverend George Rushout-Bowles, gave £100 to the Bishop of London's Fund, from an estate valued at £324,977. Northwick left only seven bequests to religious charities (equalling £1,100) and 44 bequests (equalling £5,200) to welfare charities, mainly hospitals. The bequests from titled women were of larger amounts, falling in the range £25 to £5,000; the (mean) average of titled female bequest was £1,339. This reflects the fact that the size of their estate which were all in excess of £10,000 and in three instances was valued at over £100,000.[16] The largest bequest from a titled person was the £5,000 legacy to the Bishop of London's Fund from the widow Viscountess Ossington (1806–89), daughter of the William Bentinck, fourth Duke of Portland (1768–1854); she had no children. Charlotte Denison was the widow of John Evelyn Denison, first Viscount Ossington (1800–73). She inherited part of the Portland estate upon the death of her brother William John Cavendish Cavendish-Scott-Bentinck, the fifth Duke of Portland in 1879. Her brother-in-law was the High Church clergyman George Anthony Denison (1805–96). The Viscountess was one of the principal funders of the Bishop of London's Fund giving £7,500 in her lifetime and a generous supporter of the temperance movement, building two coffee houses in Marylebone and Newark, Nottinghamshire.[17]

Not unexpectedly, the London City Mission did not receive much money from titled individuals (see Table A.2.2f), partly due to the fact that Nonconformists were less likely to have titles; the average proportion of contributors to this society who were titled was under two per cent (619 out of a total of 35,250). The first Duke of Westminster, who gave £4,500, is the only landed peer listed in the 'Top 20' funders of the London City Mission (see Table A.4.1f); the other titled individuals all derived their wealth from commercial pursuits. Likewise, a very small percentage (1.5%) of its bequests came from titled legators: 32 bequests out of 2,084. For example, Lady Victoria Mary Catherine Pole-Tylney-Long-Wellesley (1819–97) left the London City Mission a legacy of £1,000. She was the unmarried daughter of the infamous William Pole-Tylney-Long-Wellesley, fourth Earl of Mornington (1788–1857) and the 'Wiltshire heiress' Catherine Tylney-Long (d. 1825). Catherine is believed to have been the richest female commoner in England with an income in excess of £1 million a year and was keenly pursued by several eligible bachelors, including the Duke of Clarence (later King William IV). Although Catherine's fortune was largely squandered by her husband during her life time, Victoria still retained at the time of her death an estate valued at £327,514 for probate purposes, mainly due to a late inheritance from her maternal aunt. The residue of Catherine's fortune was preserved for the children, thanks to the intervention of Mornington's uncle, Arthur Wellesley, the first Duke of Wellington (1769–1852) who successfully sought a Chancery Order to prevent Mornington getting custody of the children from Catherine's sisters; Catherine's fortune had been inherited by William the eldest son.[18] Lady Victoria left 55 bequests equalling nearly £40,000 in total, the larger bequests being in aid of Evangelical religious organizations such as the Church Missionary Society (£2,000), Church Pastoral-Aid Society (£1,000) and Missions to Seamen (£1,000).[19] One of first acts upon inheriting a large sum from her spinster aunt Emma Tylney-Long in 1879, was to increase the size of her charitable subscriptions and also to build a church (All Soul's Church in Eastboune); the site was donated by the Duke of Devonshire.[20]

Philanthropic Clergy

Clergy are more prominently represented in the list of top funders of the Bishop of London's Fund. This is because all of the bishops of London gave significant amounts to the Bishop of London's Fund in the period up to 1912: John Jackson gave £6,000 (Bishop of London between 1869 and 1885); Frederick Temple £4,800 (Bishop of London between 1885 and 1896); Arthur Winnington-Ingram £4,800 (Bishop of London between 1901 and 1939); Archibald Campbell Tait £2,200 (Bishop of London between 1856 and 1868) and Mandell Creighton gave £1,600 (Bishop of London between 1897 and 1901). These amounts reflected both their personal wealth and the length of their time in office. Likewise, the East London Church Fund also received large amounts from Bishop Walsham How (Bishop of Bedford between 1879 and 1888) and Bishop Winnington-Ingram (whose initial formal connection with the Fund was as Bishop of Stepney between 1897 and 1901) in the period up to 1914; Walsham How gave £2,000 and Winnington-Ingram gave £1,700.[21]

Twenty-five of the bequests to the Bishop of London's Fund and the East London Church Fund came from clergy; the majority (22) of these were made to the Bishop of London's Fund.[22] These bequests span a wide financial range from £20 to £10,000 and were either for a relatively small amount (nine of the bequests were for £100 or under) or for a larger than typical amount (seven of the bequests were for £1,000 or more). Of the 25 bequests, 19 can be traced as having a connection with London. This was either through having a London address or through having held a curacy or incumbency in the dioceses of London or Rochester. For example, the Reverend Alfred Povah (1824–1901) left £3,000 to the Bishop of London's Fund, specifically to be used for endowment. Povah's whole clerical career had been connected to London.[23] Alternatively, William Thomas Thornhill Webber, Bishop of Brisbane (1837–1903) left £50 to the Bishop of London's Fund along with another four small bequests to Anglican religious organizations, such as the Additional Curates' Society (£50) and St John the Evangelist's Church in Holborn (£100), where he had been incumbent between 1864 and 1885. The largest clerical bequests came from the Reverend John Henry Ellis (1840–1912). From his estate valued at £184,706, he left three bequests to the Bishop of London's Fund, East London Church Fund and the Bishop of St Albans' Fund for £10,000 each. He also bequeathed £90,000 to Cambridge University to use for general purposes, having studied at Trinity College.[24] Although he did not hold any London incumbencies (his clerical career was spent in the counties of Kent, Buckinghamshire, Essex and Wiltshire), his connection to London came through his family. He was born in Clapham and retired to South Kensington at the end of his life. Ellis inherited his wealth, an estate of just under £140,000 from his father, George Ellis (1794–1874), who is listed in the census returns as a 'fundholder' and 'living on his own wealth'.

Relations of clergy also feature as prominent givers to both the Bishop of London's Fund and the East London Church Fund. The widow Anne Turner (1819–1902) of Dingle Hall in Liverpool, gave the Bishop of London's Fund £4,800 during her life-time and left the Fund an additional £2,000 in her will, from an estate valued at £620,000. Her husband, Charles Turner (1803–75), was a magistrate, East India merchant and Conservative MP; their only son had died in 1871. A connection to a London clergyman can be detected through the executor of her estate: Charles Henry Turner, Bishop of Stepney (1842–1923), her nephew. Two of the principal funders of the East London Church Fund were related to clergymen. Caroline Amelia Newman (1840–1934), of

Bournemouth, gave her annual subscriptions (totalling £2,100 in the period up to 1914) under the description of 'In honoured memory of Reverend Frederick Newman'. Caroline was the widow of the Reverend Frederick Newman (1838–94), a Wiltshire clergyman; the couple had no children as they were both in their fifties when they married, Frederick Newman dying just two years later. Additionally, Caroline's brother and father were both clergymen in Somerset. It is possible that she learnt of the work of the East London Church Fund on one of the Bishop's Bournemouth campaigns. The other principal funder was Penelope Anna Monk, one of the three daughters of the James Henry Monk (1784–1856), Bishop of Gloucester and Bristol. Penelope Monk gave £2,300 to the East London Church Fund during her lifetime and an additional £1,000 as a legacy. Her legacies totalled £7,700 and were all for religious organizations, including the Walsham How Memorial Institution (£500), the Bishop of London's Fund (£1,000) and the Parochial Mission Women Association (£200). Her sister, Jane Emily Monk (who also died in 1917) left the sisters' home in Cadogan Square, Chelsea to the London Diocesan Board of Finance to be used as office space. Monk's daughters, including his married daughter Mary Mostyn (who coincidentally also died in 1917), built St James the Less church in Westminster in his memory; the church was consecrated in 1861.[25]

The Parochial Mission Women Association did not receive any contributions of a significant size from clergymen; this reflected the absence of clerical involvement in the society's committee. In contrast, the London Diocesan Deaconess Institution received several large contributions from this source. Principal among these was Edward Hood Linzee (1815–95), Vicar of Bracknell between 1854 and 1861, and member of the society's committee between 1866 and 1878; he gave £166 in the form of annual subscriptions. In 1873, he was the central committee figure involved in the search and purchase of a new home for the deaconesses; he personally loaned the London Diocesan Deaconess Institution the purchase money of £6,000 for the new deaconess home in Tavistock Crescent.[26] Also Edward Meyrick Goulburn (1818–97), Vicar of Paddington between 1859 and 1866 and later Dean of Norwich, gave the society £136.[27] The deaconesses moved to the Paddington area in the 1870s with the building of their new home in Westbourne Park. Prominent in the society's subscription lists were the names of the deaconesses and their immediate family. A survey of the surnames of the deaconesses shows that roughly half appear in the subscription lists. For example the family of Deaconess Jane Willis Field (1836–91) subscribed to the London Diocesan Deaconess Institution: those being her two brothers and her father. The first Head Sister, Elizabeth Catherine Ferard, gave £1,057, with most of this sum being given in 1874 at the height of the society's fundraising campaign for their new premises. Following the pattern of the Parochial Mission Women Association, most of the large bequests to the London

Diocesan Deaconess Institution came from people closely associated with it. Consequently, many of the bequests came from the deaconesses themselves. Of the total 13 bequests received between 1861 and 1914, five came from deaconesses: Eliza Mary Hankin (1837–1908) bequeathed £150, Marian Christiana Heale (1850–1910) £500; Eleanor Crawford Rees (1846–1913) £300; Anne Jane Woodall Field (1838–89) £274; and Mary Elizabeth Overton Field (1841–78), second Head Sister and sibling of Mary, bequeathed £119.[28]

Merchant Philanthropists

The principal source of funding across all of the societies was from commoners who derived their wealth from some form of commerce. The Bishop of London's Fund, East London Church Fund and London Diocesan Home Mission all received significant individual amounts from commoners, in particular from wealthy businessmen. Of these the most noteworthy were three bankers: Charles Morrison (1817–1909); Samuel Jones-Loyd, first Baron Overstone (1796–1883); and Francis Alexander Hamilton (1814–1907).

At his death in 1909, Charles Morrison left an estate valued at nearly £11 million, making him almost certainly the second wealthiest man in Britain at his death (the wealthiest being the first Duke of Westminster).[29] In turn, his father James Morrison (1789–1857) is also thought to have been probably the wealthiest commoner at his death. James Morrison was a self-made man, who married the boss's daughter (of the textile firm Todd and Company) and became the company's manager, eventually going on to establish a merchant banking firm in 1841 called Morrison Sons and Company. By the end of his life, James had amassed a fortune estimated to have been worth £5 million and a large estate of over 100,000 acres.[30] The family company was wound up in the 1850s and after this date Charles acted as an independent merchant banker. Charles Morrison was the most generous individual funder of Anglican home-mission in London, giving £47,600 to the Bishop of London's Fund and £9,900 to the East London Church Fund in the form of annual subscriptions.[31] Very little is known about Morrison. He died unmarried and was quite reclusive, probably due to persistent ill health.[32] Consequently, he took on very few public duties, choosing to spend most of his time at his Basildon Park estate in Berkshire where he read voraciously.[33] His reading diaries reveal his increasing preoccupation with the biographies of wealthy men and their philanthropy.[34] Morrison's vast estate was inherited by his extended family, with the bulk going to his nephew. He also left a number of sizable bequests to Church of England charities: £10,000 to the Bishop of London's Fund; £10,000 to the Bishop of St Albans' Fund; £10,000 to the East London Church Fund; £10,000 to the Rochester Diocesan Society £10,000; and £5,000 to the Poor Clergy Relief Corporation.[35] In total, he gave the Bishop of London's

Fund and the East London Church Fund a combined total of £77,500, which was enough money at that time to build about fifteen churches.

The acquisition of wealth by the Loyd family shares many parallels with the Morrison family. Samuel Jones-Loyd, first Baron Overstone (1796–1883), was also the son of a self-made man: the Reverend Lewis Loyd (1768–1858), a Welsh Unitarian clergyman who gave up his ministry to become a banker and married into the family firm. He went on found the family banking firm Jones Loyd and Company with his brothers-in-law (Samuel and William Jones). This small company eventually became one of the leading private banking firms in the country. Like James Morrison, Lewis Loyd had also amassed a large fortune by his death (estimated to have been worth several million pounds) and a large estate of property. In accordance with his father's faith Samuel Jones-Loyd's birth was registered with the Unitarians; he was, however, brought up as a member of the Church of England.[36] Boyd Hilton describes him as being 'a deeply religious man who had almost decided to take orders, and although there is no evidence that he ever called himself an evangelical, it is likely that if he had been a generation older he would have associated with the moderate evangelicalism of Wilberforce's Clapham and Simeon's Cambridge'.[37] Jones-Loyd retired from banking, on being raised to the peerage as Baron Overstone, in 1850. He contributed £11,500 to the Bishop of London's Fund and had previously subscribed to the Metropolis Churches Fund, Bethnal Green Churches and Schools Fund and the London Diocesan Church Building Society; Bishop Blomfield had been his private tutor.[38] Overstone's wealth at death was £2.1 million in securities and £3.1 million in landed property.[39] His estate was inherited by his only daughter, Harriet Sarah Loyd-Lindsay, Lady Wantage (1837–1920) who was also a generous supporter of Anglican organizations with her name appearing in the subscriptions lists of the Bishop of London's Fund, East London Church Fund and Parochial Mission Women Association. In her biography of her husband, Lady Wantage wrote a brief description of her father:

> He looked at everything in the white light of reason, yet preserved withal a warmth of heart and generosity of disposition that showed itself in constant deeds of kind thoughtfulness and large benevolence ... Born to wealth and endowed with a genius for business which caused that wealth to increase and multiply, he fully recognised the heavy responsibilities that attach to great possessions, whether in money or in land. Display and luxury had small attractions for him, yet the duties of his position as a rich man and a large landowner he discharged to the full.[40]

In contrast to these two leviathans of wealth, Francis Alexander Hamilton (1814–1907) was a less spectacularly wealthy banker; his estate at death was valued at £383,561.[41] Hamilton was a merchant banker and worked for Brown Shipley and Company until his retirement in 1904 at the age of 90.[42] He gave £500 to the London Diocesan Home Mission, £4,300 to the Bishop of London's Fund, £380 to the East London Church Fund, and £5,638 to the London City Mission plus an additional bequest of £250.[43] Hamilton's biography in the history of his firm, describes him as being 'an unostentatious but liberal giver, not only to the various forms of work in which his church was engaged, but also to almost every well-known philanthropic and charitable association in Liverpool and London'.[44] Hamilton's bequests were modest in size and were confined to evangelical societies (such as £250 each to the Scripture Readers' Association in London and Liverpool) and the Waterloo Bridge hospital. His large donations were all made in the last few years of his life; the £500 given to the London Diocesan Home Mission, for example, was given as a single sum in 1902. The *London Diocesan Magazine* praised his philanthropy and gave the following examples of his benevolence:

> Quite recently he contributed nearly the whole cost of S Luke's Church, Finchley, and provided an endowment. The Rector of Finchley relates that on one of the Sundays in the present year he preached for the Society for the Propagation of the Gospel in Foreign Parts, and that Mr Hamilton sent to him a cheque for £1,000 for its funds.'[45]

The prompt for this benevolence is likely to have been due to the death of his wife in August 1901 and his advancing age (he was 87 years old in 1901). In his will, Hamilton stated his wish to 'be buried in a quiet and unostentatious manner'. Despite this, at his funeral the streets from his home to the church and cemetery were lined with people, with 1,000 people in the cemetery alone. His biography records that local schools and shops of Finchley closed for the funeral both as 'a token of respect' and in order that people could attend the service.[46] Upon Hamilton's death, the Scripture Readers' Association commented that: 'We trust that God will raise up other friends to take the place of those who each year are thus taken from us'.[47]

In addition, to these public contributions, it is likely that Hamilton was also the identity behind the generous anonymous supporter entitled 'FAH' whose pseudonym appears in many of the subscriptions lists for these charities, giving large amounts in the same time period. The identity 'FAH' was a very generous supporter and was one of the top subscribers to the Bishop of London's Fund and the East London Church Fund. 'FAH', for example, in 1902 gave a donation of £7,000 to the Bishop of London's Fund. In 1902 the *London Diocesan Magazine* reported upon this donation to the Bishop of London's Fund: 'Receipts were swelled by one munificent contribution of £7,000 towards the cost of erecting a church and vicarage and the endowment of a new parish'.[48] 'FAH' also gave £1,350 to the East London Church Fund, of which £1,000 was given in 1900. Hamilton's biography mentions that he sometimes gave anonymously and he is known to be the identity behind an anonymous donation of £1,000 to the Waterloo Bridge Hospital.[49] This theory is supported by the fact that the minute book of the Church Pastoral-Aid Society discloses that Hamilton was the identity behind three significant donations listed in the society's subscription lists in the period 1901 to 1903: £3,000 from 'FH' in 1901; £10,000 from 'FH' in 1902; and a further £5,000 from a 'Friend' in 1903.[50] At the same time, he was publically giving the society a £50 per year subscription in his name and was listed as having given the society £1,760 in total as a life member.[51] The Scripture Readers' Association also announced in 1899 the support of a new generous anonymous donor 'desiring only to be known by his initials' which were 'FH'.[52] The use of initials was a common form of anonymity used both in subscriptions lists and as a form of authorship in literature in the nineteenth century. Robert Tener argues that the use of initials, in periodicals, allowed the author to conceal their identity from the world at large, whilst also allowing their identity to be easily penetrated by those in the inner circle.[53] The use of initials to hide philanthropic identity, in some cases, could therefore be a way of identifying yourself as a generous supporter whilst also professing to be humble. This seems a plausible explanation, as initials such as 'FAH' appear to be easily penetrated by the historian and presumably also by contemporaries. Likewise, it is possible to speculate that the 'GC' who gave the Bishop of London's Fund £4,500 was possibly George Cubitt, first Baron Ashcombe (1828–1917) who gave the Fund £4,200. Cubitt was the son of Thomas Cubitt (1788–1855), one of London's main builder developers.

Anonymity was also employed as a tool for strategic reasons. The banker, Richard Foster (1822–1910), gave contributions in various different forms: under his own name; under the description of 'A Merchant of the City of London'; and under the description of initials. Foster would sometimes make three contributions to a church-building fund: in his own name; through a church-building society; and anonymously. The strategic reason for this was because he found that money coming into a project from a variety of sources stimulated that project in a way that one large donation could not.[54] Foster felt that he had an obligation to help Londoners; and that by using the pseudonym he would 'arouse a sense of responsibility in other merchants'.[55] As a youth, Richard Foster had considered entering the clergy but instead joined the family banking firm, Messrs Foster Brothers, in 1836 at the age of fourteen. His uncles retired in 1853 and left the firm to Richard Foster and his cousin John Knowles, prompting the formation of a new family firm called Messrs Knowles and Foster. Foster was a devout supporter of church work from his early twenties, giving money to a range of church societies and donating the money for the building of St Saviour's Church in Walthamstow (Diocese of St Albans), its parsonage and an endowment; the church was consecrated in 1874.[56] Foster was also instrumental in the creation of the Bishop Suffragan for East London in 1879 and the establishment of the Queen Victoria Clergy Fund (founded in 1897 in order to supplement clergy income).[57] Foster was a treasurer of the East London Church Fund and was one of its principal funders giving £4,080 in total. The *East London Church*

Chronicle said that, 'though a High Churchman in faith and practice, he did not confine his sympathies to those like-minded, but was ready to promote whatever promised for good'.[58] The subscription lists of the Society for the Propagation of the Gospel record that he gave £11,705 between 1858 and 1909 and an additional £1,500 in 1910 (the year in which he died), of which £1,000 was given under the description 'Thankoffering, Almighty God for His continued great and many mercies during a long life.' His name also appears as a subscriber to the Bishop of London's Fund (giving £100 per annum) and Parochial Mission Women Association.[59] Notably, his biography records that he gave £5,000 to the Bishop of London's Fund in the 1870s in order to purchase sites for churches in poor areas.[60] He was also a supporter of the National Society, the Society for Promoting Christian Knowledge, Bishop of St Alban's Fund, the Free and Open Church Association, Incorporated Church Building Society, colonial bishoprics and the London Hospitals. In 1910, Foster's estate was valued for probate purposes at just over £160,000, however, like Hamilton he had chosen to give away his charity during his lifetime. The *London Diocesan Magazine* stated that it was believed that Foster had given over £100,000 to Church causes in his lifetime.[61] Instead, his biography (written by his son) suggests the much larger amount of £380,000; enough money to build as many as seventy five churches.[62] The minute book of the East London Church Fund in 1910 marked his passing by thanking 'God for a beautiful life just closed'.[63]

Likewise, Foster's friend, Charles Jacomb (1816–91) the wealthy wool broker, also supported religious causes through a combination of both public and private donations; his name appears against modest sums in both the subscription lists for the Bishop of London's Fund and the East London Church Fund; the name of his firm Messrs Jacomb Son and Company also appears as a subscriber to the East London Church Fund, of which Jacomb was a committee member. The *East London Church Chronicle* described Jacomb's philanthropic practices:

> He preferred that his gifts should be anonymous, and although sometimes under pressure he would yield for the sake of influencing others to give, his public and private charities, amounting to a very large annual sum, were usually given under his simple initials. Frequently, too, his name would appear with some modest sum attached, while a much larger donation would accompany it, but without any indication to the outside world whence it had been derived.[64]

The philanthropy of George Moore (1806–76) is a good example of the intertwining of corporate and personal contributions. Moore was a self-made man who from humble beginnings quickly made his mark in London, eventually becoming a senior partner in the firm Copestake Moore Crampton and Company.[65] The firm was a manufacturer and a wholesale trader of lace and had several warehouses in the City of London. Moore, an Evangelical, was a supporter of many religious causes and contributions appear in subscription lists in both his own name and that of his firm. His name appears in the subscription lists of the London Diocesan Home Mission (£125) and London City Mission (£925). Although Moore is not listed as a subscriber to the Bishop of London's Fund, its minute book indicates that an anonymous donation of £1,000 given in 1868, to be applied to Clarendon Square, Somers Town had come from him.[66] He was an active committee member of the Bishop of London's Fund and held drawing-room meetings at his home in aid of the London Diocesan Home Mission. He also gave sizeable bequests to the Bishop of London's Fund (£6,000), London Diocesan Home Mission (£2,000) and London City Mission (£3,000). From an estate valued at 'Under £500,000', Moore donated a fifth (£94,500) to charity.[67] Moore's philanthropic ethos was clearly articulated in his diary, in which he stated that he did not want to die a rich man. He wrote: 'The money belongs to God; let me give it back to Him'.[68] Moore's concern also extended to religious provision for his employees. The Bishop of London's Fund minute book records that in 1865 the Bishop of London visited Moore's firm to speak to the employees; Moore had collection boxes in aid of the Bishop of London's Fund placed in his firm for the employees to use.[69] In the period 1864 to 1873, Moore's firm gave £1,005 to the Bishop of London's Fund to be applied to the 'building a Church at Kensington or elsewhere besides the parsonage at Kentish Town'.[70] His firm also gave £61 to the London Diocesan Home Mission; and £1,250 to the London City Mission. These contributions from his firm stopped a few years before his death in 1876 and were not continued by the next generation of partners.[71] Moore's biography, *George Moore, Merchant and Philanthropist* (1879), was written by Samuel Smiles (1812–1904), the renowned author of many self-help books. Smiles exalted Moore, in particular, for his philanthropic work, saying that:

> George Moore had discovered what many people never find out, that man's duty in the world is not merely to 'get on' without regard for others, or to spend his accu-mulated money on mere selfish gratification; but to help those who want help, to instruct those who want instruction, and to endeavour to lift them up into the higher light of civilization and Christianity. Every year he wrote the following words in his pocket-book. They became ingrained in his soul, and to a certain extent, formed his creed: 'What I spent I had: What I saved I lost: What I gave I have.'[72]

Upon Moore's accidental death, having been knocked down by a runaway horse, the *London City Mission Magazine* lamented the death of 'a real friend'. Again, as with his other charitable work, he showed his support through active par-ticipation, giving each London City missionary a sovereign each year as a New Year's gift (at an average annual cost of £400 to £500) and guaranteeing to pay (anonymously) for any marriage fees that the society incurred through its work with people 'living together in sin'.[73] Moore is only listed in the society's annual reports as giving £925 publicly. This is certainly just a small fraction of what he actually gave; his obituary in the *London City Mission Magazine* noted a recent donation of £1,000 for disabled missionaries.

The names of the Gilliat brothers and their banking firm, J. K. Gilliat and Company, also appear across a wide range of subscription lists for religious organizations. The brothers were: John Saunders Gilliat (1829–1912), Algernon Gilliat (1837–1925) and Howard Gilliat (1848–1906). John Saunders Gilliat, Conservative MP, was Governor of the Bank of England, treasurer of the Bishop of St Albans' Fund and a Governor of the Queen Anne's Bounty.[74] The brothers were involved in the committees of the Bishop of London's Fund and London Diocesan Deaconess Institution during the 1860s. John and Algernon were both London Diocesan Deaconess Institution committee members and subscribed £5 or £10 annually to the fund. John was also a member of the Bishop of London's Fund committee, to which he subscribed £100 annually. Howard was honorary treasurer to the Bishop of London's Fund and subscribed both to the Bishop of London's Fund and East London Church Fund.[75] The family's merchant banking firm J. K. Gilliat and Company also gave £1,500 to the Bishop of London's Fund in the period 1863 to 1872. The timing of the firm's donations to the Bishop of London's Fund coincided with the committee membership of the brothers in the 1860s; their personal contributions, however, persisted into the 1880s.

Two brewing families were also prominent funders of religious activity in London: the Buxton family and the Charrington family. It can clearly be seen in these cases, that their support for religious provision was a manifestation of their concern for the locality in which their firm was situated. Foremost were the Buxton family, who have been described as being 'one of the leading evangelical families in Britain.'[76] The brewing firm of Truman Hanbury and Buxton gave £2,350 to the Bishop of London's Fund, £200 to the London Diocesan Home Mission, £753 to the East London Church Fund and £7,079 to the London City Mission. Earlier in the century, the firm had also been a major supporter of both the Metropolis Churches Fund and Bethnal Green Churches and Schools Fund giving £2,410 in total. A single sum of £1,000 was given by the firm in 1864 to the Bishop of London's Fund with the stipulation that the sum be allocated for the benefit of Spitalfields and Bethnal Green.[77] From this sum, the Fund initially granted £150 per annum for three years for an additional curate to work in the Parish of All Saints in Spitalfields where the firms' brewery was based. Supplementing these financial contributions, the names of different members of Buxton family appeared in the committee lists of several religious charities.[78] The slavery abolitionist, Sir Thomas Fowell Buxton, (1786–1845), first baronet, was treasurer of the London City Mission. His mother was a Quaker and Buxton was closely involved with leading Quaker families, such as the Gurneys and Frys; Elizabeth Fry was his wife's sister. The subsequent generations sustained this active support of religion in London and were particularly financially supportive of the London City Mission, as well as being committee members. His son, Sir Edward North Buxton, second baronet (1812–58) gave the London City Mission £8,531. In turn Edward's son, Sir Thomas Fowell Buxton, third baronet (1837–1915) gave the society £5,665 and this support was continued further by the fourth generation, Sir Thomas Fowell Buxton, fourth baronet (1865–1919) gave the society £14,040. Their relationship with the Anglican home-missionary organizations was not as involved. Not one of these Buxtons appears on the Anglican committee lists. Robert Hanbury (1796–1884), who was also the cousin of the first baronet and a partner of Trumans, held committee posts for the Scripture Readers' Association, London Diocesan Home Mission and Bishop of London's Fund. And Charles Buxton (1823–71), Liberal MP and younger brother of the first baronet, was on the committee of the London Diocesan Church Building Society and London Diocesan Home Mission. Generally, the Buxton family, personally, gave more modest amounts to the Bishop of London's Fund, London Diocesan Home Mission, London Diocesan Deaconess Institution and East London Church Fund. For example, in respect of donations to the Bishop of London's Fund: Sir Thomas Fowell Buxton, third baronet donated the largest sum giving £1,000 in total in the period 1865 to 1912; and his wife, Lady Victoria Buxton (1839–1916) donated an additional £55. In contrast, in the same period, he gave the Church Missionary Society an annual subscription of £100. Each generation of this brewing family were significantly wealthy. The first baronet left an estate valued at 'Under £250,000' in 1845, and the third baronet a sum of £420,000 in 1915. Several generations of Buxtons can be found in the subscription lists of the Church Missionary Society.

This strength of concern can also be seen in the contributions from the brewery Charrington Head and Company, which gave the East London Church Fund £1,355 and the Bishop of London's Fund £602 through annual subscriptions; it did not give any money to the London City Mission. In this case, there is less evidence of subscriptions from personal sources as well, with evidence suggesting that sums were given anonymously. None of the Charrington partners subscribed to the Bishop of London's Fund or had any committee involvement with the Bishop of London's Fund. Their main area of personal involvement was with the East London Church Fund; the Charrington brewery was situated in Mile End (Tower Hamlets) in the East End. Spencer Charrington (1818–1904) represented this area as Conservative MP between 1885 and 1904, and was treasurer of the East London Church Fund.[79] Thomas Charrington (1820–1894) was also treasurer of the East London Church Fund.[80] Thomas and Spencer both subscribed to the East London Church Fund; and the two spinster sisters of Spencer left bequests to the society: Miss Emma Charrington (1807–99) left the society £1,000 and Miss Marian Charrington (1817–1907) left £3,000; Marian requested in her will that she wanted her bequest be made anonymously as she did not want her name to appear in the newspapers.[81] Marian's bequests were extensive, leaving 37 bequests from an estate valued at £52,000: 14 totalling £14,875 to religious charities and 23 totalling £15,200 to welfare charities. Notably, their support of the Bishop of London's Fund is very minimal, giving £20 in the name of the Misses Charrington and £20 from Marian Charrington; no Charrington names appear in the committee lists for the Fund. The support of these two brewing families epitomizes the way in which religious commitment manifested itself as a paternalistic concern for a specific locality. The historian Jeffrey Cox in his discussion of corporate philanthropy by Lambeth firms, argues that the philanthropy was motivated in part by the local social improvement that came from church work: 'Churchgoing and social improvement were linked in their minds as two dimensions of one institution, and both fit into a general concept of civic responsibility in which churches played a key role as a wholesome and civilizing influence.'[82]

Although virtually all of the significant contributions came from men of property or commerce in London, one woman eclipsed all of these men with her single bequest; a bequest so large in size that it earned her a memorial in the crypt of St Paul's Cathedral. Maria Mary Fussell (1834–81) upon her death bequeathed virtually the entirety of her large fortune to the London Diocesan Home Mission, leaving just a few small annuities to her aunt, friends and servants. This one bequest, of £111,805 in consolidated stock, single-handedly rescued the society's fortune; the London Diocesan Home Mission had begun to express its concern regarding its diminishing income from the early 1870s. This stock was a useful capital reserve for the society; in the period up to 1905, the society sold £15,000 of stock in order to meet annual deficits. Most of the stock was released immediately to the society, with further sums reverting upon the deaths of the annuitants. Fussell's fortune came from the family's ironworks company in Somerset.[83] Her father, John Fussell had been a partner in the family firm of James Fussell and Company, based in Nunney in Somerset; the firm was nationally regarded for its edged tools. At his death in 1853, John left a fortune worth £200,000 to be held in trust for his two daughters and with an annuity for his wife. Maria's wealth increased considerably in the 1860s, following the deaths of her mother in 1863, and her younger sister Emma in 1865, leaving Maria with only her husband for family. Maria had married Pierre Philip Eugene de Gendre (d. 1893) in 1858, having met him on a six month long continental tour. Unfortunately, the marriage was unhappy from the outset and the divorce petition papers and a friend's account cast the husband in a very bad light. Maria was styled the Countess de Gendre until her divorce in 1871 (De Gendre vs De Gendre), when she resumed her maiden name. In life and death there were several petitions by family members attempting to gain control of the family's wealth. Briefly before her father's death in 1853, the Somerset Fussells challenged alterations that John Fussell had made to his will (Fussell vs Fussell), alleging that he was insane. In 1872, after her divorce, the Count and other parties challenged the terms of the divorce settlement (Fussell vs Dowding). And finally, after her death, her aunt challenged the financial aspects of the divorce settlement (De Gendre vs Kent).[84] None of these court cases were successful but they are likely to have been a contributing factor in Maria's decision to leave her fortune to the Church of England. *The Times*, in 1904, covered the circumstances of her bequest on the occasion of a memorial being unveiled in her name in the crypt of St Paul's Cathedral. It reported that: 'It was the sight of a street fight while she was passing in her carriage which stirred her to consider what she could do to remedy the vice and crime of London, and introduce a more Christian Spirit.'[85] The memorial records for posterity that Maria Mary Fussell 'an honoured benefactress of the Church in London' bequeathed the sum of £111,000 to the London Diocesan Home Mission; this was from an estate valued at £133,673.

The interesting aspect of Maria Mary Fussell's bequest is that there is no evidence that she was a regular supporter or that she had any other kind of connection with the society. In the case of the London Diocesan Deaconess Institution and the Parochial Mission Women Association, the principal female supporters were generally connected to the society through a family relationship with the committee members, as seen in the contributions from the family of Lady Lucy Cavendish, for example. One example of support from a particular family, in respect of the London Diocesan Deaconess Institution, can be seen in contributions given by two generations of the Doxat family between 1861 and 1903, giving a total of £1,098 during this period. The family money came from the family firm Messrs Doxat and Company which traded in wool. 'The Misses Doxat' were three spinster daughters: Lavinia (1816–90), Mary (1818–1904) and Harriet (1820–1903). The Misses Doxat subscribed annually and, in 1881, paid off the new Chapel debt of £121. Lavinia was on the society's committee from its inception in 1861 until her death in 1890; until 1882, she was the only woman on the Finance Committee other than the Head Sister.[86] Charles Doxat (1813–71), her cousin, was the society's treasurer from 1861 until his death in 1871. Additionally, their aunt Miss Jane Harriet Doxat (1792–1878), left the society a bequest of £270 in her Will.[87] This financial connection through committee work can also be observed in the subscriptions of Henry Warner Prescott (1837–1926), a solicitor, was the brother of Reverend George Frederick Prescott (1827–1917) who held several committee positions with the London Diocesan Deaconess Institution: he became secretary in 1869; the third chaplain in 1873; and the warden in 1888. In 1903, he retired from the committee and continued on as honorary treasurer and Trustee until his final retirement in 1906.[88] Prescott became Vicar of Paddington St Michael and All Angels in 1864, having previously been Curate of St John's Paddington between 1855 and 1864.

In 1895 he was made Rural Dean of Paddington. Henry Warner Prescott was one of the top funders of the London Diocesan Deaconess Institution, giving £526 in the form of annual subscriptions of £10. He is listed in the book *The Charitable Ten Thousand* (1896), along with many other of the philanthropists mentioned in this chapter, and died in 1926 with an estate valued at £120,000. This family connection with the deaconesses was continued through the generations: Ernest Prescott (1867–1933), son of the Reverend Prescott, became the society's treasurer in 1905; upon his death, he was replaced by his son Frederick John Oliver Prescott (1907–64).

Matilda Blanche Gibbs (1817–87) and her husband William Gibbs (1790–1875) were the principal funders of the London Diocesan Deaconesses Institution, giving nearly £7,500 to the society. William Gibbs was an annual subscriber to the society giving £5 each year. This annual support was reinforced with a large donation of £2,430 towards the new deaconess building, given under the description of 'William Gibbs and his family' in 1874. His widow gave a further donation of £5,000 in 1875, in the year of his death, to establish an endowment fund for the Chaplain. William Gibbs was born in 1790 in Spain, the son of Antony Gibbs who had moved his wool merchant business from Exeter a couple of years earlier because of debts. His childhood was spent divided between England and Spain until 1806 when he moved back to England to join the family firm in Bristol. He then joined the London firm Antony Gibbs and Sons in 1813 and, in 1842, became the sole partner in the firm on his brother's death. The firm had now shifted the bulk of its business interests into trade with South America and was the sole importer of guano to Britain.[89] Such was Gibbs's wealth that his obituary in *The Times* said that Gibbs: 'has been spoken of – probably erroneously – as the richest commoner in England'; his wealth at death was valued for probate purposes at under £800,000 [90] Upon Gibbs's retirement in 1858, his nephew Henry Hucks Gibbs, first Baron Aldenham(1819–1907), a director of the Bank of England, took over the running of the company. After his retirement, William concentrated his efforts on philanthropic endeavours. A strong supporter of the Oxford Movement, he financed the building of several churches for the movement, including £30,000 for the building of Keble College, Oxford, which commenced building in 1873. Lady Lucy Cavendish, Lady Manager of the Parochial Mission Women Association, records having dinner with the Gibbs in her diary for 1872:

> We dined at Portland Place, meeting the dear Keble couple, who showed off the plans of the Chapel, which are excellent. Mr Gibbs is going to build out of his own pocket - £30,000. The plans are too odd (Butterfield) for me to be sure I altogether like them; but there is to be a high-up row of windows with great space for mosaics below, which will have a capital effect.[91]

Gibbs also donated £1,000 to the Bishop of London's Fund and just a few pounds (at least £40) to the Parochial Mission Women Association. The Parochial Mission Women Association's minute book implies that Gibbs was on its Gentlemen's Committee of Reference, as he recommends which investments the society should make in 1880.[92] Unsurprisingly, given his support of the Oxford Movement, he did not support the London City Mission. His wife, Blanche Gibbs was the cousin of the High Church novelist Miss Charlotte Mary Yonge (1823–1901). Her philanthropic interests concentrated on welfare activities, for causes such as nursing and convalescent homes. She also continued to support Keble College and gave a donation in 1881 to create a scholarship fund. William's nephew, Henry Hucks Gibbs was also a strong supporter of the Oxford Movement and acted as treasurer of the East London Church Fund from the commencement of the Fund to his death, having previously been a committee member for the London Diocesan Church Building Society and the Bishop of London's Fund. Baron Aldenham became a member of the English Church Union in 1862, later becoming a trustee and President; he also financially supported Keble College.[93] The association with the Parochial Mission Women Association, was continued by his son Alban George Henry Gibbs, second Baron Aldenham (1846–1936), who acted as the society's treasurer; treat days were held at the family home for the mission women.[94]

Other prominent supporters were connected to the societies through their own active church work. In the case of the East London Church Fund, a subscriber Miss Annie Amelia Jeaffreson (1856–1910), the daughter of a surgeon, left the society a bequest of £7,000 from her £13,838 estate; this was the only charitable bequest that she left. Miss Jeaffreson, who was called 'Sister Annie' in her obituary in the *East London Church Chronicle*, was the secretary of the Twenty Minutes' Work Society. The society took its name from the fact that members were expected to do twenty minutes work each day in aid of East London. She was an active Temperance worker, and established a branch of the Church of England Temperance Society in Stoke Newington where she lived. She also built a Church Mission Hall, the Mission of the Holy Redeemer, in the parish of St Mary, Stoke Newington. Additionally, her obituary recorded that between 1894 and 1908 she worked with 'indescribable energy in the poorest streets of Hoxton, founding a hostel for workers, a Medical Mission, and involving herself in local schools'.[95]

The largest single sum known to have been given to the Parochial Mission Women Association was a donation of £1,000 given by Susannah (Susan) Trevanion (1800–86) in 1881, the daughter of the politician Sir Francis Burdett (1770–1844) and Sophia (1775–1844) who was the daughter of the banker Thomas Coutts (1735–1822).[96] More crucially, she was the elder sister of the extraordinarily wealthy Angela Georgina, Baroness Burdett Coutts (1814–1906) who at the age of only 23 inherited the Coutts fortune in 1837. Thomas Coutts left his entire fortune to his second wife, Harriot Mellon (d. 1837) who chose to name the younger sister Angela as the heiress to the fortune, making

Angela 'the richest heiress in all England' when she inherited £1.8 million in 1837. In 1830, Susannah married John Trevanion (1780–1840) a Cornish MP. Unfortunately, this is an example of another very unsuccessful marriage. John Trevanion ran up large debts gambling and also through building the property Caerhays in Cornwall. By the late 1830s, he was forced to put the property up for sale and after mortgaging the property to the Bank of England, he fled to the Continent and died there shortly afterwards.[97] Susannah's very wealthy younger sister Angela Burdett-Coutts did not financially assist the couple and this caused a rift for many years.[98] The Evangelical Burdett-Coutts was recognized for her philanthropic public service in 1871 when she was raised to the peerage as Baroness Burdett-Coutts; she is thought to have given away between £3 million and £4 million during her lifetime, and is known to have used the anonymous descriptor of 'A Lady'.[99] A strong supporter of the Church of England, she financed Church activities both at home and abroad through donations for church buildings and the establishment of foreign bishoprics. Her greatest single expense was the building and endowment of St Stephen's Church, Westminster in her father's memory; the church was consecrated in 1850, costing more than £90,000. She is only listed in the annual reports as giving £150 to the Bishop of London's Fund and £50 to the London Diocesan Church Building Society. Her biography however records that she gave £15,000 to Bishop Blomfield for churches which were built in the 1850s: St John's, Limehouse; St James', Hatcham; and St John's, Deptford.[100] In terms of the Church abroad, she established several colonial bishoprics through generous endowments. In 1845 she donated £35,000 to fund bishoprics in Adelaide and Cape Town. A decade later in 1858 she donated a further £50,000 to endow the bishopric of British Columbia.[101] In parallel, she was also a committed supporter of foreign mission societies; the Society for the Propagation of the Gospel's Annual Report for 1860 reported a £10,000 donation for the 'special purpose of securing a provision for two Archdeaconries in British Columbia'.[102] In 1881 she shocked society, at the age of 66, by marrying a much younger American who was only 29 years old. This marriage to a foreign national caused a clause in Harriot Mellon's will to be invoked; as a result she forfeited three-fifths of her income to her sister Clara. Her much reduced fortune, however, was still considerable and she continued to devote her life to philanthropic causes until her death in 1906.

Conclusion

It seems fitting that this gallery of philanthropists should be book-ended by the two of the best known philanthropists of the nineteenth century: the first Duke of Westminster and Baroness Burdett-Coutts. However, there were many other lesser-known or entirely unknown individuals, as just described, who devoted their wealth to supporting the Church. There is no reason for these lesser philanthropists to be submerged in an 'anonymous mass' forgotten by history. Unsurprisingly given the commonality of purpose of these financial gifts, all of these philanthropists shared a desire to uphold and further the progress and work of the Church of England. Despite this, the historian W. K. Jordan has argued that the motivation for philanthropic action is unknowable: 'What really animates our action when we subscribe to a hospital fund...? This most essential datum remains deep in the recesses of our nature, immune, perhaps happily from the fumbling probing of the historian, and, certainly happily, from the too arrogantly pitched enquiry of the psychoanalyst.'[103] Jordan is, of course, correct in this assertion that we cannot penetrate the actual thoughts of the philanthropist. Nevertheless, it is still possible to initiate an informed discussion regarding the reasons for individual philanthropy in the nineteenth century.

The motive of class guilt is not thought to have been a major factor behind philanthropy in the nineteenth century. Prochaska argues that middle-class guilt is actually 'a feature of our more egalitarian age' and did not make sense in an age in which the social hierarchy was an accepted feature of society.[104] This view is reinforced by David Owen, who writes that the middle- and upper-classes accepted '"the poor" as a given and permanent element in the social structure'.[105] Middle-class and upper-class culture was a culture of obligation and civic duty; their position in society entailed certain responsibilities and duties. Owen reinforces this point: 'Some recognition of the obligation at least to subscribe to charity, from whatever motives, was so widespread among the upper and upper-middle classes that philanthropy became a social imperative, a convention by those who were, or wished to be, anybody.'[106] The multi-millionaire Scottish industrialist Andrew Carnegie (1835–1919), for example, outlined what he felt were the duties of a wealthy man. He was 'to consider all surplus revenues which came to him simply as trust funds, which he is called upon to administer, and strictly bound as a matter of duty to administer in the manner in which, in his judgement, is best calculated to produce the most beneficial results for the community'.[107] Even though Carnegie had only 'a lukewarm interest in organized religion', he still included the church in his list of philanthropic priorities, albeit in seventh and last place.[108] Carnegie's top priority was the establishment of libraries. This sense of class obligation is inherent in the fundraising literature for the organizations chosen for this study.[109] In particular, organizations such as the London Diocesan Church Building Society, Bishop of London's Fund and East London Church Fund stressed the obligations that the landowners and employers of the metropolis had for the spiritual welfare of the wider population.[110] This sense of social responsibility can be seen in the contributions made by corporate bodies, such as the City banks and the East End breweries, and more public and civic bodies, such as the Commissioners of Woods, Forests and Land Revenues and the Corporation of the City of London.[111]

This idea of Christianity being a civilizing force was undoubtedly the reason that many gave money to Church societies and religious organizations often marketed themselves as such civilizing agents. Bishop Tait when launching the Bishop of London's Fund directly referenced the civilizing force of the Fund's work: 'Consider what our Metropolis is ... the certainty that, as evil breeds evil wherever men do congregate, such a mass of population must demoralize the country, and disorder our whole social system, unless it be leavened by a civilizing Christian influence.'[112] Likewise, the Parochial Mission Women Association stressed the great practical and moral influence that their parochial mission women were able to have over the poor with whom they resided, through schemes such as the penny bank and mothers' meetings.[113] This work was described in the *Sunday Times* as 'civilising lay work'.[114] The historian Jeffrey Cox suggests that the 'civilizing mission' of church work may have been the reason that commercial businesses, such as the Doulton china works in Lambeth, supported the Church. He argues that such companies had a vested interest in creating 'a sober and industrious nation'.[115] Religious voluntary organizations, therefore, promoted themselves as civilizing forces that could bring about social order and alleviate both temporal and spiritual destitution.

Such 'secular' positions that focus on guilt and civilization, however, denigrate the spiritual motivations that underpinned the philanthropic impulse. This is the subject of the next chapter and marks the contribution that this book makes to the secularization debate.

6 PHILANTHROPY IN THE LATE NINETEENTH CENTURY: THE ETHOS OF GIVING

Undoubtedly, the literature on philanthropy – with its concentration on the activity of philanthropy as 'good works' – has given short shrift to any detailed discussion or analysis of the ethos of giving. The tension between 'giving' money to religious causes and 'raising' money for religious causes (through events such as the charitable bazaar) was much debated in the late nineteenth century as a professional and mechanical system of fundraising began to supplant the ethos of giving. The effect of this was that new generations of Anglican laity were growing up uneducated in the doctrine of Christian stewardship and were, therefore, more reluctant to give up their money for charitable causes. This had repercussions on the state of the Church of England's finances. Over the course of the nineteenth century, the Church had experienced the loss of different traditional streams of funding for its societies and churches: the cessation of state funding of church building; the abolition of the mechanism of royal letters privileging certain religious organizations; the abolition of the compulsory church rate; and the abandonment of pew rents as an inefficient mechanism. The progressive loss of these different forms of revenue meant that the Church of England came to the gradual realization at the end of the nineteenth century that it was failing to educate its laity in the ethos of giving.

Philanthropic motives with a spiritual basis are essentially those based on the individual's sense of relationship with God. The renowned biographer and author of many self-help books Samuel Smiles held the wealthy businessman George Moore up as an exemplar of Christian philanthropy. Smiles reported that Moore 'believed, however, that mere money, unless it was given for the love of Jesus, would be as filthy rags in the sight of God. He looked to the heart, not to the action.'[1] It is this interaction between the use of money and man's personal relationship with God that is crucial to understanding philanthropy in the mid-nineteenth century. And central to this discussion is the doctrine of Christian stewardship and its promotion of systematic and proportionate giving which was widely discussed in this period; Christian stewardship teaches that God is the absolute owner of all property in the world, and that man simply acts as God's manager or steward.[2] As a steward, man must use the resources wisely for the benefit of all (as God would wish his resources to be used), and not solely for a man's own pleasure. The doctrine holds that man's stewardship would be judged under these criteria and that each man would be rewarded or punished in accordance to his performance. An important part of this stewardship was that the money should be given while living and not as a legacy.[3] The doctrine of stewardship, consequently, outlined how man should behave in relation to his ownership of money in his lifetime.

Regular Giving: Systematic and Proportional

In the eighteenth century the doctrine of stewardship became widely influential amongst Moravians and Methodists and was epitomized by John Wesley's ethos: 'gain all you can, save all you can, give all you can'.[4] Henry Reeves Calkins's review of the biblical teachings in respect of *A Man and His Money* (1914) argues that the 'industry and frugality' which characterize the Protestant work ethic were 'the offspring' of the ideal of stewardship.[5] A 'Renaissance' in the promotion of stewardship occurred in the mid-nineteenth century fuelled by the publication of many essays and books and by the establishment of the Systematic Beneficence Society firstly in America (1856) and then in Britain (1860). The aim of this society was to 'promote the principles and practice of systematic giving to God for pious and charitable uses' and to address 'the glaring disproportion between the well-ascertained income of the professing Christians of this country and the amount of their contributions to all religious and charitable purposes'.[6] The Systematic Beneficence Society outlined three principles of stewardship: as a steward man is accountable to God; that the tithe of a tenth be 'the general standard' for giving; and that this tenth should be at first set aside (before meeting other obligations) and should 'be offered in worship as first-fruits to God'.[7] This society and its literature crystallized a new form of systematized stewardship which advocated systematic and proportional giving.[8] Boyd Hilton argues that this approach would have been an anathema to earlier generations:

> Such views would have scandalized moralists in the earlier nineteenth century, when the application of any precise 'measure of Christian liberality' was thought to undermine the spontaneity – and anxiety – with which performance of good works needed to be accompanied if it was to go down as a mark of spiritual grace.[9]

John Wesley, for example, had been haphazard and spontaneous in his distribution of charity.[10] Hilton argues that this move, in the latter half of the nineteenth century, to systematized giving was a natural consequence of the shift in the Christian emphasis from piety to the championing of good works. The Systematic Beneficence Society, in its journal *The Benefactor*, directly addressed this change from sentiment to system:

> It is, however, frequently asked, "How are we to preserve the *freedom* and *sentiment* which characterised our former mode of giving when we were left to our own dispositions to decide what we should give, and when the only motive applied was love to

Christ and the poor?" We are free to confess that this question has often given rise to some anxiety, and we are glad to suggest what we regard as a most satisfactory and scriptural solution of this real difficulty. The habit of regarding our property as a part of our moral accountability, and of acting with regard to it as the principles of morality require, is no doubt calculated to lower the act of giving from the *devotional* to the merely *moral* platform, and consequently to deprive the giver of the special joy and blessing which is in every *devotional* act. Now, how is this to be prevented? Does scripture suggest any alternative? We answer that it does. For the offerings of the patriarchs were all *devotional* ... The benefits of such a practice are manifold. It is a corrective to covetousness, a training to liberality, a means of supply for all church and charitable contributions, a habit of thrift and economy in our own affairs, an elevating process in the social scale, and a means of thorough association in all good works of the rich and poor.[11]

Hilton's interpretation of the Systematic Beneficence Society does not reflect the society's insistence that: 'Liberality should be done out of a pure heart which remembers its stewardship, and under the felt scrutiny of an Eye that is omniscient and divine.'[12] The Systematic Beneficence Society examined three aspects of stewardship: 'the *measure* of giving, the *method* of giving, and the *motives* of giving'.[13] And it is this exactitude in measure, method and motive that was promoted by the society. In 1863, emphasising the Christian basis of charity, *The Benefactor* denounced the many self-serving motives for philanthropy that sullied its very nature. It stated that 'If the motives are impure or unworthy, the offering will be valueless, and the deed itself will have in it the nature of sin.' These debased motives were: giving to charity in order to gain credit from God (and therefore to gain worldly benefits, such as, health and prosperity); giving to charity falsely to establish yourself as a wealthy man (thereby enabling you to extend your material credit); and giving to charity because of peer pressure (either because of fear of censure, or self-promotion).[14]

The society traced the impetus for the start of this stewardship campaign to the response to the Irish potato famine of the late 1840s and early 1850s.[15] The famine prompted debates regarding 'the principles of benevolence, of the relationship between State and private contributions'.[16] It claimed that when the new principles were tried in Ireland, 'the amount of their contributions were on the average increased fivefold in amount and tenfold in cheerfulness'.[17] This experiment in Ireland prompted a flowering of literature on stewardship in the 1850s with several international essay competitions on the subject in America, Scotland and Northern Ireland.[18] In 1850, the American Tract Society published four prize-winning essays on the importance of systematic beneficence. This was followed by the Ulster prize in 1853, sponsored by the Evangelical Alliance, which resulted in the publication of a compendium of essays titled *Gold and the Gospel: Prize Essays on the Scriptural Duty of Giving in Proportion to Means and Income*.[19] The Glasgow prize published its winning essay in 1857.[20] Each of these essay prizes was open to evangelicals of all denominations. These prizes were complemented by the publication of several essays and pamphlets.

One of the most circulated was *The Duty of Giving Away a Stated Proportion of our Income* (1855) by William Arthur (1819–1901), a Wesleyan Methodist Missionary and honorary secretary of the Evangelical Alliance.[21] These essays were widely read through out America and Britain and led to the founding of the Systematic Beneficence Society in both countries.[22] In 1856, the American Systematic Beneficence Society was founded following a lecture there by William Arthur. The British version was founded in London and Belfast in 1860.[23]

The Systematic Beneficence Society was interdenominational in constitution, though slightly more balanced in favour of Nonconformists. The President of the British society was George William Frederick Howard (1802–1864), seventh Earl of Carlisle, an Anglican broad churchman with 'an inclination to evangelicalism'; Howard was a financial supporter of the Parochial Mission Women Association.[24] Reflecting its interdenominational constitution, speakers at meetings included prominent Nonconformists such as: Charles Haddon Spurgeon (1834–92), Baptist minister; Robert Smith Candlish (1806–73), Free Church of Scotland minister; Thomas Binney (1798–1874), Congregational Minister; and William Arthur.[25] Other speakers on the Systematic Beneficence Society's behalf included: the Evangelical Anglican, Anthony Ashley-Cooper, seventh Earl of Shaftesbury and supporter of the Bishop of London's Fund and committee member of the Metropolis Churches Fund, Additional Curates' Society, Church Pastoral-Aid Society, Scripture Readers' Association, London Diocesan Home Mission and Bishop of London's Fund; Sir Culling Eardley Eardley (formerly Smith: 1805–63), Liberal MP, a Congregationalist (though originally an Anglican) described as 'a lay leader of interdenominational and international evangelicalism' and who had been involved in the issue of *Gold and the Gospel*;[26] and the Evangelical Anglican Robert Culling Hanbury (1823–67), Liberal MP and partner in the brewing firm of Truman Hanbury and Buxton. Hanbury was a financial supporter of the Bishop of London's Fund and London Diocesan Home Mission and a committee member of the Scripture Readers' Association, Bishop of London's Fund, London Diocesan Home Mission and London City Mission.[27] Regular meetings of the Systematic Beneficence Society were held each year as part of the annual May meetings at Exeter Hall in London.[28] Members of the committee, in the early 1870s, included several prominent Anglican Evangelicals: Francis Close (1797–1882), Dean of Carlisle; Robert Bickersteth (1816–84), Bishop of Ripon; Edward Meyrick Goulburn (1818–97), Dean of Norwich (who financially supported the Bishop of London's Fund and London Diocesan Deaconess Institution and was a London Diocesan Deaconess Institution committee member); Robert Payne Smith (1818–95), Regius Professor of Divinity, Oxford; Drummond Percy Chase (1820–1902), Reverend Principal of St Mary Hall, Oxford; and William Weldon Champneys (1807–75), Dean of Lichfield (who had previously had a long clerical career in London, and was a committee member of the London Diocesan Home Mission, Bishop of London's Fund and Scripture Readers' Association).[29] Other high connected supporters were: Sir George Williams (1821–1905), founder of the Young Men's Christian Association and one of principal financial supporters of the London City Mission (giving nearly £9,000 during his lifetime); Thomas Dundas Harford-Battersby (1822–83), Canon of Keswick, who founded the Keswick Convention at St John's Church, Keswick and was also a close friend of the philanthropist George Moore; Arthur Penryhn Stanley (1815–81), Dean of Westminster and supporter of the Bishop of London's Fund; Charles Perry (1807–91) Bishop of Melbourne; and William Thomson (1819–90), Archbishop of York and supporter of the Bishop of London's Fund. All of these men spoke or preached sermons on behalf of the Systematic Beneficence Society.[30] Additionally, *The Benefactor* also reported that the Reverend Baptist Noel attended the society's annual meetings; he had been pivotal in the establishment of the Metropolis Churches Fund and had been a committee member of that society.[31]

In terms of influence, the society's magazine regularly reported on its campaigns and literature. In 1862 the Systematic Beneficence Society reported on a successful campaign in London in the preceding year which involved sermons and 'several nobly influential public meetings'.[32] *The Benefactor,* in 1867 reported that in the previous year, it had campaigned in Islington, Kingsland, Stepney, Bow, Camberwell, Southwark, Kennington, Brighton, Lambeth, Clapham, Battersea, Pimlico, Bayswater, Kentish Town, Camden Town and the City.[33] Local conferences (e.g., Tunbridge Wells, Bury St Edmunds, Southampton, Plymouth, Leamington, Leeds, Chester, Doncaster, Darlington and Shrewsbury) were held by the society throughout the country in 1869, with national conferences being held in London, Glasgow and Belfast. Reports of these national conferences were sent to all bishops, archbishops, and members of the House of Lords and House of Commons.[34] As well as holding meeting and services, the society distributed literature that promoted systematic giving; 5,000 copies of the publication *Gold and the Gospel* were distributed in England.[35] The work of the Systematic Beneficence Society was publicized in various evangelical religious newspapers: *The Record, Watchman, Patriot, Freeman, Nonconformist, London Quarterly Review, Christian Observer* and *Wesleyan Times*.[36] In 1864, the society stated that 10,000 copies of its journal *The Benefactor* had been issued. Some of its supporters ordered multiple copies to distribute: one lady, it reported, posted copies to 200 clergy in the East of London; a gentleman sent it to 500 ministers; and another gentleman sent copies to 100 of the principal supporters of the large charities in the area where he lived.[37]

The creation of the Systematic Beneficence Society in 1860 was symptomatic of the thinking at that time in evangelical circles that individuals should be more systematic in their attitude to giving money to charity. Many prominent Anglican Evangelicals were involved in the work of the society which initially shared offices with the Evangelical Alliance in Adam Street, Adelphi, and then in 1867 moved its offices to Old Jewry in the City of London on the grounds that it would be more effective surrounded by its supporters in the 'City of Gold'.[38] Its annual meeting (held as one of the London season of May meetings) were located at the prominent evangelical venue of Exeter Hall in London, and were publicized and reported upon in London newspapers such as *The Times, The Illustrated London News, Daily News,* and *The Standard.* In conjunction, a wide body of evangelical literature was published to promote systematized giving between 1850 to the early 1870s, of which the Anglican leaflet *What is Mine, and What is God's* (1859) was circulated to every clergyman in England and Wales. This had been written by an anonymous Church of England clergyman and had a run of four editions between 1859 and 1872.[39] Writing just two years after the society's creation, the *Christian Observer* commented on the success of the Systematic Beneficence Society: 'The seed thus liberally sown has at length grown up into a veritable tree, which seems already to have struck its roots pretty firmly into the soil of almost every orthodox church.'[40] In 1867, the Systematic Beneficence Society reported examples of how the society had impacted upon individual giving: 'Another statement, that delighted us was, that a gentleman in excellent health, and certainly not more than middle life, had altered his purpose to retire from a most successful pursuit of business by which he had attained ample means, through the formation of the Systematic Beneficence Society. The formation of the society decided him to continue in business, and thousands a year are going through his hands, as a result of that decision, to various charitable objects, such as the City Mission, and other causes that he mentioned'.[41] At the end of the nineteenth century and beginning of the twentieth century, when a new body of Anglicans were trying to revive the practice of stewardship as an answer to the Church of England's financial problems, they personally related their own experience of the work of the Systematic Beneficence Society to their attitudes to philanthropy.[42]

In 1866 the High Church *Church Magazine,* which approved of the promotion of regular giving, argued that the very need for a society such as the Systematic Beneficence Society demonstrated that the Church had failed in its task of teaching the Anglican laity the principles of giving. It proclaimed that: 'If her ministers had obeyed her clear directions, and demanded a weekly offertory from their people, they would not now find it necessary to enforce the duty of systematic almsgiving.'[43] The implication of this statement was that the Church of England's need for money was not being met and that the weekly offertory was one mechanism that could deliver much needed regular funding. Essentially though, the offertory was regarded with suspicion by evangelicals because of its association with Roman Catholicism; Jane Garnett argues that the tarnished reputation of the offertory 'did much to delay the emergence of regularity in setting money aside.'[44] In 1844, for example, a storm of controversy erupted when the curate of Hurst parish church in Berkshire tried to introduce a weekly offertory for charitable objects. *The Times* campaigned against the practice of weekly collections, running several articles during the months of November, December 1844 and January 1845.[45] In the 1860s the use of the offertory became more acceptable, however, particularly to evangelicals, and was used as an example of how to systematize giving.

In 1862 the *Christian Observer*, in an article about the Systematic Beneficence Society, advocated the use of the weekly offering citing its successful use by Nonconformists and the High Church. The article stated that 'an absurd prejudice has been excited against it, as if something dangerous must lie concealed under its very simple and practical exterior.'[46] From the mid 1860s the practice of the offertory also received strong support from the mixed Church party Free and Open Church Association which had been founded (in 1866) to campaign for the abolition of pew rents in order to makes churches free and open to all.[47] Conscious of the resultant loss of church income, the society promoted the practice of the offertory in the place of income from pew rents, describing the offertory as the 'lost act of worship':

> The scriptural system is advocated first because it *is* Scriptural. Whether it is more productive financially than the system of pew-rents is a purely secondary question, but still one which the Association is bound to meet ... But this is not all, for a great principle of worship underlies the Offertory. That almsgiving is one of the primary Christian duties, and that, to be entirely acceptable to Almighty God, alms must be offered in a spirit utterly different to that in which we make any mere payment, are truths which are widely admitted in theory, but which are not so generally reduced to practice as they ought to be ... The introduction of the Offertory, is not advocated merely as a substitute for pew-rents. It is this, but it is much more.[48]

Prejudices against the offertory were gradually overcome; in 1867 only 19 per cent of London churches (104 out of 546) used the weekly offertory, by 1876 this had increased to 48.5 per cent (389 out of 802).[49] Bishop Tait refused the presidency of the Free and Open Church Association on the grounds that its object to abolish pew rents was at odds with his role as an Ecclesiastical Commissioner; and in the years that followed, the society often clashed with the Bishop of London's Fund over the Fund's requirement that only half of church seats had to be free.[50] By the end of the nineteenth century, with the abolition of church rates and the abandonment of pew rents, the practice of weekly collections had become generally accepted.[51]

The 1860s also saw the publications of several pamphlets which advocated the use of the offertory, including *The Offertory: The Most Excellent Way of Contributing Money for Christian Purposes* (1862) by James Heywood Markland (1788–1864), High Churchman, solicitor of the Metropolis Churches Fund and Additional Curates' Society committee member; and *An Inquiry into the Principles of Church Finance* (1865) by James Hamilton, senior curate of Chipping Campden. Hamilton commented that 'in this age of advanced revival', the Church was being confined in its work by a 'vulgar want of money'.[52] He argued that a new and regular source of income was needed that would 'enable the Bishop of London to achieve the noble objects of his fund'.[53] John Sandford (1801–73), in his 1861 Bampton Lecture, also advocated the use of the offertory which would train people in the act of giving regularly to God:

> But the Church, by means of her Offertory, stately enforces them. She reminds her worshippers that they are only 'stewards of the manifold grace of God', – that 'all things come of Him', and must be rendered to Him again.[54]

Sandford referred to recent literature in support of the offertory, citing Markland's leaflet and the recent charge of the Bishop of Lincoln.[55] The Bishop of Lincoln in question was the Evangelical John Jackson who transferred to the Bishopric of London in 1869.[56] Jackson said that the offertory was 'a wholesome, a liturgical, and a scriptural method of almsgiving, in which rich and poor are encouraged to unite in the fulfilment of plain duty'.[57] Jackson also referenced man's stewardship in his sermon for the thirty-fifth anniversary service for the Church Pastoral-Aid Society, preached at St Marylebone Church in 1870: 'It is to the liberality of Christian Churchmen, and to their habitual contributions, reckoned as due offering to God's service out of their annual expenditure, that the Church must look for the means of carrying the Gospel to the homes and hearts of the masses of our people ...'[58]

The key concepts of Christian stewardship and systematic beneficence were also advocated during the 1860s in connection with home-missionary fundraising. Sandford's 1861 Bampton Lectures were on the subject of 'Home Mission', and the fourth lecture was specifically on the topic of the method of funding home-missionary work. He commented that 'in days in which the responsibilities of wealth and the Christian duty of almsgiving are becoming better understood, it may be hoped that the appeal of religion will not be made in vain', then going on to elucidate the main principles of Christian stewardship and systematic giving.[59] In addition, both Samuel Waldegrave (1817–69) the Evangelical Bishop of Carlisle, and Robert Bickersteth (1816–84), the Evangelical Bishop of Ripon, appealed for systematic forms of giving in their 1861 charges. Bickersteth was a Systematic Beneficence Society committee member.[60] The Reverend Thomas Williamson Peile (1806–82) preached a sermon specifically on the topic of stewardship at his own church of St Paul, South Hampstead (a newly created district). The sermon, preached in 1864 in aid of the Bishop of London's Fund, was entitled *Give God His Tenth*.[61] He preached that man should 'give on system' and not wait for 'the "great occasion" that shall inflame his zeal'.[62] The Bishop of London's Fund was itself occasionally mentioned in the *The Benefactor* which in 1864 stated:

> The Bishop of London at the present moment wants a hundred thousand pounds to build ten or fifteen new churches for London. Now, perhaps the members of the Established Church comprise nearly all the rank and title of the land, and supposing they acted upon this principle of Sys ben, they could give the Bishop of London in twenty-four hours, not £100,000, but half a million of money, and he might at once commence to build, and

I am persuaded that in his efforts to provide for the spiritual destitution of London he would have all the pecuniary success he desired. Would it not be a glorious thing if this good Bishop immediately found half a million of money placed to his credit at the bankers, so that he could commence the execution of his plans tomorrow morning?[63]

The Reverend Edward Lewes Cutts, secretary of the High Church Additional Curates' Society, used the concept of judgement of man's stewardship emotively and persuasively in an appeal for funds on its behalf in 1861.[64] And likewise the Church Pastoral-Aid Society, its Evangelical parallel, referenced stewardship in its literature. In 1865 an article entitled 'Go and Do Likewise', the society commended the example of parishioner who gave three or four shillings every week to charity. The society challenged the reader with the words 'could you, whom God has blessed with this world's goods, at your latter end give such an account of your stewardship?'[65] Additionally, the sermon preached at the society's fifty-first anniversary, at St Paul's Church in Onlow Square, ended with a reference to man's stewardship:

> As God gives us opportunity let us use the stewardship committed to us of means for the support and furtherance of His work. Let not custom be our rule. Let us not be content with offerings which bear small proportion to what we spend for earthly or selfish ends. Let our offerings be made as under our Great Master's eye, and let them be such as in our own solemn judgment are the best response we can make to *His* claim upon us ... [66]

The Additional Curates' Society also discussed the work of the Systematic Beneficence Society in its annual meeting of 1862 and again in 1868, when Charles Longley (1794–1868), Archbishop of Canterbury and President of the Additional Curates' Society stated:

> Speaking of the members of the Church generally, I am thankful to say that there has of late grown up as an increased sense of responsibility ... Let us thank God for it; but has it reached its *maximum*? Oh, if ever one would give a tenth of his income – if only the good example which some have set were but generally and rigidly adhered to! then, instead of having to come here to beg for this Society, we should have ample funds for everything.[67]

Both the offertory and the Systematic Beneficence Society received recognition and support from High Churchmen such as William Ewart Gladstone. His approval of the society's work is reported twice in *The Benefactor*. In 1865, when Chancellor of the Exchequer, Gladstone received the society at his home at Hawarden Castle, saying: 'I believe that the diffusion of the principles and practice of systematic ben will prove the moral specific for our age...' He further stated that 'we had made a great hit, and that we had only to persevere, and we should fill all England with these opinions.'[68] He noted in his diary for 2 January 1865 that he thought the society had a good object but 'a bad title'; the day before his diary noted that he had read Thomas Binney's *Money: Popular Exposition in Rough Notes, with Remarks on Stewardship and Systematic Beneficence* (1864).[69] Later in 1869, when he was Prime Minister, Gladstone added:

> I cordially approve of the principle involved in a combination, in which person binds himself simply to this, to devote to the purpose of alms, that is, as I understand it, of religion and beneficence, a minimum proportion of his income.[70]

Gladstone was a committee member for the Metropolis Churches Fund, Bishop of London's Fund, Additional Curates' Society and Church Pastoral-Aid Society, and contributed to the Bishop of London's Fund, East London Church Fund and Parochial Mission Women Association. He systematically set aside at least a tenth of his income at the start of each year and kept detailed notes of his acts of charity. Henry Lansdell estimates that Gladstone gave away £114,000 during his lifetime.

In addition to the examples of George Moore and William Ewart Gladstone already cited, other prominent supporters of the home-missionary societies in this study also referred to stewardship and tithing as the reason underlying their philanthropy. William Walsham How, a Broad Churchman who as Suffragan Bishop was responsible for the spiritual care of the East End of London, systematically set aside at least 10 per cent of his income. He increased the amount to 20 per cent when he became Bishop of Wakefield in 1888.[71] How wrote a poem entitled 'Our Trusteeship' about stewardship:

> We give Thee but Thine own
> Whate're the gift may be;
> All that we have is Thine alone-
> A trust, O Lord, from Thee.
> May we Thy bounties thus
> As stewards true receive;
> And gladly as Thou blessest us
> To Thee our firstfruits give.[72]

In 1896 he also wrote an article for the *Free and Open Church Advocate* on the subject of 'Proportionate Almsgiving':

> Few things are sadder than the miserly unworthy view a vast number of respectable men and women take of the duty of almsgiving. They never practice the Apostolic precept to give regularly – 'upon the first day of the week' – and proportionately – 'as God hath prospered' them. And almsgiving which is not regulated on these principals is sure to be a very poor and unworthy thing. I am quite ashamed of the niggardliness of many of our wealthy Church people. I am afraid our old endowments have taught them not to give. They have been quite content that their forefathers made some sort of provision at least for the ministrations of the Church, and they are quite content habitually to offer to God that which costs them nothing. Why have we not more persons conscientiously dedicating to God's service in almsgiving a tenth of their income? … A few of our best and truest do act on this principle, and bring blessing to thousands, not to speak of the blessing that they win for themselves. I know various people differing much in means and in social rank who make it a rule to give away regularly one-tenth at least of their income. The Jew of old had to do so by God's law. Is the Christian to be more straitened in his charity? I earnestly commend this good rule to

all who would try to do their duty in the sight of God in this matter of almsgiving. Set apart God's portion. Let that be a tenth of your income. And then seek to apportion this to the various claims which come before you so as to do the most good you can.[73]

In respect of 'our best and truest', Walsham How was undoubtedly thinking of the banker Richard Foster, one of the most regular givers to the bishop's East London Church Fund. Both Richard Foster and Lord Overstone, in the same manner of William Gladstone, kept detailed account books listing their charitable donations.[74] Foster, a merchant banker and High Churchman, gave away an estimated £380,000 during his lifetime. His obituary said that 'He looked on himself as but the steward of wealth entrusted to him, feeling strongly that at least a tithe of every man's income should be set aside for the good of others.'[75] In 1872, Foster, who was exemplified at his death for his stewardship, set aside the sum of £100,000 that he just inherited from his thrifty and uncharitable uncle.[76] Lord Overstone inscribed his charitable account books with biblical quotations relating to stewardship on the flyleaves. One quotation read: 'It requires an unusually clear, steady, noble faith to be surrounded with wordly goods; yet to be self denying; to consider ourselves but stewards of God's bounty, and to be faithful on all things "committed" to us. (Newman sermon)'; and another 'Freely ye have received, freely give (Matthew 10:8).'[77] Taking 1869 as an example year from Overstone's notebook, he gave away money to a very wide range of religious objects: the Bishop of London's Fund, Additional Curates' Society, Scripture Readers' Association, Society for the Propagation of the Gospel in Foreign Parts, a Wesleyan Chapel, and the Primitive Methodists.[78] In the last twenty years of his life, Overstone's annual income was in the region of £100,000 per year.[79] An analysis of his income and expenditure in the period 1863 to 1882 indicates that from an income of £2.1m, he gave £278,000 (13%) to charity, the largest amounts being given away in the early 1870s.[80] Francis Alexander Hamilton was also commended by his biographer for being a systematic giver. He 'was a giver from principle and not from impulse, and regularly set aside each year a goodly portion of his income for works of benevolence and charity'.[81]

Henry Lansdell in his book *The Sacred Tenth* (1906) listed many exemplars of good stewardship. Many of these individuals supported the principal home-missionary societies operating in London. Such individuals included Alfred Peache (1818–1900) Vicar of Downend, Bristol, and his sister Miss Kezia Peache (1820–99), both Evangelicals. Alfred Peache was a London Diocesan Home Mission committee member, and they both subscribed to the Bishop of London's Fund. Lansdell says that when Alfred's father died, Alfred consulted with his friends on how he could best fulfil his stewardship.[82] Other examples that Lansdell cites include the Evangelical banker Robert Cooper Lee Bevan (1809–90), one of the top funders for the London City Mission. The Mission's obituary of

Bevan commended his philanthropy, describing him as 'an almoner for Christ' and commending his philanthropy: 'Inheriting a princely fortune and high position in our commercial circles, from the date of his conversion he appears to have fully realized his stewardship for Christ and his fellow-men.'[83] Another example is the Evangelical glove manufacturer, John Derby Allcroft (1822–93), who in 1886 succeeded the Earl of Shaftesbury as President of the Church Pastoral-Aid Society. Allcroft was a subscriber to the Bishop of London's Fund and his firm Dent Allcroft gave money to the London City Mission; Allcroft's business partner Sir Francis Lycett, a Methodist, was an officer of the Systematic Beneficence Society.[84]

The 1860s therefore experienced a reconciliation in church party attitudes to giving, with both High Church support of the Systematic Beneficence Society's work and evangelical support of the offertory as suitable mechanisms for carrying out proportionate giving. This revival in stewardship coincided with the need to fund the massive expansion in home mission that occurred both in Britain and America. Charles Maxfield, in his research on early American missionary movements, argues that systematic beneficence as Christian stewardship was developed in the nineteenth century to meet the funding needs of the new founded missionary organizations because the ambitious systematic schemes of work needed regular and reliable streams of funding.[85] The Reverend William King Tweedie (1803–63), Church of Scotland minister, writing in *Man and His Money: Its Use and Abuse*, in the mid 1850s, claimed that the impact of the new Christian stewardship could be seen in the annual income figures for the 'one hundred societies in Evangelical Christendom'. He said that the increased benevolence was due to 'the progress of man's feeling of obligation to God'.[86] As the societies in this study were established in the 1860s, it is not possible to suggest a correlation between their income levels and the dialogue in the 1860s about proportionate giving. However, the launch of the Bishop of London's Fund was extremely well supported financially if considered in the context of the lacklustre support for the London Diocesan Church Building Society. In fact, the annual meeting of the Systematic Beneficence Society in 1866 claimed that the 'development in different forms of a larger spirit of liberality in every denomination of Christians, and the determined purpose to overtake, as speedily as practicable, the recently discovered arrears of charitable and evangelizing work, have manifested themselves in the Bishop of London's Fund, the Wesleyan Metropolitan Building Fund, the Peabody Benefaction, and many similar noble efforts', going on to claim that 'both in the Church and the nation, a mighty and beneficent revolution is at hand'.[87] In conjunction, the income of the London City Mission and the Church Missionary Society, both evangelical societies, both experienced a sustained boost in their income levels in the mid to late 1850s.[88] Speaking in 1869 at the ninth annual meeting of the Systematic Beneficence Society, George Williams reported that:

> Their society has done much for the city of London, and perhaps I stand in a position to be able to gauge some of the results of the operation of the society on the great mer-

chants of the city of London; having occasionally to go to them, I see the operations of this society; its principles find their way to the rich men of the city, and they are prepared to give in larger proportions than we could possibly have expected a few years ago.[89]

Unfortunately, this 'Renaissance of Stewardship' was confined to the mid-nineteenth century. In Great Britain, the revival lasted until the mid 1870s and then gradually fell into decline as the classic texts issued in the 1850s fell out of print.[90]

Although the Systematic Beneficence Society movement was interdenominational in character and arguably produced more Nonconformist than Anglican literature, it undoubtedly influenced the philanthropy of some individual Anglicans. Additionally, this mid-century campaign was clearly influential to later Anglicans at the end of the nineteenth century who saw stewardship as a means of reviving Church finance. In parallel, the mid-century dialogue on proportionate giving also influenced Anglican giving by making the High Church mechanism of the offertory acceptable to Evangelicals. These factors came together to ensure a public dialogue that focused on man's relationship with God as experienced through his stewardship of money.

Philanthropy and Secularization: the Commercialization of Giving

As the stewardship revival lost influence after the 1870s, in both Britain and America, its ethos was replaced by money-raising techniques that concentrated on different forms of entertainment and social events.[91] The essential different basis in these methods was that they involved an exchange of goods; money was being given in return for entertainment in the form of a bazaar, sale of works, concert or recital. The form of fundraising that came in for the most criticism, as being an unsavoury way of raising money for religious purposes, either for a religious charity or for a particular church, was the bazaar or fancy fair. Commercial bazaars had risen up in the 1810s: these bazaars were marketplaces where individuals (mainly women) could rent a stall to sell their wares.[92] Modelled on this format, the charity bazaar was employed on a great scale by women, particularly upper-class ladies, in the nineteenth century to raise funds for charitable objects. The bazaar differed greatly from its materially poorer cousin, the humble sale of works carried out by societies such as the London Diocesan Deaconess Institution. In contrast, these were unanimously praised as a noble effort of giving time to a charity when the individual had little money to give. Charitable bazaars however, particularly the large London bazaars, were roundly condemned for being fashionable, lavish in scale, and morally suspect.[93] William Makepeace Thackeray, Charles Dickens and James Joyce all criticized the charity bazaar in their novels.[94]

The charitable bazaar and its associated forms of fundraising (such as concerts and dramatic performances) were used to raise monies to support home-missionary organizations (such as the High Church Parochial Mission Women Association), foreign-missionary organizations (such as the Evangelical

Church Missionary Society) and church-building projects. Criticism of charitable bazaars in aid of religious objects had commenced in the 1840s and 1850s.[95] Prochaska suggested that it was mainly High Churchmen that were against bazaars, believing that the clergy should promote the offertory as a means of worship.[96] This distaste of the charitable bazaar was epitomized by the refusal, in 1887, of the High Church Society for the Propagation of the Gospel in Foreign Parts to accept funds that were being raised through this medium. The bazaar, held in Gloucester in October 1887, was themed as a Flemish market town and included stalls that involved undesirable pursuits that could be very loosely described as fortune telling and gambling. The secretary of the Society for the Propagation of the Gospel in Foreign Parts, Henry William Tucker (1830–1902), writing to the Archbishop of Canterbury (then Edward White Benson) in respect of this event, expressed the society's 'humiliation' at being connected with this 'indiscrete practice'.[97] Likewise, this anti-bazaar sentiment was echoed by the High Church banker Richard Foster. His biographer and son recalled that: 'Bazaars, especially those for building churches, or those in which palmists, fortune-tellers, and raffles were held out as attractions, my father objected to on principle, and it gave him a quiet pleasure to return in answer to appeals for them, a pamphlet he had written expressing his view on the subject'.[98]

In contrast to this High Church position, Prochaska argues that Evangelical societies were more likely to be open to charitable bazaars because higher levels of women were involved in their societies.[99] This involvement of women would indeed seem to be the key to understanding the acceptance of this fundraising method. As demonstrated in Chapter 3, the most important indicator of acceptance of entertainment forms of fundraising by the organizations in this study was gender. This view point is epitomized by the fundraising methods employed by both the Parochial Mission Women Association and the London Diocesan Deaconess Institution which both fully utilized their 'Society' contacts and social events in order to fundraise. In contrast, the male societies made very little use of such methods and relied upon the standard mechanism of collections, sermons and a network of subscribing supporters. What the evidence does seem to suggest is that as the nineteenth century progressed commercial forms of fundraising became more prevalent. So that by the early twentieth century, even the 'male' Bishop of London's Fund can be seen to accept small sums from entertainment-based sources; again, though, these were events connected to the Women's Diocesan Association and the Ladies Diocesan Orchestra. This view is supported by the fundraising efforts of the Evangelical Church Pastoral-Aid Society. The first mention of funds being raised through the medium of a bazaar is noted in the late 1870s.[100] Bazaars then became a permanent feature of this society's fundraising with the establishment of the Church Pastoral-Aid Society's female association, the Ladies Home Mission Union, in 1887, under the presidency of the Dowager Lady Dynevor.[101] As the Union expanded, forming more and more branches regionally, bazaars and sales of work became a routine occurrence; by 1910 the Ladies' association had 580 branches of 22,000 members who together raised about £4,500 for the Church Pastoral-Aid Society every year.[102] Such was the regional infrastructure that by 1898, the Union had a network of four depots in London, Bristol, Cambridge and Newcastle-on-Tyne in order to collect items of work for sales.[103] Tellingly, Lady Lucy Cavendish expressed the tension between ideology and necessity of fundraising in a diary entry for October 1864 when she was visiting Hardwick Hall. Calling the bazaar she was required to attend a 'sham charity', Lucy went on to reluctantly accept its value: 'Though I think such a thing a miserable make-shift, whereby people's grudging help towards a good object is obtained by dint of giving them in return a foolish, frivolous, wasteful, and generally tuft-hunting, day's jollification; yet of course I don't think it distinctly wrong, and would not put up my back beyond having a few little kicks about it in private.'[104] It is noticeable, in complete contrast to the *Free and Open Church Advocate* later issues (particularly of the 1890s), that the Systematic Beneficence Society's journal *The Benefactor* in the 1860s makes only the most fleeting mention of an anti-bazaar reference, thereby highlighting the fact that such fundraising mechanisms were not as prevalent earlier in the century.[105]

In the late 1880s and early 1890s, three texts were published which expressed the dangers inherent to the Church in these new fundraising methods. In England, the major text on the evils of the charitable bazaar, *Fancy Fair Religion* (1888), was written by the Reverend John Priestly Foster. Foster argued that 'Fancy Fair Religion' was destroying Christian charity because 'Christians now-a-days are not exhorted to support their Religion on principle, but they are to be enticed to do so through pleasure'.[106] In America, at the same time Newton Wray was making the same point in *Fun and Finance* (1890). Wray stated that the 'young grow up and enter the Church with no idea of systematic and liberal giving, naturally supposing the demands of Christian work are to be met by some system of exchange'.[107] Also in Scotland, the Reverend Charles Jerdan, a United Presbyterian Church minister in Greenock, published the pamphlet *The Counterfeit in Church Finance and Christian Giving* (1891). Foster, Wray and Jerdan all argued that the clergy needed to preach from their pulpits the doctrine of systematic giving and stewardship.[108] Such an education in stewardship, they argued, would eradicate the need for these unsuitable means of fundraising.

This strong condemnation of the charitable bazaar at the end of the nineteenth century coincided with attempts to revive the doctrine of stewardship and systematic giving. In 1886, the mixed Church party Society of the Treasury of God was established in London, a Canadian version having been established in the previous year.[109] In its first meeting, the British society stated that it had been 'formed for the purpose of restoring the law of the tenth and awakening the minds of Churchmen to the fact that a tenth of all income or increase is due to God not as a matter of gift but as of debt'.[110] The Society of the Treasury of God advertised in a wide range of newspapers: the *Guardian, The Record, Church Times, Church Review, Church Bells, Weekly Churchman, The Church in the West,* and *Irish Ecclesiastical Gazette*.[111] Its members gave papers at meetings of the English Church Union in 1892 and raised the issue at diocesan conferences and through the publication of leaflets.[112] However, the growth of the society was slight and its fifth annual report in 1894 stated that the 'growth of our Society is not what we could wish. Our objects, work, and rules are not popular, and do not attract members, or even associates, in great numbers. This is not to be wondered at, when we consider the laxity of Church teaching and practice concerning the tithe.'[113] The society fell into decline in the period after 1895, and in 1914 a meeting was held in order to revive it; Henry Lansdell (1841–1919), an Evangelical, was elected as the new Master.[114] The Society of the Treasury of God members Henry Lansdell and Charles Ashwell Boteler Pocock (1829–99) both credited the book *Gold and the Gospel* and the work of the Systematic Beneficence Society in the 1850s and 1860s for awakening their initial interest in stewardship and systematic giving.[115] In addition to the Society of the Treasury of God, the Evangelical clergyman Edwin Arthur Watkins (1827–1907) established the Proportionate Giving Union in 1887. Watkins was Vicar of Ubbeston in Suffolk and had previously been a missionary in Canada for the Church Missionary Society. His impetus to establish the Proportionate Giving Union was to revive the state of the funds raised for foreign missions; by the early 1900s the society had about 500 members.[116] Between 1887 and 1907, the Proportionate Giving Union estimated that it had distributed 430,000 copies of the society's publications.[117] This society, despite its extensive distribution of tracts, appears to have been principally the work of one man; there is no hint in its literature of committee members, influential patrons, or of national meetings. A Society of the Treasury of God member commented in 1893 that he had joined the Proportionate Giving Union but was 'disappointed at its inaction'.[118]

Both the Society of the Treasury of God and Proportionate Giving Union shared the American model of stewardship society membership which required all members to take a pledge that they would give a proportionate amount of income.[119] The work of these two small societies had no noticeable impact on the income levels of the diocesan societies in this study. The value of their work was in raising concerns regarding the Church's deficiency in promoting stewardship in conferences nationally, thereby highlighting the concern that the current generations of Christians were growing up without a strong ethos of giving and were, therefore, giving less. Likewise throughout the same period of the 1890s and early 1900s, the Free and Open Church Association, in its campaign to eradicate pew rents and make churches free and open, constantly supported proportionate and systematic giving in opposition to the charitable bazaar. In its annual report published in 1897, the association stated that:

> He has given, not to please himself, not to combine godliness and pleasure, but deliberately, carefully, and unostentatiously, as a good steward should give, who thinks of the day when he will have to bring in his accounts for his Master's approval. The raising of money for spiritual work is a great present-day want of the Church; but we are always beginning at the wrong end, begging before teaching, expecting to reap where we have not sown. Depend upon it, that no good will be done till the education of Church-people in "the art and mystery" of Christian giving is seriously undertaken by our bishops and clergy, not for the sake of the money which they want and hope thereby to obtain, but for the sake of the underlying truths which men need to learn, and in order to raise the spiritual tone and life of Church-people.[120]

By the late 1890s the very society ladies who were such supporters of the charitable bazaar, formed together to establish the pointedly named London Society of Church Beggars in 1897. Gwendolen Talbot (1877–1960) was the society's honorary treasurer and granddaughter of Caroline Jane Talbot, founder of the Parochial Mission Women Association. Gwendolen Cecil (1860–1945) was honorary secretary and daughter of the Marquess of Salisbury. Founded by these two well-connected society ladies, the object of the organization was to 'diminish the number of charity bazaars and entertainments'. The ladies of the society promised to devote their time to writing personal letters of appeal on behalf of charities.[121]

From the late 1880s and throughout the 1890s, the need to encourage systematic giving was repeatedly being raised in various diocesan conferences: for example Winchester in 1887, Manchester in 1888, Chichester in 1891, Ripon in 1891, Wakefield in 1892, Worcester in 1896, Liverpool in 1896, Truro in 1896, and Peterborough in 1898.[122] In 1888 proportionate giving was one of the topics discussed at Church Congress.[123] The Liverpool Diocesan Conference of 1896 passed a resolution saying that the clergy should encourage proportionate giving and should discourage 'questionable methods' of Church fundraising (both in the sense of parish funding and missionary funding). This thought was echoed by the Worcester Diocesan Conference of 1896 which also resolved that 'the necessity and blessing of proportionate and systematic almsgiving should be earnestly and frequently pressed upon all church people'.[124] The Society of the Treasury of God was instrumental in raising this as an issue at many of the conferences held in 1891 and 1892.[125] In 1891 for example, Frederick Henry Rooke (1842–99), a Society of the Treasury of God member, addressed the Rochester Diocesan Conference. He said that: 'The duty of vigorously denouncing in sermons the sins of covetousness, and the frequent teaching of the law of tithing, is much neglected in the present day by the clergy; and until this duty is taught and practiced, the Church will ever suffer from impecuniosity and starvation.'[126] In 1892, the Free and Open Church Association held a meeting at Church

House on the subject of giving which discussed: 'The instruction or education of Church people in giving (especially for the support of the ministry). (a) on the principle of some definite proportion to income (b) with regularity (c) with appreciation of the relative importance of claims'.[127] In 1897, a full meeting of the Central Council of Diocesan Conferences was held in London to discuss the problem of clerical incomes. The meeting was chaired by Wilbraham Egerton, first Earl Egerton (1832–1909), a financial supporter of both the Bishop of London's Fund and East London Church Fund. Egerton argued that the whole question of Church finance was in great need of reorganization because 'the Church of England had never, of recent years certainly, taught in her pulpits the duty of systematic Church finance'.[128] This reawakened interest in systematic almsgiving was employed for the benefit of the Bishop of London's Fund in 1895 when William Boyd Carpenter, the Bishop of Ripon preached a sermon entitled 'Our Lord's Teaching with Regard to Beneficence' in aid of the Bishop of London's Fund at Westminster Abbey. He preached that too many people gave money only in response to emotional appeals; instead, he advocated the practice of systematic giving.[129] These examples highlight the increasing debate regarding proportionate giving at the end of the nineteenth century, in the context of the Church's concerns about the state of its finances and how the laity should be doing more financially to support it. It also highlights the fact that the men endeavouring to raise the subject were all of the same generation, born in the late 1820s to early 1840s; these men would all have been in their adulthood at the time of the mid-century renaissance in stewardship.

In 1906, Lansdell attempted to reinvigorate the subject with the publication of his book *The Sacred Tenth*; a revised version of this book was issued in 1908 under the title *The Tithe in Scripture*. The monthly journal, *The Philanthropist*, promoted the publication of Lansdell's book, and hoped that it would give the subject a much needed impetus. It said: 'The subject is one which is singularly appropriate for discussion at the present time when so large a proportion of the public have apparently forgotten this eminently desirable duty of systematic giving to the causes of religion and charity.'[130] Commenting upon the relevance of stewardship to missionary funding, the London Missionary Society in its review of Lansdell's book declared that: 'We badly need a new crusade on the subject of systematic and proportionate giving.'[131] The reissue of a revised version of the book in 1908 coincided with Lansdell's address to the Pan-Anglican Congress of 1908.[132] At the Pan-Anglican Tithers' Garden Party of 1908, several Bishops expressed their wish 'that the giving of Anglican Churchmen may return to more habitual, Scriptural, and systematic methods than at present prevail.'[133] These writers of the late nineteenth century and early twentieth century recognized that the ethos of stewardship had waned and was in need of fresh reinvigoration, and that as a consequence of this the Anglican laity had forgotten its financial obligations; this tallies with the evidence presented here of a clear decline in giving to the societies in this study. The timing of this reawakened dialogue regarding stewardship coincided with a radical restructure of diocesan church finance which encompassed both the funding of diocesan home-missionary organizations and individual parishes.

A New Financial Structure: The Diocesan Board of Finance

The germ of the idea for centralized finance for the Church of England came from two sources. Firstly, a Church of England committee, formed in 1907, found that the crisis regarding low levels of ordinations had underlying causal financial factors. The investigating committee recommended an overhaul of the financial system that provided money for clergy pensions and training.[134] Secondly, in the subsequent year a Pan-Anglican Congress was convened to survey the work of the Anglican Church both at home and abroad. The lesson taken from this 1908 Congress was that the Church in England at home could learn from the Church overseas in terms of efficiency and finance.[135] The Church overseas was entirely reliant on voluntary contributions and could not afford to mismanage its funds, or withstand its contributions drying up. In 1908 the magazine *The Philanthropist* aptly commented, regarding the upcoming Pan-Anglican Congress, that the Church's growth was being stunted by lack of 'food'. Instead it argued that the Church should stop begging for money and should instead introduce a 'solid system of finance'.[136]

In response to the Pan-Anglican Congress, the Archbishop of Canterbury and the Archbishop of York appointed a committee in 1909 'to consider the position, administration, and mutual relation of the various funds which are raised for Church purposes by voluntary subscription, whether Diocesan, Provincial or General, and the most effectual means of using such funds to supplement endowments of the Church'.[137] The principal rationale behind the work of the committee was that the provision of the needs of the Church was 'the duty of the whole Church and not of the individual Parish' and that in order to carry this out effectively the Church must make the diocese 'its financial unit'.[138] The Evangelical Reverend Edward Grose Hodge, speaking subsequently as a committee member of the new London Diocesan Board of Finance, set out the circumstances for the new scheme: 'the Church has lived hand to mouth; it has been beg, beg, beg, with very inadequate response – all very unbusinesslike and very unworthy ... Whatever may be said of the past, it is clear that the present methods will not avail for the future.'[139] Hodge was the voice of experience, having had lengthy exposure of the issue of finance in the Diocese of London as both an incumbent and rural dean. The Archbishops' Committee produced its report in 1911 which recommended the creation of a Central Board of Finance with subsidiary Diocesan Boards of Finance.[140] The seven objects that the Diocesan Board of Finance was responsible for funding were: training for the ministry; maintenance of the ministry; pensions for the ministry; provision for needy clergy, and widows and orphans of clergy; church buildings and church extension; religious education for children; and general diocesan expenses.[141] The scheme therefore provided both financially for the parish and financially for diocesan home-missionary work.

Under the new structured system, the diocese assessed each rural deanery and calculated a sum (called the apportionment) that the deanery was required to pay to the Board. Each deanery would then allocate a sum (called the parochial quota) to be raised by every parish according to the size of its congregation and its financial condition.[142] The parish in turn raised its quota through the introduction of the church due; this was a 'voluntary' amount to be paid by the parishioner according to his or her means. The 'suggested' rate of the church due was not to be less than one half penny per week. This new system, therefore, made the Diocesan Board of Finance the controlling and organizational force behind all aspects of diocesan finance and crucially it took overall responsibility for raising the money for diocesan needs. In this radical diocesan restructure, the diocesan organizations that became part of the London Diocesan Board of Finance were the Bishop of London's Fund, East London Church Fund, Ordination Candidates Council, Queen Victoria Clergy Fund, Clergy Pensions Institution, Clergy Widows Fund, Clergy Schools Association, and the Sunday School Council. In the first few years of the scheme, there was a period of transition when subscriptions continued to be paid directly to these voluntary organizations. Consequently, the parish quotas were initially much lower to reflect this financial shift. The London Diocesan Board of Finance commenced its integration with the diocesan societies in January 1914.[143] This absorption was not unanimously welcomed: John Henry Nelson (1850–1926), the honorary secretary of the Bishop of London's Fund, resigned on principle in the weeks before the transfer. His statement was recorded in full in the society's executive committee minute book:

> In the spring of last year, when the scheme of the Archbishop's Committee on Church Finance was considered by a small committee appointed by the Bishop, I recorded my opinion in the following terms:- "That the reasons given in the report of the Archbishop's Committee, on which their recommendations are based, obviously do not apply to the Diocese of London and certainly not as far as regards the work assigned to the Bishop of London's Fund and East London Church Fund. That to try to raise any considerable sum by assessment or apportionment would in this Diocese end in failure. That the experiment, if tried, would have a disastrous effect upon the work carried on by the two funds, for which they raise about £50,000 a year – the greater part of which, once lost, would be lost altogether." I still adhere to that opinion ... This Fund has been, beyond comparison, the greatest of all Diocesan Funds, and has a unique record of services. One might have thought that it would have been treated with great care and consideration; and further that, the wants of the Diocese being so great, so fruitful a source of help could not have been lightly dispensed with.[144]

The diocesan wide church collections from 1914 were held in aid of the Diocesan Board of Finance, and from this date could no longer be held in aid of societies such as the Bishop of London's Fund and East London Church Fund. In January 1914, the executive committee of the Bishop of London's Fund recorded its concern regarding the potential loss of income but presumably its hands were officially tied, the Bishop's Fund could hardly opt out of the new diocesan scheme.[145] On 1 January 1918 the Bishop of London's Fund merged fully with the London Diocesan Board of Finance (and ceased to exist as a separate entity) to form a newly reconstituted body called the Bishop of London's Diocesan Fund, known generally in its shortened form of the London Diocesan Fund.[146]

The report of the Archbishops' committee emphasized 'the need to arouse a sense of responsibility among church people, and upon the need for a higher standard of giving and systematic instruction in the principles of the matter'.[147] William Cunningham (1849–1919), Archdeacon of Ely, commenting on the Archbishops' report, argued that the current mixture of almsgiving and popular entertainment fundraisers was inadequate to the Church's needs, instead the 'one hope for the development of sources on which the Church can rely, is to be found in creating a definite and intelligent understanding of the work in which she is engaged'.[148] To explain the new scheme to parishioners, the Diocese of London produced three leaflets. Leaflet No. I entitled *Paying for Religion* took a rather strident tone saying to the reader:

> If you want *Recreation* you must pay for it ... If you want *Amusement*, you must pay for it ... If you want *Medical* services, you must pay for them...If you want *Legal* services, you must pay for them ... Then, when you get *Religious* services, is it reasonable to expect to get them for *nothing* – or next to nothing? ... Is it fair or just that the absentees from church (who at least expect the Church's services to be ready for them at call) should escape their rightful share of yearly Church expenditure? Is it fair to leave the burden of responsibility on the shoulders of a few generous people, who actually have to pay for other people's religion? Have you ever thought about this? What proportionate part of your wage, salary or income are you giving in order to provide for the spiritual privileges which you receive? What proportionate part *ought you* to give? [149]

This leaflet, which lumped religious provision with leisure and business services, was devoid of any sense of stewardship. Any sense of a relationship with God had been eliminated and was replaced with an economic exchange of goods, an exchange which made the Church simply one product amongst many. Overall, the whole initiative seemed more concerned with how the money was to be raised than the motive for giving; God barely gets a mention. Instead, the emphasis was on getting people to give systematically and regularly in order to pay for the services that the church supplied to the individual and to others. David Alan Hunter Johnston, a layman and member of the Central Board of Finance, in his evaluation of the implementation of the recommendations of the

Archbishops' committee, argued that its achievements were mainly in relation to organization and machinery and that it failed in its aim to 'arouse a sense of responsibility among church people'.[150] In 1918, a book produced by the clergy and laymen of the Diocese of London, entitled *The Gospel of Giving*, lamented the continuing lack of a strong ethos of stewardship in the Church: 'It is a truism that whatever we possess belongs to God; that we are merely stewards, and that nothing is really our own. Everyone knows this and admits it, but few act upon it.'[151] The introduction of the measures of the Archbishops' committee was recognition of the fact that the Church needed to create a sense of financial responsibility in the Anglican community.[152] Unfortunately, the overall effect of the new Diocesan Board of Finance was that it introduced a new mechanism for payment rather than an ethos for giving.

Conclusion

The Christian stewardship campaign of the mid-century sought to systematize and regulate philanthropic giving by making it a regular habit rather than an occasional emotional response. The timing of the launch of the Christian stewardship campaigns, in terms of the literature and the establishment of the Systematic Beneficence Society, was opportune for the new voluntary organizations established in Bishop Tait's episcopacy in London which were poised to reap the rewards of this newly awakened spirit of systematized giving. It is possible that this was one of the reasons that Tait's new organizations were responded to so enthusiastically; the financial success of the Bishop of London's Fund was marked in contrast with the lacklustre support of the London Diocesan Church Building Society. Writing in 1908, Lansell looked back to the vibrant stewardship ethos of the mid-nineteenth century:

> Much was done, generally, forty years ago, by means of lectures, addresses, and literature, by the Systematic Beneficence Society ... Individuals, as we know, were influenced, and fruit appeared'.[153]

By the 1870s, however, the ethos of stewardship had begun to wane and in the place of the Christian stewardship, secular fundraising methods such as the charitable bazaar became more commonplace. The problem of this shift to commercial fundraising was being widely discussed from the late 1880s in Church Congress, diocesan conferences, in different publications and through the work of the Society of the Treasury of God and Proportionate Giving Union. At the start of the twentieth century, writers such as Lansdell recognized that new efforts were needed to reawaken this ethos.

This chapter has set out to emphasize the explicitly religious based impulses that motivate philanthropy through a discussion of the underlying theology of giving in the late nineteenth century. Motive is an important indicator of the strength and longevity of the philanthropic relationship. Individuals (such as Lord Overstone or Richard Foster) who gave principally from religious conviction gave more because their philanthropy was underpinned by a systematic structure. Such individuals regarded their stewardship of money as being an essential part of their Christian life. The financial analysis in Chapter 4 demonstrated that the Anglican organizations sampled for this case study experienced a decline in giving at the end of the century. And in particular, the analysis pinpointed the loss of the wealthy male supporter towards the end of the nineteenth century as a key factor in this decline. This chapter has argued that such a decline in financial support can be attributed to changing attitudes to giving in the second half of the nineteenth century. Furthermore, this chapter has identified the Church's anxiety regarding the absence of both the teaching and practice of Christian stewardship in the same period. This theme will be developed in the Conclusion which will argue that, as the Victorian age progressed and finally ended, so with it passed a generation of philanthropic and wealthy businessmen who viewed the funding of the Church as an obligation.

CONCLUSION

The economist and social reformer Beatrice Webb (1858–1943), writing in the 1920s, commented that one of the most striking changes that she had observed in her lifetime was the decline in the practice of charity. Recalling the 'enlightened philanthropist of mid-Victorian times' she remarked upon the charitable ethos of her youth:

> To the unsophisticated Christian; even of the nineteenth century, almsgiving was essentially a religious exercise; a manifestation of his love of God, and his obedience to the command of his Lord and Saviour ... Yet this universal and unquestioning yielding up of personal possessions for common consumption was thought to be the ideal conduct; the precious fruit of divine compassion. The spirit of unquestioning, of unrestricted – in short, of infinite – charity was, to the orthodox Christian, not a process by which a given end could be attained, but an end in itself – a state of mind – one of the main channels through which the individual entered into communion with the supreme spirit of love at work in the universe.[1]

The giving of alms, referred to by Webb, reflected something more meaningful than just a financial transaction between two people. It involved a sense of obligation by those in the middle- and upper-classes for those in the working-class.[2] It is this loss of obligation – in combination with how individuals thought about their money – that is the core subject of this book. By the turn of the century the majority of the voluntary organizations in this study were experiencing financial difficulties. In most cases the number of financial supporters had declined and in conjunction with this the annual income of the societies had suffered. In parallel with this, various local case studies have shown that the parish churches themselves, in this period, were also experiencing a decline in financial support. This conclusion will reflect upon the changes experienced by these voluntary organizations in order to consider whether they are symptoms of a wider phenomenon.

The Changing Ethos of Giving

The decline in giving to the diocesan home-missionary organizations in London coincided with a national debate in the late nineteenth century regarding the most effective and ethically appropriate way to raise money for religious causes.[3]

At the heart of this debate was the issue that new fundraising methods were more concerned with the amount of money being raised rather than the motive: it was the money that mattered, not how it was obtained. In the late 1880s, John Priestly Foster summed this up nicely by saying that the 'morality of Fancy Fair Religion is based almost entirely upon one Article of its Creed, namely, "The End justifies the Means".[4] Foster argued that it was specifically this slow destruction of the ethos of giving that was responsible for the poor state of the funds of both churches and charitable institutions. Foster dismissed the view that economic reasons could be responsible for this poor financial state, arguing logically that if the economy was the reason, then bazaars would also struggle to raise funds for charitable objects. Foster's particular concern was that the new generation of Anglicans was growing up equating Christian charity with bazaars and other fundraising methods that coaxed money from individuals.[5] This sentiment is expressed by Gwendolen Cecil, the honorary secretary of the London Society of Church Beggars, who in 1897 wrote: 'When clergy or charity-promoters are asked why they tolerate such a degradation of Christian almsgiving and so gross a waste of the charity fund of the country, they reply desperately that people will not give unless they get something in return'.[6]

Foster and other writers argued that the Anglican laity achieving adulthood in the late nineteenth century had grown up with the view that money should be given in exchange for some form of entertainment that would act as a form of motivation to prompt their philanthropy. William Boyd Carpenter, the Bishop of Ripon speaking at the 1891 diocesan conference on the topic of almsgiving, regretted what he called the 'miserable' shift that had occurred in Church fundraising. He said: 'Sales of work and Bazaars are unfortunate necessities, they are not charity in its highest sense, they give rise to a totally false conception of charity. Every Bazaar, which is advertised as a mode of raising money, is in itself an indictment against the liberality of Churchmen.'[7] This view was echoed in the annual report of the Free and Open Church Association in 1905 which felt the need to make a formal resolution on the subject, in an article produced under the title of 'Unworthy Methods of Church Finance'.

> That the Council views with apprehension the growing practice of raising money for Church purposes by means of un-Scriptural and unworthy methods, which are often a scandal to the Church, injurious to those who take part in them, and calculated to lower Christian standards of stewardship and responsibility. The Council further desire to record their conviction that the time has come when the whole subject of Church Finance should be fully considered by the authorities of the Church, and that Convocation and the Houses of Laymen should be respectfully asked to consider the desirability of putting forward a scheme for the systematization of parochial finance, coupled with suggestions for the teaching by the clergy of true principles of Christian giving, and the adoption of such means only as can be justified by the high end in view, namely, the Worship and Glory of Almighty God.[8]

In the absence of case studies relating to the state of parish finances in the Diocese of London, it is necessary to relate the findings of this study to Simon
Green's study of religion in industrial Yorkshire (in the period 1870–1920), Jeremy Morris' study religion in Croydon (in the period 1840–1914), and Stephen
Yeo's study of voluntary religious and secular organizations in Reading (in the
period 1890–1914).[9] Each of these case studies recorded a financial crisis of debt
in local churches in the late nineteenth century.[10] Furthermore, Morris makes the
significant point that this crisis in parish finances was occurring at a time when
the number of communicants in the Anglican Church was increasing.[11] Of these
works, Green makes the most concerted effort to fully analyse parish finance;
a subject that, given the overall paucity of research on church finance, is much
neglected and worthy of dedicated study. Green reports that after the mid 1870s
bazaars became a significant mode of raising money for parish churches, becoming particularly significant as a proportional source of church funding after the
1890s.[12] This increase in the use of bazaars was in the context of the abolition of
the compulsory church rate in 1868 and the phasing out of pew rents in the late
nineteenth century. Green argues that this change in financing local churches
constituted a fundamental ethical change in the 'doctrine of voluntary beneficence', in other words that it affected the foundation of the ethos of giving.[13] He
argues that 'in the moral scale of the mid-Victorian ideal' receipts (the mutual
exchange of money for goods) were the lowest form of revenue. The highest and
most ethically superior forms of giving were those that involved obligation and
commitment.[14] In particular, Green argues that the end of pew rents resulted in
the fracturing of the financial relationship between parishioner and church. He
says that the pew rent 'was something more because the act (or the promise) of
payment represented something greater than simply the exchange of financial
tokens for the supply of religious services. It constituted a statement of allegiance by an individual to a society'.[15] Essentially, this shift from forms of finance
that involved a financial relationship and commitment, to forms of finance that
involved an exchange of goods, meant that this important sense of obligation was
lost. The churches had 'shifted their base of supply. They had ceased to depend
on their members, at least as the real foundation of their financial organization'
and therefore precipitated their own demise.[16] Green concluded that:

> To shift the efficient organisation of the political economy of religious association from
> the fruits of individual generosity to the product of common enterprise, and also to trans-
> fer it from the moment of devotion to the hour of specialised fund-raising, was not merely
> to dabble with the symbolic peripheries of voluntary beneficence. It was systematically to
> redefine the 'price of faith', for it redefined who gave; and it redefined how they gave.[17]

Green therefore argues that the increasing reliance of parish churches upon
forms of fundraising (such as the bazaar) fundamentally affected the Anglican
laity's sense of financial obligation. The commodifying effect of the financial

transaction has received much attention from behavioural economists in recent years. Michael Sandel's recent book *What Money Can't Buy: The Moral Limits of Markets* (2012) highlights, through a series of case studies, the corrosive effect of money. Sandel argues that 'some of the good things in life are corrupted or degraded if turned into commodities.'[18] This theory of the 'commercialization effect' was first emphasized by the British economist Fred Hirsch who described this effect as being 'the effect on the characteristics of a product or activity of supplying it exclusively or predominantly on commercial terms rather than on some other basis – such as informal exchange, mutual obligation, altruism or love, or feelings of service or obligation.'[19] Sandel's and Hirsch's work, therefore, reinforces Green's argument. To use Sandel's terminology, the shift from systematic payments through the mechanism of the pew rate to commercialized fundraising shifted the basis of motivation from 'intrinsic motivations (such as moral conviction or interest ...)' to 'external ones (such as money or other tangible rewards).'[20] The financial payment should, instead, be anchored within a deeper relationship rather than being given as part of a material exchange of goods.

The argument presented here is that this fracturing of the financial relationship between individual and Church was compounded by the fact that a new generation of Christians had grown up without an education in Christian stewardship. The loss of financial obligation meant that when the traditional financial bond between the laity and the Church was abandoned, the new generation of Christians had no solid ethos of giving to fall back upon. This concern regarding the failure to educate later generations in stewardship can repeatedly be found in literature from the 1880s onwards. Foster complained:

> And we consider that the youth of English Christendom are being reared in the belief that the needs of the Church of Christ can be met, and may be met, by the methods of the Fancy Fair Religion, which methods give them a certain amount of pleasure and excitement, is not the outlook a gloomy one for the principles of true Christian liberality? ... How can we suppose that the rising generation, when subjected practically to such misguided instruction, will ever give liberally, systematically, and of their own will, free from any inducements but those of the love of God and love to man?'[21]

Nearly twenty years later the same complaint regarding the failure of the Church to lay down a proper education in stewardship was being made by the Free and Open Church Association:

> As a well-known friend of our movement recently expressed it, "the duty of the clergy is to raise motive, not money." When the education of a race of Christian givers is thus taken in hand – but not till then – will the Church find herself in sufficient funds to carry on her work at home and abroad.'[22]

This absence of an education in stewardship was critical because it meant that more people came to view money as being their own property and consequently, they gave it up more reluctantly. Henry Lansdell, writing in 1906, shared this view:

Christians, in fact, are stewards: and a good steward ought so to manage the property entrusted to him as to make the most of it for his employer; whereas the average Christian nowadays, in too many cases, places the money passing through his hands into his own private banking account, draws upon it for his own wants, wishes, and whims, and then has the audacity to present the balance (if there be one) to his Master, as if that were worthy the name of stewardship![23]

Coincidentally, at the same time in America, Harvey Reeves Calkins (1866–1941), stewardship secretary of the Methodist Episcopal Church, in his book *A Man and His Money* (1914), was recommending that it was education in stewardship that was needed rather than financial drives.

In the late nineteenth century, the churches stopped relying on the 'theology of giving' and turned instead to secular and commercial forms of fundraising.[24] This situation was further exacerbated, when in 1911, the Church reorganized diocesan and central finance. This reorganization introduced a new form of church finance that prioritized system over ethos. The decline in giving in this period experienced by both the diocesan voluntary organizations in London and the parish churches regionally highlights a shift in the Anglican laity's attitude to financing their religion.

An End of an Era: the Deaths of the Paternalists

The point that needs reinforcing here is that the different generations of Victorians held different attitudes to financially supporting the Church of England. The loss of the paternalists of the Victorian age was observed in case studies relating to Reading, Lambeth, Croydon, and Yorkshire.[25] Yeo says that: 'It is clear from the local press, particularly from obituaries, that the passing of a generation meant the passing of a whole local style of life.'[26] Cox notes that when they died 'no one stepped forward to replace' them.[27] Morris tentatively suggests that this loss may have had an impact on church finance. Lastly, both Cox and Morris suggest that the influential laymen of the early twentieth century preferred to commit their time to civic affairs rather than church affairs.[28] This suggests that lay energies of a new generation of laymen had transferred to other secular areas. This shift is echoed in the motivations of female philanthropists in this period. Poole, in her study of Lucy Cavendish and Emma Cons, suggests that there was a change in how women articulated their philanthropy: 'a broader shift in perceptions took place in the latter third of the nineteenth century, replacing women's charity as "a Christian duty" with women's philanthropy as a display of their citizenship.'[29]

The research in this study has established that the societies generally experienced, despite their best efforts, a decline in financial support from both individuals and from corporate sources. From the 1880s, the London Diocesan Home Mission, London Diocesan Deaconess Institution and Parochial Mission Women Association all experienced a slow decline in their income from donations and annual subscriptions. The East London Church Fund (which was not

established until 1880) suffered from a similar decline from the start of the twentieth century, with income falling off more dramatically in the 1910s as local
association income began to decline. The Bishop of London's Fund, which also
suffered such a decline through the 1880s, experienced an upturn in its fortunes
at the start of the twentieth century due to increased contributions from women.
All of the societies attributed their waning finances to the fact that their wealthy
benefactors were dying and were not being replaced with a new generation of
philanthropists. The loss of these wealthy middle-class supporters was keenly
felt by the societies: every Charles Morrison or Richard Foster that died was the
equivalent of hundreds of female supporters. The deaths of such men, therefore,
left gaping holes in the societies' accounts. In 1911 the East London Church
Fund referred to the substantial decline in subscriptions: 'It points unmistake-
ably to the fact that gaps which appear in the list, chiefly through the deaths of
old friends, have not been filled up with new names.'[30] The Golden Jubilee report
of the Bishop of London's Fund, in 1913, said that its receipts had been, in the
last few years, 'greatly affected by the passing away of old and very large contributors'.[31] This was echoed by the Parochial Mission Women Association which
started commenting on the loss of subscribers through death in 1896. In 1908, in
its entry in the *London Diocesan Magazine*, the committee reported: 'The income
has been seriously diminished by the death and removal of old subscribers, and
the Committee earnestly appeal for new annual subscriptions, that they may not
only maintain, but also extend their useful work.'[32] This phenomenon was also
commented upon by the London Diocesan Deaconess Institution in 1904 which
diagnosed their financial problems as being due to the fact that their 'older and
wealthier friends are in the natural course of things, passing away'.[33]

Analysis of the subscription lists of the Bishop of London's Fund of 1912[34]
and the East London Church Fund of 1914[35] highlights the fact that the
remaining wealthy male supporters were principally titled landowners, clergymen and the sons of deceased subscribers. The financial support of the landed
peers, who owned substantial amounts of London property, had generally been
maintained in this period. In some cases the individual amount of the contribution had diminished because of the impact of the new form of death duties; in
1894 the process of collecting probate duties had been reassessed and simplified
to include all property passing on death.[36] However, the overall continuance of
support suggests that they continued to feel obliged by virtue of their position in
society to maintain the Established Church and support religious provision for
their tenants.[37] Analysis of the businessmen giving large sums to the Bishop of
London's Fund and East London Church Fund in the 1910s shows that most of
them were born in the 1830s and 1840s; these men were of the same generation
as Henry Lansdell (1841–1919) who made great efforts to revive proportionate giving and Christian stewardship in the early twentieth century. Likewise

the only male subscriber giving £10 or more to the London Diocesan Deaconess Institution in the period 1900 to 1914 was a committee member who had been giving to the organization for over 40 years.[38] This analysis highlights the complete absence of a new generation of businessmen coming forward to support these organizations financially. This shared commonality of experience is significant because it highlights the fact that a particular generation of wealthy supporters were passing away and were not being replaced by a new younger generation. Tellingly, the Bishop of London speaking in 1911 at a meeting of the East London Church Fund prayed that a new generation of philanthropists would come forward, saying: 'God grant that in the City there would rise up for the Church many more men like Richard Foster'.[39]

These models of financial decline and loss of support are also mirrored in the accounts of the Scripture Readers' Association (an Evangelical society established in 1844). The society first mentions its anxiety regarding the death of its supporters in the mid 1880s: 'During the past year we have lost by death a very large number of Annual Subscribers and Donors, whose contributions to the Society have amounted in the aggregate to something like £420', and 'We have lost many old contributors of late through death and removal. May we hope their place will be filled by many new annual subscribers.'[40] By the early 1890s, very much like the Parochial Mission Women Association, the committee was expressing its concern regarding its overdraft; the situation escalated to the extent that by 1899 the society's treasurer, the brewer Edmund Smith Hanbury (1850–1913), made himself personally liable to the bank for the society's 'considerable' overdraft.[41] Luckily a 'generous' anonymous donor, known only by his initials of 'FH' (undoubtedly Francis Alexander Hamilton again) came forward to help.[42] Appeals throughout the 1890s, in the *Record*, *The Times* and personal appeals, had all met with a 'disappointing response'.[43] The July 1900 issue of the *Scripture Readers' Journal* upon reporting the deaths of further generous supporters stated that the Committee wanted to 'make a special effort to obtain others in their place. They venture, therefore, to invite each present Subscriber to obtain one new Annual Contributer.'[44] The most prominent supporters 'lost' at this time were: the first Duke of Westminster; third Earl of Harrowby and Sir Walter Rockliffe Farquhar (the society's original treasurer). The Society's financial desperation continued right up to World War One, with occasional alleviation from 'well-timed' legacies and the ever-dependable support of their treasurer Robert Hanbury and other committee members.[45] As succinctly put by the society in 1903: 'The first six months of our financial year have been the reverse of flourishing'.[46] In 1909 the society lamented its constantly declining annual income over the previous twenty years, from £13,084 in 1889 to £10,805 in 1899 and a further decline again to £9,462 in 1908.[47] Furthermore, an appeal in *The Times* in 1911 to clear the overdraft summed up what was needed: 'We trust this will meet the eye of some of "God's stewards," so that our need may be met'.[48] This appeal was obviously unsuccessful because in 1913 the society appealed again in *The Times* stating that the 'Society's financial position is at present strained almost to breaking point ... '[49]

The Church Pastoral-Aid Society (a High Church society established in 1836) also lamented the loss of many of its principal supporters in the early 1900s. The *Seventy-Second Church Pastoral-Aid Society Annual Report,* for the budget year 1906–7, noted the recent deaths of the 'princely donor' Francis Alexander Hamilton, the landowner Horace Smith-Bosanquet (1829–1907) and the titled William Brodrick, eighth Viscount Midleton (1830–1907), saying that the 'Committee deplore the loss of many generous friends. One by one they are called home, and their places are hard to fill'.[50] In 1910 and 1912 it also noted the loss of the brewer Ralph James Fremlin (1834–1910) and the tea dealer James Inskipp (1836–1912) who were both 'staunch and generous supporters' and the engineering maunfacturer and landowner William Donaldson Cruddas (1832–1912), adding that 'the loss of his frequent gifts will be a serious one to face'.[51] In 1911 the society reported that 'the state of the Society's funds is not without ground for anxiety. There is a regrettable falling off in the amount received both from Donations and Associations ... the fact remains that the income of the Association this year is the smallest since the year 1857'.[52] Notably, only three men gave amounts of £100 or more in 1910: a clergyman, a member of the Buxton family and a member of the Barclay family.

In contrast, it is important to note that the London City Mission's income levels remained robust during the period of decline for the Anglican organizations. In its annual report for 1904–5, the London City Mission commented that 'The Committee are deeply thankful to God that, during a year when the nation has been tried, not only by depression in trade, but also by heavy taxation, the contributions to the Society's funds have been so well sustained'.[53] In fact the London City Mission annual reports often took a cheerful tone when reporting its buoyant finances. However, in parallel with the other organizations in this study, the London City Mission supporter numbers also experienced a decline in support which mainly consisted of male supporters but crucially this decline was less marked than in the case of the Bishop of London's Fund and East London Church Fund. This would support the argument that the decline of stewardship was a factor. The London City Mission had a mix of both Anglican and Nonconformist supporters and therefore any change in an Anglican ethos of giving would be less marked in the London City Mission subscription lists. In addition, the buoyancy in the London City Mission income can be explained by the fact that Nonconformists had a longer history of voluntaryism.

This financial buoyancy was also mirrored in the financial health of the foreign missionary societies of the Church Missionary Society and the Society for the Propagation of the Gospel. Both societies, like the London City Mission, were shored up by a large collecting infrastructure and saw rapidly expanding income levels in the late nineteenth and early twentieth centuries: with the Evangelical Church Missionary Society's income rising from £129,409 in 1860 to £403,610 in 1910; and the High Church Society for the Propagation of the Gospel's income rising from £116,430 in 1859 to £209,481 in 1910. Interestingly though, this increased support did not come from wealthy individuals, instead it came from a groundswell of thousands of people giving small amounts. Neither society received very much in the way of financial support from the large property owners that dominated the London societies (for example, the dukes of Westminster, Devonshire or Bedford). Again, mirroring the age profile of the wealthy male supporters (giving large sums to the diocesan societies in this study), the few men giving to these foreign missionary societies in the late nineteenth and early twentieth century were also quite elderly.[54] It is also notable that the younger generation of larger donors did not contain any London bankers but instead were more likely to come from professional or retail trades. But it must be stressed, as in the case of the London City Mission, that the number people giving large sums was very small, particularly when considering that these were national (and not just diocesan) charities. Consequently, the deaths of these wealthy men had no impact on the financial health of the two societies. There is no indication that the wealthy men that supported the Anglican diocesan societies switched their financial allegiance to Anglican foreign missionary societies. A new generation of wealthy men giving large sums, born post 1860, is absent both from home-missionary and foreign-missionary subscription lists in the early twentieth century. Finally, it is useful to reiterate the point that Beatrice Webb made at the start of this chapter: she commented that in her experience people had become less charitable, not that they had transferred their charitable concerns elsewhere.[55]

Conclusion

Back in the Introduction, I commented that the old adage 'put your money where your mouth is' makes the point that serious dedication is demonstrated with actions and not just words, and that if you really are committed to cause you will back up your words with actual financial support. This book takes the view that a decline in financial commitment can be a measure of changing public attitudes towards religion. Money is vital to an organization's survival, and religious organizations are no different in this respect, be they individual churches or religious voluntary organizations. In the late nineteenth century, the evidence demonstrates that there was a decline in giving to Anglican home-missionary organizations and that this decline was in parallel with a crisis in the state of parish finances. In particular, the analysis has highlighted that the wealthy businessman at the start of the twentieth century no longer felt financially responsible for upholding the Church. This loss of financial obligation suggests a wider loss of commitment to the Church of England.

It is important not to consider these findings in isolation as wider factors could also have a bearing on philanthropic behaviour. Various economic factors impacted upon disposable income in the early twentieth century. These were the higher taxation rates imposed during the Boer War (1899–1902) and the implementation of the welfare reforms (1906–1914) of the new Liberal Government which were funded by higher taxation rates.[56] In particular, this burden was increased with the introduction of further compulsory contributions under the National Insurance Act in 1911, which provided unemployment and sickness benefit. The impact of these measures on church finance, particularly the National Insurance Act, was commented upon by the Vicar of Christ Church in North Brixton, and the local newspaper the *Brixton Free Press*. Cox suggests that it is perhaps the 'cumulative effects' of all of these reforms that impacted on the state of parish finances.[57] These various economic factors are, therefore, likely to have had an additional impact on levels of giving in the early twentieth century. It is noteworthy that this period, relating to the introduction of welfare measures and their associated financial burdens, coincided exactly with the financial crisis being experienced by the East London Church Fund. However, it should be noted that many of the Anglican voluntary organizations chosen for this study, were in financial distress from the 1880s.[58]

It is also possible that the decline in giving to Anglican organization was because the Anglican laity had relocated their financial commitment to different charitable concerns, such as welfare charities or foreign-missionary organizations. This would still, however, indicate that financially supporting the Church of England had become less important to the Anglican laity of the late nineteenth century and early twentieth century. However, analysis of the subscription lists of (both the Church Missionary Society and the Society for the Propagation of the Gospel in Foreign Parts) foreign missionary societies demonstrates that neither society was supported in any great degree by large contributions from wealthy individuals.[59] Both societies had financial models like that of the London City Mission: models that depended upon a multitude of very small sums collected through a vast collecting network. Consequently, the deaths of their principal funders failed to even slightly dent the financial health of these societies.[60]

This study's contribution to the secularization debate, is the claim that a study of philanthropy can attest to the religious commitment of the Anglican laity. The sociologists Charles Glock and Rodney Stark argue that different religious groups vary in their degree of response to the different dimensions. Green reinforces this point: 'Different kinds of religious commitment, in other words, were (and still are) skewed by disparate cultural values, reflecting diverging social priorities.' This theory, which Green calls 'divergence theory', appreciates that different social groups participate in their religion in different ways.[61] Glock and Stark argue that studies have found that such differences can be found in class relationships with religion, with the upper-class and middle-class scoring more highly in the 'ritual-istic dimension' of religiosity and with the lower-class scoring more highly in the 'experiential dimension' of religion.[62] For example, Sarah Williams found that the working-class model of religiosity in Southwark did not conform to the middle-class model of formal church involvement.[63] In addition, Hugh McLeod's research found different class levels of religious observance in London in the period between 1880 and 1914.[64] This idea of the different expressions of religion is valuable meth-odologically in the secularization debate. Glock and Stark comment that:

> Religion is not necessarily the same thing to all men; perhaps, therefore, the source of the disagreement is that different observers are defining religion in different ways. Some may equate it with belief, others with practice and still others with experience. If it should turn out that there has been an increase in one, a decline in the second, and no change in the third, much of the disagreement would be explained if not resolved.[65]

A study of philanthropic giving naturally focuses on the middle- and upper-classes; the significance of this research is that the findings specifically illuminate the reli-gious commitment of middle-class and upper-class men. In the period 1880 to 1910, this sector of the Anglican laity demonstrated a marked change in the 'con-sequential dimension' of their religion. This is the dimension that relates to the behaviour of people as a consequence of their faith, so how people live out their Christians standards or ethical stance in their day-to-day lives. A change in financial behaviour was most strongly observed in the mercantile male middle-classes who, to borrow Callum Brown's phrase, 'cancelled their mass subscription' to Angli-can home-missionary organizations.[66] The fracturing of the financial relationship between the layman and the Church could be also taken to be another indicator in the shift towards 'believing without belonging'.[67] The timing of this shift in ethos, from the promotion of the doctrine of Christian stewardship to a reluctant reli-ance upon secular forms of fundraising, corresponds with that covered by Dominic Erdozain's research on the growth of leisure services provided by churches. He places secularization at the end of the nineteenth century 'when Evangelical social morality dissolved'.[68] It also corresponds with Hugh McLeod's research on religion and class in London, where he argues that: 'around 1880 is a significant turning-point in the history of middle- and upper-class attitudes, because it is about then that the "Victorian" façade of religious consensus began to crumble.'[69]

After the 1870s, the new generations of Christians growing up did not have a close financially supportive relationship with the Church of the England. Cru-cially, Johnston a committee member of the Central Board of Finance, argued that it did not re-establish such a relationship until the 1950s, a century after the first successful stewardship impulse.[70] Research in America has argued that a reinforced promotion of stewardship results in higher levels of contributions to the Church, and that those denominations that placed an emphasis on the theology of Christian stewardship were also more likely to institutionalize this concept in practices such as annual pledge cards.[71] In particular, research has also shown that the teaching in stewardship needs to be periodically repeated otherwise its import will be forgotten.[72] This was also the view of *The Benefactor*, the magazine of the Systematic Beneficence Society, which in 1869 said: 'The habit of giving has to be acquired, like other habits, by repetition and rule.'[73] Nearly 50 years later in 1906, Lansdell campaigned for a new stewardship campaign to reinvigorate giving: 'In other words, I suppose we want some present-day Apostle of tithe-paying to stir up the Church and country, as did Dr Cather and the Systematic Beneficence Society forty years ago.'[74] Unfortunately for the Church of England, this campaign failed to galvanize a new generation of the Anglican laity to respond with great generosity in order to fulfil its financial obligations. Writing in the 1990s, the Central Board of Finance's booklet, *Receiving and Giving: The Basis, Issues and Implications of Christian Stewardship* commented that it 'has been said that the Church of England has not so much a problem of finance as a problem of giving.'[75] This 'problem of giving' was a problem that the Church created for itself through its lack of a consistent ongoing education in stewardship. The Church, therefore, accelerated its own decline by failing to establish in its laity strong and lasting foundations of financial obligation. Every charitable bazaar or concert held to raise funds for a religious cause served to further alienate the Anglican laity from the doctrine of Christian stewardship and an ethos of charity with embedded Christian values. The rise in commercialized and secularized mechanisms of fundraising, in parallel with a decline in a Christian ethos of giving, resulted in the commodification of religion. Religion became just one more leisure product on the market, as epitomized in the London Diocesan Board of Finance *Paying for Religion* leaflet of 1914.[76] As damningly put by the Bishop of Rochester, and quoted on the title page of Foster's book *Fancy Fair Religion* (1888): 'To vulgarize the great cause of religion is to destroy it.'[77]

APPENDIX 1

Timeline of Home Mission in London, 1818 to 1914

1818 Parliamentary grant of £1,000,000 for church building.
Establishment of the Church Building Commissioners.
Establishment of the Incorporated Church Building Society.

1824 Parliamentary grant of an additional £500,000 for church building.

1828 Bishop Blomfield succeeded Bishop Howley.
Repeal of Test and Corporation Act.

1829 Catholic Emancipation Act.

1835 Establishment of the London City Mission.

1836 Establishment of the Metropolis Churches Fund.
Establishment of the Church Pastoral-Aid Society.

1837 Establishment of the Additional Curates' Society.

1839 Establishment of the Bethnal Green Churches and Schools Fund.

1841 First use of a temporary church in the Metropolis (in Kentish Town).

1843 Peel Act (New Parishes Act 1843) simplified district formation.

1844 Establishment of the Church of England Scripture Readers' Association.

1851 Religious Census was held on Sunday 30 March 1851.

1853 Royal letters (church briefs) were abolished.

1854 Publication of 1851 Census ReportCensus, Religious 1851.
Reconstitution of the Metropolis Churches Fund as the London Diocesan Church Building Society.

1855 Open air preaching was legalised (Religious Worship Act 1855).

1856 Bishop Tait succeeded Bishop Blomfield.

1857 Establishment of the London Diocesan Home Mission.
Formal opening of the first school church (in Stepney).

1858 of Select Committee of the House of Lords on the Spiritual Condition Large Towns.

1860 Establishment of the Parochial Mission Women Association.

1861	Establishment of the London Diocesan Deaconess Institution (now known as the Community of St. Andrew).
1863	Establishment of the Bishop of London's Fund.
1864	Establishment of the Ladies' Diocesan Association.
1865	Establishment of the Lay Helpers' Association.
1869	Bishop Jackson succeeded Bishop Tait.
1873	Bishop of London's Fund was made a permanent institution.
1874	First General Mission held throughout the Diocese.
1879	Creation of Bishop Suffragan of Bedford.
1880	Establishment of the East London Church Fund.
1882	First London Diocesan Conference held.
1885	Bishop Temple succeeded Bishop Jackson.
1886	Publication of the *London Diocesan Magazine*.
1888	Church House was opened.
1895	Creation of Bishop Suffragan of Stepney.
1896	Bishop Creighton succeeded Bishop Temple.
1897	Reconstitution of the Ladies' Diocesan Association as the Women's Diocesan Association.
1898	Creation of Bishop Suffragan of Islington.
1901	Bishop Winnington-Ingram succeeded Bishop Creighton. Establishment of the Girls' Diocesan Association.
1911	Report of the Archbishops' Committee on Church Finance.
1914	Establishment of the Central Board of Finance and the Diocesan Boards of Finance.

APPENDIX 2

The heart of this book is a financial analysis of a range of home-missionary organizations operating in the Diocese of London. This is carried out with the ambition of evaluating the Anglican community's support of these organizations during the period of study, in terms of who gave financial support and how this changed.

The purpose of this appendix is to present the data that is used to evaluate the financial health of the diocesan organisations selected for this study, within the period 1856 to 1914. The tables, therefore, outline the changes in the funding levels of these societies through an analysis of the different streams of funding. This is used in order to determine whether the level of financial support given to these organisations by the Anglican laity declined or remained stable during the period.

This appendix of tables presents the overall results of the analysis of the data gathered from the supporters' philanthropic payments. The information contained in the subscription lists of the societies' annual reports is also presented in a variety of ways in order to discern whether there were any demographic changes in the source of contribution and level of contribution.

The source documents for the contributor analysis are the subscription lists from the societies' printed annual reports. In the case of the London Diocesan Home Mission, it has also been possible to recreate the subscriptions lists from their manuscript cash books. The cash books were the source used by the London Diocesan Home Mission to record its subscription lists. In the tables that follow, every financial payment listed as a donation or subscription has been interrogated by examining the size and source of the payment.

Section 1 – Funding Stream Analysis

A brief explanation on the use of the income figures published in charitable guides follows. The editors of the main charitable directories compiled their statistics from the published annual reports of charities in London. These figures, however, can be unreliable guides to the financial health of specific charitable organizations. For example, in *Herbert Fry's Royal Guide to the London Charities* directory for 1865–6, the income for the London Diocesan Home Mission for the year 1864–5 was reported as being £5,300. This, however, is a deceptive figure. The end of year financial reconciliation for the London Diocesan Home Mission, in its annual report published in 1865, shows that the £5,300 actually represented the total cash assets of the Fund at 30 December 1864 rather than reflecting a statement of income for the year. The figure of £5,300 included a brought forward balance of £273 from the previous accounting year and an additional £1,495 realised from the sale of £1,500 nominal of Exchequer Bills. The actual 'raised' income figure for the year of 1864 was £3,569. This demonstrates that the publicly reported figures should be used only as a guide figure when evaluating the financial health of a charity. The most reliable sources, from an accounting perspective, are the printed annual reports and manuscript general ledgers of a society. The annual income figures stated are, unless otherwise specified, based on the society's statement of receipts and expenditure. For accounting purposes the statement of receipts and expenditure has to show how the society's expenditure for that year was funded. For this reason the 'receipts' in accounts include items that do not represent newly raised income for that year: loans, petty cash and sale of stock. As this work is concerned with the financial success of these particular Anglican home-missionary organizations (in terms of the amount of income raised each year), these types of sources have been stripped from the receipt figures shown in the tables. The funding stream categories, in the following analysis, differ from table to table according to how the societies reported their finances. This means that in some instances church collection income is combined with subscription and donation income.

Table A.1.1: BLF Funding Stream Analysis

Year	Subscriptions & Donations	Interest	Legacy Income	Church Collections	Total Income
1863–4	£90,043	£1,198	–	£9,216	£100,457
1865	£41,476	£2,806	–	£3,967	£48,249
1866	£32,102	£2,749	£10	£6,229	£41,090
1870	£28,140	£1,040	£90	£7,011	£36,281
1872	£23,959	£1,016	£20	£6,040	£31,035
1873	£29,923	£919	–	£7,133	£37,975
1876	£15,710	£1,499	£4,806	£6,540	£28,555
1878	£14,174	£821	£300	£5,721	£21,016
1879	£11,362	£923	£2,200	£5,579	£20,064
1884	£12,315	£811	£2,022	£4,767	£19,915
1895	£12,224	£1,484	£655	£6,329	£20,692
1896	£12,405	£1,475	£2,388	£6,609	£22,877
1897	£12,091	£1,460	£2,553	£6,793	£22,897
1904	£14,387	£1,876	£1,472	£7,814	£25,549
1905	£18,512	£1,778	£3,443	£8,089	£31,822
1906	£18,339	£1,971	£24,493	£8,423	£53,226
1908	£17,386	£2,386	£2,685	£7,152	£29,609
1912	£20,768	£3,546	£4,770	£6,539	£35,623

Source: This table shows the information for all available years. Figures for 1904, 1905, 1906 and 1908 have been extracted from the *London Diocesan Magazine*. All other figures are taken from Bishop of London's Fund [hereafter BLF] Annual Reports.

Table A.1.2: ELCF Funding Stream Analysis

Year	Subscriptions & Donations	Subscriptions, Donations & Church Collections	Church Collections	Church Collections & Local Associations	Interest	Legacy Income	Misc.	Diocese Board of Finance Grant	Total Income
1880–1	–	£11,408	–	–	£119	–	–	–	£11,527
1885	–	£9,222	–	–	£79	–	–	–	£9,301
1887	£9,950	–	£2,706	–	£40	–	–	–	£12,696
1890	£10,135	–	£7,681	–	£510	£11	–	–	£18,337
1892	£7,857	–	£6,597	–	£224	£120	–	–	£14,798
1894	£10,978	–	£6,824	–	£131	£850	–	–	£18,783
1899	£11,055	–	–	£8,720	£246	£762	–	–	£20,783
1902	£8,496	–	–	£9,944	£302	£1,189	–	–	£19,931
1905	£8,933	–	–	£0,104	£325	£1,336	–	–	£20,698
1907	£8,467	–	–	£9,579	£424	£1,934	–	–	£20,404

Year	Subscriptions & Donations	Subscriptions, Donations & Church Collections	Church Collections	Church Collections & Local Associations	Interest	Legacy Income	Misc.	Diocese Board of Finance Grant	Total Income
1910	£9,632	–	–	£9,462	£824	£1,537	–	–	£21,455
1913	£6,588	–	–	£8,613	£821	£791	£40	–	£16,853
1914	£5,838	–	–	£5,469	£600	£978	£32	£4,500	£17,417

Source: All information is taken from East London Church Fund [hereafter ELCF] Annual Reports. Only selected years (at regular intervals) have been chosen for this table. 'Misc.' relates to the sale of the ELCF Kalendar (a calendar of daily quotations).

Table A.1.3: LDHM Funding Stream Analysis

Year	Subscriptions & Donations	Interest	Legacy Income	Church Collections	Mission Payment	Grants: BLF & ELCF	Inland Revenue & Misc.	Total Income
1857–8	£1,716	–	–	–	–	–	–	£1,716
1860	–	–	–	–	–	–	–	£1,549
1864	£1,204	£49	£422	£672	£219	£1,000	£3	£3,569
1894	£287	£2,500	–	–	£255	£1,500	£65	£4,607
1897	£184	£2,675	–	–	£493	£1,500	£94	£4,946
1899	£190	£2,697	£45	–	£290	£1,700	£100	£5,022
1902	£690	£2,636	–	–	£179	£1,500	£164	£5,169
1904	£160	£2,622	–	£18	£240	£1,500	£127	£4,667
1907	£131	£2,686	–	–	£187	£1,500	£141	£4,645
1909	£137	£2,703	£50	£5	£322	£1,500	£142	£4,859
1912	£84	£2,886	–	£8	£439	£1,500	£172	£5,089
1914	£55	£3,115	–	–	£441	£1,500	£193	£5,304

Sources and notes: This table shows the information for all available years. Figures for 1858 to 1864 are taken from London Diocesan Home Mission Annual Reports. The annual report for 1860 does not categorise the income. Figures for 1894 to 1914 are taken from the LDHM General Ledger: London Metropolitan Archives, DL/A/H/020/MS31994. The category 'Inland Revenue and Misc.' relates to Tax refunds and an unspecified refund of £3 in 1864.

Table A.1.4: LDDI Funding Stream Analysis

Year	Subscriptions & Donations	Interest	Legacy Income	Church Collections	Sisters' Payment	Mission Payment	Misc.	Total Income
1864–5	£705	–	–	–	£211	£57	£103	£1,076
1869–70	£750	–	–	–	£388	£56	£130	£1,324
1874–5	£913	–	–	–	£329	£137	£140	£1,519
1879–80	£663	£187	–	–	£327	£315	£104	£1,596
1884–5	£399	£186	£300	–	£340	£441	–	£1,666
1889–90	£298	£187	£274	£7	£545	£469	£186	£1,966
1894–5	£183	£185	–	–	£547	£679	£115	£1,709
1900	£139	£184	–	£23	£647	£560	–	£1,553
1905	£183	£282	–	£13	£846	£736	–	£2,060
1910	£105	£281	–	–	£1,085	£421	£16	£1,908
1914	£87	£221	–	–	£923	£516	£34	£1,781

Source: Only selected years (at regular intervals) have been chosen for this table. All figures are taken from London Diocesan Deaconess Institution [hereafter LDDI] Annual Reports. The 'Misc' category includes: payments from patients; revenue from the school and the girls' industrial school; contributions from retreats and sales of works. Grants from the BLF are included in the 'Mission Payments' category.

Table A.1.5: PMWA Funding Stream Analysis

Year	Subscriptions & Donations	Interest	Legacy Income	Church Collections	Grants	Event Income	Inland Revenue	Total Income
1861–2	£599	£22	–	£38	–	–	–	£659
1865	£2,142	£28	£100	£21	£528	–	–	£2,819
1917–18	£1,545	£110	£200	–	£179	£337	£20	£2,391

Source: This table shows the information for all available years. The 1861–62 figures come from: C. J. S. Talbot, *Parochial Mission-Women; Their Work, and its Fruits* (London, 1862), p. 170. The other information comes from Parochial Mission Women Association [hereafter PMWA] Annual Reports

Table A.1.6: LCM Funding Stream Analysis

Year	Donations, Subscriptions, Local Associations & Interest	Subscriptions & Donations	Metropolitann Associations	Provincial Associations	Legacy Income	Interest	Misc.	Total Income
1860–1	£32,325	–	–	–	£2,692	–	£76	£35,093
1865–6	£33,390	–	–	–	£2,027	–	£43	£35,460
1870–1	£32,891	–	–	–	£3,693	–	£32	£36,616
1875–6	–	£11,818	£23,963	£6,221	£8,519	–	£26	£50,547
1879–80	–	£10,893	£23,437	£5,701	£6,684	£159	£116	£46,990
1885–6	–	£11,025	£25,859	£5,888	£15,058	£12	£45	£57,887
1890–1	–	£10,319	£24,636	£5,745	£14,269	£2,054	£105	£57,128
1895–6	–	£10,720	£22,622	£6,047	£14,373	£1,441	£52	£55,255
1900–1	–	£10,265	£23,844	£6,967	£23,022	£1,708	£17	£65,823
1905–6	–	£14,141	£21,323	£6,231	£9,481	£1,444	£11	£52,631
1910–1	–	£6,826	£20,771	£5,999	£16,307	£1,615	£727	£52,245
1913–14	–	£10,163	£20,714	£6,130	£15,258	£1,250	£592	£54,107

Source: All figures are taken from London City Mission [hereafter LCM] Annual Reports. Only selected years (at regular intervals) have been chosen for this table. Miscellaneous includes rent, sale of magazines and sale of books.

Section 2 – Subscription List Analysis

Source Categorization and Financial Size of Contribution (Tables A.2.1a–A.3.2)

In the analysis found in these tables, every financial payment listed as a donation or subscription has been interrogated by examining the size and source of the payment. Firstly, each subscription and donation payment has been categorised by size into the following bands: '<£1'; '£1 to <£2'; '£2 to <£10'; '£10 to <£50'; '£50 to <£100'; '£100 plus'. The reason for distinguishing between '£1 to <£2' and '<£1' is because a significant proportion of all contributions were for the amount of one guinea (e.g., the Million Guineas Fund). This is because a guinea was commonly the amount given to charity. Secondly, payments were then categorised by source. These categorizations are: male, female, both male and female (i.e. a married couple), anonymous, corporate bodies and groups. The categories of 'Groups' and 'Corporate Bodies' need further clarification. Companies (such as banks, solicitors, breweries) are classified as being corporate bodies. 'Groups' includes payments from groups of individuals and includes descriptions such as 'Mrs Ley's children', 'Mrs F. G. Davidson's servants' and the 'Chester Deaconesses'. The payments from individuals categorised as 'Male', 'Female' or 'Both' were all then assigned a sub-classification to indicate their status; this was based on their form of address. This sub-classification categorises all people as being either clergy (e.g., Reverend, Bishop), titled (e.g., Lady, Sir, Duke) or commoner (e.g., Esq., Miss). This categorization makes it possible to establish the main demographic of the funder-base (in terms of gender and status) for each organization and then, consequently, to evaluate whether the demographic of this funder-base experienced any changes within the period. The information from these sources is presented in this Appendix in a number of different tables. These tables analyse the information in terms of the specifications of each contribution. For example, Table A.2.1a shows a breakdown of payments to the Bishop of London's Fund by year; these payments are analysed by the various categories (male, female, both male and female, anonymous, corporate bodies and groups). This approach is taken because the number of contributors gives a better representational gauge of public support than analysis in terms of how much money came from different sources. In the case of the East London Church Fund in the 1910s, for example, the relatively stable income from subscriptions and donations masks the fact that the society was being propped up by large donations (often anonymous) to balance the society's books at the end of the year and prevent a deficit.

Anonymity (Tables A.2.1a to A.2.1f)

Before presenting the data analysis tables, it is necessary to take a moment to discuss the phenomenon of anonymity and how it has been dealt with. The category of 'Anonymous' causes problems when wanting to indicate the percentage of supporters that were male or female. To take an example from the analysis of the subscription lists, Table A.2.1a analyses the source of the contributions listed in subscription lists in the Bishop of London's Fund's annual reports: these are categorised (as male, female, both, anonymous, corporate body or group) by year, thereby reflecting the supporter base year-by-year. In 1865, for example, from a total of 2,509 contributions, the payments have been categorised as: 1,611 (64.2 per cent) from men; 602 (24.0 per cent) women; 24 (1.0 per cent) from married couples; 189 (7.5 per cent) from anonymous sources; 69 (2.8 per cent) from corporate bodies; and 14 (0.6 per cent) from groups. The selected method has been to take the female sector as a proportion of gender identified contributions (male contributions plus female contributions). For example, in 1865, 1,611 (72.8 per cent) came from men and 602 (27.2 per cent) contributions came from women. As anonymous contributions only make up a small overall percentage of contributions, their categorization has no impact on the observed supporter trends in the book which have involved either large demographic swings (from male to female supporters) or straightforward decline across all sectors.

Status Analysis (Tables A.2.2a to A.2.2f)

These tables show the number of payments per year from individuals; these have been categorised by the form of address. This categorises all people as being either clergy (e.g., Reverend, Bishop), titled (e.g., Lady, Sir, Duke) or commoner (e.g., Esq., Miss). In the rare event that a clergyman was also a baronet, the individual has only been categorised as clergy. As for couples, if the husband was a clergyman, the couple have been categorised as 'Clergy'. This is a further analysis of the contributions categorised as 'Male', 'Female' and 'Both Male and Female'.

Section 2.1 – Contributions Analysed by Source Category and by Year

Table A.2.1a : BLF Contributions Analysed by Source Category and Year

Year	Male	Female	Both Male & Female	Anonymous	Corporate Body	Group	Total
1863	382	78	0	25	24	2	511
1864	2087	906	29	271	86	13	3392
1865	1611	602	24	189	69	14	2509
1866	1570	604	25	191	50	12	2452
1867	1742	705	32	190	50	16	2735
1868	1716	730	29	195	43	22	2735
1869	1565	652	19	151	39	18	2444
1870	1538	647	20	149	41	12	2407
1871	1406	610	19	111	35	9	2190
1872	1467	627	19	100	34	11	2258
1873	1365	595	17	117	32	9	2135
1876	601	295	6	54	13	2	971
1878	505	248	4	45	9	1	812
1879	517	249	4	49	10	3	832
1884	424	204	6	47	11	6	698
1897	492	447	19	70	12	3	1043
1912	789	1725	34	145	10	9	2712
Total	19777	9924	306	2099	568	162	32836

Table A.2.1b: ELCF Contributions Analysed by Source Category and Year

Year	Male	Female	Both Male & Female	Anonymous	Corporate Body	Group	Total
1881	147	81	4	40	8	1	281
1885	299	292	8	94	6	8	707
1890	776	1182	20	150	17	40	2185
1899	760	1329	11	163	29	65	2357
1902	790	1715	15	205	24	54	2803
1905	938	2527	32	325	21	88	3931
1910	723	2245	37	254	18	73	3350
1914	612	1985	32	168	13	54	2864
Total	5045	11356	159	1399	136	383	18478

Table A.2.1c: LDHM Contributions Analysed by Source Category and Year

Year	Male	Female	Both Male & Female	Anonymous	Corporate Body	Group	Total
1858	119	28	1	9	1	0	158
1859	40	18	0	21	2	1	82
1861	231	84	2	51	4	5	377
1864	186	67	2	10	1	4	270
1893	49	37	1	1	1	1	90
1894	50	40	1	3	2	1	97
1895	40	25	1	2	1	2	71
1896	42	20	1	2	2	2	69
1897	34	20	1	1	1	2	59
1898	39	19	0	2	1	2	63
1899	35	18	0	0	2	2	57
1900	34	16	0	0	1	2	53
1901	32	15	0	0	1	2	50
1902	43	13	0	1	3	2	62
1903	37	13	0	1	1	2	54
1904	36	12	0	4	1	2	55
1905	38	10	0	2	1	2	53
1906	36	12	0	3	1	2	54
1907	32	10	0	2	1	2	47
1908	28	10	0	1	1	2	42
1909	28	9	1	2	1	2	43
1910	22	8	0	2	0	1	33
1911	25	8	0	2	0	2	37
1912	23	7	0	3	0	2	35
1913	22	5	0	3	0	2	32
1914	22	5	1	1	0	1	30
Total	1323	529	12	129	30	50	2073

Table A.2.1d: LDDI Contributions Analysed by Source Category and Year

Year	Male	Female	Both Male & Female	Anonymous	Corporate Body	Group	Total
1862	61	115	0	18	0	0	194
1863	81	161	0	25	0	0	267
1864	104	142	1	14	0	0	261
1865	90	360	6	23	3	0	482
1866	88	399	8	22	1	1	519
1867	100	439	7	31	2	0	579
1869	96	361	11	23	2	1	494
1870	95	352	11	14	2	0	474
1871	95	359	9	14	2	2	481
1872	97	336	7	23	1	1	465
1873	124	352	8	36	1	2	523
1874	126	369	8	49	3	2	557
1875	107	366	7	29	2	2	513
1876	90	315	8	25	5	0	443
1877	100	345	7	28	4	0	484
1878	101	347	7	22	7	1	485
1879	94	334	6	19	3	2	458
1880	93	331	6	22	4	0	456
1882	87	278	5	13	3	0	386
1884	53	176	3	13	3	1	249
1886	49	175	1	6	1	0	232
1888	53	166	1	7	1	0	228
1890	36	132	3	6	1	0	178
1892	31	121	1	7	1	1	162
1894	22	114	2	2	1	1	142
1896	16	105	2	2	1	0	126
1898	10	85	1	2	1	0	99
1900	13	87	1	2	1	0	104
1902	9	86	1	4	1	0	101
1903	10	86	1	2	0	0	99
1904	12	95	1	8	0	0	116
1905	12	108	1	16	0	0	137
1906	11	93	1	2	0	0	107
1907	11	97	1	5	0	0	114
1908	11	96	1	4	0	0	112
1909	10	90	1	5	0	0	106
1910	9	90	0	2	0	0	101
1911	9	79	0	5	0	0	93
1912	10	80	0	4	0	0	94
1913	9	79	0	4	0	0	92
1914	5	78	0	5	0	0	88
Total	2240	8379	145	563	57	17	11401

Table A.2.1e: PMWA Contributions Analysed by Source Category and Year

Year	Male	Female	Both Male & Female	Anonymous	Corporate Body	Group	Total
1861	83	287	10	28	0	0	408
1865	121	257	9	18	0	3	408
Total	204	544	19	46	0	3	816

Table A.2.1f: LCM Contributions Analysed by Source Category and Year

Year	Male	Female	Both Male &Female	Anonymous	Corporate Body	Group	Total
1859–60	6366	6814	193	719	174	238	14504
1889–90	4600	7253	255	486	242	111	12947
1913–14	3409	5988	372	659	193	152	10773
Total	14375	20055	820	1864	609	501	38224

Section 2.2 – Clergy/ Titled/ Commoner Analysis by Year

Table A.2.2a: BLF Clergy/ Titled/ Commoner Analysis by Year

Year	Titled	Clergy	Commoner	Total
1863	102	82	276	460
1864	326	245	2451	3022
1865	199	210	1828	2237
1866	200	225	1774	2199
1867	198	255	2026	2479
1868	209	250	2016	2475
1869	169	237	1830	2236
1870	168	236	1801	2205
1871	153	226	1656	2035
1872	153	221	1739	2113
1873	144	206	1627	1977
1876	79	113	710	902
1878	67	107	583	757
1879	64	115	591	770
1884	63	86	485	634
1897	93	97	768	958
1912	203	99	2246	2548
Total	2590	3010	24407	30007

Table A.2.2b: ELCF Clergy/ Titled/ Commoner Analysis by Year

Year	Titled	Clergy	Commoner	Total
1881	21	42	169	232
1885	30	87	482	599
1890	61	199	1718	1978
1899	94	219	1787	2100
1902	93	212	2215	2520
1905	111	261	3125	3497
1910	94	203	2708	3005
1914	85	171	2373	2629
Total	589	1394	14577	16560

Table A.2.2c: LDHM Clergy/ Titled/ Commoner Analysis by Year

Year	Titled	Clergy	Commoner	Total
1858	17	50	81	148
1859	5	10	43	58
1861	31	82	204	317
1864	18	57	180	255
1893	9	11	67	87
1894	9	14	68	91
1895	8	10	48	66
1896	5	15	43	63
1897	6	12	37	55
1898	6	14	38	58
1899	7	13	33	53
1900	6	11	33	50
1901	6	12	29	47
1902	5	15	36	56
1903	6	11	33	50
1904	6	14	28	48
1905	7	13	28	48
1906	8	14	26	48
1907	8	11	23	42
1908	8	9	21	38
1909	8	8	22	38
1910	6	6	18	30
1911	8	6	19	33
1912	6	7	17	30
1913	6	7	14	27
1914	6	7	15	28
Total	221	439	1204	1864

Table A.2.2d: LDDI Clergy/ Titled/ Commoner Analysis by Year

Year	Titled	Clergy	Commoner	Total
1862	5	18	153	176
1863	9	24	209	242
1864	9	28	210	247
1865	45	26	385	456
1866	39	21	435	495
1867	47	34	465	546
1869	41	32	395	468
1870	42	28	388	458
1871	38	30	395	463
1872	28	26	386	440
1873	28	29	427	484
1874	31	37	435	503
1875	34	26	420	480
1876	27	24	362	413
1877	28	28	396	452
1878	30	27	398	455
1879	27	29	378	434
1880	27	27	376	430
1882	19	27	324	370
1884	13	17	202	232
1886	14	13	198	225
1888	12	17	191	220
1890	10	15	146	171
1892	8	11	134	153
1894	7	8	123	138
1896	8	7	108	123
1898	7	3	86	96
1900	8	4	89	101
1902	6	5	85	96
1903	5	5	87	97
1904	5	6	97	108
1905	4	6	111	121
1906	3	5	97	105
1907	3	6	100	109
1908	3	6	99	108
1909	2	5	94	101
1910	2	4	93	99
1911	2	4	82	88
1912	2	4	84	90
1913	2	3	83	88
1914	2	2	79	83
Total	682	677	9405	10764

Table A.2.2e: PMWA Clergy/ Titled/ Commoner Analysis by Year

Year	Titled	Clergy	Commoner	Total
1861	207	14	159	380
1865	134	57	196	387
Total	341	71	355	767

Table A.2.2f: LCM Clergy/ Titled/ Commoner Analysis by Year

Year	Titled	Clergy	Commoner	Total
1859–60	250	638	12485	13373
1889–90	207	510	11391	12108
1913–14	162	292	9315	9769
Total	619	1440	33191	35250

Section 2.3 – Contribution Band by Category

Table A.2.3a: BLF Contribution Band by Category

Category	Male	Female	Both Male & Female	Anonymous	Corporatie Body	Group	Total
£100 plus	859	79	3	139	135	2	1217
£50 to <£100	603	121	5	56	69	2	856
£10 to <£50	4127	1094	71	380	179	17	5868
£2 to <£10	6602	3099	112	645	114	62	10634
£1 to <£2	5702	3076	80	355	57	43	9313
<£1	1884	2455	35	524	14	36	4948
Total	19777	9924	306	2099	568	162	32836

Table A.2.3b: ELCF Contribution Band by Category

Category	Male	Female	Both Male & Female	Anon.ymous	Corporatie Body	Group	Total
£100 plus	52	49	1	55	21	0	178
£50 to <£100	46	41	0	44	14	2	147
£10 to <£50	400	396	11	183	41	20	1051
£2 to <£10	1442	2354	60	322	43	78	4299
£1 to <£2	1667	3390	45	244	10	73	5429
<£1	1438	5126	42	551	7	210	7374
Total	5045	11356	159	1399	136	383	18478

Table A.2.3c: LDHM Contribution Band by Category

Category	Male	Female	Both Male & Female	Anonymous	Corporatie Body	Group	Total
£100 plus	5	0	0	10	4	0	19
£50 to <£100	23	2	2	5	1	4	37
£10 to <£50	151	40	0	18	20	21	250
£2 to <£10	437	224	5	67	3	17	753
£1 to <£2	679	213	4	12	2	8	918
<£1	28	50	1	17	0	0	96
Total	1323	529	12	129	30	50	2073

Table A.2.3d: LDDI Contribution Band by Category

Category	Male	Female	Both Male & Female	Anonymous	Corporate Body	Group	Total
£100 plus	1	5	0	14	0	1	21
£50 to <£100	4	7	0	16	1	0	28
£10 to <£50	174	69	1	40	6	3	293
£2 to <£10	715	1275	48	105	30	1	2174
£1 to <£2	1039	3132	48	189	20	3	4431
<£1	307	3891	48	199	0	9	4454
Total	2240	8379	145	563	57	17	11401

Table A.2.3e: PMWA Contribution Band by Category

Category	Male	Female	Both Male & Female	Anonymous	Corporate Body	Group	Total
£100 plus	1	0	0	0	0	2	3
£50 to <£100	2	2	1	0	0	0	5
£10 to <£50	36	29	3	5	0	0	73
£2 to <£10	104	222	11	14	0	1	352
£1 to <£2	50	226	4	9	0	0	289
<£1	11	65	0	18	0	0	94
Total	204	544	19	46	0	3	816

Table A.2.6f: LCM Contribution Band by Category

Category	Male	Female	Both Male & Female	Anonymous.	Corporate Body	Group	Total
£100 plus	54	23	0	34	2	1	114
£50 to <£100	97	73	2	65	11	12	260
£10 to <£50	514	244	16	176	64	34	1048
£2 to <£10	2150	1983	169	365	192	90	4949
£1 to <£2	4991	5207	242	407	192	88	11127
Under £1	6569	12525	391	817	148	276	20726
Total	14375	20055	820	1864	609	501	38224

Section 2.4 – Contribution Band by Year

Table A.2.4a: BLF Contribution Band by Year

Year	<£1	£1 to <£2	£2 to <£10	£10 to <£50	£50 to <£100	£100 plus	Total
1863	10	22	96	187	62	134	511
1864	339	648	1193	884	139	189	3392
1865	224	580	914	591	91	109	2509
1866	278	625	872	527	71	79	2452
1867	452	746	892	489	66	90	2735
1868	464	789	888	454	62	78	2735
1869	393	753	753	411	58	76	2444
1870	393	737	746	405	56	70	2407
1871	329	712	691	350	50	58	2190
1872	368	748	687	351	46	58	2258
1873	333	733	680	291	46	52	2135
1876	109	296	320	174	32	40	971
1878	77	247	272	163	15	38	812
1879	88	255	278	163	16	32	832
1884	52	219	258	117	20	32	698
1897	156	360	352	129	10	36	1043
1912	883	843	742	182	16	46	2712
Total	4948	9313	10634	5868	856	1217	32836

Table A.2.4b: ELCF Contribution Band by Year

Year	<£1	£1 to <£2	£2 to <£10	£10 to <£50	£50 to <£100	£100 plus	Total
1881	20	41	100	69	22	29	281
1885	101	209	268	90	22	17	707
1890	819	616	556	152	23	19	2185
1899	828	718	616	149	22	24	2357
1902	1084	873	654	148	19	25	2803
1905	1764	1199	764	171	14	19	3931
1910	1488	941	716	155	16	34	3350
1914	1270	832	625	117	9	11	2864
Total	7374	5429	4299	1051	147	178	18478

Table A.2.4c: LDHM Contribution Band by Year

Year	<£1	£1 to <£2	£2 to <£10	£10 to <£50	£50 to <£100	£100 plus	Total
1858	3	41	63	40	6	5	158
1859	7	21	31	19	3	1	82
1861	14	94	149	90	20	10	377

Year	<£1	£1 to <£2	£2 to <£10	£10 to <£50	£50 to <£100	£100 plus	Total
1864	24	126	84	30	4	2	270
1893	3	48	34	4	1	0	90
1894	9	48	34	6	0	0	97
1895	2	39	24	5	1	0	71
1896	3	35	25	5	1	0	69
1897	1	30	24	4	0	0	59
1898	3	32	22	6	0	0	63
1899	2	29	22	4	0	0	57
1900	1	28	22	2	0	0	53
1901	1	26	21	2	0	0	50
1902	1	33	23	4	0	1	62
1903	2	31	18	3	0	0	54
1904	3	28	22	2	0	0	55
1905	3	29	19	2	0	0	53
1906	3	29	19	3	0	0	54
1907	2	25	17	3	0	0	47
1908	1	23	14	3	1	0	42
1909	2	23	15	3	0	0	43
1910	1	19	11	2	0	0	33
1911	1	23	10	3	0	0	37
1912	2	20	11	2	0	0	35
1913	1	18	11	2	0	0	32
1914	1	20	8	1	0	0	30
Total	96	918	753	250	37	19	2073

Table A.2.4d: LDDI Contribution Band by Year

Year	<£1	£1 to <£2	£2 to <£10	£10 to <£50	£50 to <£100	£100 plus	Total
1862	42	74	56	21	1	0	194
1863	74	101	66	26	0	0	267
1864	82	108	63	8	0	0	261
1865	234	167	76	4	0	1	482
1866	260	173	71	15	0	0	519
1867	298	174	96	11	0	0	579
1869	219	173	89	11	1	1	494
1870	205	180	82	7	0	0	474
1871	198	177	94	11	1	0	481
1872	181	181	89	11	2	1	465
1873	181	198	116	19	3	6	523
1874	178	198	145	24	5	7	557
1875	176	210	108	18	0	1	513
1876	146	182	98	10	6	1	443
1877	158	211	99	11	3	2	484
1878	166	193	105	19	2	0	485
1879	150	209	86	11	2	0	458

Year	<£1	£1 to <£2	£2 to <£10	£10 to <£50	£50 to <£100	£100 plus	Total
1880	155	205	86	10	0	0	456
1882	128	175	78	5	0	0	386
1884	70	119	57	3	0	0	249
1886	68	103	56	5	0	0	232
1888	66	100	57	5	0	0	228
1890	50	82	44	2	0	0	178
1892	47	74	36	4	0	1	162
1894	49	60	32	1	0	0	142
1896	43	58	24	1	0	0	126
1898	36	39	23	1	0	0	99
1900	39	44	20	1	0	0	104
1902	42	38	18	2	1	0	101
1903	49	37	12	1	0	0	99
1904	58	41	15	2	0	0	116
1905	74	44	15	3	1	0	137
1906	63	33	10	1	0	0	107
1907	66	36	11	1	0	0	114
1908	69	34	8	1	0	0	112
1909	61	36	7	2	0	0	106
1910	59	36	5	1	0	0	101
1911	57	31	4	1	0	0	93
1912	54	35	4	1	0	0	94
1913	53	33	5	1	0	0	92
1914	50	29	8	1	0	0	88
Total	4454	4431	2174	293	28	21	11401

Table A.2.4e: PMWA Contribution Band by Year

Year	<£1	£1 to <£2	£2 to <£10	£10 to <£50	£50 to <£100	£100 plus	Total
1861	59	138	182	26	3	0	408
1865	35	151	170	47	2	3	408
Total	94	289	352	73	5	3	816

Table A.2.4f: LCM Contribution Band by Year

Year	<£1	£1 to <£2	£2 to <£10	£10 to <£50	£50 to <£100	£100 plus	Total
1859–60	7591	4736	1681	405	65	26	14504
1889–90	6886	3801	1783	338	95	44	12947
1913–14	6249	2590	1485	305	100	44	10773
Total	20726	11127	4949	1048	260	114	38224

Section 2.5 – Number of Large Contributions (£100 plus) per Year Analysed by Supporter

Table A.2.5a: BLF Number of Large Contributions (£100 plus) per Year Analysed by Supporter

Year	Male	Female	Both Male & Female	Anon.	Corporate Body	Group	Total
1863	106	6	0	6	15	1	134
1864	136	13	2	14	23	1	189
1865	75	5	0	12	17	0	109
1866	58	4	0	6	11	0	79
1867	58	7	1	14	10	0	90
1868	46	6	0	18	8	0	78
1869	54	5	0	10	7	0	76
1870	47	5	0	11	7	0	70
1871	47	3	0	3	5	0	58
1872	45	2	0	7	4	0	58
1873	37	3	0	9	3	0	52
1876	29	3	0	3	5	0	40
1878	28	1	0	5	4	0	38
1879	24	2	0	3	3	0	32
1884	23	3	0	3	3	0	32
1897	21	5	0	5	5	0	36
1912	25	6	0	10	5	0	46
Total	859	79	3	139	135	2	1217

Table A.2.5b: ELCF Number of Large Contributions (£100 plus) per Year Analysed by Supporter

Year	Male	Female	Both Male & Female	Anon.	Corporate Body	Group	Total
1881	14	5	0	5	5	0	29
1885	5	4	1	5	2	0	17
1890	5	4	0	9	1	0	19
1899	6	6	0	9	3	0	24
1902	7	7	0	8	3	0	25
1905	6	6	0	5	2	0	19
1910	8	11	0	11	4	0	34
1914	1	6	0	3	1	0	11
Total	52	49	1	55	21	0	178

Table A.2.5c: LDHM Number of Large Contributions (£100 plus) per Year Analysed by Supporter

Year	Male	Female	Both Male & Female	Anon.	Corporate Body	Group	Total
1858	1	0	0	3	1	0	5
1859	0	0	0	0	1	0	1
1861	3	0	0	5	2	0	10
1864	0	0	0	2	0	0	2
1902	1	0	0	0	0	0	1
Total	5	0	0	10	4	0	19

Table A.2.5d: LDDI Number of Large Contributions (£100 plus) per Year Analysed by Supporter

Year	Male	Female	Both Male & Female	Anon..	Corporate Body	Group	Total
1865	0	0	0	1	0	0	1
1869	0	0	0	1	0	0	1
1872	0	0	0	1	0	0	1
1873	0	2	0	4	0	0	6
1874	1	2	1	3	0	0	7
1875	0	1	0	0	0	0	1
1876	0	0	0	1	0	0	1
1877	0	0	0	2	0	0	2
1892	0	0	0	1	0	0	1
Total	1	5	1	14	0	0	21

Table A.2.5e: PMWA Number of Large Contributions (£100 plus) per Year Analysed by Supporter

Year	Male	Female	Both Male & Female	Anon.	Corporate Body	Group	Total
1865	1	0	0	0	0	2	3
Total	1	0	0	0	0	2	3

Table A.2.5f: LCM Number of Large Contributions (£100 plus) per Year Analysed by Supporter

Year	Male	Female	Both Male & Female	Anon.	Corporate Body	Group	Total
1859	15	4	0	6	1	0	26
1889	21	10	0	12	1	0	44
1913	18	9	0	16	0	1	44
Total	54	23	0	34	2	1	114

Section 3 – Comparative Analysis Of All Societies (Including London City Mission)

For the purposes of this study, it was felt that it would be useful to provide comparative data (across all of the organisations) that focused solely on the size of the donation or subscriptions paid. Such analysis gives an indication of the typical support. Consequently, these tables show side-by-side comparative data from: the Bishop of London's Fund; East London Church Fund; London Diocesan Home Mission; London Diocesan Deaconess Institution; Parochial Mission Women Association; alongside the London City Mission. This data highlights, for example, the disparity in the amounts give to the Bishop of London's Fund and the London City Mission. This comparative analysis then focuses further on the source of support for the large '£100 plus' payments, again highlighting the disparity in large sums from titled individuals.

Table A.3.1: Contribution Band Comparison

Society	<£1	£1 to <£2	£2 to <£10	£10 to <£50	£50 to <£100	£100 plus	Total
BLF	4948	9313	10634	5868	856	1217	32836
ELCF	7374	5429	4299	1051	147	178	18478
LDHM	96	918	753	250	37	19	2073
LDDI	4454	4431	2174	293	28	21	11401
PMWA	94	289	352	73	5	3	816
LCM	20726	11127	4949	1048	260	114	38224

Table A.3.2 Analysis of the Contribution Band '£100 plus' by Clergy/ Titled/ Commoner Categorization

£100 plus	Titled	Clergy	Commoner	Anonymous	Corporate Body	Group	Total
BLF	341	91	509	139	135	2	1217
ELCF	17	13	72	55	21	0	178
LDHM	2	2	1	10	4	0	19
LDDI	0	0	6	14	0	1	21
PMWA	1	0	0	0	0	2	3
LCM	7	2	68	34	2	1	114

Section 4 – Top 20 Funders For Each Company

This section shows the 'league table', so to speak, of the top 20 funders for each organisation. Most of these philanthropists will be mentioned, with additional biographical information, within the main body of the book. Those individuals who have bibliographical information reported in the endnotes of this Appendix, do not receive fuller treatment within the book. The purpose of presenting this information together was to highlight any shared funder-base across organisations and to highlight the very large sums given by certain individuals.

Table A.4.1a: BLF Top 20 Funders

Rank	Name	Amount (accumulated figures)
1	Charles Morrison	£47,600
2	Hugh Lupus Grosvenor, 1st Duke of Westminster	£35,050
3	The Commissioners of Woods, Forests and Land Revenues	£25,000
4	William Henry Berkley Portman, 2nd Viscount Portman	£13,595
5	Samuel Jones-Loyd, 1st Baron Overstone	£11,600
6	The Worshipful Company of Grocers	£10,955
=7	William Russell, 8th Duke of Bedford	£10,000
=7	Dowager Lady Lucy Howard de Walden	£10,000
9	Charlotte Denison, Viscountess Ossington	£7,500
10	F. A. H	£7,000
=11	K. P.	£6,000
=11	Bishop John Jackson	£6,000
13	Anonymous for a free church and a free school	£5,000
=14	Bishop Arthur Winnington-Ingram	£4,800
=14	Archbishop Frederick Temple	£4,800
=14	Anne Turner	£4,800
17	Cecil Henry Oliverson	£4,700
18	G. C.	£4,500
19	Francis Alexander Hamilton	£4,300
=20	George Cubitt, 1st Baron Ashcombe	£4,200
=20	The Worshipful Company of Drapers	£4,200

Source: These figures are taken from the BLF Annual Report for 1912 which shows the accumulated total of money given as donations and subscriptions between 1863 and 1912. These amounts do not include legacies.

Table A.4.1b: ELCF Top 20 Funders

Rank	Name	Amount (accumulated figures)
1	Charles Morrison	£9,900
2	Hugh Lupus Grosvenor, 1st Duke of Westminster	£6,000
3	Worshipful Company of Grocers	£5,505
4	A Friend	£5,000
5	Richard Foster	£4,080
6	An East End Worker - A Thankoffering	£3,000
7	Gertrude Scholfield[1]	£2,600
8	William Henry Berkley Portman, 2nd Viscount Portman	£2,400
9	Miss Monk	£2,300
10	Caroline Amelia Newman – 'In honoured memory of Reverend Frederick Newman'	£2,100

Rank	Name	Amount (accumulated figures)
=11	Bishop William Walsham How	£2,000
=11	Anonymous	£2,000
=13	MSD	£1,700
=13	Worshipful Company of Goldsmiths	£1,700
=13	Bishop Arthur Winnington-Ingram	£1,700
16	Worshipful Company of Mercers	£1,680
17	Richard Fellowes Benyon[2]	£1,650
18	MHF	£1,450
19	Messrs Charrington Head & Co	£1,355
20	F. A. H.	£1,350

Sources and notes: The figures in this table are taken from a virtually complete set of ELCF annual reports covering the period 1880 to 1914. The figures, therefore, do not include income for all years.

Table A.4.1c: LDHM Top 20 Funders

Rank	Name	Amount (accumulated figures)
1	Francis Alexander Hamilton	£ 500
=2	Anonymous	£ 300
=2	Anonymous	£ 300
4	Worshipful Company of Leathersellers	£ 268
5	Archbishop Archibald Campbell Tait	£ 210
=6	Messrs Truman Hanbury Buxton & Co	£ 200
=6	DC	£ 200
=6	Anonymous	£ 200
=6	Messrs Hoare and Co	£ 200
10	Hugh Lupus Grosvenor, 1st Duke of Westminster	£ 170
11	Abel Smith MP[3]	£ 127
12	Jessie Margaret Richards[4]	£ 103
=13	A Lady (per the Reverend William Pitt Wigram)	£ 100
=13	RH	£ 100
=13	Anonymous	£ 100
=13	Anonymous	£ 100
=13	Anonymous	£ 100
=13	Anonymous	£ 100
=13	F Sargent Esq[5]	£ 100
=13	William Page Wood, 1st Baron Hatherley	£ 100
=13	William Bingham Baring, 2nd Baron Ashburton[6]	£ 100
=13	William Pleydell-Bouverie, 3rd Earl of Radnor[7]	£ 100

Sources and notes: The figures in this table are based on figures taken from the available LDHM Annual Reports and General Ledger and Cash Books for the period 1857 to 1914. The figures, therefore, do not include income for all years.

Table A.4.1d: LDDI Top 20 Funders

Rank	Name	Amount (accumulated figures)
1	Matilda Blanche Gibbs	£5,000
2	William Gibbs	£2,490
3	A Friend	£1,400
4	Deaconess Elizabeth Catherine Ferard	£1,057
5	Henry Warner Prescott	£526
6	The Misses Doxat	£514
=7	A Friend	£500
=7	A Friend	£500
9	Lord Josceline Percy	£345
10	Joseph Sherwood[8]	£202
11	The Worshipful Company of Salters	£173
12	Reverend Edward Hood Linzee	£166
13	Lady Louisa Percy	£155
=14	AT	£150
=14	ZZ	£150
16	Elizabeth Von Mumm[9]	£145
17	The Misses Loveday[10]	£140
18	Reverend Edward Meyrick Goulburn	£136
19	'A Lady gave all her jewels'	£110
20	Lavinia Godwin Doxat	£101

Source: The figures in this table are based on a virtually complete set of LDDI Annual Reports for the period 1861 to 1914. The figures, therefore, do not include income for all years.

Table A.4.1e: PMWA Top 20 Funders

Rank	Name	Amount (accumulated figures)
1	Susannah Trevanion	£1,000
2	Society for the Relief of Small Debtors	£895
3	Lady Lucy Cavendish	£700
4	Roundell Palmer, 1st Earl Selborne	£378
5	Ladies' Diocesan Association	£200
6	Miss Bampton[11]	More than £100
=7	Hugh Lupus Grosvenor, 1st Duke of Westminster	£100
=7	Samuel Jones-Loyd, 1st Baron Overstone	£100
=7	Miss Rawson[12]	£100
=7	HE	£100
=7	PH	£100
12	Worshipful Company of Mercers	£157
13	Worshipful Company of Fishmongers	£52
=14	Sir William Earle Welby-Gregory	£50

Rank	Name	Amount (accumulated figures)
=14	Lady Victoria Welby-Gregory	£50
=14	Lady Harriet Sarah Wantage	£50
=17	Lady Harriet Duncombe[13]	£40
=17	William Gibbs	£40
19	Sir Edward Hulse[14]	£31

Source: The figures in this table are based on information from the 1861 and 1868 annual reports and entries made in the PMWA Minute Books 1862–1923, Lambeth Palace Library, 1682–1693A and 2664, regarding large donations or subscriptions. The figures, therefore, do not include income for all years.

Table A.4.1f: LCM Top 20 Funders

Rank	Name	Amount (accumulated figures)
1	Joseph Gurney Barclay[15]	£ 24,966
2	Robert Cooper Lee Bevan	£ 24,182
3	"FAITH"	£ 15,000
4	Thomas Fowell Buxton (4th Baronet)	£ 14,040
5	Francis Augustus Bevan	£ 13,015
6	Sir George Williams	£ 8,926
7	Sir Edward North Buxton (2nd Baronet)	£ 8,531
8	John William Berry[16]	£ 8,039
9	Messrs Truman Hanbury & Buxton	£ 7,079
10	Joseph Hoare	£ 5,803
11	Sir Thomas Fowell Buxton (3rd Baronet)	£ 5,665
12	Francis Alexander Hamilton	£ 5,638
13	Sir Harry James Veitch[17]	£ 5,374
14	William Cooke[18]	£ 5,045
15	T. E. E.	£ 4,984
16	Mrs Lawton[19]	£ 4,800
17	William Ellice & Lady Jane Ellice[20]	£ 4,763
18	Miss Sophia Portal[21]	£ 4,720
19	Hugh Lupus Grosvenor, 1st Duke of Westminster	£ 4,500
20	John Marnham[22]	£ 4,072

Sources: LCM Annual Reports for the period 1859/60 to 1913/14.

Section 5 – Bequest Analysis (1860–1914)

This section analyses the bequests made to all of the societies in this study in the period 1860 to 1914 (and does not therefore include any bequests made to the London City Mission before 1860). The bequest analysis initially examines the bequests by volume and amount of money bequeathed, before going on to break this information down into further subsets looking at gender, the size of the bequest and size of probate estate. (It was not possible to analyse the size of probate estate for the London City Mission due to the high volume of bequests made to this organisation). The largest ten bequests made to each organisation are listed in separate tables. Those individuals who have bibliographical information reported in the footnotes of this Appendix, are not mentioned in the main body of the book text.

Section 5.1 – Bequest Analysis by Gender

Table A.5.1: Bequest Analysis by Gender for Each Organization

Gender & Total Amount	Female	Male	Unknown	Total
BLF	£76,859	£142,329	£10	£219,198
	(84 legacies)	(87 legacies)	(1 legacy)	(172 legacies)
ELCF	£32,883	£26,817	(0)	£59,700
	(54 legacies)	(20 legacies)		(74 legacies)
LDHM	£113,700	£2,604	(0)	£116,304
	(11 legacies)	(6 legacies)		(17 legacies)
LDDI	£2,633	£500	(0)	£3,133
	(12 legacies)	(1 legacy)		(13 legacies)
PMWA	£1,780	£45	(0)	£1,825
	(17 legacies)	(1 legacy)		(18 legacies)
LCM	£447,653	£260,056	£2,423	£710,132
	(1396 legacies)	(674 legacies)	(14 legacies)	(2084 legacies)

Sources: Annual Reports and Minute Books

Section 5.2 – Bequest Analysis by Size

Table A.5.2: Bequest Analysis by Size of Bequest for Each Organization

Company	Not known	>£50	£50 to £99	£100 to £499	£500 to £999	£1,000 to £9,999	£10,000 to £99,999	£100,000 plus	Total
BLF	1	19	22	55	31	39	5	0	172
ELCF	1	12	13	25	6	15	2	0	74
LDHM	0	2	4	6	3	1	0	1	17
LDDI	0	1	1	10	1	0	0	0	13
PMWA	0	5	1	11	1	0	0	0	18
LCM	0	673	387	716	149	152	7	0	2084

Sources: Annual Reports and Minute Books

Section 5.3 – Bequest Analysis by Size and Gender

Table A.5.3: Bequest Analysis by Size of Bequest and Gender (combined for BLF, ELCF, LDHM, LDDI and PMWA)

Bequest Band	Female	Male	Anonymous	Total
£100,000 plus	1	0	0	1
£10,000 to £99,999	0	7	0	7
£1,000 to £9,999	32	18	1	51
£500 to £999	27	16	0	43
£100 to £499	61	45	1	107
<£100	55	28	1	84
Unknown	0	1	0	1
Total	176	115	3	294

Sources: Annual Reports and Minute Books

Section 5.4 – Bequest Analysis by Probate Estate Size

Table A.5.4 Bequest Analysis by Probate Estate Size for Each Organization

Company	Unable to trace	<£1,000	£1,000 to £4,999	£5,000 to £9,999	£10,000 to £49,999	£50,000 to £99,999	£100,000 to £999,999	£1m plus	Total
BLF	17	5	12	16	61	24	34	3	172
ELCF	18	4	7	8	21	5	8	3	74
LDHM	1	2	4	2	2	2	4	0	17
LDDI	2	3	0	3	3	0	2	0	13
PMWA	14	0	1	1	2	0	0	0	18

Sources: Annual Reports and Minute Books

Section 5.5 – Bequest Analysis by Decade

Table A.5.5: Bequest Analysis by Decade for Each Organization: Showing Financial Value of Total Bequests and (Number of Bequests)

Company	Unable to trace	1860s	1870s	1880s	1890s	1900s	1910 to 1914	Total
BLF	£5,035 (8)	£10,271 (14)	£47,154 (21)	£25,670 (24)	£26,464 (38)	£67,578 (47)	£37,026 (20)	£219,198 (172)
ELCF	(0)	(0)	(0)	£280 (2)	£8,908 (19)	£28,767 (33)	£21,745 (20)	£59,700 (74)
LDHM	(0)	£522 (1)	£1,616 (3)	£111,905 (3)	£1,993 (6)	£268 (4)	(0)	£116,304 (17)
LDDI	(0)	(0)	£1,039 (4)	£870 (4)	£274 (2)	£150 (1)	£800 (2)	£3,133 (13)
PMWA	(0)	£100 (1)	£935 (7)	£490 (7)	(0)	£200 (2)	£100 (1)	£1,825 (18)
LCM	(0)	£49,523 (233)	£83,236 (303)	£141,425 (434)	£123,227 (440)	£233,205 (449)	£79,516 (225)	£710,132 (2084)

Sources: Annual Reports and Minute Books. This table only shows LCM bequests for the period 1860 to 1914.

Section 5.6 – Top 10 Bequests Made to Each Organization

Table A.5.6a: BLF Top 10 Requests

Rank	Name	Year of Bequest	Amount of Bequest
1	Joshua Lockwood[23]	1907	£21,989
2	Edward Arnold[24]	1911	£17,500
3=	Charles Morrison	1909	£10,000
3=	John Brenchley[25]	1870	£10,000
3=	Reverend John Henry Ellis	1912	£10,000
6	Reverend William Peace[26]	1908	£8,087
7	Captain Edward William Harris[27]	1867	£7,571
8	Reverend John Back[28]	1891	£7,087
9	Mrs Mary Ellis[29]	1887	£5,142
10=	George Moore	1876	£5,000
10=	Charlotte Denison, Viscountess Ossington	1889	£5,000

Sources: 49th BLF Annual Report and *London Diocesan Magazine*.

Table A.5.6b: ELCF Top 10 Requests

Rank	Name	Year of Bequest	Amount of Bequest
=1	Charles Morrison	1909	£10,000
=1	Reverend John Henry Ellis	1912	£10,000
3	Miss Annie Amelia Jeaffreson	1910	£7,000
4	Anonymous (Miss Marian Charrington)	1907	£3,000
5	Miss Ellen Augusta Gray[30]	1899	£2,871
6	Reverend Robert George Swayne[31]	1901	£2,533
7	Mrs Agatha Gresham Wells[32]	1903	£2,500
=8	Francis Libress Brine[33]	1897	£2,000
=8	Miss Mary Doxat	1904	£2,000
=8	George John Fenwick[34]	1913	£2,000

Sources: ELCF Annual Reports and *London Diocesan Magazine*.

Table A.5.6c: LDHM Top 10 Requests

Rank	Name	Year of Bequest	Amount of Bequest
1	Miss Maria Mary Fussell	1882	£111,805
2	George Moore	1876	£ 2,000
3	Mrs Anna Ardlie Salisbury[35]	1892	£ 833
=4	George Churchill[36]	1890	£ 500
=4	Alexander Davidson[37]	1890	£ 500
6	Miss Harriet Hurst[38]	1878	£ 484

Rank	Name	Year of Bequest	Amount of Bequest
7	Richard Emerson[39]	1864	£ 422
8	Joseph Headland[40]	1907	£ 149
9	Maurice Bernays[41]	1877	£ 132
=10	Miss Marian Sarah Jackson[42]	1900	£ 100
=10	Miss Mary Frances Wood-burn[43]	1865	£ 100

Sources: LDHM Annual Reports, *London Diocesan Magazine* and Minute Books.

Table A.5.6d: LDDI Top 10 Requests

Rank	Name	Year of Bequest	Amount of Bequest
1	Marian Christiana Heale	1910	£500
2	Constance Rose Bradford[44]	1876	£450
=3	Mary Lake[45]	1885	£300
=3	Joseph Sherwood[46]	1888	£300
=3	Eleanor Crawford Rees	1913	£300
6	Anne Jane Woodall Field	1890	£274
7	Jane Harriet Doxat	1879	£270
8	Hannah Brackenbury[47]	1875	£200
9	Eliza Mary Hankin	1909	£150
10	Mary Elizabeth Overton Field	1878	£119

Sources: LDDI Annual Reports and *Ancilla Domini*.

Table A.5.6e: PMWA Top 10 Requests

Rank	Name	Year of Bequest	Amount of Bequest
1	Lady Charlotte Hatherley	1879	£500
2	Lady H Cox[48]	1906	£200
3	Lady Anne Manningham-Buller[49]	1876	£155
=4	Adele Eleonere d'Henin[50]	1885	£100
=4	Anne Helen Erskine[51]	1887	£100
=4	Miss Larcom[52]	1885	£100
=4	William Marshall[53]	1882	£100
=4	Laura Oldfield[54]	1876	£100
=4	Mrs E Palmer[55]	1874	£100
=4	Miss Roper[56]	1911	£100
=4	Isabella Thompson[57]	1906	£100

Sources: PMWA Minute Books.

Table A.5.6f: LCM Top 10 Requests

Rank	Name	Year of Bequest	Amount of Bequest
1	Miss Laura Gowland[58]	1900	£40,215
2	Miss Mary Tanner[59]	1887	£13,662
3	Reverend James Spurrell[60]	1893	£11,373
4	Mrs Sarah Hancock[61]	1912	£11,078
=5	Thomas Kincaid Hardie[62]	1902	£10,000
=5	Mrs Emily Leifchild[63]	1901	£10,000
=5	Douglas Henty[64]	1893	£10,000
8	George Brightwen[65]	1907	£9,090
9	Mrs Harriet Sophia Shaw-Hellier[66]	1909	£9,037
10	William Dollin Alexander[67]	1888	£9,000

Sources: LCM Annual Reports. Only bequests for the period 1860 to 1914 analysed.

Section 6 – Corporate Bodies As Subscribers

The term 'corporate body' is used loosely, in the statistical analysis, to refer to all contributions which were not made in the names of individuals or groups of individuals (e.g., 'Mrs F. G. Davidson's servants'). The category encompasses businesses, charities, educational establishments, livery companies and public bodies. The purpose of this analysis is to add to the evidence gathered in Section 2 and to specify which types of corporate bodies supported Anglican home-missionary organisations in this period. Mirroring Section 4, this section shows a 'league table' of the top 20 corporate funders for each organisation. This information is supplemented by a composite table showing combined figures for the Anglican organisations in this study.

Section 6.1 – Top 20 Corporate Funders

Table A.6.1a: BLF Top 20 Corporate Funders

Rank	Name	Type	Amount
1	The Commissioners of Woods, Forests and Land Revenues	State Department	£25,000
2	The Worshipful Company of Grocers	Livery Company	£ 10,955
3	The Worshipful Company of Drapers	Livery Company	£4,200
4	The Worshipful Company of Goldsmiths	Livery Company	£3,820
5	The Worshipful Company of Mercers	Livery Company	£3,750
6	The Worshipful Company of Merchant Taylors	Livery Company	£3,705
7	The Worshipful Company of Clothworkers	Livery Company	£2,700
8	Messrs Truman Hanbury Buxton & Co	Brewery	£2,350
9	Messrs Charles Macintosh & Co	Rubber manufacturers (rubberised textiles)	£2,183
10	The Honourable Society of Lincoln's Inn	Professional Association	£1,665
=11	Messrs JK Gilliat & Co	Merchant Bank	£1,500
=11	Messrs Marshall & Snelgrove	Department Store	£1,500
13	The Governors of the Charterhouse	Charity	£1,250
14	The Worshipful Company of Salters	Livery Company	£1,039
15	Messrs Copestake Moore Crampton & Co	Textile wholesaler	£1,005
=16	Messrs Baring Brothers & Co	Bank	£1,000
=16	Messrs Reid & Co	Brewery	£1,000
18	The Worshipful Company of Leathersellers	Livery Company	£609
19	Messrs Charrington Head & Co	Brewery	£602
20	Messrs Leaf & Sons	Warehousemen	£553

Source: BLF Annual reports. Only Top 20 funders listed.

Table A.6.1b: ELCF Top 20 Corporate Funders

Rank	Name	Type	Amount
1	The Worshipful Company of Grocers	Livery Company	£5,505
2	The Worshipful Company of Goldsmiths	Livery Company	£1,700
3	The Worshipful Company of Mercers	Livery Company	£1,680
4	Messrs Charrington Head & Co	Brewery	£1,355
5	Messrs Hoare & Co	Bank	£998
6	The Worshipful Company of Clothworkers	Livery Company	£800
7	The Worshipful Company of Merchant Taylors	Livery Company	£758
8	Messrs Truman Hanbury Buxton and Co	Brewery	£753
=9	The Worshipful Company of Drapers	Livery Company	£567
=9	The Worshipful Company of Leathersellers	Livery Company	£567
11	Messrs Mann Crossman & Paulin	Brewery	£415
12	Messrs Fruhling & Goschen	Bank	£361
13	Marlborough College	Education	£345

Rank	Name	Type	Amount
14	Messrs Robartes Lubbock & Co	Bank	£300
15	The Worshipful Company of Skinners	Livery Company	£273
16	The Worshipful Company of Salters	Livery Company	£210
17	Messrs William Brown & Co	Publisher	£179
18	The Worshipful Company of Armourers & Brasiers	Livery Company	£130
19	Messrs HJ Bliss & Sons	Surveyor & estate agent	£126
20	Messrs Bryant & May Limited	Match manufacturer	£113

Sources: ELCF Annual reports and *London Diocesan Magazine*. Only Top 20 funders listed.

Table A.6.1c: LDHM Top 8 Corporate Funders

Rank	Name	Type	Amount
1	Worshipful Company of Leather Sellers	Livery Company	£267
=2	Messrs Hoare	Bank	£200
=2	Messrs Truman Hanbury Buxton & Co	Brewery	£200
4	Messrs Copestake Moore & Co	Textile wholesaler	£61
5	Worshipful Company of Merchant Taylors Company	Livery Company	£21
6	Worshipful Company of Salters	Livery Company	£11
7	Messrs Laurence & Mortimer	Leather seller	£10
8	Worshipful Company of Skinners	Livery Company	£5

Sources: LDHM Annual Reports. The table only includes corporate bodies that gave £5 or above.

Table A.6.1d: LDDI Top 10 Corporate Funders

Rank	Name	Profession	Amount
1	Worshipful Company of Salters	Livery Company	£176
2	Small Debts Society	Charity	£50
3	Worshipful Company of Clothworkers	Livery Company	£46
4	Worshipful Company of Grocers	Livery Company	£25
5	Worshipful Company of Mercers	Livery Company	£21
6	Messrs W & A Gilbey	Distiller	£20
=7	Worshipful Company of Skinners	Livery Company	£11
=7	Windham Club	Gentleman's Club	£11
8	Express Milk Company	Milk Supplier	£8
9	Welch Margetson & Company	Menswear manufacturer	£6

Sources: LDDI Annual Reports. The table only includes corporate bodies that gave £5 or above.

Table A.6.1e: LCM Top 20 Corporate Funders

Rank	Name	Type	Amount
1	Messrs Truman Hanbury Buxton & Co	Brewer	£7,079
2	Messrs ED & F Man	Commodities trader (sugar, coffee etc)	£2,623
3	Messrs Wells & Perry	Brewer	£2,456
4	Messrs Wimbush & Co	Job Master (supplier of coaches, horses and drivers)	£2,078
5	Corporation of the City of London	Local Government	£1,500
6	Messrs Peek Frean & Co	Biscuit maker	£1,420
7	Messrs Copestake Crampton & Co	Textile wholesaler	£1,250
8	Messrs Swan and Edgar	Department Store	£1,196
9	Messrs Trotter	Engineers	£1,080
10	Worshipful Company of Goldsmiths	Livery	£1,050
11	Messrs Stone and Kemp	Silk manufacturer	£777
12	Worshipful Company of Leathersellers	Livery	£741
13	Price's Patent Candle Co	Candle Maker	£670
14	Messrs Matheson & Co	Merchant Bank	£644
15	Worshipful Company of Salters	Livery	£629
16	Messrs Hayward-Tyler & Co Ltd	Hydraulic engineer	£601
17	Worshipful Company of Clothworkers	Livery	£600
18	Messrs Dent Allcroft & Co	Glove maker	£578
19	Worshipful Company of Mercers	Livery	£510
20	Messrs WH Smith & Son	Stationer	£494

Sources: LCM Annual reports for the period 1859/60 to 1913/14. Only Top 20 funders listed.

Section 6.2 – Combined Figures for Top 20 Corporate Funders

Table A.6.2: Top 20 Corporate Funders for BLF, LDHM, LDDI & ELCF (combined figures)

Rank	Name	Occupation	Organizations	Amount
1	The Commissioners of Woods, Forests and Land Revenues	State Department	BLF	£25,000
2	The Worshipful Company of Grocers	Livery Company	BLF, ELCF, LDDI	£16,485
3	The Worshipful Company of Goldsmiths	Livery Company	BLF, ELCF	£ 5,520
4	The Worshipful Company of Mercers	Livery Company	BLF, ELCF, LDDI	£ 5,451
5	The Worshipful Company of Drapers	Livery Company	BLF, ELCF	£ 4,767
6	The Worshipful Company of Merchant Taylors	Livery Company	BLF, ELCF, LDHM	£ 4,484
7	The Worshipful Company of Clothworkers	Livery Company	BLF, ELCF, LDDI	£ 3,546
8	Messrs Truman Hanbury Buxton & Co	Brewers	BLF, ELCF, LDHM	£ 3,303
9	Messrs Charles Macintosh & Co	Rubber manufac- turers	BLF	£ 2,183
10	Messrs Charrington Head & Co	Brewers	BLF, ELCF	£ 1,957
11	The Honourable Society of Lincoln's Inn	Professional Association	BLF	£ 1,665
=12	Messrs JK Gilliat & Co	Merchant Bank	BLF	£ 1,500
=12	Messrs Marshall & Snelgrove	Department Store	BLF	£ 1,500
14	The Worshipful Company of Leathersellers	Livery Company	BLF, ELCF, LDHM	£ 1,443
15	The Worshipful Company of Salters	Livery Company	BLF, ELCF, LDHM, LDDI	£ 1,436
16	Messrs Hoare	Bank	BLF, ELCF, LDHM	£ 1,298
17	The Governors of the Charterhouse	Charity	BLF	£ 1,250
18	Messrs Reid & Co	Brewers	BLF, ELCF	£ 1,100
19	Messrs Copestake Moore Crampton & Co	Textile wholesaler	BLF, LDHM	£ 1,066
20	Messrs Baring Brothers & Co	Bank	BLF	£ 1,000

Sources: Annual Reports of BLF, LDHM, LDDI and ELCF.

Section 7 – Population Figures for the Diocese of London

The figures in this section have been drawn from a range of diocesan sources in this period: bishops' charges, *Report of the Proceedings of Church Congress, Official Yearbook of the Church of England*; and Blomfield's *Proposals for the Creation of a Fund* [the Metropolis Churches Fund]. The figures highlight the dramatic population growth in every decade throughout the nineteenth century. It is also important to note that the diocese lost 340,000 people to the Diocese of Rochester when a number of parishes were transferred in 1867 on the death of Bishop Wigram of Rochester; this was under the terms of the London Diocese Act of 1863.

Table A.7 – Population Figures for the Diocese of London

Year	Diocese of London Population Figures
1836	1,137,000
1851	2,143,340
1858	2,422,300
1861	2,570,079
1871	2,655,408
1881	2,918,814
1891	3,251,475
1901	3,585,209
1911	3,811,827

Sources: *Report of the Proceedings of Church Congress, 1899*, pp. 34, 37 (Archdeacon Sinclair takes the diocesan population figure for 1836 from C. J. Blomfield, *Proposals for the Creation of a Fund to be Applied to the Building and Endowment of Additional Churches in the Metropolis* (London: B. Fellowes, 1836), p. 5); A. C. Tait, *Charge Delivered in November 1858 to the Clergy of the Diocese of London, at his Primary Visitation by Archibald Campbell, Lord Bishop of London* (London: Rivingtons, 1858), pp. 15–16; A. C. Tait, *A Charge Delivered in December, 1862, to the Clergy of the Diocese of London, etc.* (London: Rivingtons, 1862), p. 61; J. Jackson, *The Parochial System: A Charge Delivered to the Clergy of the Diocese of London in November 1871* (London, 1871), p. 11; and *Official Yearbook of the Church of England*, 1884, p. 20; 1903, p. 595; 1913, p. xxviii.

WORKS CITED

Manuscript And Archive Sources

Cadbury Research Library, University of Birmingham

Church Pastoral-Aid Society: minute books, CPAS 1/4/1/24.

Church of England Scripture Readers' Association: minute book, CPAS 4/1/1.

Community of St Andrew, London

London Diocesan Deaconess Institution: papers and minute books. (Uncatalogued; due to be transferred to Lambeth Palace Library).

Lambeth Palace Library, London

Fulham Papers, Blomfield.

Benson papers.

Parochial Mission Women Association: minute books, 1682–1693A, 2664.

Wordsworth papers.

Lewisham History and Archives Centre, London

The Society of the Treasury of God: minute books, letter books, account books, membership records and miscellaneous papers, A/68/18.

London Metropolitan Archives, London

Bishop of London Fund: minute books and miscellaneous papers, DL/A/K/09.

Church Extension Fund: minute book and letter book (Uncatalogued).

East London Church Fund: minute books and miscellaneous papers, DL/A/K/11.

London Diocesan Church Building Society: minute books and miscellaneous papers, DL/A/H/054.

London Diocesan Home Mission: minute books, cash books, general ledgers and miscellaneous papers, DL/A/H/018.

Metropolitan Churches Fund: minute books and miscellaneous papers, DL/A/H/052.

London School of Economics and Political Science, Archives and Special Collections, London

Booth papers, survey notebooks, Booth B67; Booth B158.

The National Archives, London

    Office of Woods, Forests and Land Revenues: papers, CRES 40/103.

Senate House Library, London

    Loyd family papers, 804.

Annual Reports

Annual reports are referenced without mention of a date in order not to cause confusion in relation to whether the date relates to the accounting year or publication date; there is no standardisation in the way that they are catalogued by libraries. Instead, in this work, only the number of the annual report is specified. For example, *Forty-Ninth Bishop of London's Fund Annual Report*.

Bishop of London's Fund.

Church Missionary Society.

Church Pastoral-Aid Society.

East London Church Fund.

Free and Open Church Association.

Islington Church Home Mission.

Ladies Home Mission Union.

Lay Helpers' Association.

Lily Mission.

London City Mission.

London Diocesan Church Building Society.

London Diocesan Home Mission.

London Diocesan Deaconess Institution.

Metropolis Churches Fund.

Metropolitan Female Asylum.

National Society for Promoting the Education of the Poor in the Principles of the Established Church in England and Wales.

New Hospital for Women.

Open Air Mission.

Parochial Mission Women Association.

Royal Society for the Prevention of Cruelty to Animals.

Society for Promoting Christian Knowledge.

Society for the Propagation of the Gospel in Foreign Parts.

Society for the Suppression of Mendicity.

Society of the Treasury of God.

Parliamentary Papers

Census of Great Britain, 1851: Religious Worship in England and Wales, 1852–53 (1690).

From His Majesty's Commissioners Appointed to Consider the State of the Established Church with Reference to Ecclesiastical Duties and Revenues: With a Synopsis of Both Reports, 1836 (86).

Hansard, Commons Debates.

Hansard, Lords Debates.

Report from the Select Committee of the House of Lords, Appointed to Inquire into the Deficiency of Means of Spiritual Instruction and Places of Divine Worship in the Metropolis, and in Other Populous Districts in England and Wales, Especially in the Mining and Manufacturing Districts; and to Consider the Fittest Means of Meeting the Difficulties of the Case; and to Report thereon to the House; together with the Proceedings of the Committee, Minutes of Evidence, and Appendix, 1857–8 (387; 387-I).

Newspapers, Periodicals, Directories

Ancilla Domini

Belfast-Newsletter.

The Benefactor.

Berrow's Worcester Journal.

British Magazine.

Central Press.

Christian Observer.

The Church Builder.

Church Magazine.

Church of England Scripture Readers' Association Quarterly Paper.

Church Work among the Masses.

The Classified Directory to the Metropolitan Charities.

Daily Express.

Daily News.

East London Church Chronicle.

Free and Open Church Advocate.

The Financial Times.

The Guardian.

The Hampshire Advertiser.

Herbert Fry's Royal Guide to the London Charities.

Huddersfield Chronicle and West Yorkshire Advertiser.

Illustrated London News.

John Bull.

The Lancaster Gazette.

The Leicester Chronicle and the Leicester Mercury.

Lighten Our Darkness.

London City Mission Magazine.

London Diocesan Magazine.

The Lord's Portion.

Mission Life.

The Morning Post.

The Musical Times

The Musical Times and Singing Class Circular.

The Nonconformist.

The Official Yearbook of the Church of England.

The Philanthropist.

The Record

The Royal Cornwall Gazette Falmouth Packet

Report of the Proceedings of Church Congress.

Scripture Readers' Journal.

The Spectator

The Standard.

The Sunday Times

The Times.

The Yorkshire Herald.

Other Primary Printed Sources

Anglican and International Christian Moral Science Association, *Science and the Gospel; or the Church and the Nations* (London: Macmillan, 1870).

Anonymous, *Go and Do Likewise. A Short Account of Elizabeth, a Parochial Mission Woman. By a Lady Superintendent* (London, 1875).

Anonymous, *Robert Culling Hanbury: A Sketch of His Life and Work* (London: George Hunt, 1867).

Anonymous, *Systematic Giving* (London: Nisbet, 1864).

Anonymous, *What is Mine? What is God's? By a Clergyman of the Church of England* (London, 1859).

Archard, C. J., *The Portland Peerage Romance* (London: Greening and Company, 1907).

Archbishops' Committee on Church Finance, *Report, with Recommendations and Appendices* (London: Longmans, 1911).

Arthur, W., *Duty of Giving Away a Stated Proportion of our Income: An address etc* (Philadelphia, PA: Presbyterian Board of Publication, 1857 [1855]).

Bailey, J. (ed.), *The Diary of Lady Frederick Cavendish*, 2 vols (London: John Murray, 1927).

Barry, O., *The Lady Victoria Tylney Long Wellesley: A Memoir* (London: Skeffington and Son, 1899).

Benson, E. W., *Phoebe the Servant of the Church: a Sermon ... 1873, in Aid of the Parochial Mission-Women Fund* (London: Macmillan, 1873).

Bethnal Green Churches and Schools Fund (London: Clowes, 1854).

Bewes, W. A., *Church Briefs or Royal Warrants for Collections for Charitable Objects* (London: Black, 1896).

Binney, T., *Money: Popular Exposition in Rough Notes, with Remarks on Stewardship and Systematic Beneficence* (London: Jackson, Walford and Hodder, 1864).

Bishop of London's Fund, *Statistics as to the Religious Condition of London, Ascertained by Inquiries in Connexion with the Bishop of London's Fund for Providing for the Spiritual Wants of the Metropolis and its Suburbs* (London: Rivingtons, 1864).

—, *The Bishop of London's Fund for Providing for the Spiritual Wants of the Metropolis and its Suburbs,* (London, 1866).

—, *The Bishop of London's Fund: Some Account of Work since Midsummer 1863,* no. 1–18 (London, 1866–71).

—, *The Bishop of London's Fund for Making Further Provision for the Spiritual Needs of the Diocese of London* (London, 1913).

—, *The Origin of the Bishop of London's Fund ... and its Work for Fifty Years* (1913).

Blomfield, A. (ed.), *A Memoir of C. J. Blomfield, Bishop of London, with Selections from his Correspondence*, 2 vols (London: John Murray, 1863).

Blomfield, C. J., *Proposals for the Creation of a Fund to be Applied to the Building and Endowment of Additional Churches in the Metropolis* (London: B. Fellowes, 1836).

—, *Charge Delivered to the Clergy of the Diocese of London, at the Visitation in November MDCCCLIV* (London: B. Fellowes, 1854).

Blunt, J. J., *The Duties of the Parish Priest* (London: John Murray, 1856).

Booth, C., *Life and Labour of the People in London,* 3rd series: Religious Influences, 17 vols (London: Macmillan, 1902), vol. 7: Summary.

Brown, J. C., *A Hundred Years of Merchant Banking* (New York: n. p., 1909).

Burdett-Coutts, A. (ed.), *Woman's Mission: A Series of Congress Papers on the Philanthropic Work of Women by Eminent Writers* (London: Sampson Low Marston, 1893).

Calkins, H. R., *A Man and His Money* (New York: Methodist Book Concern, 1914).

Carnegie, A., 'Wealth', *The North American Review*, 148:391 (June 1889), pp. 653–64.

—, *The Gospel of Wealth* (London, 1890).

Carpenter, W. B., *Two Addresses Delivered at the Diocesan Conference, 1891: I. The Presidential Address. II. Systematic Almsgiving* (Knaresborough: A. W. Lowe, 1891).

—, *Our Lord's Teaching with Regard to Beneficence: A Sermon Preached by the Lord Bishop of Ripon, in Westminster Abbey, June 19th, 1895, on Behalf of the Bishop of London's Fund* (London: Brettel, 1895).

Cather, R. G., *The Origin and Objects of the Systematic Beneficence Society* (London, 1862).

The Charitable Ten Thousand (London: H. Grant, 1896).

The Charitable Ten Thousand (London: H. Grant, 1904).

Church Extension in the Diocese of London: Remarks on the Present State of the Metropolis Churches' Fund, by a Layman (London: Rivingtons, 1853).

Church Finance Leaflet No. I - III (London: Longmans, 1912).

Church of England Central Board of Finance, *Receiving and Giving: The Basis, Issues and Implications of Christian Stewardship* (London: General Synod of the Church of England, 1990).

Church Pastoral-Aid Society, *Abstract of Reports and Speeches at the Twenty-Ninth Meeting of the Church Pastoral-Aid Society held at St James's Hall, Piccadilly, on Thursday, May 5, 1864* (1864).

Churton, E., *Memoir of Joshua Watson* (Oxford and London: J. H. and J. Parker, 1861).

Crosland, N., *Rambles Round My Life: An Autobiography, 1819–1896* (London: E. W. Allen, 1898).

Cunningham, W., *Efficiency in the Church of England: Remarks Suggested by the Report of the Archbishops' Committee on Church Finance* (London: Murray, 1912).

Cutts, E. L., *On Church Extension and New Endowments* (London: Rivingtons, 1860).

—, *Home Missions and Church Extension* (London: Rivingtons, 1861).

Dale, H. P. (ed.), *The Life and Letters of Thomas Pelham Dale,* 2 vols (London: George Allen, 1894).

Davidson, R. T., *Life of Archibald Campbell Tait,* 2 vols (London: Macmillan, 1891).

Dickens, C., *Our Mutual Friend,* Daily News Memorial edn (London: Chapman and Hall, 1900 [1865]).

Evans, R. W., *The Bishopric of Souls* (London: Rivingtons, 1841).

Foster, J. P., *Fancy Fair Religion: or, The World Converting Itself* (London: Swan Sonnenschein, 1888).

Foster, W. F., *Richard Foster* (London: Eyre Spottiswoode, 1914).

Girdlestone, C., *A Letter to the Right Hon. and Right Reverend the Lord Bishop of London* (London: Rivingtons, 1863).

Gold and the Gospel; The Ulster Prize Essays on the Scriptural Duty of Giving in Proportion to Means and Income (London, 1853).

The Gospel of Giving: Sermons, Outlines, and Papers by Clergymen and Laymen of the Diocese of London (London: SPCK, 1918).

Gurney, S., *Charitable Societies of London: A Paper Read to the International Philanthropic Conference of June 1862* (London : McCorquodale & Co, c.1862).

Hamilton, J., *Prize Essay: An Inquiry into the Principles of Church Finance* (n. p.: n. p., 1865).

Harrison, W. (ed.), *All Saints' Day and other Sermons by the Rev. Charles Kingsley* (London: Macmillan, 1890).

Hodge, E. G., *Church Finance in the Diocese of London: A Popular Explanation of the Scheme adopted by the Diocesan Conference on June 29th, 1913* (London: Christian Knowledge Society, 1913).

How, F. D., *Bishop Walsham How: A Memoir* (London: Isbister, 1898).

Incorporated Church Building Society, *Refusal of Royal Letters to the Church Building Society* (London, 1855).

Inglis, R. H., *Church Extension: Substance of a Speech Delivered in the House of Commons on Tuesday 30th June 1840* (London: J. Hatchard and Son, 1840).

Islington Church Extension Society, 'Report of Proceedings at the Inaugural Meeting of the Islington Church Extension Society with Speeches delivered by the Rt. Hon. and Rt. Rev the Lord Bishop of London', *Occasional Papers*, 1 (1 January 1857).

Jackson, J., *A Charge Delivered to the Clergy of the Diocese of Lincoln, in October, 1861* (London, 1861).

—, *The Parochial System. A Charge Delivered to the Clergy of the Diocese of London in November 1871* (London, 1871).

—, *Letter from the Bishop of London on the Prospects and Future Work of the Bishop of London's Fund* (London: T. Brettel, 1874).

—, *A Charge Delivered to the Clergy of the Diocese of London, at his Fourth Visitation (London:* Skeffington, 1884).

Jerdan, C., *The Counterfeit in Church Finance and Christian Giving* (London: James Nisbet, 1891).

Lansdell, H., *The Sacred Tenth: or, Studies in Tithe-giving, Ancient and Modern,* 2 vols (London: SPCK, 1906).

—, *The Tithe in Scripture: Being Chapters from 'The Sacred Tenth'* (London: SPCK, 1908).

—, *Back to the Tithe: An Address Delivered to the Pan-Anglican Congress* (London, Burnside: 1909).

Lectures Delivered in the Establishment of Messrs Copestake, Moore, Crampton and Co … 1860–61 (Routledge: London, 1861).

Liddell, C. C., *Work in Dark Places* (London, n. p., n. d.).

—, *The Poverty-Stricken Clergy and the Society of the Treasury of God. A Paper by Rev Edward Liddell (Hon Canon of Durham). Read at the Gen meeting of the Society at the Church House, Westminster on 12 June 1893* (London: Society of the Treasury of God, 1893).

Liddon, H. P., *Life of Edward Bouverie Pusey,* 2 vols (London, Longmans Green, 1893).

Londinensis [William Rivington], *Our Church Extension Societies, General and Diocesan* (London: Harrison, 1855).

London Congregational Union, *Religious Statistics of London* (London: Warren Hall and James J. Lovitt, 1879).

London Diocesan Association of Lay Helpers, *Diocesan Organisation of Lay Help: A Paper Read at the Conference of the London Diocesan Association of Lay Helpers* (London: Rivingtons, 1868).

London Diocesan Church Building Society, *Special Appeal to the Landowners and Others Interested in the Welfare of the Metropolis* (London, 1855).

London Diocesan Conference, *Report of the Funds Committee, 1883–84* (London, 1884).

Loyd-Lindsay, H. S., *Lord Wantage: A Memoir* (London: Smith, Elder and Company, 1907).

Markland, J. H., *The Offertory: The Most Excellent Way of Contributing Money for Christian Purposes* (Oxford: Parker, 1862).

Mearns, A., *The Bitter Cry of Outcast London* (London: James Clarke, 1883).

Metropolis Churches Fund, *Spiritual Destitution in the Metropolis: An Appeal on Behalf of the Metropolis Churches Fund* (London, 1845).

Miles, A. H. (ed.), *Sacred Poets of the Nineteenth Century* (London: Routledge, 1907).

Moxon, T. A., *Reform in Church Finance: Four Papers on the Report of the Archbishops' Committee on Church Finance* (London: Christian Knowledge Society, 1912).

Mudie-Smith, R., *The Religious Life of London* (London: Hodder Stoughton, 1904).

Muir, J., *Bazaars and Fancy Fairs; Their Organisation, etc.* (London: L. Upcott Gill, 1896).

Nesbitt, R. C., *Church Finance, with Reference to the Diocese of London* (London: Wells Gardner, 1917).

Noel, B., *The State of the Metropolis Considered: A Letter to the Bishop of London* (London: James Nisbet, 1835).

Paley, W., *The Principles of Moral and Political Philosophy (London, 1785).*

Palmer, R., *Memorials: Part I Family and Personal 1766–1865, Part II Personal and Political 1865–1895* (London: Macmillian, 1896–8).

Peile, T. W., *Give God His Tenth: The Way to Lay by in Store for Ends at this Time Specially Sought through the Bishop of London's Fund: a Sermon [on 1 Cor xvi 2], etc.* (London, 1864).

Pocock, C. A. B., *Why Give? Or a Public Confession, as to the Right Motives for Proportionate Giving* (London: Charles Cull, c.1899).

Pusey, E. B., *Churches in London: Past and Present Exertions of the Church and Present Needs, with an Appendix containing Answers to Objections raised by the "Record" and Others to the Plan of the Metropolis Churches' Fund* (London: Baxter, 1837).

Rooke, F. H., *Systematic Almsgiving; a Paper, Revised, with Notes* (London, 1890).

Sandford, J., *The Mission and Extension of the Church at Home Considered in Eight Lectures Preached before the University of Oxford in the Year 1861 at the Lecture Founded by the late Rev John Bampton* (London: Longman, 1862).

Silvester, J., *A Pioneer of Proportionate Giving: A Brief Memoir of the Rev. E. A. Watkins* (Clacton-on-Sea, 1912).

Sinclair, J., *Church Difficulties of 1851: A Charge Delivered to the Clergy of the Archdeaconry of Middlesex, at the Visitations held at St. Paul's, Covent Garden, on the 12th and 13th of May, 1851* (London, 1851).

Smiles, S., *George Moore, Merchant and Philanthropist* (London: Routledge, 1878).

Society of the Treasury of God, *Society of the Treasury of God: A Monthly Paper* (Toronto: 1885).

Spencer, C. F. F., *East and West* (London: Longmans Green, 1871).

Stock, E., *History of the Church Missionary Society,* 2 vols (London: Church Missionary Society, 1899).

Tait, A. C., *Charge Delivered in November 1858 to the Clergy of the Diocese of London, at his Primary Visitation by Archibald Campbell, Lord Bishop of London* (London: Rivingtons, 1858).

—, *From the Bishop of London to the Laity of the Diocese: Claims of the London Diocesan Church Building Society* (London: Brettell, 1860).

—, *A Charge Delivered in December, 1862, to the Clergy of the Diocese of London, etc.* (London: Rivingtons, 1862).

—, *The Spiritual Wants of the Metropolis and its Suburbs. A Letter to the Laity of the Diocese of London ... With a Statement by the Executive Committee of "The Bishop of London's Fund"* (London: Rivingtons, 1863).

Talbot, C. J. S., *Parochial Mission-Women; Their Work, and its Fruits* (London, 1862).

Talbot, J. G., *Memorials of Hon Mrs John Chetwynd Talbot* (London, Spottiswoode, 1876).

Tweedie, W. K., *Man and His Money: Its Use and Abuse* (London, 1855).

Walford, C., 'Kings' Briefs: Their Purposes and History', *Transactions of the Royal Historical Society,* Vol. 10 (1882), pp. 1-74.

Walsh, W., *Progress of the Church in London During the Last Fifty Years* (London: Rivingtons, 1887).

—, *Progress of the Church in London: From the Accession of Queen Victoria to 1908* (London: SPCK, 1908).

Webb, B., *My Apprenticeship* (London: Longmans, 1926).

Wesley, J., *Sermons on Several Occasions,* 2 vols (New York: Carlton and Phillips, 1855).

Wood, W. P., *Parochial Mission Women, A Paper Read at Church Congress* (London: Emily Faithfull, 1864).

Wray, N., *Fun and Finance: A Discussion of Modern Church Novelties in Connection with the Subject of Christian Giving* (Boston, Mass: McDonald Gill, 1890).

Wylie, J. A., *The Gospel Ministry: Duty and Privilege of Supporting it* (London: James Nisbet, 1857).

Yates, R., *The Church in Danger* (London: Rivington, 1815).

Secondary Sources

Ball, M. and D. Sutherland, *An Economic History of London, 1800–1914* (London: Routledge, 2001).

[Baldwin], Sister Joanna, 'The Deaconess Community of St Andrew', *Journal of Ecclesiastical History,* 12:2 (October 1961), pp. 215–30.

Best, G., *Temporal Pillars: Queen Anne's Bounty, the Ecclesiastical Commissioners, and the Church of England* (Cambridge: Cambridge University Press, 1964).

Blackmore, H. (ed.), *The Beginning of Women's Ministry: The Revival of the Deaconess in the Nineteenth-century Church of England*, Church of England Record Society 14 (Woodbridge: Boydell Press, 2007).

Brown, C. G., 'The Costs of Pew-renting: Church Management, Church-Going and Social Class in Nineteenth Century Glasgow', *Journal of Ecclesiastical History*, 38:3 (July 1987), pp. 347–61.

—, *The Death of Christian Britain: Understanding Secularisation, 1800–2000* (London: Routledge, 2007).

—, *Religion and the Demographic Revolution: Women and Secularisation in Canada, Ireland, UK and USA since the 1960s* (London: Boydell and Brewer, 2012)

Brown, S. J., *The National Churches of England, Ireland, and Scotland, 1801–1846* (Oxford: Oxford University Press, 2001).

Burnett, J., *A History of the Cost of Living* (1969, Aldershot: Gregg Revivals, 1993).

Burns, A., *The Diocesan Revival in the Church of England, c1800–1870* (Oxford: Clarendon Press, 1999).

—, 'My Unfortunate Parish: Anglican Urban Ministry in Bethnal Green 1809- c.1850', in M. Barber, G. Sewell, Stephen Taylor (eds), *From the Reformation to the Permissive Society: A Miscellany in Celebration of the 400th Anniversary of Lambeth Palace Library*, Church of England Record Society Record Series 18 (Woodbridge: Boydell Press, 2010).

Cannadine, D., *Lords and Landlords: The Aristocracy and the Towns, 1774–1967* (Leicester: Leicester University Press, 1980).

Chadwick, O., *The Victorian Church,* 2 vols (London: Adam and Charles Black, 1970 [1966]).

Chaves, M., 'The Financing of American Religion Initiative Evaluation: Final Report', Institute for the Study of American Evangelicals, November 1997 (unpublished).

Checkland, O., *Philanthropy in Victorian Scotland: Social Welfare and the Voluntary Principle* (Edinburgh: Donald, 1980).

Clark, J. C. D, 'Secularization and Modernization: the Failure of a "Grand Narrative"', *Historical Journal*, 55 (2012), pp. 161–94.

Coleman, B. I., *The Church of England in the Mid-Nineteenth Century: A Social Geography* (London: Historical Association, 1980).

Covert, J. T. (ed.), *Memoir of a Victorian Woman: Reflections of Louise Creighton, 1850–1936* (London: Hambledon London, 2000).

Cox, J., *The English Churches in a Secular Society: Lambeth, 1870–1930* (Oxford: Oxford University Press, 1982).

—, 'Master Narratives of Long-term Religious Change', in H. McLeod and W. Ustorf, *The Decline of Christendom in Western Europe, 1750–2000* (Cambridge: Cambridge University Press, 2003), pp. 201–17.

Cropper, M., *The Girls' Diocesan Association 1901–1961 and Spearhead 1961–1964* (London, 1976).

Currie, R., A. Gilbert, and L. Horsley, *Churches and Church-Goers: Patterns of Church Growth in the British Isles since 1700* (Oxford: Oxford University Press, 1977).

Dakers, C., *A Genius for Money: Business, Art and the Morrisons* (New Haven, CT: Yale University Press, 2011).

Daunton, M. J., *House and Home in the Victorian City: Working Class Housing 1850–1914* (London: Edward Arnold, 1983).

Davie, G., *Religion in Britain Since 1945* (Oxford: Blackwell, 2002).

Dawson, D. G., 'Funding Mission in the Early Twentieth Century', *International Bulletin of Missionary Research*, 24:4 (October 2000), pp. 155–8.

Dyer, G. R., 'The "Vanity Fair" in Nineteenth Century England: Commerce, Women and the East in the Ladies' Bazaar', *Nineteenth-Century Literature*, 46:2 (September 1991), pp. 196–222.

Ellens, J. P., *Religious Routes to Gladstonian Liberalism: The Church Rate Conflict in England and Wales, 1832–1868* (University Park, PA: Pennsylvania State University Press, 1994).

Erdozain, D., *The Problem of Pleasure: Sport, Recreation and the Crisis of Victorian Religion* (Woodbridge: Boydell, 2010).

Erdozain, D., 'The Secularisation of Sin in the Nineteenth Century', *Journal of Ecclesiastical History*, 62:1 (2011), pp. 59–88.

Eskridge, L. and M. Noll (eds), *More Money, More Ministry: Money and Evangelicals in Recent North American History* (Grand Rapids, MI: W. B. Eerdmans, 2000).

Flew, S., 'Money Matters: The Neglect of Finance in the Historiography of Modern Christianity', in P. Clarke and C. Methuen (eds), *The Church on its Past*, Studies in Church History Volume 49 (Woodbridge: Boydell and Brewer: 2013), pp. 430–43.

Garnett, J., "Gold and the Gospel': Systematic Beneficence in Mid-Nineteenth Century England', in W. J. Sheils and D. Wood (eds), *The Church and Wealth*, Studies in Church History 24 (Oxford: Basil Blackwell, 1987), pp. 347–58.

Gilbert, A. D., *Religion and Society in Industrial England: Church, Chapel and Social Change, 1740–1914* (London: Longmans, 1976).

Gill, S., *Women and the Church of England* (London: SPCK, 1994).

Glock, C. Y. and R. Stark, *Religion and Society in Tension* (Chicago, IL: Rand McNally, 1966).

Gordon, B., *Bazaar and Fair Ladies: The History of the American Fundraising Fair* (Knoxville, TN: University of Tennessee Press, 1998).

Gorsky, M., *Patterns of Philanthropy: Charity and Society in Nineteenth-Century Bristol* (New York: Boydell Press, 1999).

Green, S. J. D., 'The Death of Pew Rents, the Rise of Bazaars, and the End of the Traditional Political Economy of Voluntary Religious Organisations: the Case of the West Riding of Yorkshire, c.1870–1914', *Northern History*, 27 (1991), pp.198–235.

—, *Religion in the Age of Decline: Organisation and Experience in Industrial Yorkshire, 1870–1920* (Cambridge: Cambridge University Press, 1996).

—, *The Passing of Protestant England: Secularisation and Social Change, c. 1920–1960* (Cambridge: Cambridge University Press, 2011).

Greenbank, A. J., '*This is the Lord's Doing!': An account of 150 years of Open-Air Evangelism through the Work of the Open Air Mission 1853–2003* (London: Open Air Mission, 2003).

Heeney, B., *The Women's Movement in the Church of England, 1850–1930* (Oxford: Clarendon, 1988).

Hilton, B., *The Age of Atonement: The Influence of Evangelicalism on Social and Economic Thought* (Oxford: Clarendon, 2001).

Hirsch, F., *The Social Limits of Growth* (London: Routledge Kegan and Paul, 1977).

Hoge, D. R., C. Zech, P. McNamara, and M. J. Donahue, 'Giving in Five Denominations', in M. Chaves and S. L Miller (eds), *Financing American Religion* (1999, New York: Rowman Littlefield, 2008), pp. 3–10.

Huxley, G., *Victorian Duke* (London: Oxford University Press, 1967).

Inglis, K. S., *Churches and the Working Classes in Victorian England* (Toronto: University of Toronto Press, 1963).

Jeremy, D. J. (ed.), *Dictionary of Business Biography: A Biographical Dictionary of Business Leaders Active in Britain in the Period 1860–1980* (London: Butterworths, 1984).

—, *Capitalists and Christians: Business Leaders and the Churches in Britain, 1900–1960* (Oxford: Clarendon, 1990).

— (ed.), *Religion, Business, and Wealth in Modern Britain* (London: Routledge, 1998).

Johnston, D. A. H., *Stewardship and the Gospel*, abridged 2nd edn (Exeter: Short Run Press, 1995).

Jones, G. S., *Outcast London: A Study in the Relationship between Classes in Victorian Society* (Oxford: Clarendon Press, 1971).

Jordan, W. K., *Philanthropy in England 1480–1660: A Study of the Changing Pattern of English Social Aspirations* (New York: Russell Sage Foundation, 1959).

Knight, F., *The Nineteenth Century and English Society* (Cambridge: Cambridge University Press, 1998).

Lewis, D. M., *Lighten their Darkness: The Evangelical Mission to Working-Class London, 1828–1860* (London: Greenwood, 1986).

— (ed.), *The Blackwell Dictionary of Evangelical Biography, 1730–1860,* 2 vols (Oxford: Blackwell Reference, 1995).

Luddy, M., *Women and Philanthropy in Nineteenth-Century Ireland* (Cambridge: Cambridge University Press, 1995).

Mangion, C. M., 'Developing Alliances: Faith, Philanthropy and Fundraising in Nineteenth-Century England', in M. Van Dijck, J. de Maeyer, J. Koppen and J. Tyssens (eds), *The Economics of Providence: Management, Finances and Patrimony of Religious Orders and Congregations in Europe 1773–1931* (Leuven, Belgium: Leuven University Press, 2013), pp. 205–26.

Matthew, H. C. G., *The Gladstone Diaries,* 14 vols (Oxford: Clarendon Press, 1978).

McLeod, H., *Class and Religion in the Late Victorian City* (London: Croom Helm, 1974).

—, 'White Collar Values and the Role of Religion', in G. E. Crossick, *Lower Middle Class in Britain, 1817–1914* (London: Croom Helm, 1977), pp. 61–88.

—, *The Religious Crisis of the 1960s* (Oxford: Oxford University Press, 2007).

Michie, R. C., 'Income, Expenditure and Investment of a Victorian Millionaire: Lord Overstone, 1823–83', *Historical Research*, 58 (1985), pp. 59–77.

Miller, S. L., 'The Meaning of Religious Giving', in M. Chaves and S. L. Miller (eds), *Financing American Religion* (New York: Rowman Littlefield, 2008), pp. 37–45.

Mole, D. E. H., 'The Victorian Town Parish: Rural Vision and Urban Mission', in D. Baker (ed.), *The Church in Town and Countryside*, Studies in Church History 16 (Oxford: Basil Blackwell, 1979), pp. 361–71.

Morris, J., 'The Strange Death of Christian Britain: Another Look at the Secularization Debate', *Historical Journal*, 46: 4 (2003), pp. 963–76.

—, 'Secularization and Religious Experience: Arguments in the Historiography of Modern British Religion', *Historical Journal*, 55:1 (2012), pp. 195–219.

Morris, J. N., *Religion and Urban Change: Croydon, 1840–1914* (Woodbridge: Boydell, 1992).

Morris, R. J., *Class, Sect and Party: The Making of the British Middle Class, Leeds 1820–1850* (Manchester: Manchester University Press, 1990).

Morris, R. M. (ed.), *Church and State in 21st Century Britain: The Future of Church Establishment* (Basingstoke: Palgrave Macmillan, 2009).

Mumm, S., *Stolen Daughters, Virgin Mothers: Anglican Sisterhoods in Victorian Britain* (London: Leicester University Press, 1999).

Noll, M. A. (ed.), *God and Mammon: Protestants, Money, and the Market, 1790–1860* (Oxford: Oxford University Press, 2002).

Orton, D., *Made of Gold: A Biography of Angela Burdett Coutts* (London: Hamish Hamilton, 1980).

Oxford Dictionary of National Biography.

Owen, D. E., *English Philanthropy, 1660–1960* (Cambridge, MA: Harvard University Press, 1965).

Poole, A. G., *Philanthropy and the Construction of Victorian Women's Citizenship* (Toronto: University of Toronto Press, 2014).

Port, M. H., *Six Hundred New Churches: The Church Building Commission, 1818–1856* (Reading: Spire Books, 2006).

Prochaska, F. K., *Women and Philanthropy in Nineteenth Century England* (Oxford: Oxford University Press, 1980).

—, *The Voluntary Impulse: Philanthropy in Modern Britain* (London: Faber, 1988).

Ralls, W., 'The Papal Aggression of 1850: A Study in Victorian Anti-Catholicism', *Church History*, 43 (1974), pp. 242–56.

Rubinstein, W. D., *Men of Property: The Very Wealthy in Britain Since the Industrial Revolution* (London: Croom Helm, 1981).

—, *Wealth and Inequality in Britain* (London: Faber, 1986).

Sabine, B. E. V., *A History of Income Tax* (London: George Allen and Unwin, 1966).

Sandel, M. J., *What Money Can't Buy: The Moral Limits of Markets* (London: Penguin Books, 2013).

Sheils, W. J., and D. Wood (eds), *The Church and Wealth*, Studies in Church History 24 (Oxford: Basil Blackwell, 1987).

Smart, N., *The World's Religions* (Cambridge: Cambridge University Press, 1989).

Smith, M., *Religion in Industrial Society: Oldham and Saddleworth, 1740–1865* (Oxford: Clarendon Press, 1994).

Soloway, R. A., *Prelates and People: Ecclesiastical Social Thought in England, 1783–1852* (London: Routledge and Kegan Paul, 1969).

Tener, R. H., 'Breaking the Code of Anonymity: The Case of the "Spectator", 1861–1897', *The Yearbook of English Studies*, Literary Periodicals Special Number 16 (1986), pp. 63–73.

Thompson, K. A, *Bureaucracy and Church Reform: The Organizational Response of the Church of England to Social Change, 1800–1965* (Oxford: Clarendon, 1970).

Thornes, R., *Men of Iron: The Fussells of Mells* (Frome: Frome Society for Local Study, 2010).

Travis, J. F., *The Rise of the Devon Seaside Resorts, 1750–1900* (Exeter: University of Exeter Press, 1993).

Walsh, J., 'Wesley and the Poor', *Revue Francaise de Civilisation Britannique*, 6:3 (1991), pp. 17–30.

Walton, J. K., *The English Seaside Resort: A Social History, 1750–1914* (Leicester: Leicester University Press, 1983).

Whitlock, T. C. *Crime, Gender and Consumer Culture in Nineteenth Century England* (Aldershot: Ashgate, 2005).

Wickham, E. R., *Church and People in an Industrial City* (London: Lutterworth, 1957).

Wilks, M., 'Thesaurus Ecclesias (Presidential Address)', in W. Sheils and D. Wood (eds), *The Church and Wealth*, Studies in Church History 24 (Cambridge: Boydell and Brewer, 1987), pp. xv–xlv.

Williams, S. C., *Religious Belief and Popular Culture in Southwark, c. 1880–1939* (Oxford: Oxford University Press, 1999).

Williams, S., 'The Language of Belief: An Alternative Agenda for the Study of Victorian Working-Class Religion', *Journal of Victorian Culture*, 1:2 (1996), pp. 303–17.

Wilson, B., *Contemporary Transformations of Religion* (Oxford: Oxford University Press, 1979).

Wuthnow, R., and V. A. Hodgkinson, 'Introduction', *Faith and Philanthropy in America: Exploring the Role of Religion in America's Voluntary Sector* (San Francisco, CA: Jossey-Bass, 1990).

Yates, N., *Anglican Ritualism in Victorian Britain, 1830–1910* (Oxford: Clarendon, 1999).

Yeo, S., *Religion and Voluntary Organisations in Crisis* (London: Croom Helm, 1976).

Unpublished Theses

Baud, H., 'Laura Ridding (1849–1939): The Life and Service of a Bishop's Wife' (PhD thesis, University of Gloucestershire, 2003).

Bennett, J. C., 'The English Anglican Practice of Pew-Renting, 1800–1960' (PhD thesis, University of Birmingham, 2011).

Coleman, B. I., 'Church Extension Movement in London *c.*1800–1860' (PhD thesis, University of Cambridge, 1968).

Coolidge, C. W., 'The Finance of the Church of England, 1830–50' (PhD thesis, Trinity College, Dublin, 1958).

Cooper, P. H. M., 'The Church in St. Pancras, 1811–1868' (PhD thesis, University of London, 1976).

Flew, S., 'Philanthropy and Secularisation: The Funding of Anglican Religious Voluntary Organisations in London, 1856 to 1914' (PhD thesis, The Open University, 2013).

Garnett, J., 'Aspects of the Relationship between Protestant Ethics and Economic Activity in Mid-Victorian England' (DPhil thesis, University of Oxford, 1986).

Lankford, J. E., 'Protestant Stewardship and Benevolence, 1900–1941: A Study of Religious Philanthropy' (PhD thesis, University of Wisconsin, 1962).

Maxfield, C. A., 'The "Reflex Influence" of Missions: The Domestic Operations of the American Board of Commissioners for Foreign Missions, 1810–1850' (PhD thesis, Union Theological Seminary, 1995).

Orr-Nimmo, K. W., 'Changes in the Methods of Financing of the Church of England, *c.*1870–1920 with Special Reference to the Parochial Clergy' (DPhil thesis, University of Oxford, 1983).

Stanley, B., 'Home Support for Overseas Missions in Early Victorian England, *c.*1838–1873' (DPhil thesis, University of Oxford, 1979).

NOTES

Introduction

1. M. Wilks, 'Thesaurus Ecclesias (Presidential Address)', in W. Sheils and D. Wood (eds), *The Church and Wealth*, Studies in Church History 24 (Cambridge: Boydell and Brewer, 1987), pp. xv–xlv, on p. xv.

2. S. Flew, 'Money Matters: The Neglect of Finance in the Historiography of Modern Christianity', in P. Clarke and C. Methuen (eds), *The Church on its Past*, Studies in Church History 49 (Woodbridge: Boydell and Brewer: 2013), pp. 430–43.

3. B. Wilson, *Contemporary Transformations of Religion* (Oxford: Oxford University Press, 1979), p. 25.

4. See Table A.7 for population figures for the Diocese of London.

5. E. L. Cutts, *On Church Extension and New Endowments* (London: Rivingtons, 1860), p. 25. Cutts was Vicar of Holy Trinity, Haverstock Hill, 1871–1901 and secretary of the Additional Curates' Society, 1865–1871.

6. M. Gorsky, *Patterns of Philanthropy: Charity and Society in Nineteenth-Century Bristol* (New York: Boydell Press, 1999), pp. 32–4. Most of the philanthropists listed in the directory *The Charitable Ten Thousand* (published in 1896 and 1904) have London addresses.

7. Examples of such London based studies: J. Cox, *The English Churches in a Secular Society: Lambeth, 1870–1930* (Oxford: Oxford University Press, 1982); H. McLeod, *Class and Religion in the Late Victorian City* (London: Croom Helm, 1974); and S. C. Williams, *Religious Belief and Popular Culture in Southwark, c. 1880–1939* (Oxford: Oxford University Press, 1999).

8. D. E. Owen, *English Philanthropy, 1660–1960* (Cambridge, MA: Harvard University Press, 1965), p. 479.

9. For example, Olive Checkland refers to the Dick bequest saying it was 'one of the most interesting of the educational endowments in Victorian Scotland', and yet supplies only the briefest information about James Dick. O. Checkland, *Philanthropy in Victorian Scotland: Social Welfare and the Voluntary Principle* (Edinburgh: Donald, 1980), p. 105.

10. R. Wuthnow and V. A. Hodgkinson, 'Introduction', *Faith and Philanthropy in America: Exploring the Role of Religion in America's Voluntary Sector* (San Francisco, CA: Jossey-Bass, 1990), p. xiii.

1 The Earlier Stages Of Home Mission In London, 1800–56

1. Walsh, in 1887, held the post of Superintendent of Missionaries and Clerical Secretary to the London Diocesan Home Mission [hereafter LDHM] and had been the Vicar

of St Matthew, Newington (1879–86). W. Walsh, *Progress of the Church in London During the Last Fifty Years* (London: Rivingtons, 1887), pp. 3–4. This volume was updated in 1908 to cover the extended period 1837 to 1908; this timeframe coincided to include the LDHM's fiftieth Jubilee of 1907: W. Walsh, *Progress of the Church in London: From the Accession of Queen Victoria to 1908* (London: SPCK, 1908). Walsh went on to become Bishop of Mauritius (1891–7) and Bishop of Dover (1898–1916).

2. In 1801, the population of in England and Wales stood at nine million; by 1851 this figure had doubled to eighteen million. J. Burnett, *A History of the Cost of Living* (Aldershot: Gregg Revivals, 1993 [1969]), p. 191; and M. Ball and D. Sutherland, *An Economic History of London, 1800–1914* (London: Routledge, 2001), p. 44.

3. D. E. H. Mole, 'The Victorian Town Parish: Rural Vision and Urban Mission', in D. Baker (ed.), *The Church in Town and Countryside*, Studies in Church History 16 (Oxford: Basil Blackwell, 1979), pp. 361–71, on p. 364.

4. R. A. Soloway, *Prelates and People: Ecclesiastical Social Thought in England, 1783–1852* (London: Routledge and Kegan Paul, 1969), pp. 286–8.

5. M. H. Port, *Six Hundred New Churches: The Church Building Commission, 1818–1856* (Reading: Spire Books, 2006), p. 26.

6. R. Yates, *The Church in Danger* (London: Rivington, 1815).

7. W. Walsh, *Progress of the Church in London During the Last Fifty Years* (London: Rivingtons, 1887), p. 11; and Port, *Six Hundred New Churches*, p. 9.

8. Walsh, *Progress of the Church in London During the Last Fifty Years*, pp. 12–13; and Port, *Six Hundred New Churches*, p. 227.

9. Port, *Six Hundred New Churches*, pp. 231, 325–47; this lists the cost of each church and the amount of the grant given.

10. F. Knight, *The Nineteenth Century and English Society* (Cambridge: Cambridge University Press, 1998), p. 64; and Port, *Six Hundred New Churches*, p. 253.

11. J. P. Ellens, *Religious Routes to Gladstonian Liberalism: The Church Rate Conflict in England and Wales, 1832–1868* (University Park, PA: Pennsylvania State University Press, 1994), p. 2.

12. The permanent body of the Ecclesiastical Commissioners sprang from the earlier 1832 Ecclesiastical Revenues Commission which was formed to investigate Church finance. S. J. Brown, *The National Churches of England, Ireland, and Scotland, 1801–1846* (Oxford: Oxford University Press, 2001), p. 189.

13. Brown, *National Churches*, p. 235.

14. Brown, *National Churches*, pp. 235–36. *The Times* also mentions petitions from Nonconformists against the proposed grant for church extension: *The Times*, 30 June 1840, p. 6. See also R. H. Inglis, *Church Extension: Substance of a Speech Delivered in the House of Commons on Tuesday 30th June 1840* (London: J. Hatchard and Son, 1840), pp. 49–50, 324–5, 340.

15. Occasionally individuals continued to raise the subject. In the wake of the publication of Mann's census report, in 1854, George William Finch-Hatton (1791–1858), tenth Earl of Winchilsea called for new state funds for church building. See Sir George Grey's speech in a debate on church extension. Hansard, Commons Debates, fifth series, vol. 118, cc. 30–102: 01 July 1851; and Londinensis [William Rivington], *Our Church Extension Societies, General and Diocesan* (London: Harrison, 1855), p. 3.

16. This form of collecting funds was introduced as a replacement for the church brief. Church briefs were an official instruction directing collections to be made in churches or in the form of house-to-house collections. In 1828 they were abolished (9 Geo IV c.

42) because of abuses of the scheme, and because of the smallness of the sums collected. At the instigation of the High Churchmen Joshua Watson and Christopher Wordsworth (1774–1846), the church brief was replaced by the royal letter. E. Churton, *Memoir of Joshua Watson* (Oxford: J. H. and J. Parker, 1861), pp. 191–2, 297.

17. W. A. Bewes, *Church Briefs or Royal Warrants for Collections for Charitable Objects* (London: Black, 1896), pp. 1, 45–6; and C. Walford, 'Kings' Briefs: Their Purposes and History', *Transactions of the Royal Historical Society*, 10 (1882), pp. 1–74, on p. 1.

18. 'Church Briefs and King's Letters', *British Magazine*, October 1832, pp. 164–5.

19. Bewes, *Church Briefs*, p. 1, 45–6.

20. Incorporated Church Building Society, *Refusal of Royal Letters to the Church Building Society* (London, 1855), pp. 4–11.

21. *Guardian,* 16 October 1855, p. 377; *Guardian* 24 October 1855, p. 789.

22. *The Times,* 22 September 1856, p. 7; *Guardian,* 16 October 1855, p. 377; *Daily News,* 23 September 1856, p. 2.

23. S. J. Brown, *The National Churches of England, Ireland, and Scotland, 1801–1846* (Oxford: Oxford University Press, 2001), p. 208; and A. Burns, *The Diocesan Revival in the Church of England, c.*1800–1870 (Oxford: Clarendon Press, 1999), p. 116.

24. S. J. Brown, 'Chalmers, Thomas (1780–1847)', ODNB.

25. B. Noel, *The State of the Metropolis Considered: A Letter to the Bishop of London* (London: James Nisbet, 1835), pp. 34–5.

26. Noel, *State of the Metropolis Considered*, pp. 51–2.

27. E. B. Pusey, *Churches in London: Past and Present Exertions of the Church and Present Needs, with an Appendix Containing Answers to Objections Raised by the 'Record' and Others to the Plan of the Metropolis Churches' Fund* (London: Baxter, 1837); and H. P. Liddon, *Life of Edward Bouverie Pusey*, 2 vols (London, Longmans Green, 1893), vol. 1, p. 327.

28. C. J. Blomfield, *Proposals for the Creation of a Fund to be Applied to the Building and Endowment of Additional Churches in the Metropolis* (London: B. Fellowes, 1836), pp. 8–9.

29. Blomfield, *Proposals for the Creation of a Fund*, p. 9. Chalmers' scheme in Glasgow was established in 1819; Chester Diocesan Church Building Society was established in 1834. Burns, *The Diocesan Revival,* p. 116.

30. Blomfield, *Proposals for the Creation of a Fund*, p. 5; *From His Majesty's Commissioners Appointed to Consider the State of the Established Church with Reference to Ecclesiastical Duties and Rrevenues. With a Synopsis of Both Reports,* 1836 (86), p. 6.

31. *Final Report of the Metropolis Churches Fund* [hereafter MCF], pp. 3–4.

32. This echoed the scheme introduced by act of parliament in 1711, to build fifty new churches in the reign of Queen Anne. R. H. Inglis, *Church Extension: Substance of a Speech Delivered in the House of Commons on Tuesday 30th June 1840* (London: J. Hatchard and Son, 1840), p. 44.

33. Pusey, *Churches in London*, p. 15.

34. A. Blomfield (ed.), *A Memoir of C. J. Blomfield, Bishop of London, with Selections from his Correspondence,* 2 vols (London: John Murray, 1863), p. 237.

35. Blomfield, *A Memoir of C. J. Blomfield*, vol. 1, p. 236. An example of another High Church member: the barrister John Duke Coleridge, first Baron Coleridge (1820–1894); and another Evangelical member: Sir Robert Harry Inglis (1786–1855).

36. Blomfield, *A Memoir of C. J. Blomfield*, vol. 1, p. 235; R. A. Soloway, *Prelates and People: Ecclesiastical Social Thought in England, 1783–1852* (London: Routledge and Kegan Paul, 1969), p. 313; and M. H. Port, *Six Hundred New Churches: The Church Building Commission, 1818–1856* (Reading: Spire Books, 2006), p. 255. This was a

traditional method for raising money for church building but was rejected on the grounds that it was a heavy burden for the poor; this method of funding church building had been used previously in the reigns of Charles II and Queen Anne. W. Walsh, *Progress of the Church in London During the Last Fifty Years* (London: Rivingtons, 1887), p. 9.

37. Blomfield, *A Memoir of C. J. Blomfield*, vol. 1, p. 237.
38. Walsh, *Progress of the Church in London During the Last Fifty Years*, p. 20.
39. *Final Report of the MCF.*
40. Blomfield gave an additional £750 to the BGCSF.
41. *First MCF Annual Report*, p. 9.
42. *Fourth MCF Annual Report*, p. 16.
43. *Fourth MCF Annual Report*, p. 7.
44. 'Ten Years of Church Extension in London', *The Church Builder* (1865), pp. 57–64.
45. See A. Burns, 'My Unfortunate Parish: Anglican Urban Ministry in Bethnal Green 1809- *c.*1850', in M. Barber, G. Sewell, and S. Taylor (eds), *From the Reformation to the Permissive Society: A Miscellany in Celebration of the 400th Anniversary of Lambeth Palace Library*, Church of England Record Society Record Series 18 (Woodbridge: Boydell Press, 2010).
46. *Bethnal Green Churches and Schools Fund* (London: Clowes, 1854), pp. 21, 42, 45.
47. *Final Report of the MCF*, p. 5.
48. B. L. Fitzpatrick, 'Rivington Family (per. *c.*1710–*c.*1960)', *ODNB*.
49. Walsh, *Progress of the Church in London During the Last Fifty Years*, p. 25.
50. Burns, 'My Unfortunate Parish', p. 287.
51. *Third London Diocesan Church Building Society Annual Report*, pp. 26–7.
52. D. E. H. Mole, 'The Victorian Town Parish: Rural Vision and Urban Mission', in D. Baker (ed.), *The Church in Town and Countryside*, Studies in Church History 16 (Oxford: Basil Blackwell, 1979), pp. 361–71, on p. 363.
53. Port, *Six Hundred New Churches*, p. 23.
54. R. A. Soloway, *Prelates and People: Ecclesiastical Social Thought in England, 1783–1852* (London: Routledge and Kegan Paul, 1969), pp. 322–3, 340.
55. D. M. Lewis, *Lighten their Darkness: The Evangelical Mission to Working-Class London, 1828–1860* (London: Greenwood, 1986), pp. 36–8.
56. B. I. Coleman, 'Church Extension Movement in London *c.*1800–1860' (PhD thesis, University of Cambridge, 1968), p. 118.
57. H. P. Liddon, *Life of Edward Bouverie Pusey*, 2 vols (London, Longmans Green, 1893), vol. 1, p. 329.
58. Church Pastoral-Aid Society [hereafter CP-AS], *Abstract of Reports and Speeches at the Twenty-Ninth Meeting of the Church Pastoral-Aid S held at St James's Hall, Piccadilly, on Thursday, May 5, 1864*, p. 7. Its objects were extended to include female lay help in 1890; *Fifty-Sixth Church Pastoral-Aid Society Annual Report*, p. 37.
59. Brown, National Churches, p. 211.
60. Lewis, Lighten Their Darkness, pp. 112–13.
61. Lewis, *Lighten Their Darkness*, pp. 110–11. For Scripture Readers' Association [hereafter SRA] work in Bethnal Green, see *Third Scripture Readers' Association Annual Report*, p. 25.
62. SRA Minute Book, March 1844–June 1847, 18 March 1844, Cadburys Reaearch Library [hereafter CRL], CPAS 4/1/1. Curiously, the minute of 6 April 1844 records that the High Churchmen William Cotton is to be added to the list of committee members; he does not, however, attend any of the meetings.

63. SRA Minute Book, March 1844–June 1847: St John's (minute 21 May 1844); St Phillips and St Matthias (minute 24 May 1844); St James the Less (4 June 1844); St Matthew (7 June 1844); St Bartholomew (11 June 1844); St James the Great (19 July 1844); St Judes (13 September 1844), CRL, CPAS 4/1/1.

64. Walsh, *Progress of the Church in London During the Last Fifty Years*, pp. 24–5.

65. *Illustrated London News*, 7 September 1844, p. 156.

66. The later London diocesan societies (the London Diocesan Church Building Society [hereafter LDCBS] and Bishop of London's Fund [hereafter BLF]) both gave grants for the erection of temporary churches.

67. The census had been commissioned in order to obtain figures regarding the provision of church accommodation for public worship. The report stated that a large percentage of the population did not attend church on census Sunday; even allowing for the non-attendance of the young, the sick and elderly, and those that lived in isolated rural areas. Coleman's reworking of the census statistics calculates that 60.8 per cent of the population of England and Wales attended worship on the census day; and roughly half (48.6 per cent) of these worshippers attended worship in Anglican facilities. In London, only 37 per cent of the population attended worship on the census day; and again roughly half (56.6 per cent) attended in Anglican facilities. B. I. Coleman, *The Church of England in the Mid-Nineteenth Century: A Social Geography* (London: Historical Association, 1980), pp. 7, 41; and *Census of Great Britain, 1851: Religious Worship in England and Wales*, 1852–53 (1690), 89, p. clxii.

68. *Report from the Select Committee of the House of Lords, Appointed to Inquire into the Deficiency of Means of Spiritual Instruction and Places of Divine Worship in the Metropolis, and in Other Populous Districts in England and Wales, Especially in the Mining and Manufacturing Districts; and to Consider the Fittest Means of Meeting the Difficulties of the Case; and to Report thereon to the House; together with the Proceedings of the Committee, Minutes of Evidence, and Appendix*, 1857–58 (387) (387-I), pp. cxxi, cxlviii.

69. *Census of Great Britain*, 1852–53 (1690), p. clxii.

70. Lewis, *Lighten their Darkness*, p. 225; *Census of Great Britain*, 1852–53 (1690), p. clxii.

71. Lewis, *Lighten their Darkness*, p. 225; and *London City Mission Magazine*, June 1854, p. 107.

72. A. J. Greenbank, '*This is the Lord's Doing!': An Account of 150 Years of Open-Air Evangelism through the Work of the Open Air Mission 1853–2003* (London: Open Air Mission, 2003), p. 7.

73. *Second Open-Air Mission Annual Report*, pp. 5–6.

74. *Second Open-Air Mission Annual Report*, p. 11. The Islington Church Home Mission [hereafter ICHM] was eventually absorbed by CP-AS in 1892: *Fifty-Eight CP-AS Annual Report 1892–93*, p. 38.

75. *Sixth ICHM Annual Report*, p. 5.

76. *Sixth ICHM Annual Report*, pp. 29–33.

77. *Christian Observer*, December 1856, p. 840.

78. A. Blomfield (ed.), A Memoir of C. J. Blomfield, Bishop of London, with Selections from his Correspondence, 2 vols (London: John Murray, 1863), vol. 2, p. 165; and C. J. Blomfield, *Charge Delivered to the Clergy of the Diocese of London, at the Visitation in November MDCCCLIV* (London: B. Fellowes, 1854), p. 44.

79. *Christian Observer*, December 1856, p. 841; and leaflet on Islington Church Home Mission, January 1855, Fulham Papers, Blomfield, Lambeth Palace Library, 62 f. 286–7.

80. The Metropolis Churches Fund [hereafter MCF] continued to exist as dormant body within the London Diocesan Church Building Society [hereafter LDCBS] until both

societies were formally closed in 1925. The reason for the continued existence of the MCF was the possibility of the society receiving a large legacy. See LDCBS: minute books and miscellaneous papers, London Metropolitan Archives [hereafter LMA], DL/A/H/052/04/001-002 and DL/A/H/054/04/007.

81. W. Ralls, 'The Papal Aggression of 1850: A Study in Victorian Anti-Catholicism', *Church History*, 43 (1974), p. 243. The Protestant Alliance was established as a consequence of the Papal Aggression.

82. *The Times*, 8 April 1851, p. 2. See also J. Sinclair, *Church Difficulties of 1851: A Charge Delivered to the Clergy of the Archdeaconry of Middlesex, at the Visitations held at St. Paul's, Covent Garden, on the 12th and 13th of May, 1851* (London, 1851), p. 39.

83. The committee included: Bishop Blomfield; William Cotton; Sir Robert Harry Inglis; Lord Robert Grosvenor, first Baron Ebury (1801–93); Anthony Ashley Cooper, seventh Earl of Shaftesbury; Philip Cazenove (1798–1880); Henry Robert Kingscote (1802–82); George William Lyttelton, fourth Baron Lyttelton (1817–76); Sir Walter Rocliffe Farquhar (1810–1900); the Reverend John Hampden Gurney (1802–62); the Reverend Richard Burgess (1796–1881); and Archdeacon John Sinclair (1797–1875). *The Times*, 8 April 1851, p. 2.

84. This later became the office address of the LDCBS and London Diocesan Home Mission [hereafter LDHM].

85. Church Extension Fund, Minute Book, 1851–6, 6 March 1851, London Metropolitan Archives (uncatalogued).

86. Church Extension Fund, Letter Book, 1851–63, letter dated 2 January 1852, LMA (uncatalogued).

87. Church Extension Fund, Minute Book, 1851–6, letter dated 24 March 1852, LMA (uncatalogued).

88. *Church Extension in the Diocese of London: Remarks on the Present State of the Metropolis Churches' Fund, by a Layman* (London: Rivingtons, 1853).

89. *Church Extension in the Diocese of London*, pp. 11, 20. By 1853, the traditional sources of funding church-extension activities in London had dried up. The funds of the Church Building Commissioners were exhausted and the income of the MCF was inconsequential. In addition, the Incorporated Church Building Society's financial situation was now seriously limited by the recent abolition of royal letters.

90. *Church Work among the Masses*, Old Series, 3 (April 1862), pp. 28–9.

91. C. J. Blomfield, Charge Delivered to the Clergy of the Diocese of London, at the Visitation in November MDCCCLIV (London: B. Fellowes, 1854), p. 32.

92. In 1860 Tait's appeal attempted to dispel this perception, saying that it should be thought of as a 'parochial extension society' rather than a church building society. A. C. Tait, *From the Bishop of London to the Laity of the Diocese: Claims of the London Diocesan Church Building Society* (London: Brettell, 1860), p. 3.

93. A. Burns, 'Blomfield, Charles James (1786–1857)', *ODNB;* and A. Blomfield (ed.), *A Memoir of C. J. Blomfield, Bishop of London, with Selections from his Correspondence*, 2 vols (London: John Murray, 1863), vol. 2, pp. 235–9. LDCBS, *Special Appeal to the Landowners and Others Interested in the Welfare of the Metropolis* (London, 1855).

94. *Church Work among the Masses*, Old Series, 4 (July 1862), p. 39.

95. *Church Work among the Masses*, Old Series, 4 (July 1862), p. 39. This magazine ran from May 1861 to August 1865.

96. A. Blomfield (ed.), *A Memoir of C. J. Blomfield, Bishop of London, with Selections from his Correspondence*, 2 vols (London: John Murray, 1863) vol. 2, p. 167; and *Third London Diocesan Church Building Society Annual Report*, pp. 14–15.

97. Blomfield, *A Memoir of C. J. Blomfield*, vol. 2, p. 167.
98. G. Best, *Temporal Pillars: Queen Anne's Bounty, the Ecclesiastical Commissioners, and the Church of England* (Cambridge: Cambridge University Press, 1964), pp. 401–2.
99. Walsh, Progress of the Church in London During the Last Fifty Years, pp. 77–87.
100. *Final Report of the Metropolis Churches Fund*, p. 8.

2 The Consolidation and Further Development of Home Mission under Bishop Tait, 1856–68

1.   R. T. Davidson, *Life of Archibald Campbell Tait,* 2 vols (London: Macmillan, 1891), vol. 1, p. 498.
2.   D. M. Lewis, *Lighten their Darkness: The Evangelical Mission to Working-Class London, 1828–1860* (London: Greenwood, 1986), p. 253; and Davidson, *Life of Archibald Campbell Tait,* vol. 1, p. 255.
3.   Davidson, *Life of Archibald Campbell Tait,* vol. 1, p. 498.
4.   In contrast to the relatively low income of the London Diocesan Church Building Society [hereafter LDCBS], the annual income of the interdenominational London City Mission rose through this period from around £20,000 a year in 1850, to around £32,000 in 1856. See D. M. Lewis, *Lighten their Darkness: The Evangelical Mission to Working-Class London, 1828–1860* (London: Greenwood, 1986), p. 277.
5.   The 1858–9 receipts were still at a modest level of £5,554, and this figure includes £216 in repaid loans. *Fifth LDCBS Annual Report*, p. 5.
6.   A. C. Tait, *Charge Delivered in November 1858 to the Clergy of the Diocese of London, at his Primary Visitation by Archibald Campbell, Lord Bishop of London* (London: Rivingtons, 1858).
7.   *Census of Great Britain, 1851: Religious Worship in England and Wales*, 1852–3 (1690), 89, pp. cxxv, cxxix.
8.   *Census of Great Britain*, p. cxxxix, appendix 'Detailed Tables', p. 7.
9.   *Report from the Select Committee of the House of Lords*, 1857–8 (387) (387-I), p. iii; and *The Times*, 12 August 1858, p. 6.
10. Stook's list of 'Parishes and Districts in the Metropolis with Populations from 1,000 to upwards of 30,000', in *Report from the Select Committee of the House of Lords*, p. 88.
11. *The Times*, 12 August 1858, p. 6.
12. *Church Work among the Masses*, New Series, 5 (December 1863), p. 70.
13. LDCBS General Committee Minute Book, vol. 1: 1854–64, 8 July 1859, London Metropolitan Archives, DL/A/H/054/01.
14. A. C. Tait, *From the Bishop of London to the Laity of the Diocese: Claims of the London Diocesan Church Building Society* (London: Brettell, 1860), p. 3.
15. This object was introduced in the summer of 1857. *Third LDCBS Annual Report*, pp. 10–11, 19. See also LDCBS General Committee Minute Book, vol. 1: 1854–64, 10 April 1863, London Metropolitan Archives, DL/A/H/054/01; LDCBS Sub-Committee Minute Book, 1855–66, 19 January 1857, London Metropolitan Archives, DL/A/H/054/02/001.
16. *Bethnal Green Churches and Schools Fund* (London: Clowes, 1854), p. 30.
17. *Church Work among the Masses*, Old Series, 3 (April 1862), pp. 29–30; and *Third LDCBS Annual Report,* p. 3. The school-church, a new initiative first used in that year, was a multi-purpose building which could be used on weekdays as a school and on Sundays as a church. Walsh, *Progress of the Church in London During the Last Fifty Years*, pp. 34–5; and *The Times*, 2 February 1857, p. 7.

18. Islington Church Extension Society [hereafter ICES], 'Report of Proceedings at the Inaugural Meeting of the ICES with Speeches delivered by the Rt. Hon. and Rt. Rev the Lord Bishop of London', *Occasional Papers, 1 (1 January 1857),* p. 9.

19. ICES, Occasional Papers, 1 (1 January 1857), p.10.

20. ICES, Occasional Papers, 1 (1 January 1857), pp. 2, 6–7.

21. ICES, Occasional Papers, 1 (1 January 1857), pp. 9–11; and E. Stock, *History of the Church Missionary Society,* 2 vols (London: Church Missionary Society, 1899), vol. 2, p. 27.

22. *First London Diocesan Home Mission* [hereafter LDHM] *Annual Report,* p. 4.

23. A. C. Tait, *Charge Delivered in November 1858 to the Clergy of the Diocese of London, at his Primary Visitation by Archibald Campbell, Lord Bishop of London* (London: Rivingtons, 1858), p. 86.

24. *Eighth LDHM Annual Report,* p. 34.

25. *Eighth LDHM Annual Report,* pp. 40–1. Ryder was a committee member of Church Pastoral-Aid Society [hereafter CP-AS], Scripture Readers' Association [hereafter SRA], LDHM and Bishop of London's Fund [hereafter BLF].

26. *Eighth LDHM Annual Report,* pp. 10–12. The total cost of the church (site, fabric and fittings) was £6,300.

27. R. T. Davidson, *Life of Archibald Campbell Tait,* 2 vols (London: Macmillan, 1891), vol. 1, p. 260; *The Times,* 24 December 1857 p. 7; LDHM Committee Minute Book, vol. 1: 1857–87, 23 December 1857, London Metropolitan Archives [hereafter LMA], DL/A/H/MS31992.

28. *Eighth LDHM Annual Report,* p. 34.

29. W. Walsh, *Progress of the Church in London During the Last Fifty Years,* pp. 4, 67; LDHM Committee Minute Book, vol. 1: 1857–87, 11 Dec 1873, LMA, DL/A/H/MS31992.

30. Examples of Evangelical committee members: the brewer Robert Culling Hanbury (1823–67); Arthur Fitzgerald Kinnaird, tenth Baron Kinnaird (1814–87); Reverend Thomas Dale; Reverend John Sinclair, Archdeacon of Middlesex; Reverend John Hampden Gurney; Reverend Edward Rhys Jones (1817–99); and Reverend William Weldon Champneys (1807–75). Several of these Evangelicals were also Scripture Readers' Association committee members: Dudley Ryder, second Earl of Harrowby (1798–1882); Lord Robert Grosvenor, first Baron Ebury; Anthony Ashley Cooper, seventh Earl of Shaftesbury; William Francis Cowper-Temple, Baron Mount-Temple (1811–88), and Sir Walter Rockliffe Farquhar. Examples of High Church committee members: Reverend Richard William Jelf (1798–1871); George William Lyttelton, fourth Baron Lyttelton; and Henry Howard Molyneux Herbert, fourth Earl of Carnarvon (1831–90).

31. Davidson, *Life of Archibald Campbell Tait,* vol. 1, p. 261; and *Guardian,* 25 November 1857, p. 910.

32. D. M. Lewis, *Lighten their Darkness: The Evangelical Mission to Working-Class London, 1828–1860* (London: Greenwood, 1986), p. 258. *The Record,* 8 January 1858, p. 2; 11 January 1858, p. 4; 3 March 1858, p. 1.

33. See N. Yates, *Anglican Ritualism in Victorian Britain, 1830–1910* (Oxford: Clarendon, 1999).

34. Davidson, *Life of Archibald Campbell Tait,* vol. 1, p. 440.

35. P. T. Marsh, 'Tait, Archibald Campbell (1811–1882)', ODNB.

36. A. C. Tait, *Charge Delivered in November 1858 to the Clergy of the Diocese of London, at his Primary Visitation by Archibald Campbell, Lord Bishop of London* (London: Rivingtons, 1858), pp. 98–9.

37. Davidson, *Life of Archibald Campbell Tait*, vol. 1, p. 501.

38. Davidson, *Life of Archibald Campbell Tait*, vol. 1, p. 444.

39. A. C. Tait, *A Charge Delivered in December, 1862, to the Clergy of the Diocese of London, etc.* (London: Rivingtons, 1862), p. 62.

40. *Church Work Among the Masses*, New Series, 5 (December 1863), p. 69. This article was written by the Reverend James Edward Kempe, Rector of St James, Piccadilly.

41. *Church Work Among the Masses*, New Series, 5 (December 1863), p. 69. A list of the churches consecrated by Blomfield can be found in Tait, *Charge Delivered in November 1858*, Appendix A.

42. Tait, *A Charge Delivered in December, 1862*, p. 62.

43. Girdlestone owned some chambers in Lincoln's Inn. *The Church Builder*, 1864, p. 65; and C. Girdlestone, *A Letter to the Right Hon. and Right Reverend the Lord Bishop of London* (London: Rivingtons, 1863).

44. *The Times*, 30 April 1863, p. 14.

45. *The Times*, 2 May 1863, p. 10; 4 May 1863, p. 5.

46. A. C. Tait, *The Spiritual Wants of the Metropolis and its Suburbs. A Letter to the Laity of the Diocese of London ... With a statement by the Executive Committee of "The Bishop of London's Fund"'* (London: Rivingtons, 1863).

47. The more modestly sized committee (46 members plus the rural deans) of the London Diocesan Church Building Society in 1856 had only two marquises and three earls (no dukes or viscounts). Likewise the Metropolis Churches Fund [hereafter MCF] committee of 1837 numbered 43 individuals, of which there was only one Earl (no dukes, marquises or viscounts).

48. *The Record*, 26 June 1863, p. 2.

49. Also: Henry Hucks Gibbs, first Baron Aldenham (1819–1907); Reverend Frederick George Blomfield (1823–79); the banker Philip Cazenove (treasurer of several religious charities: Society for the Propagation of the Gospel in Foreign Parts, Society for Promoting Christian Knowledge [hereafter SPCK], National Society, Additional Curates' Society [hereafter ACS]; William Tatton Egerton, first Baron Egerton (1806–83); Sir Walter Rockliffe Farquhar; William Page Wood, first Baron Hatherley (1801–81); Reverend Dr James Augustus Hessey (1814–92), chair of the SPCK; Alexander James Beresford Beresford Hope; Reverend William Gilson Humphry (1815–86), treasurer of the SPCK; William Henry Leigh, second Baron Leigh (1824–1905); Horatio Nelson, third Earl Nelson (1823–1913); Walter Charles James, first Baron Nortbourne (1816–93); and the printer William Rivington.

50. BLF, *Statistics as to the Religious Condition of London, Ascertained by Inquiries in Connexion with the Bishop of London's Fund for Providing for the Spiritual Wants of the Metropolis and its Suburbs* (London: Rivingtons, 1864), pp. 3–4. Fifteen years later, in 1879, Andrew Mearns (of the London Congregational Union) published a statistical review of all church accommodation in London. This set out the current church accommodation provided by all denominations, area by area, with a view to calculate the current level of deficiency. Overall, it calculated that the denominations in London were still only supplying accommodation for 31% of the population instead of the accepted standard of 58% population. And of this 31% the Church of England had lost some of its market share (Church of England provision 16%; all other provision 15%). See London Congregational Union, *Religious Statistics of London*, (London: Warren Hall and James J. Lovitt, 1879); see file relating to the Commissioners of Woods and Forests,Office of Woods, Forests and Land Revenues: papers, The National Archives, CRES 40/103.

51. BLF, *Statistics as to the Religious Condition*, pp. 7, 9.
52. BLF, *Statistics as to the Religious Condition*, pp. 6–7.
53. BLF, *Statistics as to the Religious Condition*, pp. 7–9.
54. C. J. Blomfield, *Proposals for the Creation of a Fund to be Applied to the Building and Endowment of Additional Churches in the Metropolis* (London: B. Fellowes, 1836), p. 5. See also D. E. H. Mole, 'The Victorian Town Parish: Rural Vision and Urban Mission', in D. Baker (ed.), *The Church in Town and Countryside*, Studies in Church History 16 (Oxford: Basil Blackwell, 1979), pp. 361–71, on p. 362.
55. BLF, *Statistics as to the Religious Condition*, p. 5; and *Report from the Select Committee of the House of Lords*, 1857–58 (387) (387-I), p. vii.
56. *Twenty-Ninth CP-AS Annual Report 1863–64*, pp. 17–18.
57. BLF Origination Committee Minute Book, 1864–6, LMA, DL/A/K/09/04/001.
58. *Fifteenth BLF Annual Report*, pp. 15–16. See development of the Queen's Park Estate.
59. The BLF did also occasionally give small grants for endowment. By 1913 the BLF had only given about £15,000 for this object (from a total income of £1.5 million).
60. *Ninth BLF Annual Report*, pp. 16–22.
61. BLF Origination Committee Minute Book, 1864–6, 24 May 1864; 21 June 1864, LMA, DL/A/K/09/04/001.
62. *First BLF Annual Report*, pp. 16, 37.
63. *Second BLF Annual Report*, p. 17; and *Thirteenth London Diocesan Deaconess Institution* [hereafter LDDI] *Annual Report*, pp. 9-10.
64. *London Diocesan Magazine* [hereafter *LDM*], December 1907, p. 381.
65. *First BLF Annual Report*, p. 13.
66. BLF, *The BLF: Some Account of Work since Midsummer 1863*, 14 (London, 1866–71), p. 2.
67. *The Church Builder*, 1869, p. 61. This figure for the first five years is very similar to the London City Mission equivalent expenditure in this five-year period of about £190,000. The BLF grants given for churches, parsonages and mission buildings were for both the acquisition of sites and the cost of building or hire of temporary building. The grants given for schools were for the acquisition of sites, and for the building of and fitting out of schools. (The school figure includes the annual block grant given to the Diocesan Board of Education). The grants given for living agents were mainly given in the form of annual block grants to societies, such as, ACS, CP-AS, LDDI, Parochial Mission Women Association and SRA. Some grants were also given directly to incumbents to fund the cost of these living agents.
68. BLF, *The BLF for Providing for the Spiritual Wants of the Metropolis and its Suburbs* (London, 1866), p. 1. £7,000 is the average cost for building a church cited by William Walsh (secretary of the LDHM) for both the site and building of a church. Walsh, *Progress of the Church in London During the Last Fifty Years*, p. iv.
69. LDM, July 1895, p. 237.
70. J. Jackson, *Letter from the Bishop of London on the Prospects and Future Work of the Bishop of London's Fund* (London: T. Brettel, 1874), p. 6; and BLF, *The Origin of the Bishop of London's Fund ... and its Work for Fifty Years* (1913). Figure for end of 1873 was £467,910.
71. For comparison, the MCF and the Bethnal Green Churches and Schools Fund together had funded the building of 78 churches (with an additional seven churches funded by individual benefactors) and the employment of 146 additional clergymen.
72. Walsh, *Progress of the Church in London During the Last Fifty Years*, p. 42; J. Jackson, *The Parochial System. A Charge Delivered to the Clergy of the Diocese of London in*

November 1871 (London, 1871), p. 11; and Church Congress, *Report of the Proceedings of Church Congress, 1899*, pp. 34–5.

73. Jackson, *Letter from the Bishop of London,* pp. 4–5. Jackson was referring to 'spiritual destitution' which was a commonly used phrase. See for example, MCF, *Spiritual Destitution in the Metropolis: An Appeal on Behalf of the Metropolis Churches' Fund* (London, 1845).

74. Jackson, *Letter from the Bishop of London,* pp. 9–10.

75. *The Times,* 6 May 1913, p. 6; and BLF, *Origin of the BLF,* p. 9.

76. BLF, *Origin of the BLF,* pp. 5–9.

77. 'Permanent' and 'transient' are the terms used by the Earl of Harrowby, see Chapter 2.

78. *LDM,* December 1907, p. 381.

79. *LDM,* May 1902, pp. 162–3; March 1911, p. 70.

80. London Diocesan Association of Lay Helpers, *Diocesan Organisation of Lay Help: A Paper read at the Conference of the London Diocesan Association of Lay Helpers* (London: Rivingtons, 1868), p. 6.

81. *LDM,* May 1886, pp. 3–7.

82. *LDM,* May 1886, pp. 3–7.

83. *LDM,* May 1886, pp. 3–7.

84. In 1887 it was proposed that the Lay Helpers' Association should become self-supporting. The BLF grant ceased entirely in 1900 and from this point on all costs were met by income raised from membership contributions. *LDM,* June 1887, p. 55; August 1900, p. 342.

85. *Official Yearbook of the Church of England,* 1883, pp. 112–13; 1891, pp. 98–9. In 1891, the Diocesan Readers' Board was formed with the object of supervising the nomination, examination and admission of lay readers in the Diocese of London.

86. *Official Yearbook of the Church of England,* 1909, pp. 101–2.

87. Walsh, *Progress of the Church in London During the Last Fifty Years,* p. 62.

88. East London Church Fund [hereafter ELCF], *Statement of the ELCF 1880–81,* p. 5.

89. *Eighth ELCF Annual Report,* p. 6.

90. *The Times,* 7 June 1882, p. 5.

91. *East London Church Chronicle* [hereafter ELCC], 21:1 (Easter 1909), p. 3.

92. *ELCC,* 14:1 (Lady Day 1902), p. 2.

93. *Seventh ELCF Annual Report,* p. 7. In 1899, the ELCF took over the management of the Rosenthal Fund (also known as the East London Mission to the Jews) and renamed it as the Church of England Fund for Work among the Jews in East and North London. The Rosenthal Fund took its name from its founder Reverend Michael Rosenthal (d. 1907) who had served as curate and as vicar in predominantly Jewish parishes in the East End. Rosenthal was a Lithuanian Jewish rabbi who converted to Christianity; he was ordained as deacon in 1877. ELCF Committee Minute Book, vol. 4: 1896–1900, 30 December 1898; 24 February 1899, LMA, DL/A/K/11/01.

94. Walsh, *Progress of the Church in London During the Last Fifty Years,* p. 47.

95. *LDM,* March 1901, p. 97; ELCF Committee Minute Book, vol. 1: 1880–5, 29 December 1882, LMA, DL/A/K/11/01; and *ELCC,* 3:4 (June 1891), p. 5.

96. L. Williamson, 'Ranyard, Ellen Henrietta (1810–1879)', *ODNB.*

97. C. C. Liddell, *Work in Dark Places* (London: n. p., n. d.), p. iii.

98. R. Palmer, *Memorials: Part I Family and Personal 1766–1865, Part II Personal and Political 1865–1895* (London: Macmillian, 1896–8); Part 1, pp. 352–3; Sankey, 'Talbot, Edward Stuart (1844–1934)', rev. G. Rowell, *ODNB*; J. G. Talbot, *Memorials of Hon. Mrs. John Chetwynd Talbot* (London, Spottiswoode, 1876), p. 6; Parochial Mission Women Association [hereafter PMWA] Committee Minute Book 1876–9, 23 June

1876, Lambeth Palace Library, 1686; and PMWA Minute Committee Book 1909–16, 6 May 1915, Lambeth Palace Library, 1693. Lady Charlotte Hatherley (1804–78) was married to the Liberal politician William Page Wood, first Baron Hatherley (1801–81) who was Lord Chancellor from 1868 to 1872. Lady Laura Selborne (1821–85) was the wife of the Conservative politician Roundell Palmer, first Earl Selborne (1812–95) who succeeded Hatherley as Lord Chancellor. Lady Cecily Susan Montagu of Beaulieu (1835–1915) was married to Conservative politician Lord Henry John Douglas-Scott-Montagu (1832–1905). And finally, the society's president was Caroline Jane Talbot (1809–76) who was the widow of John Chetwynd Talbot (1806–52), leader of the parliamentary bar. She was also the daughter of James Archibald Stuart-Wortley, first Baron Wharncliffe (1776–1845) and Tory politician, thereby making her the aunt of her co-founder Lady Montagu of Beaulieu.

99. Lady Maud Caroline Hamilton (1846–1938) was the wife of Conservative politician Lord George Francis Hamilton (1845–1927).

100. W. P. Wood, *Parochial Mission Women, A Paper Read at Church Congress* (London: Emily Faithfull, 1864), p. 10.

101. A. G. Poole, *Philanthropy and the Construction of Victorian Women's Citizenship* (Toronto: University of Toronto, 2014), p. 76.

102. Wood, *Parochial Mission Women*, p. 5

103. Anonymous, *Go and Do Likewise. A Short Account of Elizabeth, a Parochial Mission Woman. By a Lady Superintendent* (London, 1875), pp. 2–3.

104. *Official Yearbook of the Church of England*, 1915, p. 74.

105. *Official Yearbook of the Church of England*, 1883, pp. 70–1.

106. Bishop of London's Fund [hereafter BLF] Executive Committee Minute Book, vol. 1: 1863–66, 11 January 1864, London Metropolitan Archives, DL/A/K/09/02/001.

107. *Mission Life*, 2:2 (1871), pp. 619–20; PMWA Committee Minute Book 1869–72, 18 Jan 1872, Lambeth Palace Library, 1683.

108. *Official Yearbook of the Church of England*, 1884, p. 75. The western branch was organized by the Lady Louisa Elizabeth Fortescue (1814–99), the maternal aunt of Lady Montagu of Beaulieu.

109. C. F. F. Spencer, *East and West* (London: Longmans Green, 1871), pp. vii–ix. Again, reinforcing the family connections between the PMWA committee members and supporters, Charlotte Spencer was married to Lucy Cavendish's cousin.

110. H. Blackmore, *The Beginning of Women's Ministry: The Revival of the Deaconess in the Nineteenth-Century Church of England*, Church of England Record Society 14 (Woodbridge: Boydell Press, 2007), p. xxi.

111. Sister Joanna [Baldwin], 'The Deaconess Community of St Andrew', *Journal of Ecclesiastical History*, 12:2 (October 1961), p. 225.

112. Ferard, the daughter of a solicitor, was related by marriage to Pelham Dale; her brother was married to his sister. Thomas Pelham Dale was the son of Thomas Dale (Rector of St Pancras).

113. H. P. Dale (ed.), *The Life and Letters of Thomas Pelham Dale*, 2 vols (London: George Allen, 1894), vol. 1, p. 74.

114. T. J. White, 'The (Deaconess) Community of St. Andrew', London Diocesan Deaconess Institution: papers and minute books, 1861–2011, p. 29, Community of St Andrew, London (uncatalogued; due to be transferred to Lambeth Palace Library). The deaconesses introduced vows in 1917; White, 'The (Deaconess) Community of St. Andrew', p. 14.

115. Dale, *Life and Letters of Thomas Pelham Dale*, vol. 1, p. 73; and *Tenth London Diocesan Deaconess Institution* [hereafter LDDI] *Annual Report*, p. 7.

116. *Second LDDI Annual Report*, p. 6; *Fifth LDDI Annual Report*, pp. 5-6; *Eleventh LDDI Annual Report*, pp. 7-8; and *Fifteenth LDDI Annual Report*, p. 8.

117. Baldwin, 'Deaconess Community of St Andrew', p. 229; Blackmore, *Beginning of Women's Ministry*, p. xx.

118. *First LDDI Annual Report*, p. 7.

119. *Ancilla Domini* [hereafter *AD*], 20 (July 1892), p. 304. See also AD, 57 (October 1901), p. 64.

120. *AD*, 31 (April 1895), pp. 179–84.

121. *Lily Mission Annual Report* for year 1882; and *Lily Mission Annual Report* for year 1883. *AD*, 6 (January 1889), p. 81. The Lily Mission had been established a decade earlier in 1878.

122. Baldwin, 'The Deaconess Community of St Andrew', p. 221.

123. *AD*, 46 (January 1899), p. 84.

124. Figures supplied by Sister Teresa Joan White of the Community of Saint Andrew. The East London Deaconess home in Stepney was established by the Bishop of Bedford.

125. B. Heeney, *The Women's Movement in the Church of England, 1850–1930* (Oxford: Clarendon Press, 1988), p. 70.

126. Heeney, *Women's Movement in the Church of England*, p. 81; F. K. Prochaska, *Women and Philanthropy in Nineteenth Century England* (Oxford: Oxford University Press, 1980), p. 179.

127. Poole, *Philanthropy and the Construction of Victorian Women's Citizenship*, p. 93.

128. D. M. Lewis (ed.), *The Blackwell Dictionary of Evangelical Biography, 1730–1860*, 2 vols (Oxford: Blackwell Reference, 1995), vol. 2, p. 1078. William Spooner's sister Barbara (1777–1847) was married to William Wilberforce (1759–1833).

129. H. Baud, 'Laura Ridding (1849–1939): The Life and Service of a Bishop's Wife' (PhD thesis, University of Gloucestershire, 2003), p. 69.

130. *London Diocesan Magazine* [hereafter LDM], May 1893, p. 163. Ackland had previously been Headmaster of Kensington School between 1869 and 1881. The society's early chaplains were the Reverend Thomas James Rowsell (1816–94), who had held a number of London incumbencies, and the Reverend William Dalrymple Maclagan (1826–1910), who was also organizing secretary of the London Diocesan Church Building Society and later Archbishop of York; both men were on the BLF committee.

131. M. Luddy, *Women and Philanthropy in Nineteenth-Century Ireland* (Cambridge: Cambridge University Press, 1995), p. 55; Prochaska, *Women and Philanthropy*, p. 25.

132. She was President of the Ladies' Diocesan Association Westminster branch and a PMWA Lady Manager.

133. *LDM*, July 1897, pp. 222–3.

134. *LDM*, May 1893, p. 163.

135. *LDM*, May 1893, p. 162. Rowsell was a BLF committee member and was instigator of the school-church.

136. R. T. Davidson, *Life of Archibald Campbell Tait*, 2 vols (London: Macmillan, 1891), vol. 1, p. 448.

137. *LDM*, May 1893, p. 163.

138. *The Times*, 28 February 1865, p. 9; 27 September 1912, p. 6. See also Poole, *Philanthropy and the Construction of Victorian Women's Citizenship*, p. 63.

139. After Catharine Tait, the role was carried out by Lucy Ellen Jackson during her father's episcopate (John Jackson, Bishop of London between 1869 and 1885), Jackson's wife having died early in his episcopacy. Beatrice Temple (1844–1915), wife of Frederick Temple (Bishop of London between 1885 and 1896) in turn handed on the responsibility to Louise Creighton, wife of Mandell Creighton (Bishop of London between 1897 and 1901). Louise Creighton held on to the vice-presidency after her husband's early death in 1901 because his successor Arthur Winnington-Ingram (Bishop of London between 1901 and 1939) did not have a wife to take on the duties. Eventually though, in 1912, Creighton handed the mantle over to Elma Paget (1871–1958), wife of Henry Luke Paget (1853–1937, Bishop Suffragan of Stepney between 1909 and 1919) because she felt that the organization was suffering through its lack of close connection to the Bishop.

140. J. T. Covert (ed.), *Memoir of a Victorian Woman: Reflections of Louise Creighton, 1850–1936* (Bloomington, IN: Indiana University Press, 1990), p. 267; *LDM*, June 1897, p. 176.

141. *LDM*, July 1897, p. 221.

142. *LDM*, April 1904, p. 114

143. *LDM*, June 1897, pp. 177–8.

144. M. Cropper, *The Girls' Diocesan Association 1901–1961 and Spearhead 1961–1964* (London, 1976).

145. *LDM*, June 1897, p. 178.

146. *LDM*, January 1894, pp. 31–3.

147. *LDM*, July 1889, pp. 85–7; July 1892, pp. 261–2.

148. *LDM*, April 1890, p. 381; April 1892, p. 136; June 1892, p. 218.

3 The Mechanics of Fundraising

1. The Charity Commission was established in 1853 to regulate and reorganize endowed charities; many of these old trusts had, by the nineteenth century, become unsuitable in purpose. The Commission was responsible for the reallocation of their objects and funds. Voluntary organizations, which raised their funds through subscriptions, were not subject to any regulation until 1960 when the Charity Commission's scope was enlarged. F. Prochaska, *The Voluntary Impulse: Philanthropy in Modern Britain* (London: Faber, 1988), p. 17; D. E. Owen, *English Philanthropy, 1660–1960* (Cambridge, MA: Harvard University Press, 1965), chapter 7: 'The "Domesday Book" and the Charity Commission'.

2. *East London Church Chronicle*, 3:4 (June 1891), p. 5.

3. *The Times*, 14 April 1884, p. 3.

4. *The Philanthropist*, 1:1 (January 1882), p. 6. *The Philanthropist* called itself 'the representative Journal of Social Philanthropic Movements and Institutions'; it was published between 1882 and 1911.

5. The 1900 edition of Howe's directory recorded the metropolitan charitable income as having risen to £6,431,062. *The Classified Directory to the Metropolitan Charities* was published by William F. Howe between 1876 and 1919; *Herbert Fry's Royal Guide to the London Charities* was published between 1863 and 1942.

6. For examples of rare works that have examined fundraising see: C. M. Mangion, 'Developing Alliances: Faith, Philanthropy and Fundraising in Nineteenth-Century England', in M. Van Dijck, J. de Maeyer, J. Koppen and J. Tyssens (eds), *The Economics of Providence: Management, Finances and Patrimony of Religious Orders and Congregations in*

Europe 1773–1931 (Leuven, Belgium: Leuven University Press, 2013), pp. 205–26; and B. Stanley, 'Home Support for Overseas Missions in Early Victorian England, *c.*1838–1873' (DPhil thesis, University of Oxford, 1979).

7. S. Gurney, *Charitable Societies of London: A Paper Read to the International Philanthropic Conference of June 1862* (London: McCorquodale and Company, *c.*1862).

8. The Bishop of London's Fund [hereafter BLF] was the only organization to have multiple bank accounts in order to make payments more convenient for the donor. These subsidiary accounts were cleared monthly or quarterly into its main account with Herries Farquhar and Company. This multiple bank account model had been set up by the Metropolis Churches Fund [hereafter MCF] and was continued by the London Diocesan Church Building Society. *Third MCF Annual Report*, p. 32.

9. S. Mumm, *Stolen Daughters, Virgin Mothers: Anglican Sisterhoods in Victorian Britain* (London: Leicester University Press, 1999), pp. 80–1. Mumm's study is based on all of the Anglican sisterhoods that gave her access to their archives and does not include the London Diocesan Deaconess Institution [hereafter LDDI].

10. Parochial Mission Women Association [hereafter PMWA] Committee Minute Book, 1909–16, 13 May 1915, Lambeth Palace Library, 1693.

11. PMWA Committee Minute Book, 1879–82, 9 February and 27 April 1882, Lambeth Palace Library, 1687; and PMWA Committee Minute Book, 1890–94, 4 February 1892, Lambeth Palace Library, 1689.

12. BLF Finance Committee Minute Book, vol.1, 1863–77, 22 January 1877, London Metropolitan Archives, DL/A/K/09/03.

13. *The Times*, 25 September 1899, p. 5.

14. D. E. Owen, *English Philanthropy, 1660–1960* (Cambridge, MA: Harvard University Press, 1965), p. 471.

15. Owen, *English Philanthropy*, p. 471. As Owen's analysis is based on newspaper reports of large bequests, it only includes very wealthy people who left charitable bequests of a noteworthy size in their wills.

16. F. K. Prochaska, *Women and Philanthropy in Nineteenth Century England* (Oxford: Oxford University Press, 1980), pp. 34–5. Prochaska's analysis of wills in the 1840s gives very similar figures to mine because his analysis was also of individual's whose names appeared in the legacy lists in annual reports.

17. *The Times*, 25 September 1899, p. 5.

18. The PMWA received 18; and the LDDI received 13. In contrast, the two large male organizations regularly received bequests making them an important source of annual funding: the BLF received 172; the East London Church Fund [hereafter ELCF] 74 and the London Diocesan Home Mission [hereafter LDHM] only 17. In total, 294 bequests were left to the BLF, LDHM, LDDI, PMWA and ELCF in the period 1860 to 1914; these bequests relate to 268 people. The interdenominational London City Mission, in the equivalent period, received a significantly larger number of 2,084 bequests.

19. The Bishop acted in an official capacity as President to the Bishop of London's Fund [hereafter BLF] and London Diocesan Home Mission [hereafter LDHM], and Patron of the East London Church Fund [hereafter ELCF] (the Suffragan Bishop acting as President).

20. J. Jackson, *A Charge Delivered to the Clergy of the Diocese of London, at his Fourth Visitation (London:* Skeffington, 1884), pp. 9–18.

21. BLF Executive Committee Minute Book, vol. 1: 1863–6, 25 April 1864, London Metropolitan Archives [hereafter LMA], DL/A/K/09/02.

22. *London Diocesan Magazine* [hereafter *LDM*], December 1895, p. 438; *LDM*, June 1898, p. 180.

23. *Sixth Parochial Mission Women Association* [hereafter PMWA] *Annual Report.*
24. *Ancilla Domini* [hereafter AD], 1 (March 1887), p. 4. See also *AD,* 31 (April 1895), p. 192. Festing became the Bishop of St Albans in 1890. PMWA Committee Minute Book, 1887–90, 17 May 1888 and 7 June 1888, Lambeth Palace Library [hereafter LPL], 1688.
25. A. Burns, *The Diocesan Revival in the Church of England, c.1800–1870* (Oxford: Clarendon Press, 1999), p. 6.
26. London Diocesan Conference, *Report of the Funds Committee, 1883–84* (London, *c.*1884), p. 3.
27. LDHM Committee Minute Book, vol. 1: 1857–87, 23 December 1857, London Metropolitan Archives, DL/A/H/MS31992.
28. BLF Finance Committee Minute Book, Vol. 1: 1863–77, 19 July 1869 and 30 August 1869, LMA, DL/A/K/09/03.
29. PMWA Committee Minute Book, 1890–94, 14 December 1893, LPL, 1689.
30. PMWA Committee Minute Book, 1904–09, 19 November 1908, LPL, 1692.
31. PMWA Committee Minute Book, 1887–90, 6 February 1890; 20 March 1890, Lambeth Palace Library, 1688; Booth papers, survey notebooks, pp. 114–15, London School of Economics and Political Science [hereafter LSE], Archives and Special Collections, Booth B67; Booth papers, survey notebooks, p. 17, LSE, Archives and Special Collections, Booth B158.
32. See A. Burdett-Coutts (ed.), *Woman's Mission: A Series of Congress Papers on the Philanthropic Work of Women by Eminent Writers* (London: Sampson Low Marston, 1893), pp. 140, 411. PMWA Committee Minute Book, 1890–4, 5 May 1892; 12 May 1892; 15 June 1893; 22 June 1893, LPL, 1689.
33. *The Times,* 17 May 1906, p. 4. For a LDHM example, see *The Times,* 18 May 1898, p. 9. For an ELCF example, see *Daily News,* 2 November 1883, p. 3.
34. For example: *The Times,* 26 November 1864, p. 10; 23 May 1888, p. 11; 3 December 1894, p. 3. In contrast to the other organizations the London Diocesan Deconess Institution [hereafter LDDI] did not have any editorial letters published.
35. *East London Church Chronicle* [hereafter *ELCC*], Vol. 21, No. 4, December 1909, p. 1.
36. BLF Finance Committee Minute Book, vol. 1: 1863–77, 22 June 1868 and 20 July 1868, LMA, DL/A/K/09/03.
37. BLF Finance Committee Minute Book, vol. 3: 1889–1902, 15 December 1890, London Metropolitan Archives, DL/A/K/09/03. For an example see: BLF, *The BLF for Making Further Provision for the Spiritual Needs of the Diocese of London* (London, 1913).
38. BLF, *Origin of the BLF;* W. Walsh, *Progress of the Church in London During the Last Fifty Years* (London: Rivingtons, 1887); W. Walsh, *Progress of the Church in London: From the Accession of Queen Victoria to 1908* (London: SPCK, 1908).
39. *Mission Life,* 9:2 (1878), p. 455. See *AD,* 4 (July 1888), pp. 54–5 for an LDDI example.
40. *AD,* 4 (July 1888), p. 54.
41. D. E. Owen, *English Philanthropy, 1660–1960* (Cambridge, MA: Harvard University Press, 1965), p. 166.
42. *LDM,* May 1893, p. 150; PMWA Committee Minute Book, 1890–94, 7 April 1892, LPL, 1689; *The Times,* 14 May 1891, p. 9; *The Times,* 26 May 1894, p. 12; *The Times,* 4 March 1899, p. 4; *The Times* 12 December 1904, p. 9.
43. *LDM,* May 1893, p. 150; July 1889, p. 73. For an example see BLF bundle of secretary's correspondence, LMA, DL/A/K/09/010.

44. *The Times*, 23 April 1904, p. 13.

45. LDHM Committee Minute Book, vol. 1: 1857–87, 26 June 1861; 8 February 1866, LMA, DL/A/H/MS31992.

46. *AD*, 2 (November 1887), p. 17; PMWA Committee Minute Book, 1879–82, 1 June 1882; 13 July 1882, LPL, 1687.

47. *LDM,* June 1906, pp. 176–7.

48. PMWA Committee Minute Book, 1894–98, 21 March 1895; 31 Mar 1898, LPL, 1690; PMWA Committee Minute Book, 1904–09, 23 March 1905 and 6 May 1909, LPL, 1692.

49. C. Dickens, *Our Mutual Friend,* Daily News Memorial edn (London: Chapman and Hall, 1900 [1865]), p. 173.

50. *ELCC*, 16:2 (Midsummer 1904), p. 1.

51. J. Muir, *Bazaars and Fancy Fairs; Their Organisation, etc.* (London: L. Upcott Gill, 1896), p. 13.

52. *Daily Express*, 13 February 1913, p. 4.

53. *AD*, 22 (January 1893), p. 39. See also *The Musical Times and Singing Class Circular*, 1 July 1877, pp. 341–2.

54. *East London Church Chronicle* [hereafter *ELCC*], 1:3 (April 1889), p. 4.

55. *London Diocesan Magazine* [hereafter *LDM*], December 1908, p. 373.

56. *ELCC,* 18:1 (Easter 1906), p. 7; *Daily Express*, 3 January 1913, p. 4.

57. The society's most successful provincial associations were in Bournemouth, Tunbridge Wells, Brighton, Eastbourne and Torquay. Examples taken from the East London Church Fund [hereafter ELCF] 1910 accounts year: Bournemouth £1,010; Tunbridge Wells £512; Brighton £428; Eastbourne £387 and Torquay £358.

58. D. Cannadine, *Lords and Landlords: The Aristocracy and the Towns, 1774–1967* (Leicester: Leicester University Press, 1980), p. 63.

59. Cannadine, *Lords and Landlords*, p. 72; J. K. Walton, *The English Seaside Resort: A Social History, 1750–1914* (Leicester: Leicester University Press, 1983), p. 105.

60. J. F. Travis, *The Rise of the Devon Seaside Resorts, 1750–1900* (Exeter: University of Exeter Press, 1993), p. 116.

61. Travis, *The Rise of the Devon Seaside Resorts*, p. 116.

62. R. C. Nesbitt, *Church Finance, with Reference to the Diocese of London* (London, 1917), p. 5.

63. *LDM,* August 1904, p. 237. The connection to Ross-on-Wye came through Bishop Winnington-Ingram whose brother Edward Henry Winnington-Ingram (1849–1930) was Rector of Ross. *LDM,* September 1903, p. 279.

64. Examples taken from the London City Mission [hereafter LCM] 1889–90 account year: Bournemouth £188; Leamington Spa £173; Eastbourne £163; Torquay £148 and Cheltenham £137.

65. A. Mearns, *The Bitter Cry of Outcast London* (London: James Clarke, 1883), chapter 7.

66. *Scripture Readers' Journal*, 180 (January 1889), p. 40.

67. Mearns, *The Bitter Cry of Outcast London,* p. 28.

68. ELCF Committee Minute Book, vol. 1: 1880–5, 26 October 1883. See *Daily News*, 2 November 1883, p. 3, London Metropolitan Archives [hereafter LMA], DL/A/K/11/01.

69. *London City Mission Magazine*, 567:1 February 1884, p. 40. The Church Pastoral-Aid Society [hereafter CP-AS] was quick to point out, in an article in 1884, that London was in fact much improved from the 1830s when its society was founded: *Forty-Ninth CP-AS Annual Report 1883–84*, p. 9.

70. I was able to trace the identities of 58 legators, of which 11 had addresses that related to the largest local associations. An example of a bequest to the ELCF, which can be identified as coming from an ex-Londoner, came from a wealthy widow Elizabeth Mason (1826–1907) who was born in the parish of St George-in-the-East. Mrs Mason gave her bequest in response to the Bishop's visit to her seaside town of St Leonards-on-Sea, near Hastings. She left a £1,000 bequest to the ELCF and an additional £20,000, jointly to the Bishop of London and the Bishop of Stepney. The bequest was to provide a church, hall and vicarage in a poor district in north east London, plus an endowment. *The Times,* 27 February 1911, p. 7. Her estate was valued at £115,228. The church that was built with this funding was St Martin's Church in Lower Edmonton.

71. *LDM,* April 1893, pp. 111–16.

72. The *Fifty-Ninth Parochial Mission Women Association* [hereafter *PMWA*] *Annual Report* (covering the year 1917–18) lists only seven contributions for the Western Fund and ten for the Northern Fund.

73. *Ancilla Domini* [hereafter *AD*], 26 (January 1894), p. 96.

74. M. Gorsky, *Patterns of Philanthropy: Charity and Society in Nineteenth-Century Bristol* (New York: Boydell Press, 1999), p. 172; B. Heeney, *The Women's Movement in the Church of England, 1850–1930* (Oxford: Clarendon, 1988), p. 39; M. Luddy, *Women and Philanthropy in Nineteenth-Century Ireland* (Cambridge: Cambridge University Press, 1995), pp. 54–7; F. K. Prochaska, *Women and Philanthropy in Nineteenth Century England* (Oxford: Oxford University Press, 1980), p. 24.

75. *LDM,* May 1900, p. 227.

76. *Forty Ninth Bishop of London's fund* [hereafter *BLF*] *Annual Report,* p. 171. For an example of a Women's Diocesan Association collecting book see BLF bundle of secretary's correspondence, LMA, DL/A/K/09/010.

77. *LDM,* August 1905, p. 250.

78. *ELCC,* 5:2 (June 1893), p. 11.

79. Not to be confused with 'associate deaconesses' who were deaconesses that received the deaconess training but chose not to become a formal member of the community.

80. *AD,* 6 (January 1889), p. 96; *AD,* 61 (January 1903), p. 126.

81. PMWA Committee Minute Book, 1883–6, 12 July 1883, Lambeth Palace Library [hereafter LPL], 2664.

82. In 1899, 898 sums came from collecting cards or boxes.

83. For example, for the accounting year of 1859–60, the LCM elicited only 634 sums from that source.

84. *Ninth London Diocesan Deaconess Institution* [hereafter *LDDI*] *Annual Report,* pp. 7–8; *Eleventh LDDI Annual Report,* pp. 8–9; *and AD,* 41 (October 1897), p. 15.

85. PMWA Committee Minute Book, 1869–72, 20 June 1872, LPL, 1683; PMWA Committee Minute Book, 1883–86, 18 March 1886, LPL, 2664.

86. London Diocesan Home Mission [hereafter LDHM] Committee Minute Book, vol. 1: 1857–87, 14 June 1866, LMA, DL/A/H/MS31992.

87. For example, the annual date for the BLF church collection was Rogation Sunday.

88. *LDM,* April 1894, p. 129; *LDM,* May 1902, p. 162.

89. *ELCC,* 2:2 (December 1889), p. 13. See balance sheet *Ninth ELCF Annual Report.*

90. LDHM Committee Minute Book, vol. 1: 1857–87, 13 March 1873, LMA, DL/A/H/MS31992.

91. BLF Finance Committee Minute Book, vol. 3 1889–1902, 22 June 1891, LMA, DL/A/K/09/03.

92. PMWA Committee Minute Book, 1876–9, 27 June 1877, LPL, 1686. Other prominent speakers who preached in aid of the PMWA: in 1871, the Reverend Charles Kingsley (1819–75) at the Chapel Royal in Whitehall; and in 1873, Edward White Benson
(1829–96), then Chancellor of Lincoln Cathedral. See W. Harrison (ed.), *All Saints'
Day and Other Sermons by the Rev. Charles Kingsley* (London: Macmillan, 1890), pp.
395–410; and E. W. Benson, *Phoebe the Servant of the Church: A Sermon ... 1873, in
Aid of the Parochial Mission-women Fund* (London: Macmillan, 1873).

93. For example, in 1888 Herbert Hensley Henson (1863–1947), then Head of the Oxford
House settlement, preached a sermon in aid of the ELCF entitled 'The Responsibility of
the City to East London' at St Margaret's, Lothbury. See *LDM,* May 1888, pp. 10–15.

94. For example, in 1888 St John-at-Hackney Grammar School at Clapton held a perfor-
mance of 'Christ and his Soldiers' in aid of the Fund; and 1906 a concert in aid of the
Fund was held at Hove Town Hall raising just £8. *The Musical Times and Singing Class
Circular,* 1 May 1888, p. 297; *East London Church Chronicle* [hereafter *ELCC*], 17:2
(Silver Anniversary 1905), p. 10; *ELCC,* 12: 4 (Christmas 1900), p. 7; *ELCC,* 10:4
(Christmas 1898), p. 9.

95. East London Church Fund, Committee Minute Book, vol. 7: 1911–16, 25 April 1913,
London Metropolitan Archives, DL/A/K/11/01.

96. These three events were: a concert held in 1906 by the Ladies Diocesan Orchestra; and
two events organized by the Hampstead Association (a concert in 1910; and a sale of
work, in 1911, organized by the Women's Diocesan Association). *London Diocesan
Magazine,* February 1906, p. 53 and March 1906, p. 88; *The Musical Times,* 1 May
1910, p. 311; *Forty Ninth Bishop of London's Fund Annual Report,* p. 11. The sale raised
£131 in 1911.

97. *Ancilla Domini* [hereafter *AD*], 16 (July 1891), pp. 111, 241, 248; *AD,* 29 (October
1894), p. 156; *AD,* 49 (October 1899), p. 159.

98. *AD,* 48 (July 1899), p. 142; *AD,* 68 (October 1904), pp. 128–9; *AD,* 93 (January
1911), pp. 5–6.

99. PMWA Committee Minute Book, 1876–9, 17 May 1877, Lambeth Palace Library,
1686; PMWA Committee Minute Book, 1883–6, 6 March 1884 and 9 July 1885,
Lambeth Palace Library, 2664; and *The Times,* 30 April 1883, p. 8.

100. Parochial Mission Women Association [hereafter PMWA] Committee Minute Book,
1904–9, 13 June 1907, Lambeth Palace Library [hereafter LPL], 1692; PMWA Committee Minute Book, 1876–9, 15 May 1879, LPL, 1686; PMWA Committee Minute
Book, 1879–82, 22 June 1882, LPL, 1687.

101. PMWA Committee Minute Book, 1887–90, 23 February 1888, LPL, 1688.

102. PMWA Committee Minute Book, 1890–4, 9 March 1893 and 14 December 1893,
LPL, 1689.

103. *AD,* 16 (July 1891), p. 241.

4 Waning Financial Support

1. M. Chaves, 'The Financing of American Religion Initiative Evaluation: Final Report', Institute for the Study of American Evangelicals, November 1997, pp. 1, 6–10 (unpublished).

2. L. Eskridge and M. Noll (eds), *More Money, More Ministry: Money and Evangelicals
in Recent North American History* (Grand Rapids, MI: W. B. Eerdmans, 2000); and
M. A. Noll (ed.), *God and Mammon: Protestants, Money, and the Market, 1790–1860*
(Oxford: Oxford University Press, 2002).

3. Chaves, 'The Financing of American Religion Initiative Evaluation', pp. 15–16; D. R. Hoge et al., 'Giving in Five Denominations', in M. Chaves and S. L. Miller (eds), *Financing American Religion* (New York: Rowman Littlefield, 2008), pp. 3–10.

4. Chaves, 'The Financing of American Religion Initiative Evaluation', pp. 19–29.

5. G. Best, *Temporal Pillars: Queen Anne's Bounty, the Ecclesiastical Commissioners, and the Church of England* (Cambridge: Cambridge University Press, 1964); R. M. Morris (ed.), *Church and State in 21ˢᵗ Century Britain: The Future of Church Establishment* (Basingstoke: Palgrave Macmillan, 2009); and K. A. Thompson, *Bureaucracy and Church Reform: The Organizational Response of the Church of England to Social Change, 1800–1965* (Oxford: Clarendon Press, 1970).

6. J. Garnett, 'Aspects of the Relationship between Protestant Ethics and Economic Activity in Mid-Victorian England' (DPhil thesis, University of Oxford, 1986); B. Hilton, *The Age of Atonement: The Influence of Evangelicalism on Social and Economic Thought* (Oxford: Clarendon, 2001 [1988]); D. J. Jeremy, *Capitalists and Christians: Business Leaders and the Churches in Britain, 1900–1960* (Oxford: Clarendon Press, 1990); D. J. Jeremy (ed.), *Religion, Business, and Wealth in Modern Britain* (London: Routledge, 1998); and W. J. Sheils and D. Wood (eds), *The Church and Wealth*, Studies in Church History 24 (Oxford: Basil Blackwell, 1987). See also J. P. Ellens, *Religious Routes to Gladstonian Liberalism: The Church Rate Conflict in England and Wales, 1832–1868* (University Park, PA: Pennsylvania State University Press, 1994), which explores the abolition of the compulsory church rate in 1868.

7. Examples of works that consider laity funding through the mechanism of the pew rent are: S. J. D. Green, 'The Death of Pew Rents, the Rise of Bazaars, and the End of the Traditional Political Economy of Voluntary Religious Organisations: The Case of the West Riding of Yorkshire, c.1870–1914', *Northern History*, 27 (1991), pp. 198–235; C. G. Brown, 'The Costs of Pew-renting: Church Management, Church-going and Social Class in Nineteenth Century Glasgow', *Journal of Ecclesiastical History*, 38:3 (July 1987), pp. 347–61; and J. C. Bennett, 'The English Anglican Practice of Pew-renting, 1800–1960' (PhD thesis, University of Birmingham, 2011).

8. For work on the Ecclesiastical Commissioners see C.W. Coolidge, 'The Finance of the Church of England, 1830–50' (PhD thesis, Trinity College, Dublin, 1958).

9. J. Cox, 'Master Narratives of Long-term Religious Change', in H. McLeod and W. Ustorf, *The Decline of Christendom* (Cambridge: Cambridge University Press, 2003), pp. 204, 208. See also J. Morris, 'Secularization and Religious Experience: Arguments in the Historiography of Modern British Religion', *Historical Journal*, 55:1 (2012), pp. 195–219.

10. See H. McLeod, *The Religious Crisis of the 1960s* (Oxford: Oxford University Press, 2010).

11. J. C. D. Clark, 'Secularization and Modernization: the Failure of a 'Grand Narrative', *Historical Journal*, 55 (2012), pp. 161–94.

12. E. R. Wickham, *Church and People in an Industrial City* (London: Lutterworth, 1957); K. S. Inglis, *Churches and the Working Classes in Victorian England* (Toronto: University of Toronto Press, 1963); A. D. Gilbert, *Religion and Society in Industrial England: Church, Chapel and Social Change 1740–1914* (London: Longmans, 1976); and R. Currie, A. Gilbert and L. Horsley, *Churches and Church-Goers: Patterns of Church Growth in the British Isles since 1700* (Oxford: Oxford University Press, 1977).

13. J. Cox, *The English Churches in a Secular Society: Lambeth, 1870–1930* (Oxford: Oxford University Press, 1982); M. Smith, *Religion in Industrial Society: Oldham and Saddleworth, 1740–1865* (Oxford: Clarendon Press, 1994); and S. J. D. Green, *Religion*

in the Age of Decline: Organisation and Experience in Industrial Yorkshire, 1870–1920 (Cambridge: Cambridge University Press, 1996).

14. S. Williams, 'The Language of Belief: An Alternative Agenda for the Study of Victorian Working-Class Religion', *Journal of Victorian Culture*, 1:2 (1996), pp. 307, 312.

15. C. G. Brown, *The Death of Christian Britain: Understanding Secularisation, 1800–2000* (London: Routledge, 2007); and C. G. Brown, *Religion and the Demographic Revolution: Women and Secularisation in Canada, Ireland, UK and USA Since the 1960s* (London: Boydell and Brewer, 2012). The planned third book is an analysis of the loss of faith as articulated in personal testimonies.

16. Brown, *Death of Christian Britain*, pp. 8, 12.

17. Brown, *Death of Christian Britain*, p. 30.

18. Brown, *Death of Christian Britain*, p. 195.

19. D. Erdozain, 'The Secularisation of Sin in the Nineteenth Century', *Journal of Ecclesiastical History*, 62:1 (2011), pp. 59–88, on p. 59.

20. D. Erdozain, *The Problem of Pleasure: Sport, Recreation and the Crisis of Victorian Religion* (Woodbridge: Boydell, 2010), p. 7.

21. J. Morris, 'The Strange Death of Christian Britain: Another Look at the Secularization Debate', *Historical Journal*, 46:4 (2003), pp. 963–76, on p. 967.

22. C. Y. Glock and R. Stark, *Religion and Society in Tension* (Chicago, IL: Rand McNally, 1966), p. 70.

23. Glock and Stark, *Religion and Society*, pp. 20–1.

24. N. Smart, *The World's Religions* (Cambridge: Cambridge University Press, 1989), pp. 12–20.

25. See McLeod, *Class and Religion*; and H. McLeod, 'White Collar Values and the Role of Religion', in G. E. Crossick, *Lower Middle Class in Britain 1817–1914* (London: Croom Helm, 1977).

26. Brown, *Religion and the Demographic Revolution*, p. 265.

27. McLeod, *Class and Religion*, p. xi.

28. S. J. D. Green, *The Passing of Protestant England: Secularisation and Social Change, c.1920–1960* (Cambridge: Cambridge University Press, 2010), p. 313. See Green's other work which considers the laity's financial relationship with the Church: Green, *Religion in the Age of Decline*, pp. 152–78.

29. *Forty-Ninth Bishop of London's Fund* [hereafter BLF] *Annual Report*, p. 34.

30. List of all new churches in *Forty-Ninth BLF Annual Report*, pp. 74–76.

31. *London Diocesan Magazine* [hereafter *LDM*], April 1893, pp. 111–16.

32. *East London Church Chronicle* [hereafter *ELCC*], 2:2 (December 1889), p. 13. See balance sheet *Ninth East London Church Fund* [hereafter ELCF] *Annual Report*.

33. *ELCC*, 22:4 (December 1910), p. 9.

34. See Chapter 5 for information on the bequest from Maria Mary Fussell (1834–81).

35. A more detailed analysis can be found in Chapter 5 of S. Flew, 'Philanthropy and Secularisation: The Funding of Anglican Religious Voluntary Organisations in London, 1856 to 1914' (PhD thesis. The Open University, 2013).

36. The proportion of male contributors remained virtually constant in the range 67 to 73 per cent until 1878 (for example, in 1866 there were 1,570 male supporters and 604 female supporters).

37. As previously stated, there was one large £4,000 anonymous donation in 1912 which skews the cash value proportions. 1897, 492 men and 447 women). 1912, 789 contributions came from men and 1,725 from women.

38. 1885, 299 men and 292 women. 1890, 776 men and 1,182 women. 1914, 612 men and 1,985 women.
39. 1859, 6,366 men and 6,814 women. 1913, 3,409 men and 5,988 women.
40. B. Heeney, *The Women's Movement in the Church of England, 1850–1930* (Oxford: Clarendon Press, 1988), pp. 92–3.
41. *Forty Ninth BLF Annual Report*, p. 171.
42. F. K. Prochaska, *Women and Philanthropy in Nineteenth Century England* (Oxford: Oxford University Press, 1980), pp. 29, 231.
43. The financial supporters of the BLF in later years, on average, gave a smaller amount than the supporter of the 1860s and 1870s. In 1865, 68 per cent of contributions were for sums below £10 per annum (1,718 out of a total of 2,509); the comparative figure for 1912 was 91 per cent (2,468 out of a total of 2,712). The bulk (92 per cent) of contributions in the band '£100 plus' came from men (859 out of a total of 938). This statistic is replicated in the next two bands: 83 per cent of contributions in the band '£50 to <£100' were made by men (603 out of a total of 724) and 79 per cent of contributions in the band £10 to £50 (4,127 out of a total of 5,221).
44. *ELCC*, 26:1 (Easter 1914), p. 1.
45. *ELCC*, 23:4 (December 1911), pp. 1, 6.
46. *ELCC*, 24:4 (Christmas 1912), p. 6.
47. *ELCC*, 25:1 (Easter 1913), p. 1.
48. ELCF Committee Minute Book, vol. 7: 1911–16, 27 December 1912, London Metropolitan Archives [hereafter LMA], DL/A/K/11/01/007.
49. The peak in 1885 marked the London City Mission's [hereafter LCM] fiftieth jubilee and therefore is an atypical income figure. *Seventy-Fifth LCM Annual Report*, p. 23; *Seventy-Sixth LCM Annual Report*, p. 23; *Seventy-Seventh LCM Annual Report*, p. 35; *Eightieth LCM Annual Report*, p. 34.
50. *Fifty-Second LCM Annual Report*, p. xii. See also *Seventieth LCM Annual Report*, p. xv.
51. *Forty-Ninth LCM Annual Report*, p. 3.
52. See Chapter 6 of S. Flew, 'Philanthropy and Secularisation'.
53. For example, the six livery companies which made contributions to the BLF in 1912 also made contributions in 1897. No other subscription lists between these two dates have survived.
54. In 1870 the BLF specifically targeted insurance companies with an appeal from the Bishop. BLF Finance Committee Minute Book, vol. 1: 1863–77, 14 February 1870, LMA, DL/A/K/09/03.
55. The BLF subscription lists for 1884, 1897 and 1912 show no contributions from financial institutions.
56. Hoares gave a contribution of 50 guineas in 1899. Fruhling and Goschen gave a contribution of £25 in 1905.
57. The other two corporate supporters were the Honourable Society of Lincoln's Inn (a professional body for lawyers) and Allen and Hanbury (a pharmaceutical and surgical instrument manufacturer).
58. Volume of LCM corporate contributions: 174 in 1859–60; 242 in 1889–90; 193 in 1913–14.
59. W. D. Rubinstein, *Wealth and Inequality in Britain* (London: Faber, 1986), p. 94.
60. J. Burnett, *A History of the Cost of Living* (Aldershot: Gregg Revivals, 1993), p. 191; M. Ball and D. Sutherland, *An Economic History of London, 1800–1914* (London: Routledge, 2001), pp. 45–6.

61. Individuals such as the Duke of Westminster and the Duke of Bedford derived their income from rental on property not on agricultural land.
62. *ELCC*, 26:1 (Easter 1914), p. 1.
63. Burnett, *Cost of Living*, pp. 204–5, 254, 257.
64. Burnett, *Cost of Living*, p. 257; and M. J. Daunton, *House and Home in the Victorian City: Working Class Housing 1850–1914* (London: Edward Arnold, 1983), p. 289.
65. The boost in the 1902 subscription and donation income was due to a £500 donation from Francis Alexander Hamilton.
66. For example, the £400 deficit at the end of 1878 accounting year was covered by 'the liberality of a friend', London Diocesan Home Mission [hereafter LDHM] Committee Minute Book, vol. 1: 1857–87, 13 March 1879, LMA, DL/A/H/018/MS31992.
67. *The Times*, 19 January 1904, p. 5.
68. *The Morning Post*, 16 July 1896, p. 2; *The Standard*, 16 June 1884, p. 2.
69. *LDM*, August 1899, pp. 308–10.
70. *The Times* 26 June 1901 p. 9; 17 June 1904, p. 15.
71. *The Times* 26 June 1901, p. 9.
72. *Ancilla Domini* [hereafter *AD*], 66 (April 1904), p. 87.
73. *AD*, 94 (April 1911), p. 21.
74. *AD*, 98 (April 1912), p. 25.
75. *AD*, 1 (March 1887), p. 2.
76. *AD*, 8 (July 1889), p. 127.
77. *AD*, 30 (January 1895), p. 163.
78. As previously stated these can only be used as guide figures. Because of the absence of Parochial Mission Women Association [hereafter PMWA] annual reports it was not possible to produce a graph that illustrated the subscription income stream contextualized against the overall income amount.
79. PMWA Committee Minute Book, 1890–4, 10 March 1892, Lambeth Palace Library [hereafter LPL], 1689.
80. *LDM*, July 1899, pp. 226–7.
81. *LDM*, June 1906, p. 187.
82. *LDM*, July 1907, p. 225.
83. *LDM*, December 1908, p. 380.
84. *LDM*, July 1910, p. 219.
85. *LDM*, December 1914, p. 365; PMWA Committee Minute Book, 1909–16, 24 April 1913, LPL, 1693.
86. PMWA Committee Minute Book, 1916–23, 11 October 1917 and 30 November 1923, LPL, 1693A.
87. *Daily Express*, 7 July 1900, p. 5.
88. PMWA Committee Minute Book, 1894–8, 15 October 1896, LPL, 1690.
89. PMWA Committee Minute Book, 1909–16, 22 October 1914, LPL, 1693. This stock was the bequest from Lady Hatherley.
90. Examples of Evangelicals amongst the 30 supporters in 1914: Henry Wace (Dean of Canterbury); Arthur Fitzgerald Kinnaird, eleventh Earl Kinnaird; Sir John Henry Kennaway, third baronet; and Reverend Hanmer William Webb-Peploe.
91. J. Burnett, *A History of the Cost of Living* (Aldershot: Gregg Revivals, 1993), p. 191; and M. Ball and D. Sutherland, *An Economic History of London, 1800–1914* (London: Routledge, 2001), pp. 26, 44.
92. W. Walsh, *Progress of the Church in London During the Last Fifty Years* (London:

Rivingtons, 1887), p. 42; J. Jackson, *The Parochial System. A Charge Delivered to the Clergy of the Diocese of London in November 1871* (London, 1871), p. 11; and *Report of the Proceedings of Church Congress,* 1899, pp. 34–5.

93. S. Gill, *Women and the Church of England* (London: SPCK, 1994), pp. 76–7, 83.

94. R. Mudie-Smith, *The Religious Life of London* (London: Hodder and Stoughton, 1904), p. 446.

95. Mudie-Smith, *Religious Life of London,* p. 91.

96. C. Booth, *Life and Labour of the People in London,* 3rd series: Religious Influences, 17 vols (London: Macmillan, 1902), vol. 7: Summary, p. 424.

97. J. Cox, *The English Churches in a Secular Society: Lambeth, 1870–1930* (Oxford: Oxford University Press, 1982), p. 25.

5 The Victorian Philanthropists

1.   O. Checkland, *Philanthropy in Victorian Scotland: Social Welfare and the Voluntary Principle* (Edinburgh: Donald, 1980), p. 105.

2.   D. E. Owen, *English Philanthropy, 1660–1960* (Cambridge, MA: Harvard University Press, 1965), p. 480. Some subscription lists in charitable annual reports (such as the Society for the Propagation of the Gospel in Foreign Parts and Incorporated Church Building Society) included brief addresses for all subscribers and donors. This practice was phased out as subscription lists became more lengthy.

3.   Rubinstein found that a high proportion of wealthy Anglicans derived their income from finance and from brewing. W. D. Rubinstein, *Men of Property: The Very Wealthy in Britain Since the Industrial Revolution* (London: Croom Helm, 1981), pp. 61–3.

4.   F. M. L. Thompson, 'Grosvenor, Hugh Lupus, first duke of Westminster (1825–1899)', *ODNB.* He was the son of Richard Grosvenor, second Marquess of Westminster (1795–1869) who was a committee member of the London Diocesan Church Building Society [hereafter LDCBS]. His uncle, Robert Grosvenor (first Baron Ebury), was a committee member of the Scripture Readers' Association, London Diocesan Home Mission [hereafter LDHM], LDCBS and Bishop of London's Fund [hereafter BLF].

5.   *London City Mission Magazine,* 759:45 (February 1900), p. 45.

6.   G. Huxley, *Victorian Duke* (London: Oxford University Press, 1967), pp. 144–5.

7.   *The Times,* 25 Dec 1899, p. 5; *The Spectator,* 30 Dec 1899, pp. 979–80.

8.   See S. Flew, 'Philanthropy and Secularisation: The Funding of Anglican Religious Voluntary Organisations in London, 1856 to 1914' (PhD thesis, The Open University, 2013), chapter 5.

9.   Hansard, Commons Debates, fifth series, vol. 147, cc. 1316–64: 10 August 1857.

10. Rubinstein, *Men of Property,* p. 194.

11. For example, the Worshipful Company of Grocers gave the Society for the Propagation of the Gospel in Foreign Parts just £350 between 1877 and 1894 (it gave the BLF £10,955 between 1864 and 1912; and the East London Church Fund [hereafter ELCF] £5,505 between 1880 and 1913)); or the Worshipful Company of Drapers just £63 between 1877 and 1901 (it gave the BLF £4,200 between 1864 and 1912; and the ELCF £567 between 1880 and 1913).

12. Parochial Mission Women Association Committee Minute Book, 1909–1916, 15 April 1915, Lambeth Palace Library, 1693.

13. G. C. Boase, 'Cavendish, Lord Frederick Charles (1836–1882)', rev. H. C. G. Matthew, *ODNB.*

14. *The Times*, 25 September 1899, p. 5.
15. The one bequest to the LDHM from a titled individual came from Sir William Rose (d.1885), Clerk to the Parliaments. Rose gave £50 to the LDHM and £200 to the BLF. His estate was valued at £98,925.
16. The estates above £100,000 related to Charlotte Denison, Viscountess Ossington, (died in 1889), Lady Jane Dundas (died in 1897) and Lady Harriet Leslie Melville (died in 1898).
17. C. J. Archard, *The Portland Peerage Romance* (London: Greening and Company, 1907), chapter 4. Her sister Dowager Lady Lucy Howard de Walden (d.1899) also gave the BLF £10,000. She was the widow of Charles Augustus Ellis, sixth Baron Howard de Walden and second Baron Seaford (1799–1868).
18. O. Barry, *The Lady Victoria Tylney Long Wellesley: A Memoir* (London: Skeffington and Son, 1899); and G. Le G. Norgate, 'Pole, William Wellesley-, third earl of Mornington (1763–1845)', rev. J. J. Severn, *ODNB*.
19. Barry, *The Lady Victoria Tylney Long Wellesley*, pp. 171–3.
20. Barry, *The Lady Victoria Tylney Long Wellesley*, pp. 136–7.
21. How in his capacity as Bishop of Bedford, and Winnington-Ingram in his capacity of Suffragan Bishop of Stepney and then Bishop of London.
22. The London Diocesan Home Mission [hereafter LDHM] did not receive any bequests from clergy.
23. Curate of St James, Westminster, 1847–50; Curate of St Saviour, Southwark, 1850–52; Curate of St Alphage, London Wall, 1852–53; Lecturer and Curate of St Andrew, Undershaft, 1853–60; Headmaster St Saviour School, Southwark, 1850–58; Under Master Dulwich College, 1858–60; Rector of St Olave, 1860; Rector of St Olave with All Hallows Staining, City, 1870; Rural Dean of the East City, 1885.
24. *The Times*, 4 January 1913, p. 9.
25. W. Walsh, *Progress of the Church in London During the Last Fifty Years* (London: Rivingtons, 1887), p. 53.
26. *Seventeenth London Diocesan Deaconess Institution* [hereafter LDDI] *Annual Report*, p. 10; *Twelfth LDDI Annual Report,* p. 5; LDDI Finance Committee Minute Book, 1869–75, see minutes for period March to May 1873, Community of St Andrew (uncatalogued).
27. A. F. Pollard, 'Goulburn, Edward Meyrick (1818–1897)', rev. M. C. Curthoys, *ODNB*.
28. Their father John Field (1812–84) had been a clergyman and left an estate of £2,900.
29. D. J. Jeremy (ed.), *Dictionary of Business Biography: A Biographical Dictionary of Business Leaders Active in Britain in the Period 1860–1980* (London: Butterworths, 1984), pp. 341–5; W. D. Rubinstein, 'Morrison, Charles (1817–1909)', *ODNB*; W. D. Rubinstein, *Men of Property: The Very Wealthy in Britain Since the Industrial Revolution* (London: Croom Helm, 1981), p. 45.
30. See C. Dakers, *A Genius for Money: Business, Art and the Morrisons* (New Haven, CT: Yale University Press, 2011). Charles was the eldest child of James Morrison (1789–1857), a partner in the successful haberdashery and drapery firm Todd and Company based in the City of London.
31. Morrison did not subscribe to the London City Mission [hereafter LCM] or to either of the female associations in this study.
32. He suffered from persistent migraines and cystitis. Dakers, *A Genius for Money*, pp. 138, 220.
33. His seven reading diaries record his reviews of every book he read between 1886 and 1906, approximately 1,400 in number (an average of two books every week).

34. Dakers, *A Genius for Money,* p. 223.
35. *The Times,* 5 June 1909, p. 13.
36. M. Reed, 'Loyd, Samuel Jones, Baron Overstone (1796–1883)', *ODNB.*
37. B. Hilton, *The Age of Atonement: The Influence of Evangelicalism on Social and Economic Thought* (Oxford: Clarendon Press, 2001), p. 133.
38. A. Burns, 'Blomfield, Charles James (1786–1857)', *ODNB.* He also contributed at least £100 to the Parochial Mission Women Association [hereafter PMWA]. He did not support the East London Church Fund [hereafter ELCF] (dying within a few years of the commencement of the Fund), London Diocesan Deaconess Institution [hereafter LDDI] or the London Diocesan Home Mission and only gave ten guineas to the LCM.
39. M. Reed, 'Loyd, Samuel Jones, Baron Overstone (1796–1883)', *ODNB*
40. H. S. Loyd-Lindsay, *Lord Wantage: A Memoir* (London: Smith, Elder and Company, 1907), p. 287.
41. It must also be borne in mind that Hamilton gave away large sums in the last few years of his life. *London Diocesan Magazine* [hereafter LDM], March 1889, pp. 323–4. For a brief biography see J. C. Brown, *A Hundred Years of Merchant Banking* (New York: n. p., 1909), pp. 340–3.
42. *The Times,* 5 February 1907, p. 8; and *Financial Times,* 1 January 1904, p. 7.
43. Hamilton, being an Evangelical, was not a subscriber to either the PMWA or the LDDI. His name does, however, appear in the Society for the Propagation of the Gospel in Foreign Parts [hereafter SPG] subscription list.
44. Brown, *A Hundred Years of Merchant Banking,* p. 343.
45. *LDM,* March 1907, p. 82.
46. Brown, *A Hundred Years of Merchant Banking,* p. 342.
47. *Scripture Readers' Journal* [hereafter SRJ], 257 (April 1907), p. 751.
48. *LDM,* February 1902, pp. 57–8; and *The Times,* 16 October 1905, p. 5.
49. Brown, *A Hundred Years of Merchant Banking,* p. 343.
50. Church Pastoral-Aid Society [hereafter CP-AS] Minute Book, 1900–1903, 29 January 1901; 6 February 1902; 27 January 1903, Cadbury Research Library, University of Birmingham, CPAS 1/4/1/24.
51. *Seventy-First CP-AS Annual Report 1905–06.*
52. *SRJ,* 225 (April 1899), p. 213. Hamilton's obituary in 1907, noted that he had given the society £11,000: *SRJ,* 257 (April 1907), p. 751.
53. R. H. Tener, 'Breaking the Code of Anonymity: The Case of the 'Spectator', 1861–1897', *The Yearbook of English Studies,* Literary Periodicals Special Number 16 (1986), pp. 67–8.
54. W. F. Foster, *Richard Foster* (London: Eyre and Spottiswoode, 1914), p. 83.
55. Foster, *Richard Foster,* pp. 44–5; and *The Times,* 28 Dec 1910, p. 9.
56. Foster, *Richard Foster,* pp. 25–6.
57. Foster, *Richard Foster,* pp. 88, 108–9.
58. *East London Church Chronicle* [hereafter ELCC], Easter 1911, vol. 23 No.1, p. 2.
59. PMWA Committee Minute Book, 1879–82, 1 June 1882, Lambeth Palace Library [hereafter LPL], 1687.
60. Foster, *Richard Foster,* p. 80.
61. *LDM,* 1911 January, p19.
62. Foster, *Richard Foster,* p. 74.
63. ELCF Committee Minute Book, Vol. 6 1907–1911, 30 Dec 1910, London Metropolitan Archives [hereafter LMA], DL/A/K/11/01.

64. *ELCC*, 4:1 (September 1891), p. 2. Also see W. Walsh, *Progress of the Church in London During the Last Fifty Years* (London: Rivingtons, 1887), p. 55. Jacomb and Foster both lived in Upper Clapton.

65. D. M. Lewis (ed.), *The Blackwell Dictionary of Evangelical Biography, 1730–1860,* 2 vols (Oxford: Blackwell Reference, 1995), vol. 2, p. 787.

66. Bishop of London's Fund [hereafter BLF] Executive Committee Minute Book, vol. 2: 1866–70, 27 October 1868, LMA, DL/A/K/09/02/002. In connection to a £1,000 anonymous sum the minute book refers to "Account Anonymous [Mr G Moore Esq]".

67. Walsh, *Progress of the Church in London During the Last Fifty Years*, pp. 54, 83; and S. Smiles, *George Moore, Merchant and Philanthropist* (London: Routledge, 1878), pp. 306–7. His estate was valued for probate purposes as: 'Effects under £500,000'.

68. Smiles, *George Moore,* p. 510.

69. BLF Other Sub-Committee Minute Book, 11 May 1865 and 15 June 1865, LMA, DL/A/K/09/06. See *Lectures Delivered in the Establishment of Messrs Copestake, Moore, Crampton and Co. ... 1860–61* (Routledge: London, 1861). Price's Patent Candle Company (which had a factory in Vauxhall) also had a chaplain for employees.

70. BLF Executive Committee Minute Book, vol. 1: 1863–66, 10 July 1863, London Metropolitan Archives, DL/A/K/09/02/001.

71. His co-partner Sampson Copestake died in 1874.

72. Smiles, *George Moore,* p. 183.

73. *London City Mission Magazine*, January 1877, pp. 1–3.

74. *The Times,* 29 May 1894, p. 12; 19 October 1901, p. 11; 23 March 1907, p. 9.

75. *LDM*, January 1907, p. 20.

76. Lewis, *Blackwell Dictionary of Evangelical Biography,* vol. 1, p. 180.

77. BLF Executive Committee Minute Book, vol. 1: 1863–66, 25 January 1864, LMA, DL/A/K/09/02.

78. Lewis, *Blackwell Dictionary of Evangelical Biography*, vol. 1, pp. 179–180, 513.

79. *ELCC*, 1:4 (July 1889), p. 12.

80. *ELCC*, 6:4 (December 1894), p. 14.

81. *The Times*, 23 July 1907, p. 5.

82. J. Cox, *The English Churches in a Secular Society: Lambeth, 1870–1930* (Oxford: Oxford University Press, 1982), p. 119.

83. See R. Thornes, *Men of Iron: The Fussells of Mells* (Frome: Frome Society for Local Study, 2010), p. 59; N. Crosland, *Rambles Round My Life: An Autobiography, 1819–1896* (London: E.W. Allen, 1898), chapter 8: 'The story of the Count and Coutness de Gendre'; and *The Times*, 9 February 1871, p. 11. See S. Flew, 'Fussell, Maria Mary (1834–1881)', *ODNB*.

84. *The Times,* 21 Feb 1853, p. 6; *Central Press*, 8 Feb 1871, p. 1; *The Times*, 13 Jul 1872, p. 11.

85. *The Times*, 19 January 1904, p. 5.

86. LDDI Finance Committee Minute Book, 1869–75, 21 November 1873, Community of St Andrew (uncatalogued).

87. There have not been any LDDI deaconesses with the surname Doxat. There is possibly a family connection between the Ferards and the Doxats. The mothers of 'The Misses Doxat' and Elizabeth Ferard both had the surname Clementson.

88. LDDI Finance Committee Minute Book, 1881–1942, Community of St Andrew (uncatalogued).

89. M. Kilburn, 'Gibbs, William (1790–1875)', *ODNB*.

90. *The Times*, 6 April 1875, p. 10.

91. J. Bailey (ed.), '9 December 1872', *The Diary of Lady Frederick Cavendish,* 2 vols (London: John Murray, 1927), vol. 2, p. 142.

92. PMWA Minute Book 1879–82, 22 Jan 1880, LPL, 1687.

93. M. Daunton, 'Gibbs, Henry Hucks, first Baron Aldenham (1819–1907)', *ODNB; LDM,* October 1907, pp. 314–16.

94. PMWA Minute Book 1876–79, 6 Feb 1879, MS. LPL, 1686; PMWA Minute Book 1916–1923, 27 May 1920, LPL, 1693A.

95. *ELCC,* 22:3 (October 1910), pp. 15–16; and *ELCC,* 14:1 (Lady Day 1902), p. 13.

96. PMWA Minute Book 1879–82, 20 Jan 1881; E. Healey, 'Coutts, Angela Georgina Burdett-, suo jure Baroness Burdett-Coutts(1814–1906)', *ODNB.*

97. *The Times,* 27 May 1974, p. 6.

98. D. Orton, *Made of Gold: A Biography of Angela Burdett Coutts* (London: Hamish Hamilton, 1980), pp. 31, 54, 166.

99. Orton, *Made of Gold,* p. 105.

100. Healey, 'Coutts, Angela Georgina Burdett-', *ODNB*; Walsh, *Progress of the Church in London During the Last Fifty Years,* p. 54.

101. Orton, *Made of Gold,* pp. 105, 185.

102. *SPG Annual Report 1860* [for accounting year 1859], p. 25.

103. W. K. Jordan, *Philanthropy in England 1480–1660: A Study of the Changing Pattern of English Social Aspirations* (New York: Russell Sage Foundation, 1959), p. 144.

104. F. K. Prochaska, *The Voluntary Impulse: Philanthropy in Modern Britain* (London: Faber, 1988), p. 47. See also R. J. Morris, *Class, Sect and Party: The Making of the British Middle Class, Leeds 1820–1850* (Manchester: Manchester University Press, 1990), p. 178.

105. D. E. Owen, *English Philanthropy, 1660–1960* (Cambridge, MA: Harvard University Press, 1965), p. 4.

106. Owen, *English Philanthropy,* p. 165.

107. A. Carnegie, 'Wealth', *The North American Review,* 148:391 (June 1889), pp. 661–2; and A. Carnegie, *The Gospel of Wealth* (London, 1890).

108. G. Tweedale, 'Carnegie, Andrew (1835–1919)', *ODNB.*

109. A. C. Tait, A Charge Delivered in December, 1862, to the Clergy of the Diocese of London, etc. (London: Rivingtons, 1862), pp. 66–7.

110. A. Blomfield (ed.), *A Memoir of C. J. Blomfield, Bishop of London, with Selections from his Correspondence,* 2 vols (London: John Murray, 1863), vol. 1, p. 237; A. C. Tait, *From the Bishop of London to the Laity of the Diocese: Claims of the London Diocesan Church Building Society* (London: Brettell, 1860; *The Times,* 30 April 1863, p. 14; and *First Bishop of London's Fund Annual Report,* p. 12.

111. See S. Flew, 'Philanthropy and Secularisation: The Funding of Anglican Religious Voluntary Organisations in London, 1856 to 1914' (PhD thesis, The Open University, 2013), chapter 5.

112. A. C. Tait, *The Spiritual Wants of the Metropolis and its Suburbs. A Letter to the Laity of the Diocese of London ... With a Statement by the Executive Committee of "The Bishop of London's Fund"* (London: Rivingtons, 1863).

113. *Official Yearbook of the Church of England,* 1883, pp. 70–1; A. Burdett-Coutts, A. (ed.), *Woman's Mission: A Series of Congress Papers on the Philanthropic Work of Women by Eminent Writers* (London: Sampson Low Marston, 1893), p. 411.

114. *Sunday Times,* 31 January 1869, p. 2.

115. J. Cox, *The English Churches in a Secular Society: Lambeth, 1870–1930* (Oxford: Oxford University Press, 1982), pp. 112, 119.

6 Philanthropy in the Late Nineteenth Century: The Ethos of Giving

1. S. Smiles, *George Moore, Merchant and Philanthropist* (London: Routledge, 1878), pp. 311–12.

2. There is very little secondary literature on this subject. See J. Garnett, 'Aspects of the Relationship between Protestant Ethics and Economic Activity in Mid-Victorian England' (DPhil thesis, University of Oxford, 1986) on the mid nineteenth century; J. Garnett, '"Gold and the Gospel': Systematic Beneficence in Mid-Nineteenth Century England', in W. J. Sheils and Diana Wood (eds), *The Church and Wealth*, Studies in Church History 24 (Oxford: Basil Blackwell, 1987), pp. 347–58; and D. A. H. Johnston, *Stewardship and the Gospel*, abridged 2nd edn (Exeter: Short Run Press, 1995); and B. Hilton, *The Age of Atonement: The Influence of Evangelicalism on Social and Economic Thought* (Oxford: Clarendon Press, 2001), pp. 100–14.

3. H. Lansdell, *The Sacred Tenth: or, Studies in Tithe-giving, Ancient and Modern*, 2 vols (London: SPCK, 1906), vol. 2, pp. 416–18; Society of the Treasury of God, *Society of the Treasury of God: A Monthly Paper* (Toronto: 1885), p. 11.

4. See John Wesley's sermons: J. Wesley, 'The Use of Money' and 'The Good Steward', both in J. Wesley, *Sermons on Several Occasions*, 2 vols (New York: Carlton and Phillips, 1855), vol. 1, pp. 440–56.

5. H. R. Calkins, *A Man and His Money* (New York: Methodist Book Concern, 1914), pp. 78–81; and J. Walsh, 'Wesley and the Poor', *Revue Francaise de Civilisation Britannique*, 6:3 (1991), pp. 17–30.

6. *The Times*, 7 May 1861, p. 4; and R. G. Cather, *The Origin and Objects of the Systematic Beneficence Society* [hereafter SBS] (London, 1862), p. 29.

7. *The Benefactor*, 1:1 (2 November 1863), p. 11.

8. The role of the SBS was to influence the ethic of giving. It was not concerned about the mechanism that the individual chose to give through (i.e. the offertory).

9. B. Hilton, *The Age of Atonement: The Influence of Evangelicalism on Social and Economic Thought* (Oxford: Clarendon Press, 2001), pp. 104–5.

10. Walsh, 'Wesley and the Poor', p. 26.

11. *The Benefactor*, 1:5 (January 1865), pp. 74–5.

12. *The Benefactor*, 1:1 (2 November 1863), p. 6.

13. *The Benefactor*, 1:1 (2 November 1863), p. 2.

14. *The Benefactor*, 1:1 (2 November 1863), p. 6.

15. Cather, *Origin and Objects of the SBS*, p. 27.

16. J. Garnett, '"Gold and the Gospel": Systematic Beneficence in Mid-Nineteenth Century England', in W. J. Sheils and D. Wood (eds), *The Church and Wealth*, Studies in Church History 24 (Oxford: Basil Blackwell, 1987), pp. 347–58, on p. 348.

17. Cather, *Origin and Objects of the SBS*, p. 27.

18. See Garnett, 'Gold and the Gospel'; and Calkins, *A Man and His Money*, pp. 110–12.

19. Hilton, *The Age of Atonement*, p. 104.

20. J. A. Wylie, *The Gospel Ministry: Duty and Privilege of Supporting It* (London: James Nisbet, 1857).

21. W. Arthur, *Duty of Giving Away a Stated Proportion of our Income: An Address etc* (Philadelphia, PA: Presbyterian Board of Publication, 1857).

22. Calkins, *A Man and His Money*, pp. 112, 117–18. Arthur's essay was quoted in an article in the *Christian Observer*, 292 (April 1862), p. 272.

23. Cather, *Origin and Objects of the SBS*, pp. 28–9.

24. I. Machin, 'Howard, George William Frederick, seventh earl of Carlisle (1802–1864)', *ODNB*.

25. *The Times*, 7 May 1861, p. 4.

26. J. Garnett, 'Aspects of the Relationship between Protestant Ethics and Economic Activity in Mid-Victorian England' (DPhil thesis, University of Oxford, 1986), p. 207.

27. *The Times*, 25 April 1864, p. 14; 22 April 1865, p. 12; and 19 April 1866; p. 7; and Cather, *The Origin and Objects of the SBS*, p. 26. In May 1866 Hanbury chaired the SBS May meeting. Hanbury adopted the name Culling when he married the daughter of Sir Culling Eardley Eardley. See Anonymous, *Robert Culling Hanbury: A Sketch of His Life and Work* (London: George Hunt, 1867), pp. 9, 102, 103, 117.

28. *The Times*, 25 Apr 1864, p. 14; 22 April 1865; p. 12; 19 April 1866, p. 7.

29. Garnett, 'Aspects of the Relationship', p. 209; and Anglican and International Christian Moral Science Association, *Science and the Gospel; or the Church and the Nations* (London: Macmillan, 1870), p. 593.

30. *The Benefactor*, 1:16 (September 1868), p. 253; 1:18 (May 1869), pp. 297–8.

31. *The Benefactor*, 1:3 (June 1864), p. 33.

32. Cather, *Origin and Objects of the Systematic Beneficence Society*, p. 43.

33. *The Benefactor*, 1:11 (January 1867), p. 174.

34. *The Benefactor*, 1:17 (January 1869), p. 272.

35. See also Anon, *Systematic Giving* (London: Nisbet, 1864). By 1864, 100,000 copies of Arthur's essay had been published. Baptist Noel had by this time left the Church of England and had become a Baptist.

36. Garnett, 'Aspects of the Relationship', p. 210.

37. *The Benefactor*, 1:4 (September 1864), p. 60.

38. Anglican and International Christian Moral Science Association, *Science and the Gospel*, p. 593; *The Benefactor*, 1:13 (September 1867), p. 208.

39. Anon, *What is Mine? What is God's by a Clergyman of the Church of England* (London, 1859). The anonymous author of this item is identified in the National Library of Scotland catalogue as George Pope (died 1893), Professor of Maths at the Royal Military College in Sandhurst, and later Rector of Rempstone, Nottinghamshire. This authorship is attributed on the basis of manuscript notes and shared binding with other works by Pope.

40. Anon, *Systematic Giving*, p. 8.

41. *The Benefactor, 1:12* (May 1867), p. 182.

42. Society of the Treasury of God (an Anglican society established in 1886) members, Henry Lansdell and Charles Pocock (1829–1899), both credited the book *Gold and the Gospel* and the work of the SBS in the 1850s and 1860s for awakening their interest in stewardship and systematic giving. C. A. B. Pocock, *Why Give? Or a Public Confession, as to the Right Motives for Proportionate Giving* (London: Charles Cull and Son, c.1899), p. 5, Lewisham History and Archives Centre, A/69/18/6/5a; Lansdell, *The Sacred Tenth*, Vol. 2, p. 605.

43. *Church Magazine*, 1 (1866), pp. 1–4.

44. Garnett, 'Gold and the Gospel', p. 352.

45. *The Times*, 12 November 1844, p. 3; 15 November 1844, p. 5; 18 November 1844, p. 5; 25 November 1844, p. 5; 7 December 1844, p. 5; 13 December 1844, p. 5; 2 January 1845, p. 6; 6 January 1845, p. 5. See also O. Chadwick, *The Victorian Church*, 2 vols (London: Adam and Charles Black, 1970), vol. 1, pp. 216–17, 329.

46. *Christian Observer*, 292 (April 1862), p. 277.

47. *First Free and Open Church Association* [hereafter FOCA] *Annual Report*, pp. 6–7. In 1872 FOCA amalgamated with the National Association for Promoting Freedom of

Worship in the Church of England. *Free and Open Church Advocate*, 1:11 (November 1872), p. 65.

48. *Tenth FOCA Annual Report*, p. 14.

49. *Second FOCA Annual Report*, p. 11; and *Tenth FOCA Annual Report*, p. 11.

50. *First FOCA Annual Report*, p. 8; *Twenty-seventh Annual Report*, p. 11; *Twenty-Eighth Annual Report*, pp. 7–8; *Thirty-Second Annual Report*, p. 12; *Forty-Second Annual Report*, pp. 7–8; and *Free and Open Church Advocate*, 1:42 (June 1896), pp. 383–4.

51. D. A. H. Johnston, *Stewardship and the Gospel*, abridged 2nd edn (Exeter: Short Run Press, 1995), p. 32; J. N. Morris, *Religion and Urban Change: Croydon, 1840–1914* (Woodbridge: Boydell, 1992), p. 55; S. J. D. Green, *Religion in the Age of Decline: Organisation and Experience in Industrial Yorkshire, 1870–1920* (Cambridge: Cambridge University Press, 1996), pp. 155–63.

52. J. H. Markland, *The Offertory: The Most Excellent Way of Contributing Money for Christian Purpose* (Oxford: Parker, 1862); and J. Hamilton, *Prize Essay: An Inquiry into the Principles of Church Finance* (n. p.: n. p., 1865), pp. 7, 19.

53. Hamilton, *Inquiry into the Principles of Church Finance*, pp. 22, 29.

54. J. Sandford, *The Mission and Extension of the Church at Home Considered in Eight Lectures Preached Before the University of Oxford in the Year 1861 at the Lecture Founded by the Late Rev. John Bampton* (London: Longman, 1862), p. 102. Sandford was Rector of Alvechurch in Worcestershire.

55. Sandford, *Mission and Extension*, pp. 254–5; and J. Jackson, *A Charge Delivered to the Clergy of the Diocese of Lincoln, in October, 1861* (London, 1861).

56. D. M. Lewis (ed.), *The Blackwell Dictionary of Evangelical Biography, 1730–1860*, 2 vols (Oxford: Blackwell Reference, 1995), vol. 1, p. 598.

57. Quoted in Sandford, *Mission and Extension*, pp. 254–5.

58. *Thirty-Fifth Church Pastoral-Aid Society* [hereafter CP-AS] *Annual Report*, p. 16.

59. Sandford, *Mission and Extension*, pp. 99, 101.

60. Anon, *Systematic Giving*, pp. 3, 15.

61. J. H. Lupton, 'Peile, Thomas Williamson (1806–1882)', rev. M. C. Curthoys, *ODNB*. Peile had previously been Headmaster of Repton School in Derbyshire (1841 to 1854), and Vicar of Luton (1857 to 1860).

62. T. W. Peile, *Give God His Tenth: The Way to Lay by in Store for Ends at this Time Specially Sought Through the Bishop of London's Fund: A Sermon [on 1 Cor xvi 2], etc.* (London, 1864), p. 17.

63. *The Benefactor*, 1:2 (February 1864), p. 18; 1:3 (June 1864), p. 39.

64. E. L. Cutts, *Home Missions and Church Extension* (London: Rivingtons, 1861), p. 15.

65. *Thirtieth CP-AS Annual Report*, p. 50.

66. *Fifty-First CP-AS Annual Report*.

67. *John Bull*, 3 May 1862, p. 289; *The Benefactor*, 1:17 (January 1869), p. 261.

68. *The Benefactor*, 1:6 (May 1865), p. 91.

69. H. C. G. Matthew, *The Gladstone Diaries*, 14 vols (Oxford: Clarendon Press, 1978), vol. 6: 1861–8; and T. Binney, *Money: Popular Exposition in Rough Notes, with Remarks on Stewardship and Systematic Beneficence* (London: Jackson, Walford and Hodder, 1864).

70. *The Lancaster Gazette*, 30 January 1869, p. 6.

71. F. D. How, *Bishop Walsham How: A Memoir* (London: Isbister and Company, 1898), pp. 86, 319; and J. H. Overton, 'How, William Walsham (1823–1897)', rev. M. C. Curthoys, *ODNB*.

72. This was published in *The Lord's Portion*, 55 (January 1915), p. 26; and in Alfred H. Miles (ed.), *Sacred Poets of the Nineteenth Century* (London: Routledge, 1907), p. 56.
73. *Free and Open Church Advocate*, 1:43 (July 1896), p. 397.
74. Samuel Jones-Loyd's (First Baron Overstone) charitable account books, Loyd Papers, Senate House Library, 804/2167(1) and 804/2169; W. F. Foster, *Richard Foster* (London: Eyre Spottiswoode, 1914), p. 33.
75. The Late Mr Richard Foster: Special Memoir', typed manuscript (*c.*1911), London Metropolitan Archives, P94/MTS/185. See also *East London Church Chronicle* 23:1 (Easter 1911), p. 2.
76. Foster, *Richard Foster,* pp. 74–6.
77. Loyd Papers, Senate House Library, 804/2169.
78. Loyd Papers, Senate House Library, 804/2169.
79. R. C. Michie, 'Income, Expenditure and Investment of a Victorian Millionaire: Lord Overstone, 1823–83'. *Historical Research*, 58 (1985), p. 61.
80. Michie, 'Income, Expenditure and Investment of a Victorian Millionaire', p.77.
81. J. C. Brown, *A Hundred Years of Merchant Banking* (New York: n. p., 1909), p. 343.
82. H. Lansdell, *The Sacred Tenth: or, Studies in Tithe-giving, Ancient and Modern,* 2 vols (London: SPCK, 1906), vol. 2, pp. 362–3; and E. Baigent, 'Lansdell, Henry (1841–1919)', *ODNB*.
83. *London City Mission Magazine*, 646:55 (September 1890), pp. 215–16.
84. Lansdell, *The Sacred Tenth,* vol. 2, pp. 364–5, 434.
85. C. A. Maxfield, 'The "Reflex Influence" of Missions: The Domestic Operations of the American Board of Commissioners for Foreign Missions, 1810–1850' (PhD thesis, Union Theological Seminary, 1995), chapter 7.
86. W. K. Tweedie, *Man and His Money: Its Use and Abuse* (London, 1855), p. 38. It is not possible to accurately quantify contributions to voluntary organizations during the 1850s and 1860s because there are not any consistent figures in charitable directories that cover this period.
87. *The Benefactor*, 1:10 (September 1866), p. 151.
88. It is not possible to use the Society for the Propagation of the Gospel in Foreign Parts as a comparative study because its income levels were dramatically affected with the abolition of the royal letter in 1853.
89. *The Benefactor*, 1:18 (May 1869), pp. 297–8.
90. Calkins notes the same trend in America, where the stewardship revival lasted until the mid 1870s and then gradually fell into decline as the classic texts issued in the 1850s fell out of print. He comments that, consequentially, the generation after the American Civil War were not educated in the doctrine of stewardship. Calkins, *A Man and His Money,* p. 120. Lansdell suggests that the SBS fell into decline because of a 'lack of proper organisation'; he criticized it for not having an auxiliary infrastructure or a membership and pledging system. A possible factor in the decline of the SBS may have been the death of Robert Cather (the society's secretary) in 1879. Lansdell, *The Sacred Tenth,* vol. 2, pp. 527–8, 536–7; *Proceeding of the Church Congress,* 1888, p. 556; *Belfast-Newsletter,* 28 November 1879, p. 7; and *The Benefactor*, 1:18 (May 1869), p. 298.
91. H. R. Calkins, *A Man and His Money* (New York: Methodist Book Concern, 1914), p. 120.
92. T. C. Whitlock, *Crime, Gender and Consumer Culture in Nineteenth Century England* (Aldershot: Ashgate, 2005), chapter 2: 'Vanity Fairs: The Growth of Bazaars and Fancy Fairs'.
93. In the USA, the sale of commercial goods (rather than hand-made goods) became more predominant after 1885: B. Gordon, *Bazaar and Fair Ladies: The History of the American Fundraising Fair* (Knoxville, TN: University of Tennessee Press, 1998), p. 207.

94. G. R. Dyer, 'The "Vanity Fair" in Nineteenth Century England: Commerce, Women and the East in the Ladies' Bazaar', *Nineteenth-Century Literature*, 46:2 (September 1991), pp. 196–222.

95. For example see, R. W. Evans, *The Bishopric of Souls* (London: Rivingtons, 1844); and J. J. Blunt, *The Duties of the Parish Priest* (London: John Murray, 1856).

96. F. K. Prochaska, *Women and Philanthropy in Nineteenth Century England* (Oxford: Oxford University Press, 1980), p. 68.

97. A copy of the bazaar's programme is filed in these papers: Benson 46 ff. 66–72, Lambeth Palace Library.

98. W. F. Foster, *Richard Foster* (London: Eyre Spottiswoode, 1914), p. 54. Unfortunately, it has not been possible to trace this pamphlet.

99. Prochaska, *Women and Philanthropy*, p. 57.

100. Church Pastoral-Aid Society [hereafter CP-AS], *Quarterly Paper*, 115 (January 1879), p. 10; filed at end of annual report for 1878–9, Cadbury Research Library, University of Birmingham, CPAS 1/9/1/29.

101. *Fifty-Third CP-AS Annual Report*, p. 36.

102. *Seventy-Fifth CP-AS Annual Report*, p. 45; *Seventy-Sixth CP-AS Annual Report*, p. 43.

103. *Eleventh Ladies Home Mission Union Annual Report*, p. 7 [filed at the back of the *Sixty-Fourth CP-AS Annual Report*].

104. J. Bailey (ed.), *The Diary of Lady Frederick Cavendish,* 2 vols (London: John Murray, 1927), vol. 1, p. 245. See also A. G. Poole, *Philanthropy and the Construction of Victorian Women's Citizenship* (Toronto: University of Toronto Press, 2014), p. 17.

105. *The Benefactor*, 1:3 (June 1864), p. 42.

106. J. P. Foster, *Fancy Fair Religion: or, The World Converting Itself* (London: Swan Sonnenschein, 1888), pp. 121, 134.

107. N. Wray, *Fun and Finance: A Discussion of Modern Church Novelties in Connection with the Subject of Christian Giving* (Boston, MA: McDonald Gill, 1890), p. 10.

108. Foster, *Fancy Fair Religion,* p. 164; Wray, *Fun and Finance*, p. 143; C. Jerdan, *The Counterfeit in Church Finance and Christian Giving* (London: James Nisbet, 1891), p. 21. See also Society of the Treasury of God [hereafter STG] Minute Book 1886 to 1920, 12 June 1893: glued in pamphlet by E. Liddell, *The Poverty-Stricken Clergy and the Society of the Treasury of God: A Paper by Rev. Edward Liddell (Hon. Canon of Durham). Read at the Gen Meeting of the Society at the Church House, Westminster on 12 June 1893* (London: Society of the Treasury of God, 1893), p. 6, Lewisham History and Archives Centre [herafter LHAC], A/69/18/1/1.

109. The STG Master between 1890 and 1914 was the Anglo-Catholic Athelstan Riley (1858–1945); he was followed by the Evangelical Henry Lansdell who was Master between 1914 and 1919.

110. STG Minute Book, 1886–1920, 9 January 1886, LHAC, A/69/18/1/1.

111. STG Minute Book, 1886–1920, 12 December 1891, LHAC, A/69/18/1/1.

112. STG Minute Book, 1886–1920, 21 June 1892, LHAC, A/69/18/1/1.

113. *Fifth STG Annual Report*, p. 7, LHAC, A/69/18/6/5a.

114. Attempts were made to revive the Society of the Treasury of God in 1914 on the death of the honorary secretary Stephen Gunyon. See STG Minute Book, 1886–1920, 26 June 1914, LHAC, A/69/18/1/1.

115. C. A. B. Pocock, *Why Give? Or a Public Confession, as to the Right Motives for Proportionate Giving* (London: Charles Cull, *c.*1899), p. 5; H. Lansdell, H., *The Sacred Tenth: or, Studies in Tithe-giving, Ancient and Modern,* 2 vols (London: SPCK, 1906), vol. 2, p. 605.

116. J. Silvester, *A Pioneer of Proportionate Giving: A Brief Memoir of the Rev. E. A. Watkins* (Clacton-on-Sea, 1912), pp. 3–8; Lansdell, *The Sacred Tenth, v*ol. 2, pp. 439–40.

117. Silvester, *A Pioneer of Proportionate Giving*, p. 14.

118. STG Minute Book, 1886–1920, 28 October 1893, LHAC, A/69/18/1/1.

119. Lansdell, *The Sacred Tenth*, vol. 2, p. 439.

120. *Thirty-first Free and Open Church Association* [hereafter FOCA] *Annual Report*, pp. 15–16; *Twenty-seventh FOCA Annual Report*, p. 14.

121. *The Times*, 19 May 1897, p. 4; *Illustrated London News*, 29 May 1897, p. 746.

122. Lansdell, *The Sacred Tenth*, vol. 2, p. 413–14; *The Hampshire Advertiser*, 15 June 1887, p. 1; *The Huddersfield Chronicle and West Yorkshire Advertiser*, 13 October 1888, p. 8; *The Standard*, 31 October 1891, p. 3; *The Yorkshire Herald, and The York Herald*, 24 October 1891, p. 6; *The Huddersfield Chronicle and West Yorkshire Advertiser*, 22 October 1892, p. 7; *Berrow's Worcester Journal*, 3 October 1896, p. 3; *Leicester Chronicle and the Leicestershire Mercury*, 15 October 1898, p. 2.

123. *The Times*, 29 March 1888, p. 5.

124. Lansdell, *The Sacred Tenth*, Vol. 2, pp. 413–14.

125. STG Minute Book, 1886–1920, 19 November 1892; 28 October 1893, Lewisham History and Archives Centre, A/69/18/1/1.

126. Lansdell, *The Sacred Tenth, v*ol. 2, p. 455. See also F. H. Rooke, *Systematic Almsgiving, A Paper, Revised, with Note* (London, 1890).

127. *Twenty-seventh FOCA Annual Report*, p. 7.

128. *The Times*, 29 April 1897, p. 11.

129. W. B. Carpenter, *Our Lord's Teaching with Regard to Beneficence: A Sermon Preached by the Lord Bishop of Ripon, in Westminster Abbey, June 19th, 1895, on Behalf of the Bishop of London's Fund* (London: Brettel, 1895).

130. *The Philanthopist*, 27:10 (22 October 1906), p. 163.

131. Lansdell, *The Sacred Tenth, v*ol. 1, page titled a 'Catena of Brevities'.

132. H. Lansdell, *Back to the Tithe: An Address Delivered to the Pan-Anglican Congress* (London, Burnside: 1909), p. 17.

133. Lansdell, *Back to the Tithe*, pp. 20–1. The Pan-Anglican Congress of 1908 led to a recommendation by the Archbishops of Canterbury and York to review the subject of church finance in England.

134. K. W. Orr-Nimmo, 'Changes in the Methods of Financing of the Church of England, *c.*1870–1920 with Special Reference to the Parochial Clergy' (DPhil thesis, University of Oxford, 1983), p. 273.

135. W. Cunningham, *Efficiency in the Church of England: Remarks Suggested by the Report of the Archbishops' Committee on Church Finance* (London: Murray, 1912), pp. 1–2.

136. *The Philanthropist*, 29:5 (May 1908), pp. 65–6.

137. Cunningham, *Efficiency in the Church of England*, pp. 4–5.

138. T. A. Moxon, *Reform in Church Finance: Four Papers on the Report of the Archbishops' Committee on Church Finance* (London: Christian Knowledge Society, 1912), p. 15.

139. E. G. Hodge, *Church Finance in the Diocese of London: A Popular Explanation of the Scheme Adopted by the Diocesan Conference on June 29th, 1913* (London: Christian Knowledge Society, 1913), p. 3.

140. Archbishops' Committee on Church Finance, *Report, with Recommendations and Appendices* (London: Longmans, 1911).

141. Archbishops' Committee on Church Finance, *Report*, p. 10.

142. R. C. Nesbitt, R. C., *Church Finance, with Reference to the Diocese of London* (London: Wells Gardner, 1917), p. 25.

143. Diocesan Board of Finance bundle of secretary's correspondence, Draft appeal letter by London Diocesan Board of Finance (undated), London Metropolitan Archives [hereafter LMA], DL/A/K/09/09/009; and Nesbitt, *Church Finance*, p. 5. Nesbitt was the London Diocesan Board of Finance's solicitor.

144. Bishop of London's Fund [hereafter BLF] Executive Committee Minute Book 1908–12, 16 December 1913, LMA, DL/A/K/09/02/003.

145. BLF Executive Committee Minute Book 1908–12, 27 January 1914, LMA, DL/A/K/09/02/003.

146. Nesbitt, *Church Finance,* pp. 45–7.

147. D. A. H. Johnston, *Stewardship and the Gospel*, abridged 2nd edn (Exeter: Short Run Press, 1995), p. 2; Archbishops' Committee on Church Finance, *Report, with Recommendations,* p. 58; T. A. Moxon, *Reform in Church Finance: Four Papers on the Report of the Archbishops' Committee on Church Finance* (London: Christian Knowledge Society, 1912), p. 26.

148. Cunningham, *Efficiency in the Church of England*, pp. 28–9.

149. Church Finance Leaflet No. 2, '*Irresistible*', set out the need for diocesan financial reform and Leaflet No. 3, '*The Method of Raising Funds*,' explained the new system of parish apportionment and the parochial quota.

150. Johnston, *Stewardship of Money*, p. 2.

151. *The Gospel of Giving: Sermons, Outlines, and Papers by Clergymen and Laymen of the Diocese of London* (London: SPCK, 1918), p. 32.

152. K. A. Thompson, *Bureaucracy and Church Reform: The Organizational Response of the Church of England to Social Change, 1800–1965* (Oxford: Clarendon Press, 1970), p. xxi.

153. H. Lansdell, *The Sacred Tenth: or, Studies in Tithe-giving, Ancient and Modern,* 2 vols (London: SPCK, 1906), vol. 2, p. 527.

Conclusion

1. B. Webb, *My Apprenticeship* (London: Longmans, 1926), pp. 194, 198.

2. See description of gift theory in G. S, Jones, *Outcast London: A Study in the Relationship between Classes in Victorian Society* (Oxford: Clarendon Press, 1971), pp. 251–2.

3. S. J. D. Green, *Religion in the Age of Decline: Organisation and Experience in Industrial Yorkshire, 1870–1920* (Cambridge: Cambridge University Press, 1996), p. 131.

4. J. P. Foster, *Fancy Fair Religion: or, The World Converting Itself* (London: Swan Sonnenschein, 1888), p. 93.

5. Foster, *Fancy Fair Religion*, pp. 24, 30, 135–6. Foster noted that bazaars were by then prevalent across all Christian denominations except for the Quakers and Plymouth Brethren who did not allow them.

6. *The Times*, 19 May 1897, p. 4.

7. W. B. Carpenter, *Two Addresses Delivered at the Diocesan Conference, 1891: I. The Presidential Address. II. Systematic Almsgiving* (Knaresborough: A.W. Lowe, 1891), p. 14. Carpenter had held two London incumbencies before coming Bishop of Ripon: Vicar of St James, Holloway (1870–79); Vicar of Christ Church, Lancaster Gate, Paddington (1879–84). He was also a subscriber to the Bishop of London's Fund.

8. *Forty-first Free and Open Church Association* [hereafter FOCA] *Annual Report*, pp. 4–5, FOCA Council resolution dated May 1905.

9. Green, *Religion in the Age of Decline; Morris, Religion and Urban Change*, p. 55; S. Yeo, *Religion and Voluntary Organisations in Crisis* (London: Croom Helm, 1976), p. 81;

Morris, *Religion and Urban Change*. Cox's study of Lambeth makes only a brief reference to finance. He says that because of the variation of system in parochial accounts he was unable to find evidence for the decline in charity commented upon by Lambeth clergymen. Cox, *English Churches*, p. 204.

10. Yeo, *Religion and Voluntary Organisations in Crisis*, p. 81; Morris, *Religion and Urban Change*, pp. 43–4; Green, *Religion in the Age of Decline*, pp. 161–2.

11. J. N. Morris, *Religion and Urban Change: Croydon, 1840–1914* (Woodbridge: Boydell, 1992), p. 183. Brown, *The Death of Christian Britain*, pp. 161–3.

12. Green, *Religion in the Age of Decline*, p. 169. See also S. J. D. Green, 'The Death of Pew Rents, the Rise of Bazaars, and the End of the Traditional Political Economy of Voluntary Religious Organisations: the Case of the West Riding of Yorkshire, *c.*1870–1914', *Northern History*, 27 (1991), pp. 198–235.

13. Green, *Religion in the Age of Decline*, p. 131.

14. Green, *Religion in the Age of Decline*, p. 176.

15. Green, *Religion in the Age of Decline*, p. 151.

16. Green, *Religion in the Age of Decline*, p. 175.

17. Green, *Religion in the Age of Decline*, p. 177.

18. M. J. Sandel, *What Money Can't Buy: The Moral Limits of Markets* (London: Penguin Books, 2013), pp. 10, 34, 37, 120.

19. F. Hirsch, *The Social Limits of Growth* (London: Routledge Kegan and Paul, 1977), pp. 84, 87, 105.

20. Sandel, *What Money Can't Buy*, p. 122.

21. Foster, *Fancy Fair Religion*, pp. 135–6.

22. *Thirty-first FOCA Annual Report*, pp. 15–16.

23. H. Lansdell, *The Sacred Tenth: or, Studies in Tithe-giving, Ancient and Modern*, 2 vols (London: SPCK, 1906), vol. 2, p. 466.

24. Lankford calls it the 'theology of giving': J. E. Lankford, 'Protestant Stewardship and Benevolence, 1900–1941: A Study in Religious Philanthropy' (PhD thesis, University of Wisconsin, 1962), p. vi.

25. J. Cox, *The English Churches in a Secular Society: Lambeth, 1870–1930* (Oxford: Oxford University Press, 1982), pp. 110–12, 211; J. N. Morris, *Religion and Urban Change: Croydon, 1840–1914* (Woodbridge: Boydell, 1992), p. 168; S. Yeo, *Religion and Voluntary Organisations in Crisis* (London: Croom Helm, 1976), pp. 105, 300; and S. J. D. Green, *Religion in the Age of Decline: Organisation and Experience in Industrial Yorkshire, 1870–1920* (Cambridge: Cambridge University Press, 1996), p. 122.

26. Yeo, *Religion and Voluntary Organisations*, p. 105.

27. Cox, *English Churches*, pp. 211, 270.

28. Morris, *Religion and Urban Change*, pp. 167–68; and Cox, *English Churches*, p. 241.

29. A. G. Poole, *Philanthropy and the Construction of Victorian Women's Citizenship* (Toronto: University of Toronto Press, 2014), pp. 15, 222, 225.

30. *London Diocesan Magazine* [hereafter *LDM*], April 1911, p. 116.

31. Bishop of London's Fund [hereafter BLF], *Origin of the BLF*, p. 6.

32. *Official Yearbook of the Church of England*, 1896, pp. 65–6; *LDM*, December 1908, p. 380.

33. *Ancilla Domini*, 66 (April 1904), p. 87.

34. In 1912, the BLF received 25 large sums from men. (For the purposes of context, the BLF received 36 large sums from men in 1873). 14 of these sums in 1912 came from either titled landowners or clergymen, 11 sums came from businessmen. Of these 11, nine were quite elderly men who had been born in the 1830s or 1840s. The two 'younger'

men (both born in 1868) were both sons of BLF subscribers. The two were: William Frederick Danvers Smith (1868–1928), son of the stationer William Henry Smith (1825–91), both Smiths were BLF committee members; and Cecil Henry Oliverson (1868–1943) a solicitor, whose father Richard Oliverson (1831- 1901) subscribed to the BLF. The two bankers and one brewer in the BLF subscription list of 1912 were all born in the 1840s: Francis Augustus Bevan Lee (1840–1919); William Cleverley Alexander (1840–1916); and Edward Cecil Guinness, first Earl of Iveagh (1847–1927).

35. In 1914 only one man made a large contribution to the East London Church Fund [hereafter ELCF]; this was from the second Viscount Portman (1829–1919), a hereditary titled landowner. In 1899 six men made large contributions to the ELCF; these men included Charles Morrison (1817–1909) and Richard Foster (1822–1910).

36. The second Duke of Westminster wrote to the ELCF in 1901 to express his apologies that due to the 'heavy succession duties' it was not yet possible to make a contribution. ELCF Minute Book, vol. 5: 1900–06, 26 May 1901, London Metropolitan Archives, DL/A/K/11/01. The Duke did not start making contributions until 1909.

37. The BLF subscription list of 1912 listed three dukes, two marquesses, eight earls and the monarch. This was higher than the one duke, five marquesses and six earls listed in the 1873 BLF subscription list. Every generation of the Dukes of Westminster and the Dukes of Devonshire maintained their financial support of the BLF in the period up until World War I.

38. Henry Warner Prescott (1837–1926), a solicitor, was aged 77 in 1914. He had been subscribing £10 annually to the London Diocesan Deaconess Institution [hereafter LDDI] for over forty years. His brother was Reverend George Frederick Prescott (1827–1917) who held many LDDI committee positions.

39. W. F. Foster, *Richard Foster* (London: Eyre Spottiswoode, 1914), p. 119.

40. *Scripture Readers' Journal* [hereafter *SRJ*], 152 (May 1883), p. 266; 155 (January 1884), p. 327.

41. *SRJ*, 198 (July 1892), p. 3; *SRJ*, 224 (January 1899), p. 1. His grandfather Robert Hanbury has founded the Scripture Readers' Association [hereafter SRA].

42. *SRJ*, 225 (April 1899), p. 213.

43. *SRJ*, 200 (January 1893), p. 38; *SRJ*, 222 (July 1898), p. 162.

44. *SRJ*, 230 (July 1900), pp. 297–8.

45. *SRJ*, 231 (April 1903), p. 485; 254 (July 1906), p. 699.

46. *SRJ*, 243 (October 1903), p. 517.

47. *SRJ*, 265 (October 1909), p. 14. Additionally, this financial decline is highlighted by a dramatic decline in the number of financial contributors supporting the society; between 1865 and 1902 the volume of financial supporters more than halved. Unfortunately, not many SRA annual reports survive, so it is not possible to detect in which decade the decline was most serious.

48. *SRJ*, 271 (April 1911), p. 1. By 1921, the SRA had accumulated debts of £6,000: see *SRJ*, 313 (October 1921), p. 1.

49. *SRJ*, 279 (April 1913), p. 3.

50. *Seventy-Second Church Pastoral-Aid Society* [hereafter CP-AS] *Annual Report*, p. 35.

51. *Seventy-Fifth CP-AS Annual Report*, p. 43; *Seventy-Seventh CP-AS Annual Report*, p. 38.

52. *Seventy-Sixth CP-AS Annual Report*, pp. 44–5.

53. *Seventieth London City Mission Annual Report*, p. xv.

54. It was possible to identify 12 of the 14 male commoners giving £100 plus to the Church Missionary Society [hereafter CMS] in 1890–1, of which 11 were born before

1850. The donor born in the 1860s was Sir Thomas Fowell Buxton, fourth baronet (1865–1919), brewer. Of the 14 male commoners giving £100 plus to the CMS in 1910–11, it has been possible to identify 13, of which 10 were born before 1860. The three born after 1860 were: Sir Thomas Fowell Buxton, fourth baronet (1865–1919), brewer; Leonard Sutton (1864–1932), seed retailer; Theophilus Clive Davis (1871–1952), sugar merchant. It was possible to identify all of the 6 commoners giving £100 plus to the Society for the Propagation of the Gospel in Foreign Parts [hereafter SPG] in 1901, all of which were born before the 1840s (including Richard Foster, Francis Alexander Hamilton and Henry William Prescott). Of the 9 commoners giving £100 plus to the SPG in 1910, it was possible to identify 7, of which 5 were born before the 1850s. The two born in the 1860s were: William Henry Wharton (1860–1938), landowner; and John Henry Hunter (1864–1930), surveyor and auctioneer.

55. See also H. Lansdell, *The Sacred Tenth: or, Studies in Tithe-giving, Ancient and Modern,* 2 vols (London: SPCK, 1906), vol. 2, p. 466; and *The Philanthopist,* 27:10 (22 October 1906), p. 163.

56. B. E. V. Sabine, *A History of Income Tax* (London: George Allen and Unwin, 1966), pp. 128–30, 145. In 1894 the income tax rate was 8d; in 1901 (during the Boer War) it was 1s and 3d.

57. J. Cox, *The English Churches in a Secular Society: Lambeth, 1870–1930* (Oxford: Oxford University Press, 1982), pp. 203–4.

58. Additionally the *Scripture Readers' Association* (established in 1844) also started to comment on its financial decline and its loss of principal funders through death from the 1880s. Scripture Readers' Journal, 152 (May 1883), p. 266; 155 (January 1884), p. 327.

59. Except for Angela Burdett-Coutt's large sums given to endow foreign bishoprics; e.g., she gave the Society for the Propagation of the Gospel in Foreign Parts [hereafter SPG] £10,000 in 1859–60 'for the purposes of securing the provision for two Archdeacons in British Columbia'.

60. Church Missionary Society [hereafter CMS] prominent supporters: Leonard Sutton (1864–1932), seed merchant; Edward Young Western (1837–1924), solicitor; Theophilus Clive Davis (1871–1952), sugar merchant; Ebenezer Bird Foster (1839–1908), landowner; Sir Robert Williams (1848–1942), CMS President; Herbert Robinson Arbuthnot (1851–1937), East india Merchant; Joseph Hoare (1814–86), banker; Francis Alexander Hamilton (1814–1907), banker; Francis Augustus Bevan Lee (1840–1919), banker; Alfred Fowell Buxton (1854–1952), brewer; Sir Thomas Fowell Buxton (1837–1915) third baronet and brewer; Sir Thomas Fowell Buxton (1865–1919) fourth baronet and brewer. SPG prominent supporters: Henry Warner Prescott (1837–1926) solicitor; Richard Foster (1822–1910); the Rt. Hon George Cubitt, first Baron Ashcombe (1828–1917); William Lygon, seventh Earl Beauchamp (1872–1938).

61. S. J. D. Green, *Religion in the Age of Decline: Organisation and Experience in Industrial Yorkshire, 1870–1920* (Cambridge: Cambridge University Press, 1996), p. 12.

62. C. Y. Glock and R. Stark, *Religion and Society in Tension* (Chicago, IL: Rand McNally, 1966), p. 189.

63. S. C. Williams, *Religious Belief and Popular Culture in Southwark, c. 1880–1939* (Oxford: Oxford University Press, 1999), p. 162.

64. H. McLeod, *Class and Religion in the Late Victorian City* (London: Croom Helm, 1974), pp. 304–6.

65. Glock and Stark, *Religion and Society,* p. 69.

66. C. G. Brown, *The Death of Christian Britain: Understanding Secularisation, 1800–2000* (London: Routledge, 2007), p. 195.

67. G. Davie, *Religion in Britain Since 1945* (Oxford: Blackwell, 2002), p. 93.

68. D. Erdozain, *The Problem of Pleasure: Sport, Recreation and the Crisis of Victorian Religion* (Woodbridge: Boydell, 2010), p. 6.

69. McLeod, *Class and Religion*, p. xi.

70. D. A. H. Johnston, *Stewardship and the Gospel*, abridged 2nd edn (Exeter: Short Run Press, 1995), p. 3.

71. D. R. Hoge et al., 'Giving in Five Denominations', in M. Chaves and S. L. Miller (eds), *Financing American Religion* (New York: Rowman and Littlefield, 2008), pp. 3–10.

72. See D. G. Dawson, 'Funding Mission in the Early Twentieth Century', *International Bulletin of Missionary Research*, 24:4 (October 2000), pp. 155–6. For examples in late twentieth century America see: S. L. Miller, 'The Meaning of Religious Giving', in Chaves and Miller (eds), *Financing American Religion*, pp. 37–45. For a review of stewardship in America in the first four decades of the twentieth century see: J. E. Lankford, 'Protestant Stewardship and Benevolence, 1900–1941: A Study of Religious Philanthropy' (PhD thesis, University of Wisconsin, 1962).

73. *The Benefactor*, 1:19 (29 September 1869), p. 308.

74. H. Lansdell, *The Sacred Tenth: or, Studies in Tithe-giving, Ancient and Modern*, 2 vols (London: SPCK, 1906), vol. 2, p. 637.

75. Church of England Central Board of Finance, *Receiving and Giving: The Basis, Issues and Implications of Christian Stewardship* (London, General Synod of the Church of England, 1990), p. 16.

76. Church Finance Leaflet No. 2, '*Irresistible*', set out the need for diocesan financial reform and Leaflet No. 3, '*The Method of Raising Funds*', explained the new system of parish apportionment and the parochial quota.

77. J. P. Foster, *Fancy Fair Religion: or, The World Converting Itself* (London: Swan Sonnenschein, 1888), frontispiece.

Appendix 2

1. Miss Gertrude Scholfield (d. 1925) lived in Mayfair and was one of the daughters of the wealthy Liverpool brewer William Scholfield (d. 1851).

2. Richard Fellowes Benyon (1811–1897) was a Conservative MP for Berkshire. His wealth derived from an estate in Berkshire which he had inherited from his uncle. He was said to 'have built more churches than any other man of his day'. East London Church Chronicle, 2:1 (October 1889), p. 6; *The Times*, 1 January 1898, p. 3; *The Times*, 2 August 1897, p. 4.

3. Abel Smith (1829–1898), politician and JP, was the eldest son of the Evangelical banker and politician Abel Smith (1788–1859).

4. Jessie Margaret Richards (1834–1919) was the wife of a London clergyman. Henry William Parry Richards (1827–1900) was appointed Prebendary of St Paul's Cathedral in 1885 and Rector of St-Giles-in-the-Fields in 1892. Their daughter was Miss Jessie Eleanor Richards, see p. 119.

5. Unable to identify F. Sargent Esq.

6. William Bingham Baring, second Baron Ashburton (1799–1864), an Evangelical. He was a member of the Baring banking dynasty.

7. William Pleydell-Bouverie, third Earl of Radnor (1779–1869), an Evangelical.

8. Joseph Sherwood (1809–1888), a solicitor, was on the London Diocesan Deaconess Institution [hereafter LDDI] Committee in the 1880s.
9. Elizabeth Von Mumm (d. 1917) lived in the parish of St Johns, Paddington. She was born in Ireland and was the widow of a wine merchant (Mumm champagne).
10. The Misses Loveday were LDDI associates.
11. Unable to identify Miss Bampton.
12. Unable to identify Miss Rawson.
13. Lady Harriet Duncombe (1809–1902) was the wife of Reverend Augustus Duncombe (1814–80), Dean of York.
14. Sir Edward Hulse (1809–99) was the fifth baronet, his family seat was in Breamore Hampshire.
15. Joseph Gurney Barclay (1816–1898), a Quaker. *Financial Times*, 2 May 1898, p. 3.
16. John William Berry, a solicitor.
17. Sir Harry James Veitch (1840–1924), a horticulturist.
18. William Cooke, a warehouseman.
19. Unable to trace Mrs Lawton.
20. William Ellice (1817–92), a merchant and Lady Jane Ellice (1819–1903), daughter of the third Earl of Radnor.
21. Miss Sophia Portal (1790–1875) was the daughter of William Portal (1755–1846), landowner in Hampshire.
22. John Marnham (1826–1903), a Stock Exchange member, was a Baptist.
23. Joshua Lockwood (died in 1872) lived in Southampton. His estate was valued at under £70,000.
24. Edward Arnold (died in 1911), wine merchant, lived in Dorking. His estate was valued at £163,911.
25. John Brenchley (died in 1870) lived in Maidstone. His estate was valued at under £120,000.
26. Reverend William Peace (died in 1908) lived in Brighton. His estate was valued at £57,607.
27. Captain Edward William Harris was a captain in Her Majesty's Indian Navy. His estate was valued at under £40,000.
28. Reverend John Back (died in 1891) had been the Rector of St George the Martyr in Holborn. His estate was valued at under £52,800.
29. Mrs Mary Ellis (died in 1887) was a widow and lived in London. Her estate was valued at under £88,644.
30. Miss Ellen Augusta Gray (1828–99) was the daughter of the clergyman Reverend John Edward Gray (1800–87). Her estate was valued at £25,507.
31. Reverend Robert George Swayne (died 1901) was Prebendary of Slape in Sarum Cathedral. He lived in Bournemouth. His estate was valued at £30,503.
32. Mrs Agatha Gresham Wells (died in 1903) lived in Torquay. Her estate was valued at £4,965.
33. Francis Libress Brine (died in 1897) lived in Essex. His estate was valued at £5,815.
34. George John Fenwick (1821–1913) was a brewer and banker who had retired from Marylebone to live in Bournemouth. His estate was valued at £1,186,845. See W. D. Rubinstein, 'The Social Origins and Career Patterns of Oxford and Cambridge Matriculants, 1840–1900', *Historical Research*, 82:218 (November 2009), p. 727.
35. Mrs Anna Ardlie Salisbury (died in 1891) was a widow and lived in Brighton. Her estate was valued at £24,738.

36. George Churchill (died in 1889) lived in Dorset. His estate was valued at £114,314.
37. Alexander Davidson (died in 1889) lived in London. His estate was valued at £12,304.
38. Miss Harriet Hurst (died in 1889) lived in London. Her estate was valued at under £140,000.
39. Richard Emerson (died in 1863) lived in London. His estate was valued at under £4,000.
40. Joseph Headland (died in 1907) lived in Lincolnshire. His estate was valued at £189.
41. Maurice Bernays (1795–1877), born in Germany, was a resident at the Charterhouse at the time of his death. He had been a languages teacher, under Bishop Tait, at Rugby School. Bernays' bequest was in the form of a legacy to Archbishop Tait 'to be employed at the discretion of his Grace for the express purpose of preaching the Gospel to the people of London as a token of acknowledgement on my part for the participation in the benefits of a London benevolent foundation'. Quote taken from his will filed at HMRC, Probate Division, High Holborn, London. His estate was valued at under £300.
42. Miss Marian Sarah Jackson (died in 1900) lived in Kent. Her estate was valued at £8,633.
43. Miss Mary Frances Woodburn (died in 1865) lived in London. Her estate was valued at under £90,000.
44. Miss Constance Rose Bradford (died in 1876) lived in London.
45. Unable to trace Miss Mary Lake.
46. Joseph Sherwood (1809–88), a solicitor was a London Diocesan Deaconess Institution committee member. His estate was valued at £112,809.
47. Miss Hannah Brackenbury (died in 1873) lived in Hove. Her estate was valued at under £160,000.
48. Unable to trace Lady H Cox.
49. Lady Anne Manningham-Buller (1845–76) was the wife of Edmund Manningham-Buller (1828–1897), Major-General in the army; she was also the daughter of Thomas Coke, second Earl of Leicester (1822–1909).
50. Miss Adele Eleonere d'Henin (died in 1885) lived in London. Her estate was valued at £22,717.
51. Miss Anne Helen Erskine (died in 1887) lived in London and Bournemouth. Her estate was valued at £29,099.
52. Unable to trace Miss Larcom.
53. Unable to trace William Marshall. He lived in Plymouth.
54. Miss Laura Oldfield (1829–76) was the honorary secretary of the Parochial Mission Woman Association [hereafter PMWA], resigning in 1865. She lived in Kensington and left an estate valued at under £6,000. There is a long obituary for her in the PMWA minute book, entry dated 16 February 1876 (PMWA Committee Minute Book, 1874–6, London Metropolitan Archives, 1685). Her brother married another PMWA committee member Miss Susan Harriet Pitt-Rivers.
55. Unable to trace Mrs E Palmer.
56. Unable to trace Miss Roper.
57. Unable to trace Miss Isabella Thompson.
58. Miss Laura Gowland lived in Caen, France.
59. Miss Mary Tanner (died in 1886) lived in Devon. Her estate was valued at £8,151.
60. Reverend James Spurrell (died in 1892) lived in Brighton. His estate was valued at £581,742.
61. Mrs Sarah Hancock (died in 1910) was a widow and lived in London. Her estate was valued at £280,379.

62. Thomas Kincaid Hardie (died in 1901) lived in London. His estate was valued at £110,675.
63. Mrs Emily Leifchild (died in 1900) was a widow and lived in Kensington. Her husband was John Roby Leifchild (died in 1889), an annuitant. Her estate was valued at £18,918.
64. Douglas Henty (died in 1892) was a brewer and lived in Chichester. His estate was valued at £147,896.
65. George Brightwen (1820–83), a discount agent, bill broker and dealer, lived in London. His estate was valued at £177,078.
66. Mrs Harriet Sophia Shaw-Hellier (died in 1907) was the wife of Thomas Bradney Shaw-Hellier, a Colonel in the army. They lived in Tunbridge Wells. Her estate was valued at £75,831.
67. William Dollin Alexander (died in 1887) was a JP and lived in London. His estate was valued at £381,675

INDEX

For Product Safety Concerns and Information please contact our EU
representative GPSR@taylorandfrancis.com Taylor & Francis Verlag GmbH,
Kaufingerstraße 24, 80331 München, Germany

Printed and bound by CPI Group (UK) Ltd, Croydon, CR0 4YY
01/05/2025
01858355-0007